THE ROUTLEDGE
TO SOCIOLINGUISTICS

Have you ever noticed an accent or puzzled over a dialect phrase? Language can be a powerful tool with which one can create a persona; it can be a common ground between people or can be used as a divide between social groups. This *Companion* is for anyone who is interested in how and why people speak and write with such diversity.

The Routledge Companion to Sociolinguistics includes articles by leading scholars in the field on:

- Methods of observation and analysis
- Social correlates
- Socio-psychological factors
- Socio-political factors
- Language change.

They are followed by a glossary of terms with references and an index. *The Routledge Companion to Sociolinguistics* opens up the discipline to the newcomer and provides a useful reference guide for the more advanced sociolinguist.

Dr Carmen Llamas lectures at the University of Aberdeen. She is co-editing with Dominic Watt and Judy Dyer an edited collection, *Language and Identity* (forthcoming 2007). **Dr Louise Mullany** is a lecturer and academic at the University of Nottingham. She has published *Gendered Discourse in the Professional Workplace* (2007). **Professor Peter Stockwell** lectures at the University of Nottingham and has published *Sociolinguistics* (Routledge, 2002) and *Language in Theory* (Routledge, 2005).

Also available from Routledge

Language: the Basics (second edition)
R.L. Trask
0–415–34019–5

Semiotics: the Basics (second edition)
Daniel Chandler
0–415–36375–6

Key Concepts in Language and Linguistics
R.L. Trask
0–415–15742–0

Psycholinguistics: the Key Concepts
John Field
0–415–25891–X

The Routledge Dictionary of English Language Studies
Michael Pearce
0–415–35172–3

The Routledge Companion to Semiotics and Linguistics
Paul Cobley
0–415–24314–9

THE ROUTLEDGE COMPANION TO SOCIOLINGUISTICS

Edited by
Carmen Llamas, Louise Mullany
and Peter Stockwell

Routledge
Taylor & Francis Group

LONDON AND NEW YORK

First published 2007
by Routledge
2 Park Square, Milton Park, Abingdon, Oxon OX14 4RN

Simultaneously published in the USA and Canada
by Routledge
270 Madison Ave, New York, NY 10016

Routledge is an imprint of the Taylor & Francis Group, an informa business

Typeset in Times New Roman by
Keystroke, 28 High Street, Tettenhall, Wolverhampton
Printed and bound in Great Britain by
The Cromwell Press, Trowbridge, Wiltshire

British Library Cataloguing in Publication Data
A catalogue record for this book is available from the British Library

Library of Congress Cataloging in Publication Data
Llamas, Carmen.
The Routledge companion to sociolinguistics / Carmen Llamas,
Louise Mullany, and Peter Stockwell.
p. cm.
Includes bibliographical references and index.
ISBN 0–415–33849–2 (hardback : alk. paper) — ISBN 0–415–33850–6
(pbk.: alk. paper) — ISBN 0–203–44149–4 (ebook)
1. Sociolinguistics—Dictionaries. I. Mullany, Louise.
II. Stockwell, Peter. III. Title.
P40.L59 2006
306.4403—dc22

2006011286

ISBN 0–415–33849–2 (hbk)
ISBN 0–415–33850–6 (pbk)
ISBN: 0–203–44149–4 (ebk)

ISBN13: 978–0–415–33849–3 (hbk)
ISBN13: 978–0–415–33850–9 (pbk)
ISBN13: 978–0–203–44149–7 (ebk)

CONTENTS

LIST OF ILLUSTRATIONS
AND TABLES

ILLUSTRATIONS

TABLES

Notes on the Contributors

Peter Auer holds a Chair in German linguistics at the University of Freiburg, Germany. He has done extensive research on bilingualism and sociolinguistics, on phonology and dialectology, and on interaction and spoken syntax. He has authored and co-edited a number of books and has published widely in linguistic journals and edited volumes.

Allan Bell is Professor of Language and Communication and Director of the Centre for Communication Research at Auckland University of Technology, New Zealand. He has published many papers, and authored or co-edited five books. He is co-founder and editor of the international *Journal of Sociolinguistics*.

Jennifer Coates is Professor of English Language and Linguistics at Roehampton University, UK. Her published work includes *Women, Men and Language* (third edition 2004), *Women Talk* (1996), *Language and Gender: A Reader* (1998) and *Men Talk* (2003). She was made a Fellow of the English Association in 2002.

Judy Dyer is a Lecturer at the English Language Institute at the University of Michigan, USA. Her main areas of research are identity and dialect acquisition, bidialectalism and dialect contact, and she has published widely in these areas.

Barbara A. Fennell is a Senior Lecturer at the University of Aberdeen, UK. Recent books include *A History of English: A Sociolinguistic Approach* (2001) and *Language, Literature and the Negotiation of Identity: Foreign Worker German in the Federal Republic of Germany* (1997). She has written numerous papers on these research topics and is working on a book on *Language and Colonialism*.

Susan Gal is the Mae and Sidney G. Metzl Distinguished Service Professor of Anthropology and Linguistics, University of Chicago, USA. She is the author of *Language Shift* (1979), co-author of *Politics of Gender after Socialism* (2000) and co-editor of *Languages and Publics: The Making of Authority* (2001). Her research focuses on multilingualism, the political economy of language, linguistic nationalism, and political rhetoric, especially in the transformation of contemporary Europe.

Mark Garner has taught foreign languages, English and applied linguistics at universities in Australia, Britain and Indonesia. His current appointment is at the University of Aberdeen, UK. His research interests are in discourse analysis and language ecology, and he has worked on a number of research contracts for the police and other emergency services. His most recent book is *Language: An Ecological View* (2004), and he is co-writing a book on operational communication.

Peter Garrett is a Senior Lecturer in the Centre for Language and Communication Research, Cardiff University, UK. He teaches sociolinguistics, language attitudes and persuasive communication. His main research field is in evaluative and attitudinal aspects of language and communication, including language attitudes and intergenerational communication. He is editor of the journal *Language Awareness*.

Matthew J. Gordon teaches at the University of Missouri, Columbia, USA. His research explores phonological variation in American English. He is the author of *Small-Town Values, Big-City Vowels* (2001) and co-author with Lesley Milroy of *Sociolinguistics: Method and Interpretation* (2003).

Sandra Harris is now Professor Emeritus and was formerly Head of the Department of English and Media Studies at Nottingham Trent University, UK. She has a long-standing interest in institutional and strategic discourse, is the author with Francesca Bargiela of *Managing Language* (1997), and has contributed a large number of articles in this field to a wide range of international journals and edited collections.

Paul Kerswill is Professor of Sociolinguistics at Lancaster University, UK and specializes in social dialectology. He has conducted research on dialect levelling in Norway and England, where he has investigated speech in Durham, Milton Keynes, Reading and, most recently, London. His publications include *Dialects Converging* (1994) and a co-edited volume on *Dialect Change* (2005), as well as extensive research articles.

Carmen Llamas is a Lecturer at the University of Aberdeen, UK. Her main research interests are in phonological variation and change, topics in language and identity, and fieldwork methodology. She is currently researching linguistic variation and change in border localities.

Janet Maybin trained as a social anthropologist, and is now a Senior Lecturer in Language and Communication at the Open University, UK. She has written extensively for Open University courses on language, literacy and learning and also researches and writes on children's and adults' informal language and literacy practices.

James Milroy is Professor Emeritus of Linguistics at the University of Sheffield, UK, and was formerly at Queen's University Belfast. His publications include

The Language of Gerard Manley Hopkins (1977), *Linguistic Variation and Change* (1992) and, with Lesley Milroy, *Authority in Language* (third edition 1999). His interests are in language history, language standardization and linguistic ideologies.

Salikoko S. Mufwene is the Frank J. McLoraine Distinguished Service Professor of Linguistics at the University of Chicago, USA. His research is on language evolution, including the development of creoles. His books include *The Ecology of Language Evolution* (2001) and *Créoles, écologie sociale, evolution linguistique* (2005). He is also the series editor of the *Cambridge Approaches to Language Contact* series.

Louise Mullany is Lecturer in sociolinguistics at the University of Nottingham, UK. She has published in a range of international journals and edited collections on the topics of language and gender, professional discourse and politeness, and she is finalizing a monograph, *Gendered Discourse in the Professional Workplace*.

Diane Nelson teaches linguistics at the University of Leeds, UK. Her research interests include theoretical syntax, Case Theory, psych predicates, language evolution, endangered languages and syntactic language disorders. She works on Finnish and other Finnic languages, Icelandic and Khalkh Mongolian.

Jennifer Smith teaches at the University of Glasgow, UK, and works on the morphosyntax of non-standard varieties of English. She has written a number of papers on transatlantic connections between British and North American dialects and is investigating the acquisition of dialect forms in pre-school children.

Peter Stockwell is Professor at the University of Nottingham, UK. He has published extensively in the areas of sociolinguistics, literary linguistics and cognitive poetics. His recent publications include *Sociolinguistics* (2002), *Cognitive Poetics* (2002) and, with Mark Robson, *Language in Theory* (2005). He edits the *Routledge English Language Introductions* series.

Jane Stuart-Smith is a Reader in English Language at the University of Glasgow, UK. Her research interests include social aspects of phonetics/phonology; language variation and change, particularly in Scottish English; media and language change; and bilingualism, especially British Asian languages.

Donald N. Tuten is Associate Professor of Spanish and Director of the Program in Linguistics at Emory University, Atlanta, Georgia, USA. His research has focused on how dialect contact/mixing and learning affect language change. He is the author of *Koineization in Medieval Spanish* (2003).

Dominic Watt lectures in phonetics and sociolinguistics at the University of Aberdeen, UK. His research interests are in phonological variation and change, phonological acquisition, forensic phonetics, and topics in language and identity. He is researching linguistic variation in the Scottish/English border region.

Walt Wolfram is William C. Friday Distinguished Professor at North Carolina State University, USA, and Director of the North Carolina Language and Life Project. In addition to research publications of more than twenty books and 250 articles, he has co-produced a series of dialect documentaries for public television.

Sue Wright is Professor of Language and Politics at the University of Portsmouth, UK, and the author of a number of books and articles on the role of language in group formation. Her research is an investigation of how the internet may be encouraging new linguistic communities.

ACKNOWLEDGEMENTS

The editors would like to thank their colleagues at the Universities of Nottingham and Aberdeen for support and practical help and advice: Svenja Adolphs, Ron Carter, Kathy Conklin, Zoltan Dornyei, Mark Garner, Sarah Grandage, John McRae, Norbert Schmitt, and Violeta Sotirova. Particular thanks to Dominic Watt and to Craig Lee for help with glossary entries and graphics. Thanks, as always, to Joanna Gavins and Matt Green. The editors are also grateful to their universities for assistance with travel on absurdly small aeroplanes between Nottingham and Aberdeen.

Paul Kerswill would like to record his gratitude to Ronald Macaulay, for administering his first-class shears. Jane Stuart-Smith is very grateful to Claire Timmins for her tireless work and enthusiasm on her project, and to Barrie Gunter for his advice and practical help in designing the data collection. She is also grateful to the ESRC for funding the research (R000239757). Walt Wolfram's research was supported by the National Science Foundation grants BCS-0236838, BCS-9910224 and SBR-9616331.

INTRODUCTION

CARMEN LLAMAS, LOUISE MULLANY AND PETER STOCKWELL

SOCIOLINGUISTICS

This *Companion to Sociolinguistics* has been collected together for anyone who is interested in how and why diverse people speak and write differently: in other words, it is aimed at everyone. Anyone who has ever noticed an accent, or puzzled over a dialect phrase, or wondered why road signs are in several languages; anyone who adjusts their speech or writing in different situations, or cannot imitate the way that older people or younger people talk, or feels excluded by the way another group speaks; anyone who has ever tried to create an impression of themselves in an interview or e-mail, anyone who has ever made a snap decision on the basis of someone's voice, anyone who has ever been in an argument – in all these situations, you have been involved in the field of *sociolinguistics*. This book opens up this area for newcomers to the study of language, and provides a useful reference guide and resource for more advanced sociolinguists.

The field of sociolinguistics in the early twenty-first century is a mature, confident and vibrant discipline. At its core is a concern for the observable facts of language variation and principled thinking about the reasons and consequences of this variation and change. The fact that language changes is indisputable and inevitable, and it is this fact of change, spread unevenly across time and space, that leads to linguistic variation. Sociolinguistic interest in variation and change can be drawn in a straight line back to the earlier traditional concerns of *dialectology* and *philology*, which described the different varieties that make up a language and traced the historical development of particular features of vocabulary and grammar.

Though traditional dialectology was inevitably also interested in differences in pronunciation, it was largely the invention of portable recording equipment in the form of the desk-sized tape-recorder that marked the birth of sociolinguistics. This allowed researchers to compare accent variation reliably and allowed them to investigate speech directly, rather than by inference from written documents and extrapolations of sound-change rules into the past. Provided with the means of hearing and replaying speech precisely, sociolinguists could focus on individual sounds and explore correlations not just with the geographical location of speakers, but also with their age, gender, class, education, outlook, politics, and so on. In the urban settings in which most people in industrialized nations live, new sociolinguistic techniques illuminated the processes of human society and language.

Over time, sociolinguistics has developed this dialectological core interest and expanded its field of interest. In the social sciences, rigorous awareness of the principles underlying exploration and explanation led to a highly developed critical theory which sociolinguistics has also drawn on. This has resulted in macro-sociolinguistic work in the consequences for language of globalization and the multinational economy: politics, ideology and education policy have become key areas for sociolinguists. The principles of language variation and change determine the patterns of multilingualism and the shape of new language varieties, helping to define ethnicity and identity in general. Language is the means by which groups of people articulate themselves, and delineate themselves from others.

Sociolinguistics has also been enriched by developments in discourse analysis, pragmatics and ethnography. There are social and cultural dimensions to the psychological choices people make: factors of linguistic behaviour like politeness and the performance of gender, age and class connect the individual with the social in ways which are principled and explainable. The dynamics of conversations and dialogic discourse can be analysed to reveal both cultural conventions and individual speech strategies. The negotiation and manipulation of power and power-lessness, status and stigma, consensus and conflict are all matters for analysis within sociolinguistics.

Even though finer gradations can be made between core sociolinguistics and *social linguistics* and the *sociology of language*, this *Companion* reflects the international and interdisciplinary diversity of the field in representing the broad view of sociolinguistics. Together with second language research and teaching (which itself owes much to sociolinguistic work), sociolinguistics is the central discipline of applied linguistics. It has practical outcomes for education policy, government spending, social affairs, constitutional arrangements, international relations and debates on ethnicity, nationalism, multiculturalism and cultural value. This book sets out many of these key areas, and offers the reader a rapid means of exploring for yourself the rich field of sociolinguistics.

HOW TO USE THIS BOOK

The *Companion* consists of two main parts: five broad sections of articles in sociolinguistics, followed by a Glossary of terms with References and an Index. The chapters in the first part are by major figures in the field, most of whom are recognized as the leading scholars in their particular areas. We asked all the contributors to produce chapters with a very precise and full set of features, usually surveying the topic in focus from the classic studies to new work. Several of our contributors used the occasion of this *Companion* to present their most recent research findings. We also asked them to be descriptive of the topic so that new sociolinguist readers would be able to assimilate the key concepts rapidly in a way that was accessible and readable. At the same time, we wanted an argumentative dimension so that it was clear that sociolinguistic exploration is an on-going dialogue and debate rather than simply being a set of facts. Our contributors have managed to set out their own fields in precise and plain terms, and have also made it clear where the main arguments are and what their own positions entail. The combination of these two dimensions makes the contributed chapters useful for working sociolinguists as well as new students.

By arranging the chapters under broad headings, we have tried to allow quick and systematic access to the key sub-areas of sociolinguistics. It is important to realize, of course, that any sort of classification implies an ideological choice in how we have carved up the field, despite this analytical convenience. It is worth remembering that almost any extended sample of language could in principle be explored from just about every angle as articulated in every chapter. Many of our contributors have recognized the fact that aspects of language are continuous, not discrete, by pointing towards other subdisciplines. We regard these overlaps between chapters as positive and necessary for a complete picture of socio-linguistics. Where there are particularly strong and salient connections to be made, we have included cross-references from one chapter to another.

Part I sets out methods of observation and analysis in sociolinguistics. The chapters in this part serve as a mini-handbook for linguistic fieldwork. The funda-mental concept of the *linguistic variable* is presented first (Chapter 1), followed in Chapter 2 by an overview of the toolkit of field methods available to the sociolinguist. The rest of Part I sets out specific techniques of sociolinguistic analysis, organized into aspects of phonological patterning (Chapter 3), morpho-syntactic variation (Chapter 4) and the analysis of discourse (Chapter 5). While this does not exhaust the areas available for a thorough sociolinguistic exploration, it provides the essential tools for the majority of sociolinguistic work which has been undertaken to date.

Part II consists of aspects of the social correlates of language. The major social dimensions of class (Chapter 6), gender (Chapter 7), age (Chapter 8), ethnicity (Chapter 9) and speech communities across these dimensions (Chapter 10) are presented and discussed. This part largely maintains an emphasis on the hard linkage between the social factor and the variation in a language feature. To complement this approach, Part III explores the socio-psychological factors of language patterning. Individual motivation in the social context (Chapter 11), the nature of the relationship between language and identity (Chapter 12), how speakers adjust to each other's speech styles (Chapter 13), how individuals' outlooks and attitudes affect language behaviour (Chapter 14) and how individuals negotiate their way through politeness and power relationships (Chapter 15) are all addressed.

In Part IV we shift to more macro-sociolinguistic matters in considering socio-political factors of language. Standardization and the ideology which promotes and sustains it are the topics of Chapter 16. This theme is elaborated in relation to media discourse (Chapter 17), and the position of multilingual societies (Chapter 18). The consequences for education policy and practice and the overarching frame of language policy and planning are addressed in Chapters 19 and 20 respectively.

Where the *Companion* begins directly with language variation, it ends with language change in Part V. The sociolinguistics of pidgins, creoles and other new varieties are explored in Chapters 21 and 22, and set into the historical context of colonialism in Chapter 23. Lastly, the disappearance and demise of language varieties (Chapter 24) closes the contributors' part of the book.

Each of these chapters ends with a suggestion for a few directions in further reading. This is where the newcomer should go next if you are interested in developing greater depth of knowledge of the topic in focus. Of course, each chapter is also rigorously referenced to the list of original books and articles given at the end of the *Companion*, so that advanced readers can check sources to trace observations and interpretations, and get into the detail of the topic.

Where technical terms are first used in each chapter, they are presented in **bold**, and a short definition is given in the Glossary. Often the criterial definition in the Glossary is placed into a richer context, with examples and discussion, in the relevant chapter. To assist your understanding, we have also cross-referenced these Glossary items back to the chapter(s) in which they are used. Additionally, the Glossary contains words that do not originate precisely in the chapters, but which are useful sociolinguistic terms or which form part of the basic technical register used by our contributors in general.

In deciding on the extent of the Glossary, we were also aware of drawing the boundaries of the discipline. We were guided by the practical principle of trying to provide the key vocabulary that any sociolinguist would be likely to come across in the first year or two of your studies. Most terms in the Glossary have their origins firmly in core sociolinguistic work in this way. However, the basic fields of linguistics in general also provide many technical terms which sociolinguists use as part of our 'shorthand' jargon. It would have been unwieldy to have included all these terms. In any case, if you are studying sociolinguistics now, you have probably had a grounding in general linguistics or language study; and of course there are numerous excellent dictionaries, book-length glossaries and volumes of key concepts in language and linguistics that will provide this level of detail. Where a term in general linguistic use has been especially significant in sociolinguistics, though, we have included it in our Glossary. In particular, you will find many terms from the fields of phonetics and phonology, since these are used extensively in sociolinguistics and several of our contributors use these expressions in context. Throughout, we have used the International Phonetic Alphabet to indicate sounds in pronunciations.

Finally, the Index lists all the Glossary terms with page numbers for every occurrence of the item. The Glossary does not include names and biographies of famous sociolinguists, as we decided that we wanted to present the field as a set of ideas rather than personalities. Of course, the Index does include these major figures, and we recognize that sociolinguistics is a humane discipline concerned with people's lives and dependent on the intellectual and empathetic skills of sociolinguistic researchers: for this reason, we are grateful to all our contributors for their work here and in the field, and we hope their example and enthusiasm will create more sociolinguists in our readership.

CONSONANTS (PULMONIC)

	Bilabial	Labiodental	Dental	Alveolar	Postalveolar	Retroflex	Palatal	Velar	Uvular	Pharyngeal	Glottal
Plosive	p b			t d		ʈ ɖ	c ɟ	k ɡ	q ɢ		ʔ
Nasal	m	ɱ		n		ɳ	ɲ	ŋ	N		
Trill	ʙ			r					R		
Tap or Flap		ⱱ		ɾ		ɽ					
Fricative	ɸ β	f v	θ ð	s z	ʃ ʒ	ʂ ʐ	ç ʝ	x ɣ	χ ʁ	ħ ʕ	h ɦ
Lateral fricative				ɬ ɮ							
Approximant		ʋ		ɹ		ɻ	j	ɰ			
Lateral approximant				l		ɭ	ʎ	ʟ			

Where symbols appear in pairs, the one to the right represents a voiced consonant. Shaded areas denote articulations judged impossible.

CONSONANTS (NON-PULMONIC)

VOWELS

OTHER SYMBOLS

ʍ   Voiceless labial-velar fricative

w   Voiced labial-velar approximant

ɥ   Voiced labial-palatal approximant

ʜ   Voiceless epiglottal fricative

ʢ   Voiced epiglottal fricative

ʡ   Epiglottal plosive

ɕ ʑ   Alveolo-palatal fricatives

ɺ   Voiced alveolar lateral flap

ɧ   Simultaneous ʃ and x

Affricates and double articulations can be represented by two symbols joined by a tie bar if necessary.   k͡p t͡s

SUPRASEGMENTALS

ˈ   Primary stress

ˌ   Secondary stress   ˌfoʊnəˈtɪʃən

ː   Long   eː

ˑ   Half-long   eˑ

˘   Extra-short   ĕ

| Minor (foot) group

‖   Major (intonation) group

.   Syllable break   ɹi.ækt

‿   Linking (absence of a break)

DIACRITICS   Diacritics may be placed above a symbol with a descender, e.g. ŋ̊

TONES AND WORD ACCENTS

LEVEL		CONTOUR	
e̋ or ˥	Extra high	ě or ˩˥	Rising
é ˦	High	ê ˥˩	Falling
ē ˧	Mid	e᷄ ˦˥	High rising
è ˨	Low	e᷅ ˩˨	Low rising
ȅ ˩	Extra low	e᷈ ˧˦˧	Rising-falling
↓	Downstep	↗	Global rise
↑	Upstep	↘	Global fall

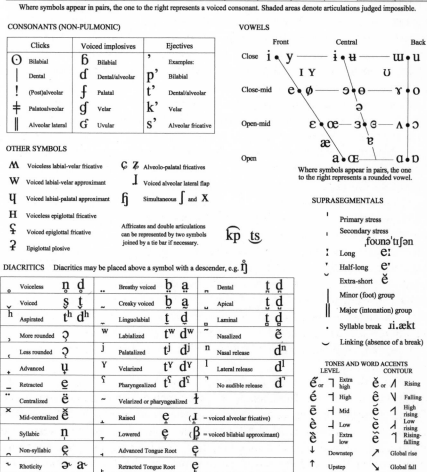

The International Phonetic Alphabet (revised to 2005) © International Phonetic Association

Part I
METHODS OF OBSERVATION
AND ANALYSIS

1

VARIATION AND THE VARIABLE

DOMINIC WATT

DEFINITION AND EXAMPLES

In all human languages, spoken and signed, we can find examples of cases in which speakers have multiple ways of saying the same thing. Some variation is accidental and transitory; it may arise from the mechanical limitations of the speech organs, for instance, and may not be fully under the speaker's control. Other, more systematic variations represent options speakers may consciously or unconsciously choose (Coulmas 2005). A choice between two or more distinct but linguistically equivalent **variants** represents the existence of a **linguistic variable**. Speakers in Aberdeen, north-east Scotland, for instance, may choose between the terms *boy*, *loon*, *loonie*, *lad* or *laddie* when referring to a young male person, or between *quine*, *quinie*, *lass*, *lassie*, or *girl* in reference to a young female. These sets exemplify lexical variables, and, following the convention of labelling variables in parentheses, we might refer to them as (boy) and (girl), respectively.

Variables are also found at all other levels of linguistic structure. Speakers may exploit **phonological** variables by choosing from different pronunciations of the same word or phrase. For example, Aberdonians may pronounce *what* using either the Scottish standard [ʍ] or the (stereotyped) local form [f] (thus [fɪtsa̠ʔ] *what's that?*). Though alternation in (wh) is typically treated as binary, other pronunciations such as [w] can also be heard in the **accent**. As discussed in Chapter 3, phonological variables may additionally be continuous rather than having discrete, clearly distinguishable variants.

Discourse variables are used as a means of structuring discourse, such as when organizing conversational **turns**. Markers in English such as *you know*, *you see*, *like* and *I mean*, **tags** (e.g. *or something*, *and that*), or **tag questions** (*innit, right, know what I mean*, etc.) have, however, been under-researched compared with lexical and, in particular, phonological variables. The study of discourse variation is still at an early stage, and while it presents challenging problems – in what sense, for example, is an utterance ending in the tag *you know* 'equivalent' to the same utterance which lacks the tag? – the fact that such variation has been found to be systematic indicates that a full understanding of how speakers construct conversations will necessitate a good deal of further research to establish more explicitly the forms, functions and uses of discourse variables (see Schiffrin 1987, 1994; Ochs *et al.* 1996; Couper-Kuhlen and Selting 2001; Macaulay 2002a; Cheshire 2005a, b; and Chapter 5).

Grammatical (morphological and syntactic) variables have, on the other hand, received much more attention in the sociolinguistics literature over the last four decades, focusing on the notion of the **variable rule** (Cedergren and Sankoff 1974; Sankoff 1978, 1988; Sankoff and Labov 1979; Wolfram 1991). Lack of space prevents fuller discussion of the hotly debated issue of the extent to which syntactic forms claimed to be functionally equivalent are in fact (or even can be) exactly synonymous; see instead Lavandera (1978), Labov (1972b, 1978); Romaine (1982); Cheshire (1987, 2005a); Cheshire *et al.* (2005); and Chapter 4. Unambiguous synonymy can none the less be found. While, for instance, Aberdonian speakers very frequently use the distal demonstrative *that* with plural noun phrases – as in example (1) – they can also use standard *those* alongside the other **non-standard** alternatives given in (3)–(6) without any difference in linguistic meaning intended or implied (McRae 2004; Beal 1997; Smith 2005).

(1) This is enough to feed all that rabbits.
(2) This is enough to feed all those rabbits.
(3) This is enough to feed all them rabbits.
(4) This is enough to feed all thae rabbits.
(5) This is enough to feed all thon rabbits.
(6) This is enough to feed all yon rabbits.

It is of course not true that all Aberdeen speakers would necessarily use *all* the forms at (1)–(6): only (2) is likely if Scottish Standard English is being used, and forms like (1) and (3) might be avoided in 'polite' speech owing to their perception as 'bad English'. To this extent a speaker's choice of variant may be constrained by non-linguistic, 'external' factors such as the social situation (an interview in a doctor's surgery, say, versus an argument at home), or the speaker's educational and economic background, age, etc., these being powerful predictors of non-standard variant usage. Alternatively, a variant's use may be constrained by an internal, linguistic factor: in Aberdeen (wh), lexical distributional constraints favour [f] in function words like *what, why, where* and *who* more highly than in content words like *white, whittle* or *whale* (see further Jones 1997: 331; Johnston 1997: 507; Smith 2005). In certain infrequent words such as *whippet, whimsical, wherewithal*, etc., [f] appears never to occur. When investigating alternations the domain of variability is circumscribed by eliminating those contexts in which variability is absent. Structural factors may assist. If, for example, a London English speaker uses the **labiodental approximant** [ʋ] as a pronunciation of (r), s/he will obviously only do so where phonological constraints allow (r) to occur, namely in pre-vocalic or **intervocalic** positions in words like *red, brown, string, around, marry, soaring* and *sawing*, across word boundaries in sequences like *soar above* and *saw it up*, and, as a consequence of **H-dropping** in the **variety**, also *sore head* and *saw himself* (Wells 1982; Foulkes and Docherty 2000, 2001; Altendorf and Watt 2005; Hughes *et al.* 2005). Whether the constraints are linguistic or non-linguistic, the fundamental premise is the same: that the distribution of the different surface forms of a **dependent variable** (the linguistic feature under scrutiny) can be correlated with bi- or multivalent **independent variables** (speaker characteristics, speech style, linguistic context, and so forth).

Identifying the social and linguistic constraints that prevent or disfavour a particular form from occurring in a given language variety and that license the use of another form instead is the central empirical preoccupation of **variationist sociolinguistics**. In this way, the social meaning of each of a variable's variants can be deduced, and their distribution within the system circumscribed. This is done by correlating patterns of variation in a community's language with the social and demographic characteristics of its speakers and the **social networks** and/or more generic categories to which they can be assigned (**social class**, **gender**, **ethnicity**, region etc.), and by noting those linguistic contexts in which certain variants are always, frequently, seldom or never found. It should be emphasized that the distribution of variants is not held to be 'either/or', but rather probabilistic. Categorical distribution of linguistic forms is clearly of secondary interest to researchers aiming to account for patterns of variation in language data.

THE HISTORY AND UTILITY OF THE (SOCIO)LINGUISTIC VARIABLE

The **sociolinguistic variable** was first systematically used for quantification of language variation in Labov's Martha's Vineyard study (1963). While in this guise it is a relatively new addition to the toolkit used by linguists for describing, analysing and modelling language structure and use, the (at least tacit) notion of the linguistic variable is as old as language study itself. Pāṇini's grammar of Sanskrit (?350 BC) incorporates variable rules that allow for differing outputs (Kiparsky 1979), and in the **dialect** geography and historical linguistics of more recent centuries the establishment of sets of 'equivalent' dialect terms and historical cognates entails identifying direct lexical and structural correspondences within and between languages. This is not at all surprising if, instead of assuming – as many modern linguists do – that variation is of only marginal significance to 'language proper', we take a more socially and historically realistic view of language structure, development and function. It hardly needs to be said that knowing that there are different ways of expressing the same idea in a given language is a fundamental element of people's everyday linguistic awareness – as Sapir (1921: 147) remarked, 'everyone knows that language is variable'. Despite this, and the fact that modern linguistics has its roots in the work of scholars who sought to provide a model of language structure and evolution to account for historical and contemporary intra- and interlinguistic differences, variability was generally marginalized or ignored by practitioners of the dominant schools of linguistics during the twentieth century, not least those working in the Chomskyan generativist tradition which continues to hold sway over large areas of the discipline. Intralinguistic variation is seen by many of the more conservative researchers in the generativist tradition to be irrelevant to an understanding of the nature of language beyond the most trivial level because, they argue, variability of the sort that interests sociolinguists is an epiphenomenon arising from the vagaries of language in use rather than a property of grammars at a deeper level (Chomsky 1986; Guy 1997; Henry 2002, 2005; Chambers 2003). But assuming, as seems reasonable, that one of the primary purposes of language acquisition is to permit social interaction, developing an awareness of the social meanings of linguistic variants and an ability to adapt one's use of variant forms according to situation and the perceived social characteristics of one's conversational partner(s) is as essential as any other aspect of language competence (Hymes 1971; Roberts and Labov 1995; Roberts 2002; Foulkes *et al.* 2005).

As suggested above, much of the value of the sociolinguistic variable in language research lies in its potential for quantifying patterns of variation: we can, that is, count how often a particular form occurs and express that frequency as a proportion of the total number of occasions on which the form *could have* occurred, even if it did not. And by comparing samples drawn from different age groups or from the same speakers at different times, we can get a sense of how the language or dialect is changing over time. The variable permits us to make statements of the sort: 'for two variants x and y of a variable (z), we find that x is used twice as much as y by older working-class men, but for young middle-class women the reverse is true.' The sociolinguistic variable thus allows us to observe changes in progress in a way that was once thought impossible (Labov 1994, 2001; Labov *et al.* 1972; Milroy 1991; McMahon 1994). Differences in the distribution of variants between casual, spontaneous speech and more closely monitored 'style-shifted' speech can likewise be captured, thereby allowing insight into speakers' attitudes towards and perceptions of the variant forms in their repertoires. This is an especially useful technique, as the researcher can thereby elicit attitudinal and perceptual information that the speaker may be unaware of, or is unable to articulate.

INDICATORS, MARKERS AND STEREOTYPES

By alluding to differing levels of 'salience' among variables and their variants, Labov (1972b) distinguishes between **indicators** (variables of which speakers other than linguists are unaware, and which are not subject to style-shifting), **markers** (variables close to speakers' level of conscious awareness which may have a role in class stratification, and which are subject to style-shifting), and **stereotypes** (forms of which speakers and the wider community are aware, but which, like other stereotyped expectations of social groups, are often archaic, misreported and misperceived). Of these, it is markers that have received, and continue to receive, the most attention from sociolinguists. These have tended to be phonological variables. This is no accident: their variants are usually more frequent than those of other sorts of variables, allowing the researcher to collect and analyse hundreds or thousands of tokens with relative ease; they can be elicited from informants without much effort; they lend themselves to **instrumental**

analysis; and they are functionally equivalent in a much less ambiguous way than are other sorts of variables. The remainder of this chapter will focus on a phonological variable that has been the object of much attention in the literature to date: (r) in English.

PHONOLOGICAL VARIATION: (r) IN BERWICK ENGLISH

Until the formalization of the sociolinguistic variable in Labov's early work, much of the surface variation in speech and writing had been treated by the majority of linguists as random, unpredictable 'free variation' that did not seem systematically to pattern with other factors. As an example, consider the use of **postvocalic (r)** in US English (the use of a **rhotic** consonant following the **vowel** in words like *car*, *turn* and *floors*). Hubbell (1950), for instance, concluded that:

> The pronunciation of a very large number of New Yorkers exhibits a pattern [. . .] that might most accurately be described as the complete absence of any pattern. Such speakers sometimes pronounce /r/ before a consonant or a pause and sometimes omit it, in a thoroughly haphazard pattern [. . .] The speaker hears both types of pronunciation about him all the time, both seem equally natural to him, and it is a matter of pure chance which one comes first to his lips.
>
> (Hubbell 1950: 48)

Such claims were made in spite of deeply held beliefs among the public that speech features of this sort were indexical of social status, ethnic group, and so forth. It is hard to see why else features such as non-rhoticity in US English would be stigmatized at the time for their perceived incorrectness, even among non-rhotic speakers themselves, as Labov's New York City studies would later demonstrate (Labov 1966).

Rhoticity works differently in the English of England. **Received Pronunciation**, which continues to enjoy the highest overall **prestige**, is a non-rhotic accent. Speakers from the few rhotic areas that remain in north-western and south-western England are not accorded much prestige, and (r)-ful pronunciations of words like *bird* and *short* are often considered amusingly rustic and old-fashioned. Rhoticity is becoming scarce in England, even in remote northern areas such as Northumberland, the accents of which were until quite recently fully rhotic and characterized by the long-standing and stereotyped 'Northumbrian burr' (**uvular fricative** or **approximant** [ʁ]; see Påhlsson 1972; Wells 1982). The accents of Scotland, lying immediately to the north, have on the other hand retained rhoticity almost universally. It is of great interest therefore to examine the interface between the two areas: since a robust **isogloss** is implausible given the plentiful cross-border interaction between Scots and Northumbrians, there is presumably a transitional area in which rhoticity is variable. Berwick upon Tweed, a town on the Northumberland coast three miles (5 km) south of the Scottish border, is cited as just such a transitional zone (Glauser 1991, 2000), and is for other historical and sociolinguistic reasons a prime site for investigating phonological variability in the region. Most intriguing is the finding of Kiely *et al.* (2000) that informants from nearby Alnwick report that they perceive Berwickers to sound Scottish; if so, rhoticity seems a good candidate as a cue to this perception. (Other possible cues are listed in Watt and Ingham 2000.)

(r) is a complex variable, as we must consider not just the presence or absence of rhoticity, we must also describe those tokens which do occur in terms of their **phonetic** identity. Berwick speakers can pronounce the word *bars* as [bɑːz] or [bɑɹz], but they also have a choice of which kind of postvocalic (r) to use should they use a rhotic pronunciation. In the present analysis, we coded for the variants [ɹ], [ʁ], [ɾ], [ʋ] and [ɹ̝], and the zero variant [Ø] to indicate non-rhoticity in postvocalic positions (we have actually simplified the analysis somewhat for present purposes; for fuller results see Watt and Pichler 2004). [ɹ] is the 'mainstream' British English variant; the **alveolar tap** [ɾ] is a traditionally Scottish form but is also found widely in northern England; [ʋ], the labiodental approximant, mentioned earlier, was until recently associated with infantile or defective speech, since when it has become extremely frequent in the English of southern England (Foulkes and Docherty 2000); [ɹ̝] differs from [ɹ] in that friction is audible.

In order first to try to establish whether or not Berwick English is undergoing a loss of rhoticity, we compared auditory **transcriptions** of spontaneous speech taken from recorded interviews with twenty male and female Berwick English-speakers ranging in age from 14 to 78 years ($n = 1,973$; average 98.7 tokens per speaker; Pichler 2005 gives further information on her fieldwork procedure). **Linking** /r/ (e.g. *sore arm*) and **intrusive** /r/ (e.g. *saw it*) contexts were of course excluded from this data set, the results for which are plotted against speaker age (Figure 1.1). Non-rhoticity appears to be (near-)categorical for all speakers. Even the eldest speaker uses non-rhotic pronunciations almost 90 per cent of the time. These data suggest, then, that Berwick English is now effectively established as a non-rhotic variety, and has thereby converged on mainstream **English English**. If Alnwick listeners hear Berwick English as 'Scottish', the perception is presumably triggered by cues other than postvocalic rhoticity.

What, then, of (r) in pre- and intervocalic positions? Figure 1.2 summarizes the pooled findings by speaker in descending order of age ($n = 1,550$; average 77.5 tokens per speaker). These results again suggest a pattern characterized by loss of traditional features. Use of [ɹ̝] and the traditional [ʁ] by all twenty speakers is negligible, and they are therefore omitted from the chart. What is most striking is the virtual loss of [ɾ] from old to young, and a corresponding upward trend (albeit a rather peaky one) in [ɹ]. Part of the reason for the peakiness lies in the modest – but perhaps growing – popularity of the innovative [ʋ] among the younger speakers, suggesting that it is finding favour among Berwick's teenage population. At any rate, it occurs at least as frequently as [ɾ] for five of the six teenage speakers.

Bringing other demographic factors (**sex**, place of residence) into the analysis as independent variables reveals additional distributional patterns that show

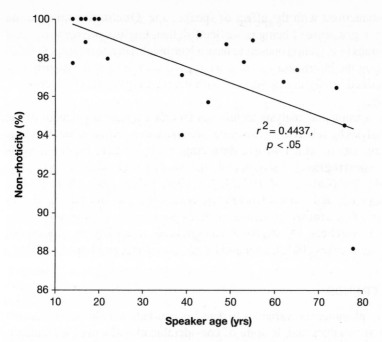

Figure 1.1 Non-rhoticity among twenty Berwick English-speakers (%)

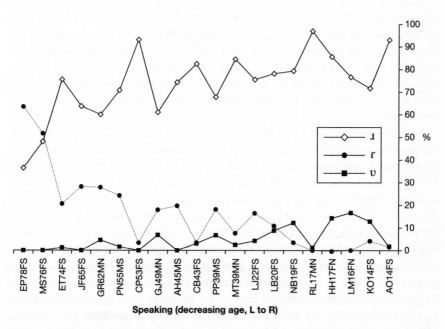

Figure 1.2 Phonetic variants of (r) in pre- and intervocalic positions (pooled) in Berwick English, by speaker (%). The speaker labels give the speaker's initials, age, sex (M/F) and place of residence (N/S, i.e. north or south of the river Tweed)

complex interactions with the effect of speaker age. **Qualitative** information on attitudes (e.g. a sense of being more Scottish than English, or vice versa) and self-perceptions (e.g. feeling oneself to have a Northumbrian rather than a Scottish accent) among the informants can also be aligned with the sort of **quantitative** results described briefly in this section, with illuminating results (Pichler *et al.*, forthcoming).

Current instrumental analysis techniques facilitate further refinement of the rhoticity analysis by subdividing the rhotic variants into narrower categories (e.g. rhotic pronunciations which involve **devoicing**, or those where friction noise is visible in a **spectrogram**). Instrumental analysis of vowel variation in English is well established (Labov *et al.* 1972; Labov 1966, 1972b, 1991; Thomas 2001; and see Chapter 3) and while it has hitherto been rather rare in analyses of consonantal variables, **acoustic** profiling methods are now being used much more widely by researchers investigating fine-grained variability in consonants (Docherty and Foulkes 2001; Carter and Local 2003; Jones and Llamas 2003).

FUTURE TRENDS

The study of phonological variables to date has concentrated almost exclusively on segmental variables and, in spite of considerable classificatory and quantificational difficulties, systematic variability in **suprasegmental** features such as **intonation**, rhythm and voice quality is starting to receive more attention (Stuart-Smith 1999; Low *et al.* 2000; Grabe *et al.* 2000). Furthermore, an emphasis on the study of production at the expense of perception has meant that we know comparatively little about how listeners selectively filter and attend to different aspects of variation in the signal (Thomas 2002a, b). It seems clear that a full account of the scope of phonological variation within a language is necessary if we are to come to understand the range of indexical resources that speakers may draw upon.

For the investigation of phonological variables and variables of other types the growing availability of searchable tagged electronic text and speech corpora is proving of enormous benefit (Garside *et al.* 1997; Oakes 1998; Sampson and McCarthy 2005; Gries 2005; Beal *et al.* forthcoming). These resources circumvent, or at least complement, intuition-based judgements of grammatical acceptability. A trend towards attempting to integrate socially conditioned variability into current theoretical models such as Optimality Theory (Nagy and Reynolds 1997; Anttila and Cho 1998) and the Minimalist Program (e.g. Adger and Smith 2005) gives an encouraging indication that as time goes on the sociolinguistic variable is being given more space as a useful analytical and explanatory device in theoretical frameworks that might previously have viewed even the most systematic variation as a 'nuisance factor'. In applications such as **forensic linguistics** and language pathology and therapy any sidelining of the role of systematic variation can be dangerously counterproductive (Nolan 1997; Foulkes and French 1999; Oetting 2005; Watt and Smith 2005), and it seems inescapable that the development of reliable human–computer interfaces – especially speech recognition systems – can progress beyond their present point only if sociolinguistic variation at multiple levels of structure is afforded a more central role. While it is still in need of refinement in some areas, as noted earlier, the sociolinguistic variable represents the means by which bringing variability in speech and language under analytical control can be achieved.

FURTHER READING

Guy, G. (1993) 'The quantitative analysis of linguistic variation', in D. Preston (ed.) *American Dialect Research*, Amsterdam: Benjamins, pp. 223–49.

Labov, W. (1980) *Locating Language in Time and Space: Quantitative Analyses of Linguistic Structure*, New York: Academic Press.

Mesthrie, R. (1999) 'Sociolinguistic variation', in R. Mesthrie (ed.) *The Concise Encyclopaedia of Sociolinguistics*, Amsterdam: Pergamon, pp. 377–88.

Milroy, L. and Gordon, M. (2003) *Sociolinguistics: Method and Interpretation*, Oxford: Blackwell.

Milroy, J. and Milroy, L. (1997a) 'Varieties and variation', in F. Coulmas (ed.) *The Handbook of Sociolinguistics*, Oxford: Blackwell, pp. 47–64.

2
FIELD METHODS

CARMEN LLAMAS

The field methods involved in a sociolinguistic study are often not reported in great detail, and are typically seen as secondary to the analysis, presentation and interpretation of the data, yet they constitute a fundamental and time-consuming step in the research process, and they can shape the findings of the study. How researchers elicit their data, and from whom, will depend on the theoretical under-pinnings and the larger objectives of the investigation. None the less, whatever the objectives, careful planning of field methods is vital to the success of the study as a whole in terms of its reliability and its replicability.

Broadly speaking, decision making in three areas influences the field methodology of a research project: the type of study being undertaken; the type of speaker required; and the type of data required. In this chapter, we will consider each of these areas in turn.

THE TYPE OF STUDY

Many of the decisions about what type of data to collect and from whom will depend on whether the study is **ethnographic** or **variationist** in nature, and whether the data collected are to be analysed **qualitatively** or **quantitatively**. The researcher may be attempting to enter the community to act as a **participant observer** (see further Johnstone 2000; for examples of studies using such methods see Cheshire 1982; Eckert 2000; Moore 2003). Alternatively, the researcher may be interested in **synchronic** variation, a snapshot of language in the community, so to speak, and what this can tell us about **language change** (see for example Labov 1972b; Trudgill 1974a; Docherty *et al.* 1997). Furthermore, the study may utilize the **apparent time** construct to investigate possible language change in the community, or it may track change in **real time** by utilizing a *panel study* or a *trend study*. A panel study investigates change in an individual's lifetime, and, using the same technique of elicitation, monitors any changes in linguistic behaviour (see for example Mees and Collins 1999). A trend study, on the other hand, tracks the speech of different but comparable individuals, offering a study of a life stage as experienced by successive age cohorts (see for example Trudgill 1988). Practicalities are such that large-scale studies in real time are rarely under-taken, and apparent time studies are more commonly used in variationist research. Such studies involve the observation of the speech of different age groups simultaneously and the evaluation of age-correlated linguistic differences as evidence of possible change in progress in the community (see Chapter 8).

Decisions made about the type of study to be undertaken, such as those outlined above, will have consequences for both the techniques of sampling and for the elicitation of speech data.

THE TYPE OF SPEAKER

In the planning stages, before the researcher even enters the 'field', decisions need to be taken on the **sampling universe** of the study. This could be a city, a neighbourhood, a business or a school, for example. Once the sampling universe has been delimited, the *population* must be *sampled*: in order to do this the researcher commonly uses a **random sample**, or some form of **judgement sample**, although in some more ethnographic or qualitative studies, such as those which take place in institutional settings like the workplace, the sample is neither random nor judgement, but is negotiated within the institutional confines of the setting.

Random samples are seldom used in sociolinguistic studies, as achieving true *representativeness* of a population, which is the aim of random sampling techniques, is rarely possible and can generate so much data as to make the study practically unmanageable (see Houck 1968 for an example of the use of a random sample in a language survey). Random sampling is based on the principle that everyone in the population has an equal chance of being selected to form part of the sample. A **sample frame** is used, such as an electoral register or a telephone directory, from which every *n*th person is selected. However, this technique does not differentiate between native speakers of the dialect (or language) and non-native speakers, local people and non-local people, willing participants and non-willing participants. Therefore certain people selected will not be suitable for the study. To replace them is to introduce bias into the sample, which, strictly speaking, no longer ensures that the sample is randomly selected from the population.

A more commonly used technique is judgement sampling. With this technique the researcher knows in advance the type of speaker required for the study (that is, the **social variables** of interest) and seeks out speakers who fulfil certain criteria to fill certain quotas. These speakers may be connected with each other in the sense of belonging to the same **social network** or **community of practice**, or they may be unconnected.

In terms of the size of the fieldwork sample required, manageability of the data is a key concern. Not all possible social variables can ever be accounted for, as samples are made up of individual speakers who bring individual factors into the mix (that is, factors which mean that their linguistic behaviour is not generalizable to other members of the community that the cohort they are in represents). None the less, in a judgement sample, every new social variable that is introduced effectively doubles the sample size. If we have five speakers per cell or cohort, say, and we have **sex** and **age** (young and old) as social variables, we need twenty speakers (five young females, five old females, five young males and five old males). If we introduce **social class** into the study and consider two groupings (working-class and middle-class), our sample size grows to forty speakers, as for

13

each of our previous cells we now need five working-class and five middle-class speakers. We therefore need to strike a balance between keeping the data that are generated by the fieldwork sample manageable whilst capturing as many social variables of interest as is possible. The level of detail of analysis will clearly have an influence here, as if we are interested in depth of analysis (for example, undertaking **acoustic** analyses of **variants** of **phonological** variables in numerous different linguistic environments) then we may lose something in terms of breadth, as the number of speakers and the number of variables that can be analysed may be restricted owing to time constraints.

Whichever sampling technique or sample size is used, **informants** must be contacted and *fieldwork* undertaken. Informants can be approached by the researcher as a stranger, or through contacts in the community. The latter of the two is generally the more successful approach. Individuals involved in youth clubs, social clubs, local societies, churches, and so on, may be extremely useful in gaining access to the community and to potential informants. The researcher may then be passed on from one informant to another as a 'friend of a friend' using a *snowball technique* which has the effect of guaranteeing the good faith of the researcher (see Milroy 1987b for further discussion). Howsoever informants are contacted, good practice in fieldwork must be followed and ethical considerations, such as gaining informed consent and guaranteeing the anonymity of the informant and restricted access to the recording, should be borne in mind.

The fieldwork can be a difficult and daunting task, particularly for the researcher new to the field. Having contact with members of the public, however, can be a rewarding and enjoyable experience, although much can depend on developing skills in successful observation and interviewing, establishing a rapport with informants and interviewees, making sure that their interests (both ethical and in terms of enjoying the experience of being observed or interviewed) are uppermost. And much can depend on what the researcher asks the informant to do.

THE TYPE OF DATA

Once we have established the types of speaker whose linguistic behaviour is to be investigated, and how they are to be contacted, we must determine how to elicit samples of their speech. This may be an on-going process of data collection over a protracted period of time, as in participant observation studies, or it may involve a dedicated period of fieldwork during which targeted speech data are collected. Data collection will probably involve the assembling of a *corpus* of spoken language or a dataset, which may include specific **elicitation tests** to investigate particular linguistic forms of interest. Depending on the interests of the study, these elicitation tests may, for instance, access intuitions about grammatical correctness or usage (see for example Cheshire *et al.* 1989), develop experimental settings to test the use of discourse strategies (see for example Freed 1996), or incorporate the elicitation of phonetic data in controlled carrier phrases (see for example Jones and Llamas 2003).

Most studies incorporate techniques to elicit different styles of speech in order to investigate intra-speaker variation (see Chapter 11), but since the work of Labov in the 1960s, interest has been, first and foremost, in accessing a style of speech which is as casual, natural and spontaneous as can be obtained. The very act of being observed, however, may have the effect of making the speech less than casual, natural and spontaneous. Overcoming this **observer's paradox** (see Labov 1972b: 61) has led to the development of many techniques which seek to access unmonitored speech. In order to lessen the effect of being observed, we may decide simply to leave recording equipment with speakers and ask them to record themselves, probably in pairs, discussing subjects of their choosing with no fieldworker participation or presence. (This method has been used effectively in many recent studies of language variation, for example, Docherty *et al.* 1997; Stuart-Smith 1999.) By eliminating any fieldworker involvement, the effects of the observer's paradox may be reduced. However, the speakers will still be aware that their conversation is being recorded – that is, observed – hence we cannot eliminate the paradox absolutely. The only way to do this would be to record speakers covertly; this would not only have serious ethical implications which would prohibit its use, but the quality of the recording would be seriously compromised by attempting to conceal the type of equipment capable of recording high-quality speech data (for example, current solid state technology). Such surreptitious recordings are therefore rarely used in sociolinguistic research.

Although informants can record themselves in their own environments, a more common technique of eliciting samples of speech data is through the **sociolinguistic interview**. The effects of the interviewer, the types of questions, modules or activities used, and the interview itself as a speech event all have implications for and place limitations on the data.

The interview may take the form of a questionnaire or may be more loosely structured around topics or modules, that is, groups of questions focusing on a particular topic on which an interviewer can draw (see further Labov 1984). The primary aim of the interview is likely to be to elicit a sample of speech from the informant which is as casual and spontaneous as possible. Therefore a formal one-to-one interview may be less than ideal for achieving this, as the asymmetrical power relationship between interviewer and interviewee determines that the interviewer controls the discourse, which may not only affect the level of self-monitoring of the interviewee's speech but may also place structural limitations on the **morphosyntactic** features which are liable to occur. (For example, **tags**, whose normal function is to compel a **minimal response** from the addressee, are unlikely to occur in the formal interview situation.)

Many attempts have been made to lessen the formality of the interview situation so as to maximize the possibility of accessing casual, unmonitored speech. One of the much cited questions used by Labov in his Lower East Side study (1972b: 93) is the 'danger of death' question. It was believed that, in the telling of an absorbing and emotional narrative of an occasion during which the speaker's life was at risk, informants would disregard the fact that they were being observed and hence forget to monitor their speech. Although seemingly successful in Labov's study, this particular question was found to be less effective for a variety of reasons when tried in other localities, however (for example, Belfast, Norwich, California). As data elicitation techniques must be usable with a variety of people, topics such as childhood games and memories are often discussed either loosely or in specific questions or modules in the interview (see Wolfram and Fasold 1974 and Labov 1984 for example questions and modules).

Furthermore, attitudinal information on identities, identifications, orientations, affiliations and perceptions of language variation can be elicited through the interview. The benefit of these types of data is that the content of the speech can be analysed in order to gain insight into the linguistic behaviour of the informants and the **indexicality** inherent in the linguistic forms of interest. (See Dyer 2000; Anderson and Milroy 1999; Llamas 2001, for examples of this in variationist studies, and Chapter 14 for examples of this in attitudinal studies.)

The length of the interview is also a consideration, and will be guided by the levels of linguistic analysis that are of interest in the research. Useful data for a phonetic/phonological analysis can be obtained from around thirty minutes of speech, for example, whereas considerably more are needed for grammatical or discoursal analyses as the relevant structures are unlikely to occur as frequently or as predictably as phonological features (see Chapters 3–5).

Eliciting data for analysis of differing linguistic levels from the same speech sample can prove difficult. Incorporating lexical variation into the elicitation technique can make the task even more problematical, as to control for lexical items in a conversation is to jeopardize the spontaneous style of speech which is of interest for phonological/grammatical analyses. A method which has been developed recently and is currently being used in a number of large-scale studies of British English involves the use of *Sense Relation Network* (SRN) sheets which are given to informants some days prior to the interview for consideration and completion. Allowing informants to know the content of the interview prior to it taking place has the effect of both increasing the amount of data captured through the method of elicitation and of lessening any feelings of unease on the part of the informant about the interview situation, thus permitting a more relaxed approach to the interaction. The SRNs contain standard notion words with space provided for the insertion of local variants (see Figure 2.1 for an example of a completed SRN – three of which are typically used in an interview).

During the interview, which is conducted with self-selected pairs of informants, local variants are discussed in terms of connotations, collocations, perceived social variation in usage, perceived etymologies, perceived geographical distribution of usage, etc., thus providing a number of variants for each standard notion word in spoken and written form, as well as a wealth of attitudinal information about the variants themselves, and all given in the context of casual speech which can be analysed for phonological and grammatical features of interest (see Llamas 1999 for full discussion).

Figure 2.1 Example of completed Sense Relation Network sheet

As well as the various techniques discussed for eliciting samples of casual speech, many other methods are available for eliciting and accessing samples of speech and perceptions of language. Space limitations restrict full discussion, but these include, amongst others, **subjective reaction tests**, **semantic differential scales**, **matched guise tests**, rapid and anonymous observations, telephone surveys, methods associated with **perceptual dialectology** (for example the use of mapping perceived language variation), methods associated with **traditional dialectology** (for example the use of written questionnaires), and so on. (Further detail and discussion of various techniques listed can be found in the Further Reading titles. Further detail on methods associated with the investigation of language attitudes can be found in Chapter 14.)

CONCLUSION

For any study which sets out to collect data in order to investigate an aspect of language variation and change in a given community, the linguistic findings and consequent interpretations and conclusions of the study depend heavily on the field methods employed, as how the data are collected and who they are collected from have consequences for the study as a whole. Empirical data form the basis of accurate descriptions from which adequate theories derive. Thus collecting 'good' data is crucial. Methodological decisions made about data collection should therefore be both transparent and based on defensible theoretical frameworks to allow both replication of the study and the efficient collection of reliable data.

A variety of methods is available for use in sociolinguistic studies, and refinements and innovations are constantly being developed. The importance of field methods in a data-driven discipline such as sociolinguistics ensures that such refinements and innovations are central to the development of the subject as a whole.

FURTHER READING

Crawford, F. (2002) 'Entering the community: fieldwork', in J.K. Chambers, P. Trudgill and N. Schilling-Estes (eds) *The Handbook of Language Variation and Change*, Oxford: Blackwell, pp. 20–39.

Johnstone, B. (2000) *Qualitative Methods in Sociolinguistics*, New York: Oxford University Press.

Labov, W. (1984) 'Field methods of the project on linguistic change and variation', in J. Baugh and J. Sherzer (eds) *Language in Use*, Englewood Cliffs, NJ: Prentice-Hall, pp. 28–53.

Mesthrie, R. (ed.) (2001) *Concise Encyclopedia of Sociolinguistics*, Oxford: Elsevier.

Milroy, L. and Gordon, M. (2003) *Sociolinguistics: Method and Interpretation*, Oxford: Blackwell.

Romaine, S. (1980) 'A critical overview of the methodology of urban British sociolinguistics', *English World Wide* 1 (1): 163–98.

3

TECHNIQUES OF ANALYSIS

I PHONOLOGICAL VARIATION

MATTHEW GORDON

Sociolinguists operate under the axiom that linguistic variation is not random but rather is shaped by social and linguistic factors. One of the goals of any sociolinguistic study is an account of the influence of these factors. Often this information is presented in the form of a statistical analysis that clearly defines the correlations among the linguistic forms and the various social and linguistic factors. When we read such an account, we rarely consider the process of analysis that went into creating it. Nevertheless, this process is in many cases the most time-consuming stage in the research.

It is easy to appreciate why this process takes so long when we remember that it typically begins with hours of recorded speech from several subjects. This is the pool of raw material in which the patterns of variation are to be found. To the casual observer, sociolinguistic variation can appear chaotic. It seems that some people use some forms more than other people and that some forms may be more common in certain words or contexts than in others, but firm generalizations are hard to deduce without a systematic analysis. That analysis is essentially a process of translating natural speech into data that allow comparison across speakers and linguistic contexts.

This chapter sketches the process for analysing phonological variables. We begin by considering issues related to how the variables to be analysed are defined. From there we turn to techniques for measuring the variation. The final section considers how variables are affected by their linguistic contexts.

DEFINING THE VARIABLES

A crucial early step in any variationist analysis is a definition of the **linguistic variables** to be examined (see Chapter 1). The research must specify the range of variation associated with each variable. This involves detailing the **phonetic variants** of the variable and their **phonological** distribution within the language or **dialect** studied.

It is common to think about phonological variation as coming in two basic flavours: *discrete* and *continuous*. Discrete variation involves phonetic variants that represent distinct alternatives. Some of the clearest examples of this type relate to the presence versus absence of a sound. Familiar examples from English include **H-dropping** in England (e.g. [hæt] ~ [æt] 'hat') and *r*-lessness in New York

City and elsewhere (e.g. [kɑr] ~ [kɑ] 'car'). Discrete variation often relies on a binary choice as in these two examples but may involve more variants. In a study of Newcastle speech, for example, Watt and Milroy (1999) identified four discrete variants of (o): [oʊ], [θː], [ʊə], and [oː].

In the case of continuous variation, there are no clear boundaries among the variants. Rather, the variable exhibits a range of realizations along a *phonetic continuum*. Many vocalic variables operate in this fashion. For example, in many varieties of American English, /æ/ is variably raised sometimes as high as [i]. Speakers do not simply alternate between [i] and [æ]. Instead they sometimes produce [æ], sometimes produce [i], and sometimes produce intermediate variants in the neighbourhood of [ɛ] and [e]; that is, they have available to them any phonetic value along the range from the low [æ] to the high [i].

In addition to defining the phonetic dimensions of the variation, the researcher must also specify the scope of the variable within the phonological system. If we think about variation as stemming from the application of rules, then the scope represents the contexts in which the rules may apply. Of course these rules may or may not apply in any given case and their likelihood of applying is influenced by social and linguistic factors (see below). Our concern here lies with defining where the variation might possibly operate. For phonological variables this is a relatively straightforward task as compared with the challenges presented by grammatical variables (see further Chapter 4).

In some instances the scope of a variable is simply that of the **phoneme** in which case the variation operates in all contexts containing that phoneme. Consider, for example, the raising of /æ/ noted above. In Chicago, Detroit, and elsewhere, this raising is part of a phenomenon known as the Northern Cities Shift (Labov 1994; Gordon 2001), a series of sound changes that lead to variable realizations of several phonemes. These changes apply across the board so that every word containing these phonemes may show the effects of the shift. Thus, the scope of the variable (æ) – parentheses are used to indicate **sociolinguistic variables** – is isomorphic with that of the phoneme /æ/.

Phonological variables often have a more restricted scope than the phonemes they involve. For instance, they are commonly subject to *phonological con-ditioning*. In the case of *r*-lessness, the /r/ is eligible for deletion only when it does not appear before a **vowel**. The raising of /æ/, while it applies across the board in the northern cities, operates within certain phonological restrictions in other locations, including Philadelphia and New York City (see Labov 1994). Thus in Philadelphia and New York the vowel may be raised when it appears before a **nasal** consonant (as in *man*) but not before a **voiceless stop** (as in *cat*).

The scope of some variables may be defined lexically, that is, in terms of particular words rather than phonological contexts. Often such variables involve alternations between phonemes (e.g. *either* and *neither* pronounced with /i/ or /aj/). In some cases the variation may apply only to a single word as in the American English examples of *aunt* which may appear with /æ/ or /ɑ/ or *ask* which may appear as [æsk] or [æks].

An exact definition of the linguistic variable is an essential prerequisite to any meaningful sociolinguistic analysis. The variation associated with a given variable is shaped by social and linguistic factors, but one cannot untangle the effects of those factors until the boundaries of the variation have been delineated. Failure to properly define the variable clouds the picture of the variation and may introduce serious bias to the results. Imagine a hypothetical study of *r*-lessness that failed to recognize the phonological conditioning of this variable and counted all instances of /r/ rather than just those potentially subject to deletion. If all of the examples from one group of speakers came from pre-vocalic /r/ (e.g. *ride, carry*), and all those from another group came from **postvocalic** contexts (e.g. *car, park*), the researcher might be led to the erroneous conclusion that the second group deleted /r/ much more frequently. Such an error is unlikely with a well studied variable like *r*-lessness, but the general caveat remains: clearly defining the variable helps ensure that one is comparing apples with apples.

MEASURING VARIATION

With the linguistic variable defined, the researcher can set about the task of measuring the variation associated with that variable. This task is essentially one of distilling the raw material of the recorded speech into usable data. These data will serve as the input for the later analysis in which the effects of social and linguistic factors are explored. Phonological variation is usually measured in one of two ways: (1) **auditorially** (by listening to the recordings), or (2) **instrumentally** (using spectrographic analysis of the acoustic signal).

Auditory coding

Over the last four decades of sociolinguistic research, the most common approach to measuring phonological variation has been to rely on the auditory judgements of the investigators who listen to the recorded speech to determine the variants used. With repeated listenings, researchers can train themselves to distinguish subtle phonetic variants reliably. A sample of speech from each subject is then reviewed and each instance of the variable under investigation is coded according to the variant produced. The goal of this coding is usually to produce some kind of statistical measure of each subject's usage.

In the investigation of discrete variables, this measurement is relatively straightforward. The researcher listens to and codes a certain number of instances or tokens of the variable, and then counts how frequently each variant appears. These raw numbers are easily translated into percentages by taking the number of tokens of each variant and dividing it by the total of all tokens. For statistical reliability it is recommended that at least thirty tokens of the variable be examined for each speaker (see further Guy 1993).

The coding of continuous variables is somewhat more complicated. The phonetic variation is too great for every variant to be transcribed. The researcher must impose a classificatory system onto the variation to break the phonetic continuum up into steps. In effect this approach treats the continuous variable as if it were discrete. Returning to the example of /æ/ raising, the analysis might propose four degrees of raising represented by unraised [æ], the slightly raised [ɛ], the more raised [e], and the most raised [i]. The tokens would then be coded according to these steps in the raising process, keeping in mind that each step represents a piece out of the phonetic continuum. The phonetic codes can be converted to a mathematical index of each speaker's usage by assigning numerical values to each step. In this example, the conservative [æ] would be assigned a zero, [ɛ] would be one, [e] would be two, and [i] would be three. The index is calculated by taking the average of all the tokens coded. In this way a speaker with an index around zero shows very little raising while one approaching three shows consistent raising to the highest degree. Like the percentages calculated for discrete variables, these indexes allow for straightforward comparison across speakers.

Instrumental measurement

Phonological variation can also be examined using the instruments and techniques of **acoustic** phonetics. This approach was pioneered in sociolinguistics by Labov *et al.* (1972), and has become increasingly popular in recent years due in part to technological advances which make acoustic analysis possible on a personal computer. A thorough account of the theoretical underpinnings of these methods is beyond the scope of this chapter, but accessible introductions can be found in Kent and Read (1992) and Johnson (1997).

In an acoustic analysis the measurements of the variation are taken instrumentally rather than by listening to the recordings. Today the process most often involves digitizing the recorded speech samples in order to enter them into a computer program to perform spectrographic analysis. This analysis produces a visual representation of the speech signal from which precise measurements can be taken. One of the most common representations used is the **spectrogram** in which shadings of light and dark are used to show degrees of acoustic energy at different frequencies across time. Research in phonetics has identified several measurable components of the acoustic signal that correlate with particular phonetic features. For example, the phonetic difference between **voiced** and **voiceless** sounds is indicated in a spectrogram by the presence or absence of a voicing bar, which appears as a dark band at low frequencies (see Figure 3.1).

Sociolinguists most commonly employ acoustic analysis in the study of vowels. This approach is especially useful in examining continuous vocalic variation such as in the case of /æ/ raising and other changes in the Northern Cities Shift. In a spectrogram, vowels appear as dark horizontal bands of energy known as *formants*. Formants are created by sound resonating in the mouth and pharynx. As the shape of the vocal tract changes by moving the tongue to produce different vowels, the sound resonates at different frequencies. For this reason, measuring the frequencies of the formants can provide indications of how the vocal tract is shaped;

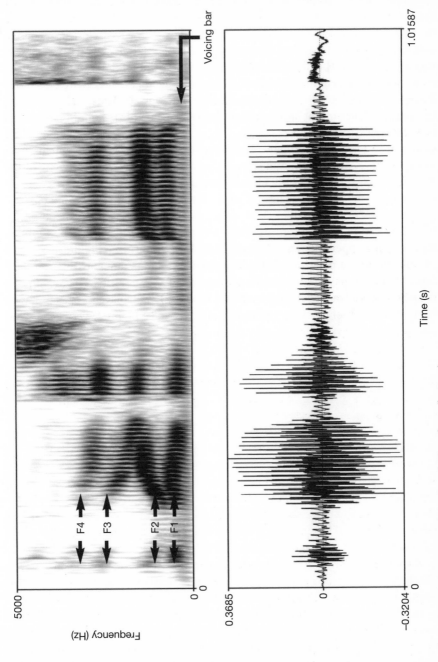

Figure 3.1 Spectrogram (top) and Waveform (bottom)

that is, of how the tongue is positioned in making the vowel sound. In this way, formant frequency measurements serve as a corollary of the position of vowels in the mouth. Of particular interest are the first and second formants, labelled F1 and F2 here, which are usually taken as corollaries of vowel height and frontness respectively. Low vowels are characterized by a high F1 frequency and high vowels by a low F1 frequency as measured in Hertz (Hz). A typical male speaker might have a high [i] with an F1 frequency of about 300 Hz and a low [æ] with an F1 around 700 Hz. For the front–back dimension, high F2 frequencies characterize front vowels and lower F2 values characterize back vowels. Thus, an [i] produced by a male speaker might have an F2 of 2,000 Hz while his [u] might have an F2 of 1,000 Hz.

Researchers can use formant frequency measurements to create a picture of a subject's vowel space by plotting the data on a graph. Individual tokens of the variable can be plotted, but for a less cluttered picture the researcher may choose to plot mean values for F1 and F2 which have been calculated on the basis of several tokens of the variable. These vowel plots can be oriented in keeping with the traditional representations of vowel articulations (i.e. the *vowel quadrangle* with [i] in the upper left corner and [ɑ] in the lower right – see Figure 3.2).

Comparing the positions of the vowels as measured acoustically with their expected positions demonstrates the progress of vowel shifts. For example, a speaker who is advanced in the Northern Cities Shift might have a vowel plot with /æ/ in the high front position (indicating a low F1 and a high F2) very near his or

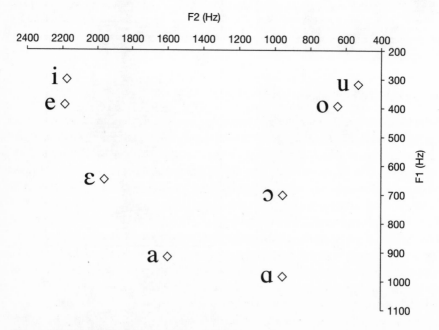

Figure 3.2 F1 and F2 plot of a male speaker's vowel space

her /i/, which is not affected by the shift (see Thomas 2001 for a collection of plots representing various American dialects).

One of the advantages of acoustic analysis is that it allows the researcher to measure variations that are too subtle to be reliably detected auditorily. Also, because the measurements are taken mechanically and therefore rely less on the researcher's judgement, they are felt to be less subjective. Still, acoustic analysis raises questions of its own (see further Milroy and Gordon 2003). One of the most important challenges posed by the use of acoustic data is cross-speaker comparison. Formant frequencies and other acoustic measures are affected by physiological differences in vocal tracts. Since no two subjects have identical vocal tracts, their formant measurements cannot be directly compared. This fact leaves the researcher with two choices: (1) compare speakers in terms of the relative positions of the vowels rather than the absolute formant frequencies, or (2) normalize the frequency measures by applying a mathematical formula.

The former approach can be useful in studying vowel shifts such as the Northern Cities Shift where progress can be measured, for example, by the position of /æ/ relative to /i/. To compare a large sample of speakers, the researcher might develop a coding system to mark degrees of shifting in much the same way as is done in an auditory analysis. Fridland (1999) presents this type of analysis in her study of another set of changes known as the Southern Shift.

The raw frequency data can be made comparable by applying a formula that normalizes the values. Several such formulas have been proposed, and their merits are the subject of ongoing debate in the field (see, for example, Adank et al. 1999). All of these normalization routines are intended to factor out the effects of physiological differences across vocal tracts. In this way, the normalized frequency values can be used to compare speakers through statistical analysis (see, for example, Labov 2001).

ANALYSING LINGUISTIC FACTORS

When we think of important sociolinguistic studies, we tend to concentrate on findings related to the social significance of linguistic variables rather than on those related to phonological conditioning. From Labov's study of New York department stores (1966), for example, we might remember that **rhotic** pronunciations were more common among the employees of the high-end store Saks though it is harder to recall that rhoticity was also more common at the end of a word than before another consonant. This is understandable since it is the focus on the social functioning of language that distinguishes this work from other areas of linguistics. We should keep in mind, however, that sociolinguistic analysis also involves a thorough exploration of linguistic factors shaping usage. Indeed, generalizations about the social distribution of a speech form cannot be made without an understanding of its internal linguistic patterning.

Phonological variables are often influenced by elements of their linguistic context. Labov's finding that /r/ is more often deleted in pre-consonantal contexts (e.g. *fourth*) than in word-final position (e.g. *floor*) illustrates the phonological conditioning that commonly shapes usage of a variable. The importance of phonological conditioning was noted above as a key element in defining a variable. The kind of conditioning at issue here differs in that it does not apply categorically but rather it contributes to tendencies. Thus, in this section we are interested in the kinds of phonological factors that make a given variant more or less likely to occur. With *r*-lessness, /r/ is more likely to be deleted pre-consonantally, but it does not have to be, and conversely it is less likely to be deleted word-finally, but it certainly can be.

The elements of the phonological context that serve as conditioning factors will vary according to the type of variable. Similar to *r*-lessness in New York, **glottalization** of /t/ in many British varieties is influenced by the position of the consonant in the word as well as by whether it is followed by a vowel or consonant (see, for example, Docherty and Foulkes 1999). In the case of vowels, adjacent consonants often play a role. The raising of /æ/, for example, has been found to be promoted by the appearance of a following nasal consonant (e.g. *ham, hand*) and retarded by a preceding **liquid** (e.g. *laugh, rat*) (Labov 1994). Such findings about phonological conditioning are arrived at by simply comparing usage across contexts as measured either auditorially or instrumentally. In the same way that one might calculate an index for an individual speaker's usage of (æ), one can break the data up by phonological context and calculate an index for all the tokens involving a following nasal, a preceding liquid, and so on.

In addition to phonological context, a variable might be influenced by individual lexical items; that is, use of some variant might be more or less common in a particular word. Ash (1997) reports a case of lexical conditioning for the process of /l/ **vocalization**, in which /l/ is pronounced as a vowel such as [o] or a **glide** such as [w] (as in [fɪo] ~ [fɪw] for 'fill'). Among the Philadelphians Ash studied, she found vocalization was not common when /l/ appeared between vowels except in the word *Philadelphia* itself.

Recognizing the influence of linguistic context, researchers often take steps to ensure they sample a range of contexts for each subject. Thus, they might limit the number of tokens of any given word to be coded. This helps to reduce the potential for skewed results from a particular lexical item or phonological context. Such measures are necessary in order to conduct a reliable comparison across speakers and thus to examine the influence of social factors.

This chapter has sketched out some of the major components of a sociolinguistic analysis of phonological variation. Readers seeking a fuller treatment of these issues may wish to consult Hudson (1996) or Milroy and Gordon (2003). My goal here has been to give a sense of the analytical process that lies behind the results we encounter when reading a sociolinguistic study. Understanding the method-ological choices that the researcher has made is essential to evaluating the validity of the study's conclusions.

FURTHER READING

Chambers, J.K. (2003) *Sociolinguistic Theory* (2nd edition), Oxford: Blackwell.

Hudson, R.A. (1996) *Sociolinguistics* (2nd edition), Cambridge: Cambridge University Press.

Johnson, K. (1997) *Acoustic and Auditory Phonetics*, Oxford: Blackwell.

Labov, W. (1972b) *Sociolinguistic Patterns*, Philadelphia, PA: University of Pennsylvania Press.

Milroy, L. and Gordon, M. (2003) *Sociolinguistics: Method and Interpretation*, Oxford: Blackwell.

4

TECHNIQUES OF ANALYSIS

II MORPHOSYNTACTIC VARIATION

JENNIFER SMITH

Since Labov's first groundbreaking study of Martha's Vineyard in the early 1960s, **phonetic** variation has been predominant in the field of **variationist socio-linguistics**. However, **morphosyntactic** variation has also garnered considerable attention, with a plethora of studies into variables which are common to a large number of **dialects**. These include *was/were* alternation as in (1) below; **negative concord**, as in (2); verbal *–s* as in (3); **non-standard** verb forms as in (4); **copula** deletion as in (5) and **quotative** *be like*, as in (6):

(1) The coppers let them go to see if they *was* the bastards. (Cheshire 1982: 44)

(2) I *ain't* got *no* money. (Howe and Walker 2000: 111)

(3) Her gives me a hug and a kiss when I *comes* in and one when I go. (Godfrey and Tagliamonte 1999: 89)

(4) My two brothers, they never *fighted*, you know. (Eisikovits 1987: 127)

(5) I feel like I ø fourteen. (Weldon 2003: 7)

(6) I'*m like* 'Joe, how's the truck? And he'*s like* 'Oh, Clarky, man, I fucked my truck up!' (Tagliamonte and Hudson 1999: 148)

Morphosyntactic variation is not confined to competition between dialect and **standard** forms. Variation occurs in all spoken varieties, even in those which can be considered to be fairly standard. For example, negative versus auxiliary contraction, as in (7); deontic **modality**, as in (8); *that* complementizer, as in (9); use of intensifiers, as in (10); relative clause markers, as in (11).

(7) He'*ll* not be better again Margaret, no . . . And you *won't* have the same interest. (Tagliamonte and Smith 2002)

(8) If she goes out she *must* have her chair, *got to* take her chair and a oxygen cylinder this height. (Tagliamonte and Smith in press)

(9) I think *that some of his family* would be the same. I *think* Ø she was lucky to get him. (Tagliamonte *et al.* to appear)

(10) It was a *really* old building . . . it was a *very* old rambling mess of a building. (Ito and Tagliamonte 2003: 269)

(11) The last meeting Ø we had in that church.
And they used the old nets which we *would* call strabbles.
Then there were a word *that* I couldn't get summat to rhyme with.
(Tagliamonte *et al.* in press)

These examples demonstrate that morphosyntactic variation is not some peripheral phenomenon confined to a handful of obscure varieties but instead is pervasive in everyday speech in every **variety**. Despite this, Labov (1991: 277) comments that '[s]yntactic change is an elusive process as compared to sound change'. This chapter aims to provide some insights into this process, setting out some of the steps involved in large-scale **quantitative** analyses of variable grammatical forms. I concentrate on issues of **transcription**, choice of **linguistic variable** for analysis, identifying the envelope of variation, coding, and statistical analysis.

TRANSCRIPTION

Although not a necessary step in the analysis, the task of identifying and analysing variable morphosyntactic forms is greatly aided by full *transcription* of the interview data. This is an extremely time-consuming initial stage, but one which is worth the effort, as the data can be mined for a number of variables without the need to return to the original recordings every time another variable is analysed.

The trick in the transcription of data for morphosyntactic analysis is to achieve a fine balance between level of detail and accessibility. A full phonetic transcription is unnecessary and, in general, phonetic or **phonological** processes are represented in standard orthography. Hence there should be no attempt to represent every nuance of speech with the inclusion of pseudo-phonetic representations and idiosyncratic spellings which makes the transcription incomprehensible (see also Macaulay 1991: 282) as in text A.

Text A

Ah hink thit it's e best hing ahv ivir saa. Thir wiz hunners o fouk ere, even tho' the tickets cos' ten powin. Ah'v got a lo' o' rispek fur a at people 'it made it happin.

On the other hand, all pertinent grammatical variation should be preserved, whether it conforms to 'standard' rules or not. Although this may seem like an extremely obvious statement to make, text B exhibits a common problem in the transcription phase: the speech has been largely standardized to what the hearer *thinks* s/he hears.

Text B

I think that it's the best show I've ever seen. There were hundreds of folk there, even though the tickets cost ten pounds. I've got a lot of respect for all those people who made it happen.

Text C is the actual words spoken during the interview, where the differences are italicized. Notice that many of the actual 'mistakes' in text B are related to variables which are so common that they are often below the level of conscious awareness – 'I think that/ø,' 'There *were/was* hundreds of folk.'

Text C

I think ø it's the best show I've ever *saw*. There *was* hundreds of folk there, even though the tickets cost ten *pound*. I ø *got* a lot of respect for all *them* people *that* made it happen.

Just how much detail goes into the transcription is in the end up to the researcher, as the final product should be guided by the goals of the study.

CHOICE OF LINGUISTIC VARIABLE

As demonstrated in the introduction, spoken data reveal a wealth of variation at the grammatical level. However, not all are ideal candidates for study. The most important issue in the choice of variable is *frequency*: morphosyntactic variables tend on the whole to be much less recurrent than phonetic variables, which can be a problem for quantitative analysis. As a guide to minimum contexts of use for quantitative analysis, Labov (1966: 181) suggests ten to twenty instances per speaker in the data, while Guy (1980) suggests more than thirty (but see further Britain 1999).

A second issue which must be dealt with in the initial stages of variable selection is functional equivalence (see Lavandera 1978; Romaine 1982; Cheshire 1987), where the differing **variants** should be 'alternat[iv]e ways of saying "the same" thing' (Labov 1972b: 118). This criterion can be easily satisfied with most phonetic variables (see Chapter 3). With many morphosyntactic variables, the same can apply, e.g. existential agreement as in (12):

(12) There *are* elephants at the party . . . there *'s* jelly sweeties for you. (Smith 2003–05)

However, there are other cases of so-called 'higher-level' variables where **semantic/pragmatic** as well as **syntactic** differences may also need to be taken into account. This is demonstrated by the 'hot news' *after perfect* in Irish English, as in (13), where the construction signals a very recent action, a meaning which the **Standard English** example in (14) does not capture:

(13) One of the farls was after breaking (Corrigan 1997: 160).
(14) One of the farls had broken.

Thus in many cases it is crucial to take into account not only the surface forms but their pragmatic inferences as well in deciding what is really equivalent (see also Milroy and Gordon 2003). This then allows the researcher to set out the envelope of variation, as discussed in the next section.

CIRCUMSCRIPTION AND EXTRACTION

Circumscription of the variable context or the envelope of variation is a major part of the analysis. In other words, what should be included in the count and what should not. These decisions come from two sources – the literature available on the forms under study and the researcher's own observations of the data. Wolfram (1979: 46) provides a perfect example of delimiting the envelope of variation in his study of *a*-prefixing as in (15):

(15)   He came *a*-running down there.

He began with Krapp's (1925: 268) observation that *a*-prefixing could occur with 'every present participle'. However, closer examination of his particular data set revealed that the contexts in which this variant could occur was far more *circumscribed*. For example, the affix could not appear on an adjective such as **a-shocking*, nor verbs which did not begin with a stressed syllable (**a-repeating*).

Another example is negative concord to indeterminates following the verb, including plural NPs, as in (16), indeterminates such as *nothing* and *no one*, as in (17), and indefinite singulars, as in (18):

(16)   There *wasn't no* lights. (Cheshire 1982: 65)
(17)   We *never* had *nothing*. (Feagin 1979: 229)
(18)   She *wasn't no* old cripple woman. (Howe and Walker 1995: 63)

Crucially, not all dialects show the full range of variability. For example, in my own analysis (Smith 2001), indefinite singulars are not a context for negative concord, thus including these in the count would have skewed the results. This is not to suggest that this is a trivial point to be ignored: why some dialects allow variation in some contexts while others do not is a crucial finding which plays a fundamental role in the final interpretation of findings.

In the examination of quotative markers in British and Canadian English, Tagliamonte and Hudson (1999) include *think* as a quotative, although in their data it is only ever used with internal dialogue, as in (19).

(19)   And I *was thinking*, 'Well, surely they can all get on.' I *thought*, 'Right, OK.' (Tagliamonte and Hudson 1999: 148)

Said, on the other hand, as in (20), and many other quotative verbs are used only with direct speech:

(20)   And she *said*, 'Would you like me to phone?' And I *said*, 'Don't do that 'cos Dad'll be furious!' (Tagliamonte and Hudson 1999: 148)

However, *be like* is used for both direct speech, as in (21), and internal dialogue, as in (22). Therefore, in order to account for the entire quotative system, they had to include all quotatives.

(21)　She's *like* 'Right, you know we're taking you out.' (Tagliamonte and Hudson 1999: 147)

(22)　And I'm like 'Oh my God, oh my God, oh my God.' I was having a heart attack. (Tagliamonte and Hudson 1999: 157)

What to include and what not to include can seem like a minefield. However, it is often the case that the researcher does not have all the answers in advance. While much of the groundwork can be carried out before extraction of the variant forms through literature sources and observation of the data, exclusion and inclusion are an on-going process. As Labov (1969: 728) observes, 'even the simplest type of counting raises a number of subtle and difficult problems. The final decision as to what to count is actually the final solution to the problem at hand. This decision is approached only through a long series of exploratory manoeuvres.'

The next step in the analysis is extraction of *all* contexts where a variant could potentially appear, in line with the 'Principle of Accountability' (Labov 1972b: 72). In other words, where a particular variant does not appear is just as important as where it does. Therefore in the case of non-standard *was* in the Buckie dialect from north-east Scotland (Smith 2000), all standard *were* contexts are included, whether they appear with *was* or with *were*, as in (23–7):

(23)　They *were* all in Gaelic.

(24)　*Was* you home?

(25)　The plans *was* drawn up,

(26)　We *wasna* actually gan thegither.

(27)　There *were* four of us gied away with her to the blueberries.

The data may be extracted automatically using a concordance (e.g. Rand and Sankoff 1990) or done manually. In many cases, extraction relies on both automatic and manual extraction. For example, in the case of quotatives, it is simple to search for lexical items such as *said* and *thought*, but what about *be like*? *Like* is multifunctional: it can be a verb, a suffix, a **discourse marker** and a conjunction. Thus this is a case where the researcher must decide on which *likes* are quotatives and which are not.

Once all possible occurrences of use have been extracted, the data are ready to be *coded*.

CODING AND STATISTICAL ANALYSIS

The first stage in the statistical analysis is to count the number of tokens overall, and the proportion of different variants within these instances of use. Numbers of tokens can literally be thousands: fortunately there are computer programs which can calculate the numbers. A range of programs exist for the analysis of variation in speech: Goldvarb (Rand and Sankoff 1990) and Varbrul (Pintzuk 1988) have been used extensively in sociolinguistic research, as they are designed to deal with the types of often 'messy' data from naturally occurring talk (as opposed to experimental data, which are highly controlled). The formats in which programs can 'read' the data differ but as it cannot 'read' straight sentences the researcher has to 'tell' the computer various pieces of information by *coding* the data. Here Goldvarb (Rand and Sankoff 1990) is used for exemplification purposes. The first piece of vital information is in the bracketed column to the left: what variant is used in the actual utterance. In the case of *was/were*, R is used to signal *were* and S *was* (the choice of code is arbitrary). This information tells the computer that in (23′) the form is *were*, but in (24′) it is *was*.

(23′) (R)   They *were* all in Gaelic.
(24′) (S)   *Was* you home?
(25′) (S)   The plans *was* drawn up.
(26′) (S)   We *wasna* actually gan thegither.
(27′) (R)   There *were* four of us gied away with her to the blueberries.

Distributional analysis

Once all the occurrences of the variable have been coded for whether they appear with *was* and *were*, we are in a position to establish (1) how many occurrences of the use of the variable under study are in the data and (2) the different numbers of variants that make up these occurrences. These initial figures are known as the *overall distributions* and are normally the first set of results reported.

Table 4.1 shows the overall distribution of *was* and *were* in standard *were* contexts (see Smith 2000). These figures establish that the variable is frequent in the data and shows robust variability between the two forms, that is, both variants are present in substantial numbers in the data, making it a good candidate for quantitative analysis.

Table 4.1 Overall distribution of *was* in *were*

Word	No.	%
was	628	46
were	723	54
Total	1,351	100

Morphosyntactic variants are not always binary, however. In the expression of necessity/strong obligation in English, four variants can be used: *must, have to, have got to* and *got to*, as in (28–31).

(28)   And we said, 'If you join the club, you *must* go to church.' (Tagliamonte and Smith, in press)
(29)   And I *have to* wear a hearing-aid, 'cos I got tinnitus as well!
(30)   You're told you'*ve got to* speak properly.
(31)   You *got to* leave it up on t' hilltop.

Table 4.2 Overall distribution of variants of deontic modality

Variant	No.	%
must	62	10
have to	277	45
have/'ve/'s got to	214	35
got to/gotta	59	10
Total	612	100

Table 4.2 shows overall distribution of these forms across a range of dialects in the British Isles (Tagliamonte and Smith, to appear).

While Tables 4.1–2 show robust competition between forms, such is not always the case. This is demonstrated in the use of the *for to* infinitival construction, as in (32):

(32)   He'd light a furnace *for to* wash the clothes. (Tagliamonte *et al*. in press)

Despite the prominence of this form in the history of English, our analysis of the same data set used for deontic modality (Table 4.2) showed that the varieties under investigation either had no occurrences of use at all or very few. Table 4.3 shows the overall distribution of use of the *for to* variant. Although there are many potential contexts of use of the *for to* infinitive (total contexts of use = 6,636), actual occurrences of the non-standard *for to* variant is miniscule (1.4 per cent). Such results are often indicative of an obsolescing feature: while in itself this is an extremely interesting finding, in reality there is little room for further analysis of forms – uncovering concurrence patterns or correlations is the next, and probably most revealing stage of the analysis.

Table 4.3 Overall distribution of *for to* infinitive

Word	No.	%
to	6,544	98.6
for to	92	1.4
Total	6,636	100

Revealing correlations

While overall distributions of forms indicate how common particular variants are, they shed little light on the processes underlying the choice mechanism. In order to do this, it is necessary to 'examine closely the forms that a linguistic variable takes, and note what features of the context co-occur with these forms' (Bayley 2002: 118). These include both surrounding linguistic environment as well as social factors (see also Chapter 3). For example, consider examples (23–7) above. In these cases, there are two forms, *was* and *were*, but note that the features of the context in which they appear also vary: in (24) the subject type is second person singular *you*. In (25) it is a plural noun phrase. (27) is an existential construction. Moreover, (26) is uttered by a young female, whereas (25) is attributed to a young male. These different features of the context – both linguistic and non-linguistic – may influence whether a speaker chooses to say *was* or *were*.

In order to find out if this is indeed true, the coding system now becomes more elaborate – not only do we code for whether the variant is *was* or *were*, but we also code for the differing contexts of use or *factor groups*. The factor groups in this analysis are speaker information, subject type, polarity (whether affirmative or negative) and verb function. The data with contextual factors coded are shown in (23″ – 27″):

(23″) (Rc6AC) They *were* all in Gaelic.
(24″) (Sr2AC) *Was* you home?
(25″) (SanAA) The plans *was* drawn up.
(26″) (St4NA) We *wasna* actually gan thegither.
(27″) (RqtAC) There *were* four of us gied away with her to the blueberries.

The computer program 'reads' the data from left to right. In (23″) *R* signals the variant is *were*; *c* indicates that the utterance was spoken by an older male; *6*, that the subject type is third person pronoun *they*; *A* records that the **utterance** is affirmative; *C*, that the verb function is copular. In (26″) the variant is *was* (S), the speaker is a middle-aged male (t), the subject type is first person plural *we* (4), the utterance is negative (N) and the verb function is auxiliary (A). From this information the statistical program computes the various correlations and frequencies of use.

Table 4.4 provides the frequencies of non-standard *was* by one factor group – **age**. The oldest speakers use the highest rates of the non-standard form (58 per cent), the middle-aged speakers the lowest (35 per cent) and the young speakers (44 per cent) are situated somewhere in between. Table 4.5 shows the results for another contextual factor – grammatical person: there are high rates of non-standard *was* in all contexts except *they*, which is categorically standard.

Tables 4.4 and 4.5 demonstrate that there are correlations both with type of subject and with age: in other words, how many times *was* (or *were*) is used depends

Table 4.4 Overall distribution of *was* in *were* by age

	No.	*%*
Old	475	58
Middle	358	35
Young	518	44

Table 4.5 Distribution of *was* in *were* by subject type

Subject type	No.	%
Second singular *you*	161	69
First plural *we*	368	67
Second plural *you*	10	10
Third p. pronoun *they*	435	0
Existential *there*	162	90
NP plural	187	56
Relative pronoun	28	71

on the age of the speaker and what subject type is in the clause. Moreover, it is now easy to see why overall distributions only can often be 'deceiving' in that they hide more than they actually reveal. Table 4.1 showed that Buckie has 58 per cent non-standard *was*, which might lead us to expect this variant can occur anywhere. Table 4.5 demonstrates that this is not the case.

Let's now look further at deontic modality. Table 4.2 suggests that *got to*, as in (31), is used 10 per cent of the time in all dialects and there is a fairly even split between *have to* and *have got to*. But what happens when we divide the data into the different communities? Do they all pattern in the same way? Figure 4.1 shows the results. It shows that Tiverton is the only community which uses *got to* to any degree. In two communities (Cullybackey and Portavogie, and Buckie) the pre-dominant form is *have to*, with much less use of *have got to*. Thus the communities are not equal with respect to the use of these four variants.

Once we begin to disentangle the correlations of these variants, we can see exactly *where* and *when* the variants occur. This allows us to go some way to explaining and interpreting the variation.

Uncovering competing influences

However, we still have one step further to go, as 'it is unlikely that any single contextual factor can explain the variability observed in natural language' (Bayley 2002: 118). The use of non-standard *was*, or zero relative, or copula deletion, or quotative *be like*, or indeed any other linguistic variable, is most likely the result of a combination of factors, whether age, speaker **sex**, subject type or polarity. Modelling this type of variation can be done by multivariate analysis, which can deal with these competing influences, as it permits us to model the combined contribution of all the contextual factors simultaneously. This type of analysis provides three important pieces of information: (1) which factor groups have a statistically significant effect on the choice of the particular variant (factor groups which are not significant are often shown in brackets), (2) which factor group has the strongest effect (shown by the largest *range*) and (3) which factors within the different factor groups favour (above 0.5) or disfavour (below 0.5) the variant.

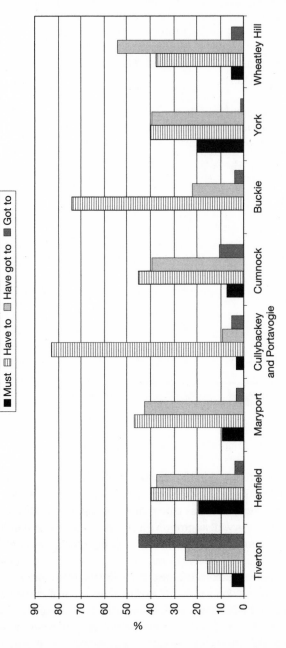

Figure 4.1 Use of forms for deontic modality across eight communities (Tagliamonte and Smith, in press)

Table 4.6 shows a multivariate analysis of the use of the probability of the *be like* quotative being used in the speech of young university students. It shows that all three contextual factors, speaker sex, grammatical person and the content of the quote (what is actually being reported), exert a statistically significant effect on the use of *be like*. The most significant factor group, that is, the one that exerts the strongest influence on the choice of *be like*, is speaker sex, with a range of 31. Moreover, it is favoured by females, in first person *I* contexts, when reporting some non-lexicalized sound, as in (33):

Table 4.6 Variable rule analysis of the contribution of speaker sex, grammatical person and content of the quote to the probability of the *be like* quotative

Speaker sex	
Female	0.67
Male	0.36
Range	31
Grammatical person	
First person	0.56
Third person	0.43
Range	13
Content of quote	
Direct speech	0.45
Internal dialogue	0.57
Non-lexicalized sound	0.67
Range	22

Source: adapted from Tagliamonte and Hudson (1999: 100–4).

(33)   And I was like 'Whaaaam!' (Tagliamonte and Hudson 1999: 163)

Table 4.7 shows the results for *was/were* in the Buckie data, this time including percentages of number of contexts of use. (Note that third person pronoun *they* has been removed from the analysis, as it was categorically standard – Goldvarb deals with variable contexts only). As well as grammatical person and age, polarity (whether the sentence is positive or negative), verb type and the speaker's sex are also considered.

Table 4.7 shows that grammatical person and age are significant in the variation, while verb function, polarity and speaker sex do not exert a statistically significant effect on the variation (indicated by the brackets round the factor weights). In other words, if the speaker is older and using an existential construction, then they are likely to use non-standard *was*. If the speaker is middle-aged, on the other hand, and the subject type is full NP, then it is more likely that *were* will be used.

Table 4.7 Variable rule analysis of the contribution of factors to the probability of *was* in *were* contexts in Buckie, all speakers

Factor	No.	Factor weight	%
Grammatical person			
Second person singular *you*	161	0.49	69
First person plural *we*	368	0.44	67
Third person plural Full NP	187	0.33	56
Existential *there*	162	0.80	90
Range		47	
Polarity			
Affirmative	838	[0.50]	69
Negative	40	[0.56]	75
Function			
Copula	602	[0.48]	69
Auxiliary	276	[0.55]	69
Age			
Old	331	0.66	81
Middle	210	0.35	57
Young	337	0.44	65
Range		22	
Sex			
Male	438	[0.50]	71
Female	440	[0.50]	68
Total No.	878		

Note: Corrected mean 0.72.

Thus multivariate analysis allows us to view the *combination* of factors that influence the use of one form over another. For the case of quotative *be like*, it is speaker sex, what is being quoted and which grammatical person is used that all go into the 'mix' in the choice of *be like* over other quotatives. With non-standard *was*, age and grammatical person are the important influencing factors.

CONCLUSION

Utilising the Labovian paradigm, I have outlined some of the steps taken in the quantitative analysis of morphosyntactic variables in a range of dialects in the British Isles and elsewhere. I started with the initial steps of how to transcribe the data in order to ensure a consistent record of what was actually said. I then described what to exclude and include in the data, how to code the data ready for statistical analysis and then how to model the multifaceted influences which are endemic in spoken data. Through these steps, the complex system of linguistic and social constraints on morphosyntactic variation can be uncovered.

FURTHER READING

Cheshire, J. (1982) *Variation in an English Dialect: A Sociolinguistic Study*, Cambridge: Cambridge University Press.

Milroy, L. and Gordon, M. (2003) *Sociolinguistics: Method and Interpretation*, Oxford: Blackwell.

Tagliamonte, S.A. (2006) *Analysing Sociolinguistic Variation*, Cambridge: Cambridge University Press.

Tagliamonte, S. and Hudson, R. (1999) 'Be like *et al.* beyond America: the quotative system in British and Canadian youth', *Journal of Sociolinguistics* 3 (2): 147–72.

5

TECHNIQUES OF ANALYSIS

III DISCOURSE

MARK GARNER

Modern linguistics, like traditional grammar before it, has tended to regard the sentence as the central element of language. Recently, however, researchers have increasingly focused on larger elements, from casual conversations to extended written texts, which are referred to by the generic term **discourse**. The concept of discourse is fundamental to understanding language as communication: it is the means by which the beliefs, values, assumptions that constitute a speaker's social and individual reality are moulded and expressed (Widdowson 2004). Not only the individual but a community defines and maintains itself by communicating, and the patterns of its communication over time form its culture (Garner 2004). In turn, the shared experiences of community and its culture make possible the continuation of communication between individuals. **Discourse analysis** therefore requires a different approach from that of sentence linguistics: it is not possible simply to apply sentence-level linguistics on a larger scale.

For example, every member of a community is able to conduct conversations in an orderly and meaningful manner with people from a variety of social groups. This requires the ability not only to create well formed **utterances**, but to connect these utterances to those of the other person(s) in the interaction, taking into account a range of social factors. A conversation with a stranger or an elderly person will differ from one with a friend or a child, in terms of, among other things, the number, length, and function of **turns**, the **topic** dealt with and what is and is not said about them. The **lexis** will vary, not only in terms of the types of words selected, but more significantly in terms of the way in which lexical items are connected throughout the discourse, making a network of explicit and implicit meanings. Conversational interactions are also influenced by factors such as: the physical setting (for example, at work, compared with in the pub); the purpose (transacting a sale, compared with entertaining); and the media of communication (e-mail, compared with face-to-face speech). Sociolinguistic analysis attempts to reveal the relation of the linguistic variation in a conversation to such social and contextual phenomena.

At a macro-sociolinguistic level, discourse analysis can be used to explore the communicative roles that different forms of discourse play within a community, or to compare their roles in different communities. These topics are researched from a range of theoretical positions, including: the **ethnography of communication** (Hymes 1972); **cross-cultural communication** (Scollon and Scollon

1997); the **ecology of language** (Haugen 1972; Fil and Mühlhäusler 2000; Garner 2004); **critical discourse analysis** (Wodak and Meyer 2002; Wodak and Chilton 2005a, b); and **multilingualism** (Edwards 1997). A micro-sociolinguistic analysis may describe, for example, the ways in which patterns of discourse vary, influenced by such things as situation, communicative function, region, **ethnicity**, **gender** and **social class**.

There are many and varied (and sometimes conflicting) definitions and approaches to discourse analysis, reflecting different theoretical orientations and the enormous range of discourse types. In this chapter, discourse analysis is used as an overarching term to cover analyses of language as communication. This broad definition enables two very influential approaches to be outlined – conversation and oral narratives – which can serve as examples of the potential of discourse analysis in sociolinguistic research. Whilst there is insufficient space here to detail further approaches, Chapter 19 illustrates another highly influential discourse analytical framework by Sinclair and Coulthard (1975). The introductory sketch provided here can be extended through the further reading recommended at the end of the chapter.

THE ANALYSIS OF CONVERSATION

Face-to-face conversation is the most basic and pervasive form of language. Through it the mother tongue is acquired, and it continues throughout life to be the most common form of language that community members engage in. **Conversation Analysis** (CA) began as the study of everyday, informal discussions (Sacks 1972; Schegloff 1968). It has since widened its field of application to include all forms of talk-in-interaction, and occasionally other, non-verbal, forms of communicative behaviour that are concomitant with the language.

Conversations are used to accomplish an almost endless range of functions, but all have some common structural features that mark them out as a specific form of discourse. Participants must contribute in a more or less orderly fashion, without interrupting or talking over each other too much: in other words, there are procedures for **turn-taking**. Each speaker's turn must be related in some readily recognizable sense to what has gone before, and contribute to the on-going shared construction of meaning: there are principles of coherence. In the natural give-and-take of conversation, however, utterances are planned at the point of articulation, and mistakes are made. Turn-taking is not always entirely orderly; coherence is not always achieved; misunderstandings arise; the intended outcome may not be achieved. Participants therefore need to be able to correct themselves and one another, using **repair** strategies that allow the negotiation of meaning to continue despite temporary set-backs or detours.

CA has developed a systematic and, despite some debate about specific issues, a generally coherent methodology. A number of excellent methodological guides can be found in the literature (for example, Sacks 1995; Psathas 1995; Have 1999;

Schegloff 2001; Renkema 2004). Schegloff *et al*. (2002) is a very useful survey of the literature.

CA methodology

There are three essential prerequisites for using CA in sociolinguistic research. The first is a good quality recording of naturally occurring interaction. Second, in addition to the linguistic data, a great deal of contextual information needs to be noted. The time and place of the interaction, what else was occurring at the same time, the social characteristics of the participants and the nature of their relationship, the purpose of the interaction, and anything else that may have a bearing on the conversation, are all potentially relevant. These should be described in as much detail and as soon after the recording as practicable. (There is a 'pure' approach to CA that argues that such extra-linguistic information is outside the purview of the analysis, which should be concerned only with the linguistic elements that occur in the interaction. From a sociolinguistic perspective, however, this information is essential.)

The third requirement is an accurate and detailed **transcription**. The process of transcribing does not simply turn the audio data into text: it also interprets the text in certain ways which influence the final analysis (Ochs 1979; O'Connell and Kowal 1994; Ashmore and Reed 2000). Transcription needs to be carefully planned in advance, and if necessary modified as it is being done. Decisions need to be made on such questions as the amount of **phonological** information to be included (for example, to indicate **non-standard** pronunciation) and what, if any, information to be included on features such as word stress, **intonation**, speed, rhythm, and variation in **pitch** and volume. How are **overlaps** between speakers, **interruptions** and **back-channelling** to be represented so as to make their sociolinguistic role in the interaction evident?

There are several transcription systems in common use (see Ashmore and Reed 2000), and the beginning researcher should become familiar with them and adept at employing at least one of them (Stockwell 2002: 127–8 is a good example), before undertaking the particular research at hand. It may be desirable to adapt one of the standard methods to the analysis.

The transcription is the first stage of the analysis. The next stage typically involves identifying and tagging the features that are being investigated. This is to a large extent an interpretative process, requiring some subjective decisions by the researcher. It should therefore be checked by other researchers working independently. The results of each then need to be compared, and divergent interpretations discussed and resolved as far as possible until there is sufficient agreement to ensure that the final analysis is valid.

The final stage of analysis next investigates relationships between the social, situational and/or cultural features of the interaction and the language used. This is often conducted manually, but for large amounts of data it may use or be replaced by computer-based analysis.

This is merely an indicative overview of how CA can be conducted within a sociolinguistic framework. A clearer idea of its possibilities can be obtained only by reading published studies: some examples can be found in the references (e.g. Schegloff *et al*. 2002; de Fina 2003; Drew *et al*. 2001).

Let us now examine a rather different approach to discourse analysis.

THE ANALYSIS OF NARRATIVE

Narratives are analysed within a range of disciplines, from social history to psychotherapy, and there is no single, unifying view, even within each discipline, of either what narrative is or the purposes and methodology of narrative analysis.

There are, none the less, some features that are characteristic of narrative as a distinct discourse type. It involves a recounting of personal experience, whether of the teller or of someone else. It exhibits temporality: a set of more or less discrete events occurring in a chronological sequence towards a culminating point – in other words, it has a 'plot'. Thus, loosely defined, narratives fulfil three broad communicative functions: entertainment, instruction, and the construction of personal **identity**. Typical of the first are jokes, artistic works such as novels, films, biographies, and the performances of story-tellers. The second function is characteristic of, for example, myths and traditional stories intended to impart religious or cultural knowledge and worldly wisdom. The third function is performed by the innumerable narratives that constitute the stuff of everyday conversations, by which community members explore the nature of the social and physical worlds and the appropriateness of their responses to them. They are thus an important aspect of how the self is constructed and negotiated.

There is no hard-and-fast distinction between the three functional types, and many narratives simultaneously serve more than one function. Furthermore, narratives of different types may co-occur: for example, a narrative about 'what happened to me yesterday' may be couched in terms of a well known joke or a fairy-story. Nevertheless, it is the third type of spontaneous, spoken narrative (or stories) that is of most interest in sociolinguistics.

At the most basic level stories can provide a rich source of linguistic data. Virtually all personal experiences are interesting; people enjoy talking about and hearing them. Asking informants to tell their own stories is one of the least constraining ways of encouraging them to talk at length. A simple cue question such as 'What is the most frightening experience you have had?' or 'When you look back on your life, are there any incidents that stick in your memory?' can result in a great deal of the sort of natural language that is the essential subject-matter of sociolinguistics. Furthermore, sharing another's experiences in this way can create a sociable bond between the researcher and the **informant**, which can make the research experience rewarding and enjoyable over and above the amount and quality of the data obtained.

The methodology of narrative analysis

Using narrative as a data-gathering technique, however, is incidental to our present concern, which is about analysis of the narratives themselves as sociolinguistic texts. There has been rather less research interest in this sort of analysis than might be predicted, and, with one notable exception (discussed below), analysis remains largely intuitive. The field offers ample opportunity for significant new discoveries to the enterprising sociolinguistic researcher.

Gathering data for analysis requires the recording and transcription of narratives, either in a free, naturalistic interaction or, more commonly, in a **sociolinguistic interview** in which the informant is prompted to recount his or her experiences. (See Wengraf 2001 for a carefully structured method of collecting biographical narratives.) The circumstances and setting in which the narratives occurred must be noted in detail, since they are important elements in the interpretation. A fairly broad transcription, which shows the words uttered and perhaps the hesitation phenomena, is usually adequate for most analyses, but a more narrow transcription (indicating phonological features, for example) may be required by the research question.

The narrative is then codified and tagged for the categories that become the basis of the analysis. Broadly speaking, two approaches to sociolinguistic codification can be identified. The first focuses on the linguistic patterns and narrative structures, guided by questions such as 'What are the principles by which narratives in general and/or this specific narrative are constructed?' 'How do narratives vary according to social categories such as social class, gender, and ethnicity?'

The classic work on the structural analysis of narrative is Labov and Waletzky (1967), which has given rise to a number of subsequent studies (JNLH 1997). Labov and Waletzky (1967: 10) started from the narrative defined as 'one method of recapitulating past experience by matching a verbal sequence of clauses to the sequence of events which actually occurred'.

The 'primary sequence' is 'a happened, then b happened', and the basic narrative clause maintains the temporal sequence of the events. Matching clauses to events does not rigidly determine the position of every clause in the narrative, however. The order of some clauses may be possible without disrupting the historical sequencing of the events. Narratives may also contain 'free clauses', which can occur anywhere within the narrative.

The transposability of clauses relative to one another reveals a number of structural principles of oral narratives. In later work, Labov (1972b) identified six components at the level of the whole text, not all of which occur in every narrative or in the same order. The 'abstract' gives a brief summary of what the story is about. The 'orientation' puts the listener in the picture, by giving the participants, setting, time, and so on. These are typically expressed by free clauses that occur before the narrative clauses start. The 'complication' is the main body, telling of the series of events, and leading to an outcome or result. 'Evaluation' expresses 'the attitude of the narrator' towards the narrative by emphasizing the relative importance of some units as compared with others. The evaluation disrupts the primary '*a* then *b*' sequence, and gives the narrative its communicative purpose. The 'resolution' defines the result of the narrated events. Finally, the 'coda' shifts the narrative focus to the present time (e.g. 'so I've always avoided him ever since').

These structural elements led Labov (1972b) to postulate an ideal or 'normal' form of narrative, one that contains all six components. The extent to which any given narrative approximates this form, and the ways in which it diverges from it, enable the researcher to make social and cultural comparisons between different **speech communities** and between individual members of one particular speech community.

The second approach to narrative analysis, which can be used in conjunction with the structural approach, focuses on content. Which events of life experience does a speaker select? What is said about them? What do they suggest about the speaker's beliefs, attitudes and sense of self? The answers shed considerable light on perceptions of self and others, the values that guide behaviour and the degree to which an individual or group conforms to and deviates from established social norms. Content analysis is therefore of interest to, for example, sociologists, social psychologists, social historians and anthropologists.

It is also a rich (though still underexplored) field for sociolinguistics, particularly with an applied and multidisciplinary orientation. The study of differences between the narratives told by, for example, a powerful majority group and a marginalized and minority group can reveal cultural and attitudinal bases for behaviour, and suggest interventions aimed at changing them. Sociolinguistic narrative research has been undertaken in, among other areas, health care (Drew *et al.* 2001) and ethnicity studies (de Fina 2003), and has potential in many other fields such as **language maintenance** and **revitalization**.

There are, however, methodological challenges that need to be met if the benefits of narrative analysis are to be fully realized. Content analysis tends to rely on intuitive descriptions for recurring topics, and many and varied systems are used. As social phenomena, narratives vary by social context (home, school, work, and so on) and data extracted from narratives will vary by the social context within which they are collected. A significant contribution that sociolinguistics can make is to identify a consistent linguistic basis for content analysis, as the Labovian approach has done for structural analysis.

One method is **systemic analysis** (Halliday 1978, 1994; Halliday and Hasan 1985), which uses the categories of **field**, **tenor** and **mode** for the description of discourse of all types, including oral narratives. *Field* expresses the topic of discourse through its 'ideational function', of which transitivity (including, for example, 'material', 'mental' and relational' processes expressed in the verb structures) is a key element. *Tenor* expresses and constitutes the relations between participants in the discourse. For example, 'mood' includes the familiar traditional categories (indicative, imperative, and so on), but also encompasses a range of **speech acts** (promising, requesting, threatening and others). Another key element is the reflexive language used by speakers to comment on their own language.

Mode is the role that the narrative is playing in a particular interaction, for example a story may be told in order to justify the speaker's actions to the listener.

Whatever approach is used, narrative analysis is ultimately an interpretative enterprise. Interpretations can be more or less valid and revealing, but there is no final measure by which an interpretation can be judged as indisputably right or wrong. It is best used for the exploration of ethical, moral and cultural ambiguities, sensitizing the researcher to critical sociolinguistic phenomena and illustrating, but not by itself validating, theory. It is, in other words, a form of hermeneutics.

CONCLUSION

Discourse is a major focus of contemporary linguistic research. It is fundamental to understanding human interaction and the ways in which meanings are negotiated through language, and in which social identities are constructed and expressed. It is a fruitful field for the conduct of sociolinguistics. This chapter has attempted to provide an outline of the basic perspectives and methods of two rather different approaches to discourse analysis, but it is only a starting point for anyone interested in engaging in this kind of research. There is a rich and growing literature on discourse analysis, and ample opportunity for researchers to explore the potential of discourse to continue to expand our knowledge of sociolinguistics in this vital aspect of communicative behaviour.

FURTHER READING

Eggins, S. and Slade, D. (2004) *Analysing Casual Conversation*, London: Equinox.
Fairclough, N. (2003) *Analysing Discourse: Textual Analysis for Social Research*, London: Routledge.
Mills, S. (2004) *Discourse*, New York : Routledge.
Thornborrow, J. and Coates, J. (eds) (2005) *The Sociolinguistics of Narrative*, Amsterdam: Benjamins.
Wooffitt, R. (2005) *Conversation Analysis and Discourse Analysis: A Comparative and Critical Introduction*, London: Sage.

Part II
SOCIAL CORRELATES

6
SOCIAL CLASS

PAUL KERSWILL

INTRODUCTION: MARX

At the core of sociolinguistics is the fact that human societies are internally differentiated, whether by **gender**, **age** or **class**. These differentiations (and there are others, including **ethnicity**) are all at a 'macro' level, that is, broad groups into which people can be categorized. Theories of class have evolved over the last 150 years, starting with that of Karl Marx (1818–83).

Discussions of class place different emphases on economic factors and more broadly cultural factors. Marx relates social structure to the position of individuals in relation to the means of production. He defines *capitalists* as those who own the means of production, while those who must sell their labour to the capitalists are the *proletariat* (Giddens 2001: 284). This theory is grounded in the circumstances of mid-Victorian industrial Britain, with its extremes of exploitation and control by many factory owners. Of direct relevance to sociolinguists today was the rise of 'class-consciousness', which led to class-specific ways of seeing the world, and talking about things. Class segregation in Britain led to a **divergence** in speech at the level of **dialect** and **accent**. The new urban **vernaculars** which emerged in places like Manchester and Leeds had powerful working-class connotations. Alongside them, there was the increasingly uniform **Received Pronunciation** of the elite, which consisted not only of the capitalists, but also traditional land-owners, senior managers and civil servants, and aristocracy. (Mugglestone 2003 is an excellent account of this process; see also Kerswill 2006.) Nineteenth-century **British English** was therefore split up not only into regional dialects, but also into social dialects or **sociolects**.

SOCIAL STATUS AND FUNCTIONALISM: WEBER AND PARSONS

The Marxian approach is the classic **conflict model**, with class struggle at its core. However, it quickly acquired critics, not least because, by the beginning of the twentieth century, Western society was changing: there were increasing numbers of people in the 'middle classes', including managers and bureaucrats, whose wealth was not linked with capital or property. The approach of Max Weber (1864–1920) allowed for this greater complexity of modern societies. According to Giddens (2001), Weber agreed with Marx in seeing class as 'founded on objectively given economic conditions', though class divisions 'derive not only from control or lack of control of the means of production, but from economic differences which have nothing directly to do with property' (Giddens 2001: 285). Weber saw people as having differing 'life chances' because of differences in skills, education and qualifications. In a capitalist society, 'status' not directly derived from Marxian 'class' must be recognized, and this leads to differences in what Weber called 'styles of life', marked by such things as 'housing, dress, manner of speech, and occupation' (Giddens 2001: 285). Thus cultural factors are brought in.

By the 1960s, Weber's notion of 'status' would become central to sociolinguists like William Labov, who are concerned with the social differentiation of phonetic and grammatical features in **speech communities** (see Chapter 10). However, Labov's adoption of status actually came about through his reading of *functionalist* sociologists in the 1950s, particularly Talcott Parsons (1902–79). American functionalism developed out of Emile Durkheim's notion that people's occupations affect their social ties in such a way that their social experience is both moulded and restricted by them. From this, social groups with different interests and values emerge along occupational lines (Bedisti 2004: 29; see Morrison 1995: 128–45). Later on, functionalist theory asserted specifically that components of society are interrelated and that, together, they form a unified entity. Thus, 'to understand any part of society, such as family or religion, the part must be seen in relation to society as a whole [. . .]. The functionalist will examine a part of society, such as the family, in terms of its contribution to the maintenance of the social system' (Holborn and Haralambos 2000: 9).

Parsons is credited with being the main theorist behind 'structural functionalism' in the United States up to the 1960s (Scott 1996). Class for Parsons is a hierarchy of esteem or status – a doctor is higher on the scale than a nurse – and is not directly connected with any economic considerations, though of course income will be a factor in this esteem.

It is easy to see the appeal of this approach for sociolinguists. From it, inventories of the relative social positions of occupations were developed, and it was a straightforward matter to adapt these for the purposes of getting a socially stratified sample of speakers. In this chapter, we will look at how sociolinguists have done this.

CLASS AND STRATIFICATION IN CONTEMPORARY WESTERN SOCIETIES

Integrated models

Since the 1970s, purely functionalist models have largely been replaced by models which combine status hierarchies, people's different relationships with the means of production (as employers and employees) and cultural factors which are characteristic of different social groups (e.g. choice of newspapers). Arguably, this is a return to a Weberian view, but it also adds a strong element of life-style choice.

That is, in our affluent, consumer society, we are now faced with a menu of possible life-styles and are (relatively) free to select from it.

A view which extends the idea of capital to both culture and language is that of the French sociologist Pierre Bourdieu (1991). **Cultural capital** gives us advantages over other people: we may 'inherit' wealth and tastes, and we 'invest' in education and in life-style choices. Bourdieu sees this investment as favouring the dominant class. Bourdieu in fact sees language as central to this form of capital: **linguistic capital** is embodied by socially highly valued language forms, such as (in Great Britain) **Standard English** and **Received Pronunciation** (see Milroy and Gordon 2003: 97).

How many classes?

In many parts of the Western world, including Canada, the United States and Scandinavia, there is only a weak 'discourse' of class (see Chambers 1991: 90; Milroy 1997, 2000). However, in Britain, a survey found that 36 per cent of adults considered themselves 'middle-class', while 46 per cent viewed themselves as 'working-class', reflecting a relatively polarized view (Argyle 1994: 4, citing Reid 1989; see also Macaulay 2005: 36). Thus, it is not surprising that these terms are routinely used without explanation by the media. Their ability to do so is doubtless grounded in what Cannadine (1998: 161) calls 'the language of class', which is employed by lay people, politicians and social commentators alike, and gives rise to the survey statistics. According to him, three basic views of social differentiation exist alongside each other in Britain: 'class as hierarchy' – essentially the Parsonian model; 'class as upper, middle and lower classes' – a 'triadic' model; and 'class as "us" and "them"' – a model of a polarized society implying a Marxian analysis. Cannadine quotes Marshall as pointing out that 'the "class consciousness" of the majority of people is characterized by its complexity, ambivalence and occasional contradictions. It does not reflect a rigorously consistent interpretation of the world' (Marshall *et al.* 1988: 187).

Gender and class

Until the 1980s, research on stratification was 'gender-blind' (Giddens 2001: 298), that is, 'it was written as though women did not exist, or [. . .] for the purposes of analyzing divisions of **power**, wealth and prestige [. . .], were unimportant'. This was because they were simply seen as economically dependent on their husbands. With the huge increase in women's participation in the economy, Giddens sees this position as untenable, and modern stratification measurements now include the main breadwinner in a household or a combination of both breadwinners. I would add that the position also fails to take into account how men and women construct **prestige** and hierarchy for themselves; it is likely that the two sexes operate with different systems in terms of how they evaluate prestige. This issue affects interpretations of some of the results of sociolinguistic research (see Milroy and Gordon 2003: 101–3).

A hierarchical model of class: the 2001 UK socio-economic classification

Since the beginning of the twentieth century, governments have published lists of occupations ranked according to either assumed status or position within the socio-economic system – or a combination. In the United Kingdom, the first was the Registrar General's Social Classes (in 1913). In Canada, a system has been developed combining a subjective ranking of 320 occupations with the income and educational level of typical people in those occupations (see Chambers 2003: 47–8). In 2001 the UK government introduced the scheme in Table 6.1. This scheme combines 'different labour market situations and work situations' (Office for National Statistics 2001) in terms of income and security. Sociolinguists use schemes similar to this, though usually with the addition of education and 'status' factors such as housing type or neighbourhood.

Table 6.1 The National Statistics Socio-economic Classification analytical classes

---

1   Higher managerial and professional occupations
   1.1   Large employers and higher managerial occupations
   1.2   Higher professional occupations
2   Lower managerial and professional occupations
3   Intermediate occupations
4   Small employers and own account workers
5   Lower supervisory and technical occupations
6   Semi-routine occupations
7   Routine occupations
8   Never worked and long-term unemployed

Source: Office for National Statistics (2001)

SOCIAL CLASS AND VARIATIONIST SOCIOLINGUISTICS

The originator of **variationist sociolinguistics** or **social dialectology** is William Labov, who in 1966 published his study of variability in the use of linguistic features, mainly phonetic but also grammatical, in the English of New York City (NYC). Labov's class index is a composite one, based on education, occupation and residence value. For each of these factors, Labov defined six levels (see Ash 2002: 407–8 for details). Labov selected his subjects from an existing social survey of the Lower East Side, and this meant that he was ensured a good social spread and a representative sample. He grouped his subjects into 'socio-economic classes' (SEC) based on their index scores, as follows: lower class; working class; lower middle class; upper middle class.

Labov devised the **sociolinguistic interview** in order to get a range of **speech styles** from his subjects, from casual chatting to the reading of formal lists. One of the features Labov investigated is the **postvocalic (r)**, in words such as *guard* or *bird*, which is usually not pronounced in working-class NYC speech. Figure

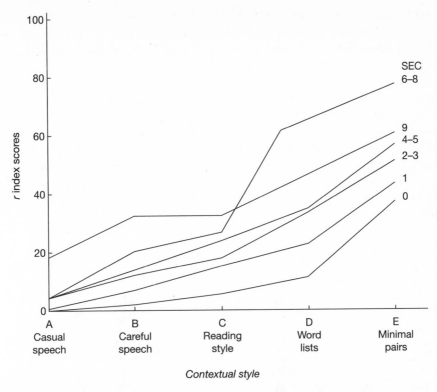

Figure 6.1 Rhoticity in various speech styles (adapted from Labov 1966)

6.1 shows the result. Note how the classes (from lower working-class 0 to upper middle-class 9) are neatly ranked in terms of the average frequency of postvocalic (r) in styles A–C, expressed as a percentage of the number of times it could have occurred. This association with language vindicates Labov's choice of socio-economic class index, because it was derived completely independently of any linguistic considerations; this is important, because accent or dialect is often *in itself* a direct cue in people's social judgement of others. A second significant finding is that **speech styles** appear to be ranked in the same way as class: in more 'formal' styles (D and E), people use more of the pronunciation with [r]. There is thus a link between high-status speakers and more monitored, formal speech. Finally, note that one of the classes, the lower middle class, uses a higher frequency of [r] than anyone else in the most formal styles. Labov sees this as evidence of the linguistic and social 'insecurity' of this group, and also a sign that these people often lead in linguistic change. All this supports a functionalist, consensus analysis of social structure. (Kerswill 2004 expands this discussion to cover the speech community and style.)

However, many sociolinguists see social class differentiation from the perspective of a conflict model. Milroy and Gordon (2003: 96) point to studies which show 'bipolar' variation, for example in the speech of villagers on a plantation in Guyana, where a social divide is reflected linguistically (Rickford 1986). It is apparent, too, that a gradient (gradual) scale of variation in one part of the language – typically **phonetics**, at least in English – is not matched by gradience in another, say the grammar. This turned out to be the case in a comparative study of two medium-sized towns in the south of England, Reading (an old, well established town) and Milton Keynes (a new town dating from 1967) (Cheshire *et al.* 2005; Kerswill and Williams 2000a, b, 2005). For this study, speakers were not selected randomly across a broad social spectrum, as Labov had done, but were instead taken from schools which had been chosen for their socially contrasting catchment areas. Adolescents from the schools were then labelled 'working-class' or 'middle-class'. Figure 6.2 shows the adolescents' scores for the use of the **glottal stop** [ʔ] for /t/ between vowels as in *letter*, the use of [f] for 'th' as in *thin*, and [v] for 'dh' as in *brother*.

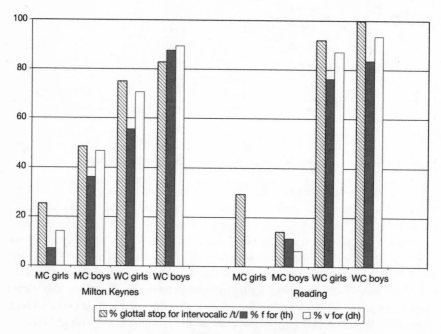

Figure 6.2 Percentage use of non-standard forms of three consonantal variables among adolescents in Milton Keynes and Reading (adapted from Cheshire *et al.* 2005: 146)

The 'middle class' (MC) use considerably fewer of the **non-standard** forms than do the 'working class' (WC). This effect is much stronger in the old town of Reading, where polarization exists in a way not found in the socially fluid new town: the two classes show extreme divergence. However, even in Milton Keynes it turns out that there is an almost categorical class divide in the use of non-standard grammatical features. Figure 6.3 shows the use of the following eight variables:

1 Negative concord, e.g. 'I don't want none'.
2 Non-standard *was*, e.g. 'we was'.
3 Non-standard *were*, e.g. 'he weren't'.
4 Non-standard *don't*, e.g. 'he don't'.
5 Preterite *come*, e.g. 'he come here yesterday'.
6 Preterite *done*, e.g. 'we done that yesterday'.
7 Non-standard relatives, e.g. 'the man what we saw'.
8 Non-standard *them*, e.g. 'look at them houses'.

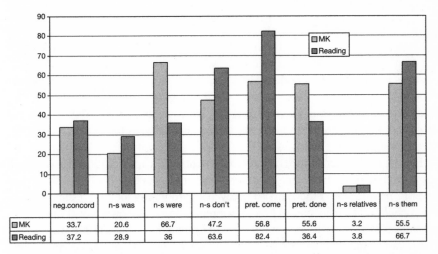

	neg.concord	n-s was	n-s were	n-s don't	pret. come	pret. done	n-s relatives	n-s them
☐ MK	33.7	20.6	66.7	47.2	56.8	55.6	3.2	55.5
☐ Reading	37.2	28.9	36	63.6	82.4	36.4	3.8	66.7

Figure 6.3 Non-standard grammatical features used by working-class adolescents in Milton Keynes and Reading (%) (from Kerswill and Williams 2005: 1041)

The figure shows that neither town has the 'advantage' over the other, and that working-class speakers in both use the features frequently. However, among the middle-class speakers the usage was so rare as to be negligible. We interpreted this result as showing that, despite the more 'standard' phonologies of the Milton Keynes working-class adolescents and the highly mobile society in which they lived, there was still a powerful class awareness, with strongly negative views expressed about 'posh' people (Kerswill and Williams 1997, 2000b: 11). Polarization, and with it a Marxian social analysis, can apparently live alongside what appears to be a more hierarchical structure. These can surely be reconciled if we regard 'class' as something which is variably relevant in different spheres of our activities: there is 'class consciousness', but it is based on an often contradictory social analysis on our part. The study of sociolects helps us understand this.

Figure 6.2 also shows that (with the exception of the Reading middle-class adolescents) the girls produce somewhat fewer of the non-standard forms than the boys. This finding has been repeated in numerous studies and is practically axiomatic, although it has been subject to criticism (see, for example, Cheshire 2002).

SOCIAL CLASS DIFFERENCES IN DISCOURSE

Since the late 1950s, a parallel track within sociolinguistics has investigated social differences in the way talk is organized. The most prominent figure is Basil Bernstein (1924–2000), who in 1958 suggested that educational failure among working-class (WC) children may be due to their use of what Bernstein later called a **restricted code**. Bernstein's main contention is that, because of supposedly 'relational' family structures where roles are implicit rather than negotiated, WC children use a much more implicit type of language, lacking in adjectives and adverbs, using stereotyped phrases, not clearly differentiating cause and effect, using commands and questions, and using 'sympathetic circularity' shown by phrases like 'It's only natural, isn't it?' (Bernstein 1971). Middle-class (MC) children can also use an **elaborated code**, which does not contain the implied deficiencies of the restricted code. (The characteristics of the codes are accessibly cited in full in Macaulay 2005: 41 and usefully paraphrased in Stockwell 2002: 56.) Bernstein has been roundly criticized, not least because of the 'deficit' that his theory implies, but also because of the weak empirical basis for it (Macaulay 2005: 40–4; Montgomery 1995: 134–46).

Is there any evidence for Bernstein's contention? Wodak (1996: 116–20) used the technique of oral retelling of news stories as a means to find out. She found that MC people would focus on accuracy, backgrounding their own stance, while WC people often incorporated the news report into their own world view, with comments like 'You can't do anything about it, anyway'. Wodak (1996: 119) found statistically significant class effects, but no **sex** or **age** effects. She attributes this to the MC speakers' years of socialization, through schooling, into producing 'oversophisticated', fact-oriented summaries, rather than the more 'natural' mode of telling narratives used by the working-class respondents. These differences are consistent with Bernstein's view, and have the potential to lead to discrimination.

Bedisti (2004) attempted to elicit experimentally the features of Bernstein's codes. She gave 11–13 year old Greek children from three socially differentiated schools map-reading and picture-description tasks. Most of the features did not show significant differences between the schools, but some did. Thus, WC children used greater 'exophoric reference', in other words, they referred to things outside the immediate context of the task. And the picture descriptions produced by the upper MC children were more explicit. Both these findings conform with Bernstein's model.

But other studies have tended to disconfirm Bernstein's predictions, and the trend now is to look beyond them and focus instead on **discourse** differences between classes, doing away with any 'deficit' notion, while focusing also on the way gender interacts with class. Macaulay (2002b) indeed finds a much greater use of adverbs by MC speakers – as Bernstein predicts – but fails to find any evidence that they are being used to make reference more explicit. Instead, they use them 'to make emphatic statements, making quite clear their opinions and their attitudes' (Macaulay 2002b: 415). This appears to contradict Wodak's finding that it is WC speakers who relate events to their own world view. However, Macaulay's MC subjects are being speaker- (i.e. self-) oriented, wanting to make their opinions clear. Wodak's WC speakers appear, from the transcripts, to be struggling to reconstruct the gist of what they have heard by relating it to their own experience, rather than reproducing the story in a disinterested way in a manner they are not trained to do. Macaulay's WC speakers give much more detail than his MC speakers, and find different ways (for example, by using changes of word order) of showing their involvement in the events and drawing attention to particular parts of the story. Hence they leave the listeners to infer what their stance is. They are being listener-oriented. Interestingly, at the same time they are arguably *more* explicit than the MC speakers (Macaulay 2002b: 415).

This tendency to allow listeners to construct their own conclusions and orientations is, according to Cheshire (2005a: 498), part of a working-class approach to conversation that is collaborative. Cheshire finds that a number of her adolescent speakers use 'bare noun phrases' to introduce new items to the discourse, for example:

(Veronica has been talking about her sister's visit to Australia.)
Interviewer: yeah my son went diving there . he went to a diving school
Veronica: my sister went to a golf course
Interviewer: oh a golf course?

(Cheshire 2005a: 490)

Here, 'a golf course' is introduced with no explanation or supporting strategy, which might have consisted of something like: 'another thing my sister did was . . .'. Cheshire finds the bare noun phrase strategy used very much more by girls than by boys, and more by WC speakers than by MC speakers. This is shown in Figure 6.4.

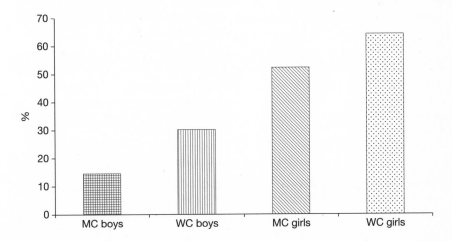

Figure 6.4 Percentage of discourse-new bare noun phrases (relative to all discourse–new noun phrases) by gender and social class (all speakers) (from Cheshire 2005: 493)

Boys – particularly MC ones – treated the questions more literally, and hence more frequently checked their understanding of the question by expanding on the noun phrase. WC girls used proportionately the most bare noun phrases. Cheshire sees the use of a bare noun phrase as part of both a cooperative and a collaborative style, where the speaker is building up the relationship with the interviewer rather than focusing on ensuring the task is conducted efficiently. Cooperativeness is part of a female style, while collaborativeness is characteristic of a WC style; it is these associations, Cheshire argues, that lead to the frequencies she observes.

Finally, we can summarise this discussion of class-related linguistic differences in Western societies in Table 6.2.

Table 6.2 Linguistic differences related to class in Western societies

Working class	Favoured by?	Middle class	Favoured by?
More use of non-standard or local forms	Males	More use of standard or prestigious forms	Females
Orientation to local identity factors – **covert prestige**	Males	Orientation to linguistic forms valued in education and the linguistic market (Bourdieu) – **overt prestige**	Females
Orientation to the listener: a collaborative style, backgrounding of own opinion	Females	*Orientation to the speaker:* explicit information, and explicit statement of own opinion	Males
Less concern for/ access to literacy and less experience of expressing factual information	No gender difference	More concern for/ access to literacy and experience through schooling of expressing factual information	No gender difference
Placing events within own world view	No gender difference	When called for, orientation to dispassionate talk	No gender difference

FURTHER READING

Ash, S. (2002) 'Social class', in J.K. Chambers, P. Trudgill and N. Schilling-Estes (eds) *The Handbook of Language Variation and Change*, Oxford: Blackwell, pp. 402–22.

Chambers, J.K. (2003) *Sociolinguistic Theory* (second edition), Oxford: Blackwell.

Milroy, L. and Gordon, M. (2003) *Sociolinguistics: Method and Interpretation*, Oxford: Blackwell.

7
GENDER

JENNIFER COATES

This chapter will focus on the social correlate known as **gender**. Readers of this *Companion* will be aware that gender – and gender differences – are topics which engage the public imagination. Tabloid newspapers and television chat shows, for example, raise questions such as 'Do women and men talk differently?' But the popular media tend to give answers which could be described as **folklinguistic**. They are likely to say that women gossip, or that men swear more than women. These answers are widely believed – but are they true, or are they myths?

In the following section I shall begin with a brief sketch of the historical background and will clarify terminology. I will then provide an overview of the field, followed by a survey of the different theoretical frameworks adopted by people working in the field. I will discuss recent developments in language and gender research, and will end with a brief discussion of the related area of language and **sexuality**.

HISTORICAL BACKGROUND

In the last twenty years, there has been an explosion of interest in the relationship between gender and language use. It is hard now to believe that early sociolinguistic work ignored gender as a **social variable**. But academic research was dominated by white, well educated males who were preoccupied with the co-variation of language and **social class**, **age** and **ethnicity**. Their androcentrism sprang from a sense that men and people were the same thing (this is sometimes called the 'male-as-norm' approach). In other words, women tended to be invisible in sociolinguistic research. This changed in the 1970s with the publication of an article – later a slim book – *Language and Woman's Place* (1975) by Robin Lakoff, a female sociolinguist based at the University of California, Berkeley. Lakoff drew attention to a wide range of gender differences in language use and argued that these differences were directly related to the relative social **power** of male speakers and relative powerlessness of female speakers. The publication of this work marked a turning point in sociolinguistics.

Lakoff's work now seems dated. In particular her emphasis on the powerlessness of female speakers is out of tune with modern attitudes. But the book remains an important landmark in the history of sociolinguistic research and has had a huge influence on subsequent research.

TERMINOLOGY

One of the ways in which Lakoff's work now seems dated is in its use of the term sex where we would now use gender. This was normal practice in the 1970s: the best-selling textbook *Sociolinguistics: An Introduction to Language and Society* (Trudgill 1974b) included a chapter entitled 'Language and Sex', and this phrase was the title of the first edited collection of articles on the topic (Thorne and Henley 1975). Writers and researchers in the 1970s did not distinguish between biological and cultural influences on the speaker. The social and linguistic behaviour of an individual was unproblematically ascribed to their sex. However, towards the end of the twentieth century, researchers became unhappy with the simplistic linking of biological sex and social behaviour: it became more and more clear that men did not prefer certain linguistic forms because they were (biologically) male but because of their alignment with the norms of the culture they lived in. In other words, speakers are born male or female but it is the social and cultural influences which surround us which determine how we speak.

Consequently, sociolinguists now distinguish between sex – a biological term – and gender, the term used to describe socially constructed categories based on sex. Most societies operate in terms of two genders, masculine and feminine, and until recently, most of the research carried out on language and gender drew on this binary distinction. (More recently there have been challenges to this binary thinking, which I shall discuss in the section 'Recent developments' below.)

SOCIOLINGUISTIC RESEARCH INTO GENDER DIFFERENCES

This is now such a popular field that it is extremely difficult to give an account which does justice to the wide range of work which has been done. Early research on gender differences in language tended to focus on mixed talk, that is, talk involving both women and men. Researchers concentrated on what were seen as core features of language: pronunciation and grammar. This early work would take a large sample of people and would record samples of their talk for analysis. This work is often referred to as **quantitative** because linguistic tokens occurring in the recorded talk were counted and the results summarized in tables and histograms, which showed diagrammatically how male and female speakers differed in their use of certain sounds or grammatical forms. Researchers might focus on **glottal stops** or on the vowel in *hit*; or they might count the incidence of **multiple negation** (sentences containing more than one negative word, such as 'I ain't seen nothing') or look at verb endings (e.g. *she loves* versus *she love*).

The first British sociolinguist to make an impact with this quantitative sociolinguistic approach was Peter Trudgill, in his work on his native city, Norwich. Trudgill (1974a) showed that, whatever their social class, men in Norwich tended to choose pronunciations which were closer to the local vernacular and less close to **Standard English**. He argued on the basis of these findings that non-standard speech must have **covert prestige**, in competition with the **overt prestige** of Standard English. In a smaller-scale study, Jenny Cheshire (1982) observed the linguistic behaviour of three groups of teenagers in adventure playgrounds in Reading, spending considerable time with them so that they came to take her for granted. Her data revealed that adolescent males were more likely to use non-standard grammatical forms than adolescent females. This finding – that male speakers are more likely than female to use non-standard **variants** – has proved very robust and has been found in studies all over the world, including Belfast (Milroy 1980) and Sydney (Eisikovits 1998), for example.

The other robust finding of quantitative sociolinguistic research is that, where linguistic change is in progress, female speakers tend to lead in the use of innovative forms. For example, an intonation contour known as the **high rising terminal** (HRT), where a speaker's voice goes up at the end of a clause, is typical of younger New Zealand speakers, and is used three times more by female speakers than by male speakers (Britain 1998). More recently, work on the **quotative** *be like* in Toronto (Tagliamonte and D'Arcy 2004) has established that this form is far more frequently used now than it was ten years ago. It is now the most common quotative, ousting *say* from its traditional place. (Quotatives are verbs which are used to introduce constructed dialogue, such as *say, go, think*; an example of *be like* would be 'I was like "Give it back!"'). This is clearly a major linguistic change, and female speakers here, as in other studies, are leading the change (see Chapter 4).

Sociolinguists in the 1980s turned their attention to broader aspects of talk: the conversational strategies characteristic of male and female speakers. The following are some of the conversational strategies that have been investigated: **minimal responses** (e.g. *yeah, mhm*), **hedges** (e.g. *I mean, you know, maybe*), **tag questions** (e.g. *isn't it?*), questions, commands and **directives**, swearing and **taboo language**, compliments, and **turn-taking** patterns. The studies focusing on these conversational strategies have shown that many of society's folklinguistic beliefs are false. For example, the notion that women are chatterboxes has not survived scrutiny: research in a range of different social contexts – in the workplace, in the classroom, in television discussion programmes, in electronic discussions via computer, for example – has revealed that in mixed groups male speakers talk more than female speakers.

More recently, researchers have begun to look at single-sex interaction, focusing on informal talk, especially talk among friends. This was an important shift of focus, because it allowed researchers to get away from comparing male and female speech patterns, and instead allowed women's and men's talk to be analysed in their own terms. In particular, women's talk was seen as part of female subculture and celebrated, rather than being labelled as powerless. There is now a growing body of research investigating women's conversational practices in a range of communities – white, African American, British Asian, deaf, hearing, gay, lesbian, straight, adult, teenage. Men remained unresearched for longer, but in the last decade the whole issue of men and **masculinity** has been problematized. So we are now beginning to build up a picture of men's talk in all-male groups, though what we know is skewed to young men and adolescents and to non-domestic contexts such as the street, the pub, the sports changing room.

This research has coincided with growing awareness of the role played by language in the construction of gender. It is apparent that when friends talk to each other in single-sex groups, one of the things that is being 'done' is gender. In other words, the fact that female speakers mirror each other's contributions to talk, collaborate in the co-narration of stories and in general use language for mutual support needs to be considered in terms of the construction of **femininity**. For many men, by contrast, connection with others is accomplished in part through playful antagonisms, and this ties in with men's need to position themselves in relation to dominant models of masculinity.

DIFFERING APPROACHES TO LANGUAGE AND GENDER

As this overview of language and gender research will have made apparent, linguists have approached language and gender from a variety of perspectives. These can be labelled the **deficit approach**, the **dominance approach**, the **difference approach** and the **social constructionist approach**. They developed in a historical sequence, but the emergence of a new approach did not mean that earlier approaches were superseded. In fact, at any one time these different approaches could be described as existing in a state of tension with each other. It is probably true to say, though, that most researchers now adopt a social constructionist approach.

The deficit approach was characteristic of the earliest work in the field. Best-known is Lakoff's *Language and Woman's Place*, which claims to establish something called 'women's language' (WL), which is characterized by linguistic forms such as hedges, 'empty' adjectives like *charming*, *divine*, *nice*, and 'talking in italics' (exaggerated intonation contours). WL is described as weak and unassertive, in other words, as deficient. Implicitly, WL is deficient by comparison with the norm of male language. This approach was challenged because of the implication that there was something intrinsically wrong with women's language, and that women should learn to speak like men if they wanted to be taken seriously.

The second approach – the dominance approach – sees women as an oppressed group and interprets linguistic differences in women's and men's speech in terms of men's dominance and women's subordination. Researchers using this model are concerned to show how male dominance is enacted through linguistic practice. 'Doing power' is often a way of 'doing gender' too (see West and Zimmerman 1983). Moreover, all participants in discourse, women as well as men, collude in sustaining and perpetuating male dominance and female oppression.

The third approach – the difference approach – emphasizes the idea that women and men belong to different subcultures. The 'discovery' of distinct male and female subcultures in the 1980s seems to have been a direct result of women's growing resistance to being treated as a subordinate group. The invisibility of women in the past arose from the conflation of 'culture' with 'male culture'. But women began to assert that they had 'a different voice, a different psychology, and a different experience of love, work and the family from men' (Humm 1989: 51). The advantage of the difference model is that it allows women's talk to be examined outside a framework of oppression or powerlessness. Instead, researchers have been able to show the strengths of linguistic strategies characteristic of women, and to celebrate women's ways of talking. However, the reader should be aware that the difference approach is controversial when applied to *mixed* talk, as was done in *You Just Don't Understand*, Deborah Tannen's best-selling book about male–female 'miscommunication' (Tannen 1991). Critics of Tannen's book (see, for example, Troemel-Ploetz 1998) argue that the analysis of mixed talk cannot ignore the issue of power.

The fourth and most recent approach is known as the social constructionist approach. Gender identity is seen as a social construct rather than as a 'given' social category. As West and Zimmerman (1987) eloquently put it, speakers should be seen as 'doing gender' rather than statically 'being' a particular gender. The observant reader will notice that the phrase 'doing gender' was also used in the paragraph above in discussion of the dominance approach. This is because the four approaches do not have rigid boundaries: researchers may be influenced by more than one theoretical perspective. What has changed is linguists' sense that gender is not a static, add-on characteristic of speakers, but is something that is *accomplished* in talk every time we speak.

The deficit approach is now seen as outdated by researchers (but not by the general public, whose acceptance of, for example, assertiveness training for women suggests a world view where women should learn to be more like men). The other three approaches have all yielded valuable insights into the nature of gender differences in language, but it is probably true to say that social constructionism is now the prevailing paradigm.

RECENT DEVELOPMENTS IN LANGUAGE AND GENDER RESEARCH

The understanding that gender is a social or cultural construction became widespread in sociolinguistics only in the early 1990s. In the years since then, notions of gender have been increasingly problematized. Gender is now conceptualized as something that is 'done': it is never static but is produced actively and in interaction with others every day of our lives. This view of gender inevitably alters the aims of the language and gender researcher. In the past, researchers aimed to show how gender correlated with the use of particular linguistic features. Now, the aim is to show how speakers use the linguistic resources available to them *to accomplish gender*. Every time we speak, we have to bring off being a woman or being a man.

But this binary distinction – being a woman or being a man – has also been challenged. It is now felt that binary pairs such as *man–woman, male–female, masculine–feminine* distort – and oversimplify – our thinking. Gender is not a matter of two separate and homogeneous social categories, one associated with being female, the other associated with being male: male and female speakers differ in many ways, but there are also many areas of overlap. The preoccupation with difference relies on an essentialist idea of gender, that is, on the idea that male and female can be reduced to unquestioned essences.

The overthrow of binary thinking has involved the deconstruction of the notion of a single masculinity or femininity. Instead, gender is conceptualized as plural. At any point in time, there will be a range of femininities and masculinities extant in a culture, which differ in terms of class, sexual orientation, ethnicity and age, as well as intersecting in complex ways. Moreover, neither femininity nor masculinity can be understood on its own: the concepts are essentially relational.

The 1990s saw seismic shifts in academic understandings of gender. As Deborah Cameron puts it, 'gender [. . .] has turned out to be an extraordinarily intricate and multi-layered phenomenon – unstable, contested, intimately bound up with other social divisions' (Cameron 1996: 34). The early years of language and gender research revolved around English-speaking cultures and around white, middle-class speakers. More recently, researchers have been encouraged to study the speech patterns of women and men in a variety of cultures. There is now emphasis on the fact that gender is constructed locally and that it interacts with race, class, sexuality and age. This has enabled researchers to 'diversify the canon' and to move away from white, middle-class and anglocentric norms.

SEXUALITY AND QUEER LINGUISTICS

Another stimulus to fresh thinking about gender is the new field of **queer linguistics**. This field 'has the sexual and gender deviance of previous generations at its centre' (Hall 2003: 354). So research on the language of gay, lesbian, bisexual and transsexual communities is at the heart of queer linguistics. Recent examples include a study of British gay slang, known as Polari (Lucas 1997), of lesbian coming-out stories in the United States (Wood 1999), of the use of sexual insults by *hijras*, a class of transgendered individuals in India (Hall 1997), of the 'polyphonous' speech of African American drag queens (Barrett 1999). The notion of gender as fluid and multiple is intrinsic to queer linguistics, since binary categories like *man–woman* are unhelpful when studying communities like these. For example, the point Barrett (1999) is making is that drag queens are *not* men who are acting like women but men who are acting like drag queens.

Language in queer linguistics is studied from the twin perspectives of gender and sexuality. For a long time, sexuality has been confused with gender – in other words, we have tended to understand sexuality in terms of gender. For example, gay men are often conceptualized as 'effeminate' men, as men who are not 'proper' men, while lesbians are seen as a masculine kind of woman.

The separation of gender and sexuality is one of the goals of queer theory, but this may prove difficult. It has become clear, for example, that heterosexuality is a central component of hegemonic masculinity (see Cameron 1997; Coates in press) and that, as the sociologist Lynne Segal has argued, the stability of contemporary heterosexual masculinity depends on the obsessive denunciation of homosexuality (Segal 1990: 137). Moreover, sexual behaviour is stereotypically gendered. So it seems that gender and sexuality are closely intertwined and that studies of language associated with sexuality will inevitably have many links with studies of language and gender.

FURTHER READING

Cameron, D. and Kulick, D. (2003) *Language and Sexuality*, Cambridge: Cambridge University Press.

Coates, J. (ed.) (1998) *Language and Gender: A Reader*, Oxford: Blackwell.

Coates, J. (2004) *Women, Men and Language* (third edition), London: Longman.

Holmes, J. and Meyerhoff, M. (eds) (2003) *The Handbook of Language and Gender*, Oxford: Blackwell.

Talbot, M. (1998) *Language and Gender: An Introduction*, Cambridge: Polity Press.

8

AGE

CARMEN LLAMAS

Of all global categories employed in investigations of language variation, **age** is perhaps the least examined and the least understood in sociolinguistic terms. Unlike **gender**, **ethnicity** or **social class**, age is often approached uncritically and treated as a biological fact with which to categorize speakers, and against which other facets of our **identity** are played out. Yet our age is as fundamental a dimension of our social and personal identities as our gender or our ethnicity. Legislatively speaking, in most societies our age will influence what we should and should not do to a greater extent than other global categories. Our age determines whether we can vote, drive, marry; whether we go to school, go to work, go on a particular holiday. It can influence what types of clothes we wear, places we go, and, importantly, ways we speak. Our age is clearly more than a number – it marks our position in and our movement through the trajectory of life, which is seen in relation to societal norms of behaviour, obligation and responsibility. It therefore impacts considerably on how we are perceived and how we are treated. Likewise, it affects how we perceive and treat others, all of which is mediated through language.

So sensitive are we to the connection between language and age that, in the absence of visual clues, as speakers and hearers we are able to hazard a reasonably close estimate at someone's age from their voice quality and their linguistic behaviour. Untrained listeners may be able to judge speaker age within five years either side of chronological age at levels considerably better than chance (see Hollien 1987). This ability suggests that we are responsive to cues from **phonetic/ phonological** features, grammatical structures and lexical items, and we use such cues to locate speakers in the span of ages.

The treatment of age in sociolinguistic studies is influenced, to a degree, by a primary concern with **language change** or with **language variation**. **Variationist, quantitative** studies investigating language change in progress may approach chronological age as a methodological device with which to group speakers and to measure sociolinguistic differences across age groups. Such differences may indicate **accent** or **dialect** change in the community. **Ethnographic, qualitative** investigations, on the other hand, may be more concerned with age as a process which affects norms of behaviour. Such work may seek to examine language variation within and across life stages. In practice, studies can employ elements of both approaches. None the less, for the purposes of this chapter we will consider the two approaches separately.

AGE AND LANGUAGE VARIATION: THE SOCIOLINGUISTICS OF AGEING

> Inasmuch as social and biological development do not move in lock step with chronological age, or with each other, chronological age can only provide an approximate measure of the speaker's age-related place in society.
>
> (Eckert 1998: 155)

The speaker's age-related place in society is often seen in terms of the life stage they are moving through. Although it is a considerable oversimplification, the life span is commonly divided into four stages: infancy/childhood, adolescence, adulthood and old age. In this section we will briefly consider characteristic linguistic behaviour at each life stage in turn.

The acquisition of language and of **communicative competence** during infancy and childhood is a vast area of enquiry. The acquisition of **sociolinguistic competence** (i.e. the ability to interpret and manipulate structured variation in language) is less well understood and is a fairly recent field of study, even though arguably the child acquires patterns of inherent variation along with contrastive phonology and grammar.

In terms of the input that infants receive, socially conditioned variation is used in **child-directed speech** (CDS) from both adult to child and from child to child. Findings from a study of Tyneside English (Foulkes *et al.* 1999) revealed that mothers used localized features such as **glottalized stops** more frequently when talking to male infants than to female infants. (Such forms are found to a greater degree in the ambient adult male population than in the female one.) Differences were not categorical, however, but were of degree. The child is therefore exposed to (and is likely to produce) more than one phonetic realization of the same underlying form. Use of the variants is likely to be similar to the gender-related frequencies to which the child was exposed, thus contributing to the perpetuation of sociolinguistic differences found in the accent.

Studies have also shown that age can affect the acquisition of certain patterns of variation. Payne's (1980) work in King of Prussia, Philadelphia, revealed that children moving into the area before the age of 8 or 9 were able to acquire certain local vowel shifts, but not ones which required the knowledge of lexical set assignment, for example, the 'short a' pattern (a complex rule in which a tensing and raising of /æ/ toward [eːə] is observed, but within a set of complicated conditioning factors). Similarly, Chambers (1992) found that 9 year old Canadian children moving to Britain were able fully to acquire the opposition between the vowels in *cot* and *caught* (which are homophonous in Canadian English, as the vowels are merged as /ɑ/), whereas children over the age of 13 were less successful.

As with the input they receive, the speech produced by children demonstrates structured variation. This is in the use of both stable sociolinguistic variables and those in which patterns of variation suggest change in progress in the community. Variation has been found in children as young as 3 (Wolfram 1989). (For further examples of structured variation in children's speech see Macaulay 1977; Romaine 1984; Roberts 1997; Roberts and Labov 1995; Kerswill 1996; Kerswill and Williams 2000a, and Ladegaard and Bleses 2003.) Importantly, children are able to recognize the sociolinguistic significance of age as a differentiator which has an effect on their linguistic behaviour. Studies suggest that from an early age they are able to adopt a CDS register and shift styles to adapt their speech to the age of their addressees (see further Sachs and Devin 1976; Shatz and Gelman 1973).

In terms of language development in children, Labov (1972b) suggests that acquisition of the local dialect takes place from the ages of 4 to 13, when speech patterns are dominated by the pre-adolescent group. However, complete familiarity with local speech norms, Labov (1972b: 138) argues, is not acquired until well into adolescence, or the age of 17 or 18.

Adolescence is perhaps the most researched life stage. Peer groups are con-sidered to exert great normative pressure at this stage of life and this is combined with a lowered susceptibility to the influence of society-wide norms as represented by the institutions of the adult and outside world. Perhaps as a result, it is widely held that adolescence is the focal period of linguistic innovation and change (Chambers 2003: 194). Indeed, according to Eckert,

> adolescents lead the entire age spectrum in sound change and in the general use of vernacular variables, and this lead is attributed to adolescents' engagement in constructing identities in opposition to – or at least independently of – their elders.
>
> (Eckert 1998: 163)

Much work has been undertaken specifically on the speech of adolescents and on their use of innovatory forms as a stylistic resource (see further Cheshire 1982; Eckert 2000; Moore 2003; Kerswill and Williams 1997). Linguistic behaviour, in such studies, is often seen in relation to the speaker's participation in a **vernacular culture** or in **communities of practice** (see further Chapter 10). Often a youth culture with identifiable youth norms is referred to as though young speakers formed a homogeneous group by virtue of their being 'young'. As with all life stages, it is important to remember that age and life stage interact with other **social variables** such as global categories of gender, ethnicity and class, or more localized groupings such as group membership or communities of practice.

Adulthood covers the gulf between adolescence and old age, and is perhaps the least explored life stage. The movement through adulthood, which can be shaped by stages in career development and parenthood, is largely unexamined. Rather, adults are customarily treated as a homogeneous mass whose linguistic behaviour represents the unmarked norm.

Young adults are at times viewed as somehow different from other adults, but they are typically seen in opposition to adolescents. Young adulthood is seen as representing a crucial life stage during which **standardization** increases and the sociolinguistic range takes the form of 'retrenchment following the adolescent years' (Chambers 2003: 195). Adults are generally thought to use more overtly prestigious or conservative linguistic forms than younger speakers. This phenomenon has been revealed in many studies which compare the speech of adults with that of younger speakers (Labov 1966; Trudgill 1974a; Macaulay 1978; Williams and Kerswill 1999, etc.). The adult is seen as participating in the standard **linguistic market** within the working life stage. Hence, the use of prestige forms is thought to peak in the middle years when the maximum societal pressure to conform is thought to be felt (Holmes 1992: 186).

Older speakers are somehow no longer seen as prototypical adults, and old age as a life stage is, again, difficult to define. In terms of language, old age is often approached from a clinical perspective: studies on the effects of loss of hearing or aphasia, for example, are undertaken. With some notable exceptions (e.g. Coupland *et al.* 1991), little sociolinguistic work has been undertaken on old age as a life stage. Studies which are undertaken within the **apparent-time** construct (discussed in the next section), routinely collect data from older speakers, but not in order to examine the state of being 'old', rather to compare the frequency of their use of linguistic forms with younger speakers' in order to investigate possible change in progress.

The pressures to conform experienced in the working, adult life stage are felt to taper off in later years, and the use of overtly prestigious forms may give way to a favouring of localized forms or those carrying covert prestige among older speakers. However, the social reasons for this, e.g. the effects of retirement, are much less examined than the actual and presumed age-related differences in language use.

The speaker's age-related place in society is complex, and the linguistic life course that he or she moves through is experienced both as an individual speaker and as part of an age cohort (see further Eckert 1998). It is therefore reasonable and convenient to group speakers by various stages in life. However, these life stages can be broad and can conceal much intragroup variation. Furthermore, life stages may influence norms of behaviour but they do not determine them. Life stages are fluid, and individuals have different experiences of movement through them: two 18 year old speakers in an adolescent cohort may demonstrate very different outlooks, behaviour and, conceivably, dissimilar linguistic usage, if one lives in the parental home and is in full-time education whilst the other is in full-time employment and is him/herself a parent, for example. Thus, grouping speakers whose chronological ages fall within a specified age range does not guarantee that those speakers will demonstrate similar behaviour or conform to assumptions associated with a life stage. Furthermore, norms of behaviour associated with life stages are also fluid and may change over time. Speakers may experience life stages differently from those who moved through them generations ago. Additionally, the distance between chronological age difference and perceived age difference varies. Certain periods of life are likely to be transitional and are punctuated by more 'life landmarks' than others. The perceived distance between 18 and 14, ages which may be a grouped in the same adolescent life stage, is much greater than that between 28 and 24, or 38 and 34, and so on. Thus, how speakers group themselves may not coincide with how they are grouped by the investigator. All these factors mean that whilst grouping speakers in terms of life stage may provide a meaningful way of separating the span of chronological ages, broad assumptions about norms of behaviour associated with life stages do not necessarily offer indubitable explanations for age-correlated variation in linguistic behaviour, and should not, therefore, be taken uncritically as though they do.

AGE AND LANGUAGE CHANGE: THE SOCIOLINGUISTICS OF AGE

When the speech of the 'young' is compared with the speech of 'older' speakers, age-correlated differences can reflect **language change** in progress (change in the **speech community** as it progresses through time), or **age grading** (change in the individual speaker as s/he progresses through life). However, whether age-correlated linguistic difference is actually evidence of change in progress or of age grading is not always, if ever, beyond doubt.

Age-correlated variation which is suggestive of change in progress can be detected by making a series of observations of similar populations over time. The value of these **real-time studies** depends on the extent to which the samples observed are comparable (see further Chapter 2). Practicalities are such that it is rarely possible to undertake large-scale real-time studies, and **apparent-time studies** are more commonly used in variationist research. Such studies involve the observation of the speech of different age groups simultaneously. The inferences drawn from the results depend upon the apparent-time hypothesis: 'the linguistic usage of a certain age group will remain essentially the same for the people in that group as they grow older' (Chambers 2003: 212). However, the common pattern of distribution of forms of a sociolinguistic variable not undergoing change is a U-curve pattern (see Figure 8.1) which sees younger and older speakers using a higher proportion of localized forms than speakers from a middle age group, as discussed in the previous section. This would seem to be in contradiction with the idea of speakers' linguistic usage remaining 'essentially the same' as the group grows older. Making strong claims that age-correlated variation in an apparent time study is unambiguous evidence for language change in progress is, therefore, problematic.

In quantitative, apparent-time studies of speech communities, speakers are often grouped into fairly broad age cohorts based on their chronological age. This can sometimes mask specific group effects, however, and what looks like a general trend can be more specifically located with fine-grained age differentiations uncovered in speech. In the linguistic behaviour of speakers defined as 'young' this can prove invaluable in identifying those responsible for the early adoption of innovations. In a study by Llamas (2001) of the British English urban variety of Middlesbrough, in the north-east of England, young speakers aged between 16 and 21 were divided into adolescents (16–17) and young adults (19–21). Differences were found between these two age groups in the use of both localized

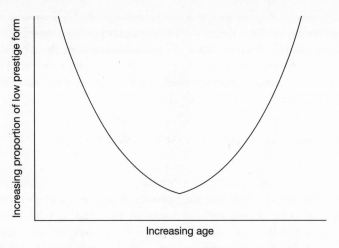

Figure 8.1 U-curve pattern of distribution as found in sociolinguistic variables not undergoing change (after McMahon 1994: 241)

forms (in this case, the use of glottalized (p) and (k), as shown in Figure 8.2 – stable sociolinguistic variables in male speech) and innovatory forms (use of fronted forms of (th) and (dh) i.e. *fink* for *think*, *bruvver* for *brother*) as seen in Figure 8.3).

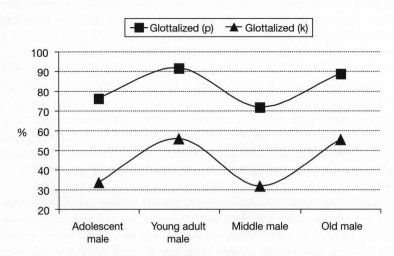

Figure 8.2 Use of glottalized (p) and (k) among male speakers

In terms of use of the localized glottalized (p) and (k) in Figure 8.2, rather than a U-curve pattern of distribution (which would have been the result of pooling the data from the adolescents and the young adults into a cohort of young speakers), an undulating pattern, or an N-shaped curve, is revealed in which the young adults

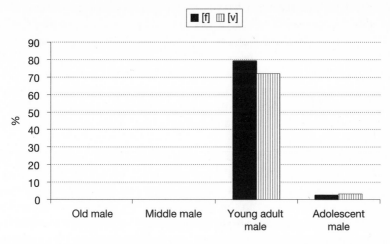

Figure 8.3 Use of fronted forms of (th) and (dh) by male speakers

show a pattern similar to that of the old males and the adolescents show a pattern which is similar to that of the middle speakers. Furthermore, contrary to conventional wisdom, speakers who are responsible for the early adoption of innovations are not always adolescents. As the data show in Figure 8.3, it is the young adult speakers who are responsible for the use of the fronted forms of (th) and (dh) in the data. This is a feature which carries **covert prestige**, and so would be unlikely to be used by characteristic speakers of the 'young adult' life stage as described in the previous section.

Although considerable evidence is available to corroborate adolescents' innovative behaviour, many studies reach this conclusion by analysing the speech of adolescents only, or by comparing the speech of adolescents with that of much older speakers. This will doubtless reveal differences. However, it does not indubitably confirm the singular role of adolescents in language innovation and change. If many of the speaker-based changes are contact-induced, as is believed to be the case in **British English**, a problem arises in accounting for how forms are introduced and diffused by speakers who experience relatively little mobility.

Again, the use of age in apparent-time studies of language change in progress can conceal an amount of intragroup variation, particularly as the groupings themselves can, at times, appear relatively arbitrary. Using fairly broad age cohorts will no doubt reveal differences, but can, at times, mask more finely stratified behaviour.

CONCLUSION

Unlike some facets of our identity, our age is never static: it is, unfortunately perhaps, constantly moving onward. Furthermore, the socio-psychological process of ageing is not fixed. Biological changes in terms of the earlier onset of puberty and better health in older age mean that younger people seem to mature at an earlier age, and older people seem to stay active for longer. This is combined with consumer-oriented factors: the emergence of lucrative new markets, such as the pre-adolescent 'tweenies' and the adult 'middle youthers', generate (and are generated by) changes in economic and life-style characteristics of age groups. Therefore, traditional assumptions of norms of behaviour in relation to position in a given life stage cannot be taken uncritically, as life stages are similarly changeable and changing, and the politics of age and ageing is likely to become more diverse and more flexible as time goes on.

Possibly because of the dynamic, elusive, ever-changing nature of age and the ageing process, the complex relationship between the movement through life and changing linguistic behaviour is not well understood in sociolinguistics. It is clear that, as a social correlate used in the investigation of language variation, the understanding of age has lagged behind that of gender, social class and ethnicity, and as a consequence, age can be considered the underdeveloped global category of sociolinguistics. However, given how important our age and our movement through the ageing process are to our changing sense of self, it is clear that the effect of age and ageing on linguistic behaviour is an area which is ripe for in-depth investigation, and is, indeed, as Coupland asserts (2001a: 201), 'a future priority for sociolinguistics'.

FURTHER READING

Bailey, G. (2002) 'Real and apparent time', in J.K. Chambers, P. Trudgill and N. Schilling-Estes (eds) *The Handbook of Language Variation and Change*, Oxford: Blackwell, pp. 312–32.

Chambers, J. (2003) *Sociolinguistic Theory* (second edition), Oxford: Blackwell.

Coupland, N. (2001a) 'Age in social and sociolinguistic theory', in N. Coupland, S. Sarangi and C. Candlin (eds) *Sociolinguistics and Social Theory*, Harlow: Pearson, pp. 185–211.

Eckert, P. (1998) 'Age as a sociolinguistic variable', in F. Coulmas (ed.) *The Handbook of Sociolinguistics*, Oxford: Blackwell, pp. 151–67.

Romaine, S. (1984) *The Language of Children and Adolescents: The Acquisition of Communicative Competence*, Oxford: Blackwell.

9

ETHNIC VARIETIES

WALT WOLFRAM

At first glance, it may appear that the association of language with ethnic group affiliation is one of the more obvious relationships between language and culture. Practically all of the approximately 6,000 languages of the world, for example, are strongly associated with an ethnocultural group of some type. But this initial transparency is betrayed by the fact that language is neither a necessary nor a sufficient condition for ethnic group membership (Fishman 1999). Like socio-cultural borders, linguistic boundaries are permeable, negotiated constructs typically defined more on the basis of sociopolitical and ideological considerations than on the basis of structural linguistic parameters. Even the dichotomy between 'language' and 'dialect' turns out to be based more on cultural and political issues than on mutual intelligibility or structural linguistic properties. Thus, Sino-Tibetan language varieties such as Cantonese and Mandarin are commonly referred to as **dialects** of Chinese even though they may not be mutually intelligible, whereas Norwegian and Swedish are considered to be different languages although speakers usually understand each other. In the former case, there is an overarching cultural unity that transcends linguistic typology whereas, in the latter case, there is a national political border that reifies minimal structural diversity in linguistic varieties. By the same token, sociopolitical struggles about language – such as those over the status of Afrikaans in South Africa, the role of French and English in Canada, or the legitimacy of African American English (so-called 'Ebonics') in the United States – are ultimately not about language, but about **ideology**, **identity**, and sociopolitical **power**.

DEFINING ETHNIC GROUP AFFILIATION

It is often difficult to separate **ethnicity** from other social factors such as historical background, region, **social class**, and other sociocultural **variables**. For example, the variety labelled Irish English may have a strong association with cultural background, region, and politics in the British Isles, and African American English in the United States is strongly linked to demographic racial categories, **social status**, and region. Invariably, ethnicity interacts with a wide array of other social, historical, and socio-psychological factors and is embedded within an intricate set of sociocultural relationships, processes, and identities. The notion of ethnicity is further complicated by the increasing number of 'mixed-ethnic' individuals and the social categories into which they may or may not fit as determined by the social hierarchies of society. Notwithstanding this array of social factors, communities in which local tradition acknowledges more than one ethnic group may expect ethnicity to be one of the factors that correlates with linguistic variation (Laferriere 1979).

The definition of an ethnic group usually involves the following kinds of parameters: (1) origins that precede or are external to the state; (2) group membership that is involuntary; (3) ancestral tradition rooted in a shared sense of peoplehood; (4) distinctive value orientations and behavioural patterns; (5) influence of the group on the lives of its members; and (6) group membership influenced by how members define themselves and how they are defined by others (National Council of Social Studies, Task Force on Ethnic Studies 1976). Though these criteria seem expansive, they still cannot ensure clearly defined ethnic categorization. In most cases, self-selection is as significant as any other criteria, thus leading Giles (1979: 253) to reduce the definition of an ethnic group to 'those who perceive themselves to belong to the same ethnic category'. At the same time, it is also important to recognize that ethnicity is defined by social practice rather than personal attributes. As Fought (2002: 445) puts it, it is 'not about what one *is* but about what one *does*' that is the primary basis for establishing ethnicity. The practice of ethnicity distinguishes this construct from demographic, institutionalized racial categories based on personal attributes, though some behavioural traits may be related to the segregation of groups based on these attributes.

In constructing ethnicity, groups form subcultures within a larger culture using a variety of behavioural practices that include language. Although it might seem that the degree of linguistic distinctiveness is determined by extent of ethnic separation, this causative equation is far too simplistic. Historical circumstance, social hierarchy, patterns of internal and external interaction, and **ideology** all help determine the construction of **ethnolinguistic** identity.

ETHNOLINGUISTIC DISTINCTIVENESS

Ethnolinguistic distinctiveness may extend from significant typological language differences to minute details of prosody or restricted lexical differences. In the case of different languages, speakers may make symbolic choices in their language use or manage **code switching** to signal ethnic identity (e.g. Zentella 1997), while in the case of intra-language variation the manipulation of particular phonological, **morphosyntactic**, or **discourse** variables may be used to signal ethnic affiliation. For the remainder of this discussion, we focus on intra-language ethnic varieties, since the examination of language choice in multilingual situations is worthy of extended study in its own right (see Chapter 18).

There is both a subjective and an objective dimension to the study of ethnic varieties, but it is often difficult to separate them in determining the basis of ethnic differentiation. Do ethnic varieties exist because sociolinguists are able to correlate linguistic variation objectively with ethnic group affiliation or because the members of society perceive these differences under the conditions of everyday social interaction? For example, in New Zealand the cultural distinction between the Maori, the indigenous people who originally inhabited the island, and the Pakeha, New Zealanders of European descent, has been a significant and discrete cultural boundary historically, but the existence of a Maori variety of English remains highly debatable after a decade of subjective and objective investigation. At best, it is manifested in subtle, **quantitative** differences that are not readily perceptible to most New Zealanders (Bell 1997, 2000). In the United States, the subjective and objective distinctiveness of African American English (AAE) is fairly well documented, but the precise nature of the perceptual cues that determine ethnic identity may be quite complex and nuanced (Thomas and Reaser 2004). Furthermore, demographic factors such as region, social status, and education are compounded by interactional factors such as interlocutors and speech situations, as well as socio-psychological factors such as **agency** and self-presentation (Wolfram and Schilling-Estes 2006). Manipulating the **linguistic variables**, **social variables**, and personal variables greatly affects the probability of reliable ethnic identification. Given a randomly selected set of content-neutral audio recordings, North American listeners can accurately identify African American speakers approximately 80 per cent of the time. At the same time, there is great variation in the accurate ethnic identification of particular speakers when the multidimensional **independent variables** are manipulated in various permutations, ranging from those who are correctly identified less than 5 per cent to those correctly identified more than 95 per cent of the time.

There are also micro and macro contextual factors relevant to the determination of ethnic identity. For example, in our study of tri-ethnic relations involving European Americans, African Americans, and Native American Indians in a Southern American rural community, we found that local listeners from the community were quite reliable in identifying the ethnicity of speakers representing all three groups, but that listeners from outside the area could identify only the difference between African American and non-African American speakers (Wolfram *et al.* 2000). In part, the explanation for this local versus non-local perceptual discrepancy may be explained in terms of underlying assumptions and beliefs about ethnic group membership in the United States. One of the reasons that AAE is so strongly defined along ethnic lines throughout the United States is no doubt the bi-racial ideology that has defined American society. Native American Indians, however, are neither white nor black in a bi-racial society, so listeners outside of the immediate tri-ethnic context are not generally attuned to the perception of such differences. We thus see that racial politics and ideology may enter into the determination of ethnolinguistic distinctiveness.

LINGUISTIC FOUNDATIONS OF ETHNIC VARIETIES

There are several different kinds of formative bases for the relationship between ethnicity and **language variation**. For ethnic groups associated with a different heritage language historically, there is the potential of language transfer from another language that may be stabilized, or **fossilized**, and integrated into the variety maintained by the ethnic group. By transfer, we mean the incorporation of language features into a non-native language based on the occurrence of similar features in the native language. For example, a comparison of ethnic varieties in which the heritage language does not have word-final **consonant** clusters (e.g. *best*, *act*, *wild*) shows that these varieties tend to maintain significantly higher levels of consonant cluster reduction (e.g. *bes'*, *act'*, *wil'*) than do native varieties of English (Wolfram *et al.* 2000). Furthermore, this pattern may persist well beyond bilingualism, in which case it is maintained as a type of **substrate** effect from the original **language contact** situation. Similarly, ethnic varieties of **speech communities** whose ancestral language produced **monophthongal** productions of **vowels** such as English /e/ in *bait* and *gate* (phonetically a **diphthong** [eɪ]) or /o/ in *goat* and *load* (phonetically the diphthong [ou]) may maintain relatively unglided versions of these vowels associated with a distinctive ethnic variety (Fought 2003; Baranowski 2006). Loan translations of words from a heritage language are also a common way in which the effects of an ancestral language can persist in an ethnic variety. Thus, the English of Pennsylvania Germans in south-eastern Pennsylvania in the United States is still characterized by direct translations of German into English, such as the use of *all* ('all gone') in 'He's going to have the cookies *all*' and *what for* ('what kind of') in 'I don't know *what for* a car you had' (Huffines 2006).

The linguistic effects of a heritage language may also be adjusted in relation to a group's shifting status as an ethnic variety. In Cajun English, spoken by the descendants of Acadian French in Louisiana in the United States, the primary features of the variety were once viewed simply as reflections of transfer effects from French. However, some of these features are now re-emerging as cultural markers at the same time that the heritage language associated with Cajun culture is rapidly receding (Dubois and Horvath 1998a, b, 1999). Several phonological features associated with transfer from French, including the stopping of **interdental fricatives**, as in *tink* for *think* or *dough* for *though*, and the use of heavy **nasalization** (a nasalized vowel instead of vowel plus nasal segment) in words like *man* and *pin*, are being recycled and intensified in the dialect of English increasingly associated with Cajun identity. The resurgence of these features is linked with the Cajun cultural renaissance that has been taking place over the last several decades, even as the traditional heritage language is lost. Furthermore, complex factors of **age**, **gender**, and **social network** correlate with the revitalization of Cajun identity through Cajun English. Older men and women show very similar use levels for Cajun English features but younger men are more likely than their female counterparts to use features associated with French influence even though they are **monolingual**. The male lead in recycling features may be explained in terms of the gendered nature of the cultural renaissance, since the hallmarks of today's Cajun culture stem from traditional male activities, including hunting, fishing, performing Cajun music, and cooking special feast-day foods.

The effects of a language contact situation may also involve a type of linguistic restructuring that leads to **interdialectal** forms, that is, forms that originally occurred in neither the source nor the target language variety (Trudgill 1986: 62). For example, the absence of **copula** and auxiliary forms in AAE (e.g. 'She nice,' 'You acting silly') is neither like the source creoles of the Caribbean and West Africa nor like the target varieties of Southern American English that provided the English dialect models for Africans brought to the United States. In AAE, the copula may be absent when the corresponding form is a contracted version of *is* (e.g. 'She's nice' → 'She nice') or *are* (e.g. 'You're acting silly' → 'You acting silly') but not when it is *am* (e.g. **I nice* from *I'm nice* is not a permissible structure in AAE), thus making the structural version of copula absence in AAE an intermediate form.

Independent language innovation may also contribute to the configuration of ethnic varieties. Lexical items are the most obvious examples, including terms for social categories and relationships endemic to the subculture, such as terms for insiders versus outsiders and different social divisions within the ethnic community, but **grammaticalization**, the encoding of a unique meaning onto a form, also can occur. In AAE, the invariant form of *be* in sentences such as 'You always *be* acting weird' is uniquely associated with 'habituality', an event that takes place intermittently over time or place. This innovation, distinct to AAE in American English varieties, took place largely during the second half of the twentieth century as an independent development, and is now uniquely associated with this ethnic variety (Labov 1998).

Though exclusive patterns of retention and innovation may be associated with particular ethnic varieties, their primary linguistic foundation is typically found not in the unique linguistic items associated with the variety but in the constellation of structures that includes regional language structures, items borrowed from other ethnic groups, and items shared with dominant social groups. The grammar of Chicano English, spoken by Hispanics in the south-west United States, is a combination of features that includes general structures shared by a wide range of vernacular English varieties, structures derived from the Spanish–English contact situation, and items shared with neighbouring regional and social dialects (Fought 2003). For example, in Chicano English the **levelling** of past tense *be* in 'We was there,' the use of **multiple negation** in 'She ain't been nowhere,' and the formation of irregular past forms in 'Yesterday he come to visit' are structural traits of **vernacular** English varieties that are found throughout the English-speaking world. At the same time, the use of prepositions such as *on* in sentences like 'She's on fifth grade' or *for* in sentences like 'She told the truth for she won't feel guilty' are traceable to fossilized transfer from the Spanish–English language contact situation. Grammatical influence from neighbouring dialects is reflected in the fact that young Chicano English-speakers in southern California may freely use the habitual form of *be* (e.g. 'The news be showing it too much'), stereotypically associated with AAE. Young Chicano English-speakers in California may simultaneously show the innovative use of quotative *be like* and *be all* in sentences such as in 'She's like, "You don't leave the house"' or 'He's all, "I'm working for you"'. The latter construction is associated stereotypically with southern California Valley

Girl Talk but is now in more widespread use throughout English worldwide, especially among younger speakers. In their linguistic composition, ethnic varieties are no different from other varieties of a language, whether they are defined primarily on the basis of a regional or a social affiliation (Wolfram and Schilling-Estes 2006).

THE SOCIAL SIGNIFICANCE OF ETHNIC VARIETIES

Ethnic varieties may serve a full range of symbolic social roles and functions, from marking relations of social dominance and subordination to constructing and negotiating individual and group identities. On one level, we may assume that these varieties will reflect the current status of the ethnic group in relation to other groups, but these roles and relationships can often be fluid, complex, and multi-dimensional.

At the negative end of the evaluative spectrum, an ethnic variety may be subjected to the application of the principle of linguistic subordination (Lippi-Green 1997), in which the speech associated with a socially subordinate ethnic group is interpreted as a linguistically inferior version of the variety spoken by the socially dominant group. Particular structures may be branded as 'ungrammatical' or 'bad grammar', and the variety as a whole may be described as 'corrupt' or 'broken'. Ethnic varieties are rarely if ever associated with the standard variety or with prescriptive language norms, since they are invariably associated with a marked, non-mainstream social group. Accordingly, the varieties associated with these groups are considered to be **non-standard** or non-normative.

Though a vernacular variety may be viewed as linguistically inferior, it may still serve positively to mark ethnic identity and group solidarity, showing how evaluative attributes related to social dominance differ from those related to social cohesion. As one Lumbee Native American Indian in the American south put it, 'We took English and corrupted it to make it our own [. . .] That's how we recognize who we are, not only by looking at someone. We know just who we are by our language' (Hutcheson 2000). Language may function as one of the most robust indicators of ethnic status, notwithstanding the application of the principle of linguistic subordination. The dualistic, seemingly schizoid status of ethnic varieties illustrates the differential roles of **overt prestige**, the positive value ascribed to language forms which is based on the value of forms in mainstream society, and **covert prestige**, the value ascribed to forms which is based on local values and associations (Trudgill 1972).

It is also essential to understand the construct of oppositional identity in ethnolinguistic differentiation, where identity is defined in terms of dissociation from another group. In African American youth culture, for example, language has taken on an oppositional role with respect to mainstream white culture. Research on the notion 'acting white' (Fordham and Ogbu 1986) shows that the adoption of **Standard English** tops the list of prominent behavioural traits cited by African American teenagers as a betrayal of indigenous culture and ethnic identity. Part of African American identity is thus defined in terms of how African Americans position themselves with respect to white society in their language behaviour.

As with other socially diagnostic linguistic variables, different linguistic items may show a range of associations in terms of their ethnolinguistic association. For example, terms like *chutzpah* 'impudence, guts', *schlep* 'haul, take', and the expression 'I need this like a hole in the head' all can be traced to Yiddish, but they have quite different social and ethnic associations with Jewish English in the United States. The ethnic association of *chutzpah* is quite strong, and those who are not part of the Jewish community would use the term only as a borrowed item from that culture. The use of *schlep* is less exclusively embedded in the Jewish community, although it still has an ethnic association; it is now an integral part of regional 'New Yorkese' apart from Jewish English. The expression 'I need this like a hole in the head', directly translated from a Yiddish expression (Gold 1981: 288), is the least ethnically associated of these items and is not nearly as regionally restricted as an item like *schlep*. We see, then, that the ethnic association of linguistic items is often a relative matter and that other social and regional factors intersect with ethnicity to varying degrees.

CONCLUSION

We have seen that ethnic varieties of a language are not nearly as self-contained and transparent as sometimes assumed. Like the definition of ethnicity itself, the linguistic manifestation of ethnicity is dynamically constructed and derived both from a group's self-definition and its relationship to other groups, in particular, socially dominant mainstream groups. Language differences run the full gamut of ethnic association, from group-exclusive, stereotypically ethnic features to group-preferential, ethnic indicators that operate below the level of consciousness. Furthermore, ethnically marked variables typically interact with a host of other social, regional, and historical factors in the configuration of the ethnic variety.

FURTHER READING

Fought, C. (2002) 'Ethnicity', in J.K. Chambers, P. Trudgill and N. Schilling-Estes (eds) *Handbook of Language Variation and Change*, Malden, MA: Blackwell, pp. 444–72.

Fought, C. (2006) *Language and Ethnicity*, Cambridge: Cambridge University Press.

Lippi-Green, R. (1997) *English with an Accent: Language, Ideology, and Discrimination in the United States*, New York: Routledge.

Mendoza Denton, N. (2002) 'Language and identity', in J.K. Chambers, P. Trudgill and N. Schilling-Estes (eds) *Handbook of Language Variation and Change*, Oxford: Blackwell, pp. 475–99.

10

SPEECH COMMUNITIES

LOUISE MULLANY

The term **speech community** is used very frequently within sociolinguistic research, and it is traditionally considered to be one of the key concepts of the discipline. Eckert (2000: 30) neatly summarizes its importance, stating that 'because sociolinguists' treatment of language focuses on its heterogeneity, they seek a unit of analysis at a level of social aggregation at which it can be said that heterogeneity is organised'. Despite this, there has been and continues to be much debate surrounding the definition and application of this term, and a number of conflicting perspectives have developed. In this chapter I will begin by examining how the term 'speech community' has been defined by some key figures in the field, including a critical consideration of the debates that surround the term. The second half of the chapter will examine other influential 'community' approaches to sociolinguistic study: **social networks** and **communities of practice**. By considering these three different community models, the development of this fundamental part of the sociolinguistic toolkit can be perceived, and differences and similarities between the frameworks can be highlighted and assessed.

DEFINING SPEECH COMMUNITIES

A good starting point for considering what constitutes a speech community is to clarify what a speech community is not. Speech communities do not exist simply because individuals share the same language or **dialect**. Although this idea was put forward as an early definition of a speech community (Lyons 1970), it is a view that is easily refuted. As Wardhaugh (2005: 120) points out, whilst English is spoken in various places throughout the world (South Africa, Canada, New Zealand, etc.), English-speakers in these countries cannot be said to constitute a speech community as they speak in a variety of different ways and are isolated from one another. Wardhaugh also makes the crucial point that if speech communities are defined solely upon the basis of linguistic criteria, then such a definition is guilty of **circularity**. In order to come to a justifiable *socio*linguistic definition of a speech community, categories other than just language need to be considered.

One of the earliest definitions of a speech community in modern-day sociolinguistics was Labov's (1972b), based on the findings of his Lower East Side New York study (Labov 1966). His significant and oft-cited classification moves the focus away from the problems associated with a purely linguistic definition:

The speech community is not defined by any marked agreement in the use of language elements, so much as by participation in a set of shared norms; these norms may be observed in overt types of evaluative behaviour, and by the uniformity of abstract patterns of variation which are invariant in respect to particular levels of usage.

Labov (1972b: 120–1)

In order for a speech community to exist, Labov makes clear, speakers do not have to agree about the language they use or speak in the same way, but they do have to be in agreement about evaluative norms. He discovered that whilst selected **linguistic variables** were being pronounced differently by members of the different **social class** groupings (see Chapter 6), when examining different **speech styles** (see Chapter 11) speakers from all social class groups style-shifted in the same way, using more **variants** that were **non-standard** when speaking in the most informal style, and vice versa. Therefore, whilst speakers were using language in different ways, there was evidence of shared evaluations, with speakers from all the differing social classes evaluating the standard language forms (see Chapter 16) in the same way, using the most prestigious forms with greater frequency in the most formal and therefore the most self-conscious situations.

Whilst Labov's definition has been highly influential, it has also been subjected to a good deal of criticism. Britain and Matsumoto (2005: 7) point out that Labov's work has been criticized for excluding non-natives of New York from his sample, which can crucially 'mask the very origins of some linguistic changes that are under way in the community'. Furthermore, they observe that Labov's framework presumes a **consensus model** of society, whereby those lower-class speakers simply share the values of the upper middle classes. The Milroys are commonly associated with the alternative **conflict model** (Milroy and Milroy 1997b) which posits that there are distinct divisions existing between unequal social groups in society, maintained by language ideologies, which result in conflict. Such conflict is hidden by the promotion of a consensus view of shared linguistic norms. Patrick (2001) disagrees with the Milroys' critique of the consensus model, arguing that Labov actually stressed the pressure of standard norms and did not intend to prescribe uniformity. However, he does acknowledge that Labov never raises the issue of speakers' resistance to standard language norms. Despite the criticisms that have been cited at Labov's work, there is no doubt that his definition was seminal, and thus still deserves detailed acknowledgement and consideration.

As well as being a key concept in larger-scale **quantitative** sociolinguistic studies such as Labov's, the speech community concept has also been used within **qualitative**, **ethnographic** sociolinguistic studies, influenced by the work of Hymes (1972, 1974). Saville-Troike (2003) highlights the centrality of the concept of the speech community to researchers working within the sociolinguistic sub-discipline of the **ethnography of communication**. She argues that research in this paradigm investigates how 'communication is patterned and organised within a speech community' (2003: 14), with the findings then being applied to wider social and cultural issues. She defines a 'community' and then a 'speech community' in the following manner:

> The essential criterion for 'community' is that some significant dimension of experience has to be shared, and for the 'speech community' that the shared dimension be related to ways in which members of the group use, value or interpret language.
>
> (Saville-Troike 2003: 15)

Echoes of Labov's ideas can clearly be seen here, with the emphasis upon a shared sense of evaluative experience, though this definition goes further than Labov's in terms of highlighting shared language use. She goes on to coin what she terms an informal typology of 'hard-shelled' and 'soft-shelled' speech communities (2003: 16). Hard-shelled communities have strong boundaries which allow only minimal interaction between outsiders and members of the speech community, thus serving to preserve the norms of language and culture. In contrast, soft-shelled communities have much weaker boundaries and are thus less likely to preserve existing language and cultural norms.

Another important issue that Saville-Troike raises is that of speech community membership. Patrick (2001) points out that she is the first to pose the question of simultaneous membership of different speech communities, as well as acknowledging that speech communities may very well overlap with one another (Saville-Troike 1982). In order to come up with a comprehensive model of a speech community, Patrick (2001: 591) argues, 'intermediate structures' of speech communities need to be conceptualized. Considering how speech communities overlap is a means of doing this, as is another related concept, termed 'nesting'. Santa Ana and Parodi (1998) develop nesting, in conjunction with adapting and reworking Labov's model. They characterize four 'nested fields' (1998: 23), used to signify points where groups of speakers are embedded with one another. They use phonological linguistic criteria to specify the differing nested levels of their model which 'reflects certain social strata and other structural features of society' (1998: 34). Their speech community typology is based upon the mutual evaluation of variables as being 'stigmatized', 'regional' or 'standard' in Mexican Spanish dialect, and from this they distinguish the four nests: 'locale', 'vicinity', 'district' and 'national' (1998: 35). They argue that their typology can be of use not just in the Mexican Spanish setting but also in a wide range of sociolinguistic settings. It is a promising model that has much research potential.

The examination of nested models concludes the first part of the chapter. I will now move on to consider social networks and communities of practice, bringing out points of comparison and contrast with the speech communities model.

SOCIAL NETWORKS

The social networks model offers a far less abstract framework than that of the speech community. It focuses on the social ties that specific speakers have with each other, and examines how these ties affect speakers' linguistic usage. A key component of the social network model is measuring its *strength*, calculated by classifying whether networks are 'dense' or 'loose', as well as whether they are 'uniplex' or 'multiplex' (Milroy 2001: 550). A network is dense if members that you interact with interact with each other – otherwise it is loose. If members know each other in more than one way, for example, they work together and are members of the same family, then the links are multiplex as opposed to uniplex. Dense and multiplex social networks tend to support localized linguistic norms, and they function as a method of norm reinforcement, whereby linguistic and other social norms are maintained by members of the network. In contrast, in loose and uniplex social networks, **language change** will be more likely to occur, owing to the lack of norm reinforcement. Milroy and Gordon (2003) argue that migration, war, industrialization and urbanization have caused disruption of close-knit, localized networks.

The social network model is most commonly associated with the Milroys' work in Belfast (Milroy and Milroy 1978; Milroy 1987). Instead of using the method of **social stratification**, the Milroys focused solely on working-class speakers. They gave each speaker a network strength score designed to measure the density and multiplexity of a network, focusing on social factors including kinship ties and whether individuals socialized with their workmates. Milroy (1980) found that those with the highest network strength scores maintained local **vernacular** norms the most. In the three different locations she examined (Ballymacarrett, the Hammer and the Clonard), she found that males in Ballymacarrett had the strongest dense and multiplex social networks and used vernacular norms most frequently, a consequence of their close social ties, resulting from good levels of male employment in the shipyard industry. This contrasted with the other two locations where male unemployment was high. Females in the Clonard also had high frequency of vernacular norms owing to employment in the linen industry, contrasting again with high levels of unemployment in the other two locations. The close social networks of the men and women in these different locations can therefore be seen to be acting as norm reinforcement mechanisms.

COMMUNITIES OF PRACTICE

The communities of practice approach was initially developed by educationalists Lave and Wenger (1991). It was brought into sociolinguistic study by Eckert and McConnell-Ginet (1992), originally for the purposes of language and gender research. Whilst it has been especially dominant in language and **gender** studies (see Holmes and Meyerhoff 2003), it has also been successfully applied in other areas of sociolinguistic research (see Mendoza Denton 1997; Holmes and Marra 2002). Eckert and McConnell-Ginet define a community of practice as:

An aggregate of people who come together around mutual engagement in an endeavor. Ways of doing things, ways of talking, beliefs, values, power relations – in short – practices – emerge in the course of this mutual endeavor.

(Eckert and McConnell-Ginet 1992: 464)

In contrast with speech communities and social networks, in the communities of practice model there is a distinct focus on examining language as a form of practice. Communities of practice can develop out of formal or informal enterprises, and members can be either 'core' or 'peripheral', depending on their levels of integration. Communities of practice can survive changes in membership, they can be small or large, and they can come into existence and go out of existence. In a later empirical study, Eckert (2000) argues that a community of practice is defined simultaneously by its membership and by the shared practices that its members partake in (see Chapter 12 for details of Eckert's findings). The value of the community of practice as a theoretical construct rests on 'the focus it affords on the mutually constitutive nature of the individual, group, activity and meaning' (2000: 35). In a further development of the original approach, Eckert and McConnell-Ginet (1999) point out that the notion of a community of practice can also extend to more global communities, such as academic fields, religions or professions. However, they point out that owing to the 'size' and 'dispersion' of these global communities, 'face-to-face interactions never link all members', and 'their "focal" practices are somewhat diffuse' (1999: 189). There is therefore a need to concentrate on how meaning is made at a more local level. In order to achieve this, Eckert and McConnell-Ginet (1992: 485) believe that researchers should adopt an **ethnographic** approach to data collection. They accuse large-scale **quantitative** studies (such as Labov's work) of overgeneralizing, resulting in the perpetuation of stereotypes.

Wenger (1998) expands upon the community of practice framework by producing a set of useful criteria. He first defines three dimensions of 'practice' that need to be fulfilled in order to make up 'community of practice': 'mutual engagement', a 'joint negotiated enterprise' and a 'shared repertoire' (1998: 73). He then further details the concept by proposing that the following fourteen points operate as 'indicators that a community of practice has formed':

1 Sustained mutual relationships – harmonious or conflictual.
2 Shared ways of engaging in doing things together.
3 The rapid flow of information and propagation of innovation.
4 Absence of introductory preambles, as if conversations and interactions were merely the continuation of an on-going process.
5 Very quick set-up of a problem to be discussed.
6 Substantial overlap in participants' descriptions of who belongs.
7 Knowing what others know, what they can do, and how they can contribute to an enterprise.
8 Mutually defining identities.
9 The ability to assess the appropriateness of actions or products.

10 Specific tools, representations and other artifacts.
11 Local lore, shared stories, inside jokes, knowing laughter.
12 Jargon and short cuts to communication as well as the ease of producing new ones.
13 Certain styles recognized as displaying membership.
14 A shared discourse reflecting a certain perspective on the world.

(Wenger 1998: 125–6)

The communities of practice approach is very useful for producing small-scale, ethnographic studies, but researchers have been accused of paying too much attention to the complexities of specific situations at the expense of being able to make broader observations concerning more than just a handful of subjects. These arguments can be seen as reflecting age-old debates concerning the pros and cons of quantitative versus qualitative research.

COMPARING THE FRAMEWORKS

Overall, when comparing the three approaches, the social network and communities of practice models immediately appear to have more in common with each other than with the speech communities framework. Both tend to favour qualitative methods for data collection, and the most high-profile figures from these approaches (Milroy for social networks and Eckert for communities of practice) have both used **participant observation** when collecting data in their studies in Belfast and Detroit respectively. Both frameworks also explicitly detail how membership of groups is constructed, which the speech community model does not do even when it considers simultaneous membership of speech communities.

Despite these differences, when considering social networks and speech communities, there are distinct parallels between dense multiplex networks and Saville-Troike's (2003) 'hard-shelled' speech communities defined above, with both categories demonstrating how high forms of integration and lack of influence from outsiders result in an established set of stable norms.

When comparing speech communities with communities of practice, Holmes and Meyerhoff (1999) highlight that whilst speech communities have their membership defined externally, membership is constructed internally within communities of practice, which also differ by stressing shared social/instrumental goals. For example, in a workplace community of practice, individuals regularly engage in social practices such as business meetings (Mullany 2006). They mutually define themselves as community of practice members when interacting in these social practices, and they simultaneously demonstrate that they share social/ instrumental goals, reflected through linguistic practices such as responding appropriately to the meeting agenda when allocated a **turn** in a meeting. The speech communities model does not require any mutual engagement in order to signify membership or any sharing of social/instrumental goals, owing to its disparate nature.

Holmes and Meyerhoff (1999) point out that social networks and communities of practice can be distinguished by considering speaker contact. Whilst the social network approach includes people who 'have limited or infrequent contact', a community of practice requires 'regular and mutually defining interaction' (1999: 179–80). Milroy and Gordon (2003) have also considered social networks with communities of practice, arguing that the differences between them are primarily of focus and method. Whilst social networks aim to discover social ties which are important to an individual, communities of practice seek to identify the 'clusters that form the crucial loci of linguistic and social practice' (2003: 119).

Despite these differences, Holmes and Meyerhoff (1999: 180) suggest that a possibility for future research may be to come up with an 'index of an individual's degree of integration into a CofP' which may then be compared with the categories that have been devised in order to measure the 'different degrees of integration into social networks'. This would be an interesting and fruitful line of further enquiry which draws upon the strengths of both frameworks.

CONCLUSION

Britain and Matsumoto (2005) observe a general trend away from the speech communities model towards the communities of practice model in recent years owing to transitions in sociolinguistic theorizing. They argue that such a change reflects the long-standing historical debate between **structure** and **agency** in the social sciences in general. Instead of favouring a top-down approach which focuses on social structure, as is the case with the speech communities model, over the last forty years they observe a 'gradual shift' towards a bottom-up model, whereby the focus is now on specific individual **identities** being jointly negotiated with one another whilst performing different practices. Britain and Matsumoto credit this change in focus to Le Page and Tabouret-Keller's (1985) work on individual identity (see Chapter 12). However, this top-down/bottom-up dichotomy oversimplifies the picture somewhat. Advocates of the communities of practice approach are quick to point out that individuals do not have total autonomy to choose how they use language, and constraints imposed by societal power structures which govern how language is used within specific communities of practice are evident. For example, both Eckert (2000) and Mills (2003) use Bourdieu's (1991) notions of **habitus** and the **linguistic market** to demonstrate how constraints are placed on language use within communities of practice.

Patrick (2001) makes an important practical point about sociolinguistic research in general when he states that 'the legitimacy of analytical choices [. . .] depends upon selection of the research question, in addition to the site' (2001: 589). He also reiterates a crucial point which can be applied to all three frameworks, that it is essential for researchers to remember that speech communities (or social networks, or communities of practice) do not already exist as 'predefined entities waiting to be researched' (2001: 593); instead it is essential to view them as tools which researchers constitute themselves.

Whilst there may have been an observable move towards the communities of practice approach, Patrick (2001) firmly argues that there is still a place for a speech communities model in current sociolinguistic research, though he does acknowledge that this may need to be in conjunction with social network or communities of practice approaches. Indeed, moving away from dichotomous thinking in order to consider more integrated community frameworks may be of real value to the discipline in future research.

FURTHER READING

Milroy, L. (1987a) *Language and Social Networks* (second edition), Oxford: Blackwell.

Patrick, P. (2001) 'The speech community', in J.K. Chambers, P. Trudgill and N. Schilling-Estes (eds) *The Handbook of Language Variation and Change*, Oxford: Blackwell, pp. 573–97.

Santa Ana, O. and Parodi, C. (1998) 'Modelling the speech community: configuration and variable types in the Mexican Spanish setting', *Language in Society* 27: 23–51.

Wenger, E. (1998) *Communities of Practice*, Cambridge: Cambridge University Press.

Part III
Socio-psychological factors

11
STYLE AND THE LINGUISTIC REPERTOIRE

ALLAN BELL

LANGUAGE STYLE

Style is the dimension of language where individual speakers have a choice. We do not always speak in consistently the same way. In fact we are shifting the way we speak constantly as we move from one situation to another. On different occasions we talk in different ways. These different ways of speaking carry different social meanings. They represent our ability to take up different social positions, and they affect how we are perceived by others.

Sociolinguistics has always had an interest in language style. One of the American founders of the field, Dell Hymes, proposed no fewer than sixteen factors which might affect the ways in which people speak differently in different situations, including purpose, genre and channel (Hymes 1974). The main factors which turn up again and again in sociolinguists' discussions of what influences a speaker's style are who the addressee is, what the **topic** is, and the nature of the setting where the interaction occurs (for example, Fishman 1972). We discuss more about these below.

STYLE AS ATTENTION TO SPEECH

In the approach of another founding American sociolinguist, William Labov, style is treated as a result of the amount of attention that speakers pay to their speech. Labov put this theory to work in the large survey he conducted of English in New York City (1966). He recorded over a hundred speakers and pioneered a means of eliciting different styles of speaking from a person within the bounds of a single interview. He had his respondents carry out a series of language tasks, each of them designed to focus increasing amounts of attention on their speech. Labov believed, that when speakers were talking to someone else rather than to the interviewer, or when they were particularly involved in the topic, they would be paying least attention to their speech – he called this 'casual' speech. When speakers were answering interview questions, they would be paying more attention to how they were speaking, and so produce a 'careful' style. When they were reading aloud a short story he gave them, Labov believed they would give still more attention to their speech. Reading out a list of isolated words focused even more attention, and reading **minimal pairs** – words which differ by only one sound, such as *batter* and *better* – would draw the maximum amount of attention.

Labov did indeed find that his interviewees shifted their pronunciation of salient **linguistic variables** as they moved across these five styles. So the choice between a **standard** *-ing* pronunciation and a conversational *-in'* pronunciation in words such as *crying* changed across the different styles. There was much more *-ing* in the minimal pairs style, and increasing amounts of *-in'* as the styles became more casual. This technique was used in many studies that followed the pattern of Labov's pioneering work, and often the researchers found the same kind of graded pattern of style shifting.

However, by 1980 some research was showing different findings. Sociolinguists began to question whether these styles were generally applicable, or whether attention to speech was the universal factor that was operating to cause style differences. Some sociolinguists began research which focused on style in its own right rather than regarding style as a secondary aspect of language variation beside differences between different speakers. An early study of this kind was by Nikolas Coupland (1984), a Welsh sociolinguist who has continued to do major research on style. For his doctoral thesis, he recorded a travel agent in conversation with a wide social range of clients. He analysed the levels of several linguistic variables in the speech of both the agent and her clients, for example, the **voicing** of **inter-vocalic** /t/ in words such as *writer*, making it sound like *rider*. The agent shifted towards more voicing with clients of a lower **social class**, who themselves used more voicing, and used less voicing when talking to higher-class clients, who used less voicing.

ACCOMMODATION THEORY

Sociolinguists like Coupland and Bell discovered that social psychologists of language were also doing research on language style. Although their linguistic analyses were unsophisticated, the social psychologists' explanations of why speakers shift style were more satisfying than Labov's. The leading British social psychologist of language, Howard Giles, put forward **Speech Accommodation Theory** (see Chapters 12–13), which maintained that speakers accommodate their speech to their addressee in order to win their approval (Giles and Powesland 1975). This means that the common form of accommodation is **convergence**, by which speakers shift their style of speech to become more like that of their addressees. A range of experiments demonstrated how speakers converge with each other in several ways such as speech rate, **accent**, content and pausing. Alternatively, instead of converging, speakers may maintain their style of speech, or even **diverge** from their addressee if they want to differentiate themselves from other individuals or groups.

The social psychological aspect of accommodation theory became increasingly complex as it developed and tried to encompass facts which do not sit easily with simple convergence or divergence. Riders to the theory proliferated; however, the basic insights of accommodation remain sound: that speakers accommodate their style to their audience. Accommodation theory is a powerful attempt to explain the causes of style, and it is paralleled by an approach within sociolinguistics which developed at the same time.

STYLE AS AUDIENCE DESIGN

Both the social psychologists (e.g. Giles 1973) and sociolinguists (e.g. Coupland 1984) were critiquing Labov's approach which held that style was controlled by the amount of attention paid to speech. New Zealand sociolinguist Allan Bell (1984) was the first to attempt an explanatory account of stylistic variation, and his **Audience Design** framework has since become the most widely used approach to language style within sociolinguistics. It proposes that the main reason speakers shift their language style is that they are responding to their listeners. This approach grew out of an early study on the language of radio news in New Zealand. At that time (1974) the organization of New Zealand public broadcasting meant that two of the radio stations being studied originated in the same suite of studios in Wellington, with the same newsreaders heard on both networks. The 'National Programme' had a higher status audience than did the 'Community Network'. A **quantitative** study of newsreaders' pronunciations showed that the newsreaders shifted their style considerably and consistently as they moved back and forth between the two stations (Bell 1991). Of all the many factors sociolinguists have suggested as possible influences on style (e.g. Hymes 1974), only differences in the stations' audiences could explain these shifts. And looking beyond this particular study, it seemed clear that the same regularities which were amplified in the media context were also operating in face-to-face communication.

The Audience Design framework can be summarized (Bell 2001) thus:

1 Style is what an individual speaker does with a language in relation to other people. Style is essentially interactive and social, marking interpersonal and intergroup relations.
2 Style derives its meaning from the association of linguistic features with particular social groups. The social evaluation of a group is transferred to the linguistic features associated with that group. Styles carry social meanings through their derivation from the language of particular groups.
3 The core of Audience Design is that speakers design their style primarily for and in response to their audience. Audience Design is generally manifested in a speaker shifting her style to be more like that of the person she is talking to – 'convergence' in terms of accommodation theory.
4 Audience Design applies to all codes and levels of a language repertoire, **monolingual** and **multilingual**.
5 Variation on the style dimension within the speech of a single speaker derives from and echoes the variation which exists between speakers on the 'social' dimension. This axiom claims that quantitative style differences are normally less than differences between social groups.
6 Speakers show a fine-grained ability to design their style for a range of different addressees, and to a lessening degree for other audience members such as auditors and overhearers.

7 Style shifts according to topic or setting derive their meaning and direction of shift from the underlying association of topics or settings with typical audience members.

8 As well as the 'Responsive' dimension of style, there is the 'Initiative' dimension where a style shift itself initiates a change in the situation rather than resulting from such a change. Sociolinguists have drawn attention to this distinction at least since Blom and Gumperz's proposal of situational versus metaphorical styles (1972). In responsive style shift, there is a regular association between language and social situation. Initiative style trades on such associations, infusing the flavour of one setting into a different context, in what Bakhtin has called 'stylization' (1981). Language becomes an **independent variable** which itself shapes the situation.

9 Initiative style shifts are in essence 'Referee Design', by which the linguistic features associated with a group can be used to express affiliation with that group. They focus on an absent reference group rather than the present audience. This typically occurs in the performance of a language or **variety** other than one's own.

Studies of whole **speech communities** of the kind that Labov conducted in New York require investigating a large number of speakers, but necessarily rather superficially. By contrast, research that focuses on style tends to look at a few speakers, but investigates them in detail. One such study is a close examination of style shifting by an African American teenager (Rickford and McNair-Knox 1994). Explicitly setting out to test some of the 'bold hypotheses and predictions' (Rickford and McNair Knox 1994: 231) of Audience Design as outlined above, the researchers found a high degree of influence by audience and by topic on the linguistic production of their informant.

Another study was designed specifically to examine the effects of **ethnicity** and **gender** on the speech of young New Zealanders (Bell 2001). It involved just four informants, a Maori (indigenous Polynesian) woman and man, and a Pakeha (white) woman and man. Each of these people was interviewed three times by different interviewers, making a total of twelve interviews. Each speaker's first interview was with an interviewer most like them – for example, the Maori man was interviewed by a Maori man. The second interview was cross-gender, the Maori man being interviewed by a Maori woman, and the third was cross-ethnicity, with a Pakeha male interviewer. By comparing the Maori man's speech in his first and third interviews, we can investigate how he may have shifted his style when talking to a Pakeha compared with talking to another Maori. It turned out that for nine linguistic features that tend to distinguish Maori English from Pakeha English (Bell 2000), the Maori man used more of the Maori-marked features to the Maori interviewer than he did to the Pakeha interviewer. This was a striking example of a speaker's ability to respond to his addressee in the way he designed his talk. It was also notable in these interviews that there tended to be clusters of 'Maori' features when the speaker was talking about topics such as family and culture. That is, when Maoriness was more salient the speaker spoke in a more Maori way.

STYLE AND IDENTITY

This kind of approach to style moves us towards an increasing relationship between linguistic performance and **identity**. The role of language in identity formation and presentation has been a prime interest of sociolinguists since the field was launched. An early classic was Labov's 1963 study of the local identity value of a single vowel sound in the English of Martha's Vineyard, an island off the coast of New England (Labov 1963). Identity has remained a focus in sociolinguistic research, increasingly so as postmodern approaches have stressed the role of language in social life and self-identity. Language is seen as having an active, constitutive role in interaction, as being very much a matter of initiative rather than response (Coupland 2001b; Schilling-Estes 2004).

The emphasis now is on how individual speakers use style – and other aspects of their language repertoire – to represent their identity or to lay claim to other identities. The thinking of the Soviet theorist Bakhtin (1981) has been particularly influential in such considerations. Bakhtin stresses how all language use in the present calls up the histories – the many prior usages – of the words and pronunciations which speakers use. Speakers use the voices of others within their own voice, constantly quoting and referencing the language of other individuals or groups. Sociolinguists have looked at phenomena such as **crossing** (Rampton 1995), by which British urban youth use fragments of languages which they do not themselves speak – such as Jamaican creole or Punjabi – as part of their identity presentation. This is the pattern of association that was termed 'Referee Design' above. Here language makes reference to a group (often an outgroup, but it may also be the speaker's own group) through intentional use of its linguistic code and claims affiliation with that group, its values and its characteristics.

The use of language for such identity representations is particularly salient in the media. Essentially such initiative style shift is a redefinition by the speaker of their own identity in relation to their audience. Thus in many New Zealand television commercials, non-New Zealand accents are used to call up desirable associations – for example, with aristocracy through use of British **Received Pronunciation**, or with the streetwise wheeler-dealer through imitation of Cockney (Bell 1991). The same phenomenon operates between as well as within languages. Advertisements in non-English-speaking countries exploit the prestige connotations of English for similar purposes, for example in Switzerland. In commercials for New Zealand's national airline, convergence towards native-like pronunciation of the words of a Maori song indexes orientation towards Maori identity (or at least empathy with that identity), and divergence signals foreignness (Bell 1999). In Wales, Coupland's work on the speech of a radio host (2001b) demonstrates how his show is to a large extent constituted by its use of local **dialect**. We can see here the common social forces that are at work regardless of a speaker's particular individual linguistic repertoire, whether monolingual style shift or **bilingual code switching**.

Use of a stylistic repertoire can be seen in face-to-face speech in the study by American sociolinguist Natalie Schilling-Estes (2004) of a single conversation between two young men from North Carolina, one African American and the other a Lumbee Indian. In her analysis of six linguistic features, Schilling-Estes found considerable evidence that these two speakers were adjusting their **speech styles** to accommodate each other at different stages of the conversation, sometimes through convergence and sometimes by divergence. Shifts in topic and in the speakers' stances towards particular topics were also reflected in their linguistic styles. Schilling-Estes was able to show how these speakers used the linguistic resources at their disposal to actively take up different stances and personas. Language was used to take the initiative in framing the encounter, the speakers' relationship and their positioning towards what they were discussing. Their linguistic usage reflected both the responsive dimension of language, in this case the ethnic identities with which they affiliated, and their ability to use language creatively for their own identity purposes.

The notable characteristic of contemporary work in style by scholars such as Coupland, Schilling-Estes and Bell is the interplay of quantitative and **qualitative** analysis in their investigations. Overall quantifying of speakers' performance on particular linguistic variables is complemented by examining their changing use of features through the course of a conversation, and how one feature relates to another. This blending of quantitative, qualitative and concurrence analysis (Bell 2001) represents a powerful combination of tools for understanding sociolinguistic style.

FURTHER READING

Bell, A. (1984) 'Language style as audience design', *Language in Society* 13: 145–204.
Bell, A. (1999) 'Styling the other to define the self: a study in New Zealand identity making', *Journal of Sociolinguistics* 3: 523–41.
Eckert, P. and Rickford, J.R. (eds) (2001) *Style and Sociolinguistic Variation*, New York: Cambridge University Press.
Rickford, J.R. and McNair-Knox, F. (1994) 'Addressee- and topic-influenced style shift: a quantitative sociolinguistic study', in D. Biber and E. Finegan (eds) *Sociolinguistic Perspectives on Register*, New York and Oxford: Oxford University Press, pp. 235–76.
Schilling-Estes, N. (2004) 'Constructing ethnicity in interaction', *Journal of Sociolinguistics* 8: 163–95.

12

LANGUAGE AND IDENTITY

JUDY DYER

In this chapter we focus on how linguistic resources, particularly **phonology** or **accent**, may be used as resources by speakers to project their **identity** in the world. As you will note in reading this chapter, identity has been defined in various ways at different times, but as a starting point let us take Norton's (1997) definition below. Although Norton's own research has been in the area of second language learning rather than sociolinguistics, she makes identity the focus of her work. According to Norton, identity is:

> how people understand their relationship to the world, how that relationship is constructed across time and space and how people understand their possibilities for the future.

(Norton 1997: 410)

Historically, sociolinguistic research has been primarily concerned not with identity itself, but with describing and understanding variation in patterns of speech, and what that variation may mean. Sociolinguists have long acknowledged that variation in speech can be used to express social meaning and to 'signal important information about aspects of speakers' social identity' (Eckert 1997: 64), yet few studies actually define or analyse the concept. In this chapter we investigate how sociolinguists have conceptualized identity from the earliest to the most recent studies, discussing how language can act as a vehicle for conveying important social information about the speaker, and the process by which certain linguistic features come to be associated with particular local social characteristics.

The main objective of most sociolinguistic research has been investigating why individuals speak differently from each other (*inter*speaker variation), and why an individual's own speech may sometimes vary (*intra*speaker variation). Developing an understanding of the *social* patterning and meaning of variation, (interspeaker variation), has been the main motivation behind much sociolinguistic work since its inception in the late 1960s. Sociolinguistic perspectives on identity are therefore unsurprisingly deeply intertwined with investigations into **language variation**, and researchers frequently refer to both variation and identity in their statements on the goals of the discipline (Milroy 1987a, b; Chambers 1995).

THE BIG PICTURE: THREE WAVES OF SOCIAL VARIATION

Eckert's (2002) theory that studies of language variation have come in three distinct waves provides a useful starting point in an overview of sociolinguistic views of identity. The first wave, initiated by Labov (1966), employed surveys and **quantitative** methods in an attempt to investigate correlations between linguistic variability and researcher-designated macro social categories, such as **social class**, **age**, **ethnicity** and **sex**. According to Eckert's theory, wave two employed more **ethnographic** methods with categories suggested by the participants themselves, in an attempt to understand more locally grounded linguistic variation, relating local variation to larger social structures like those investigated in the first wave studies. Studies in the first two waves, Eckert proposes, are concerned with language as situating the individual in a community or social group, often specifically geographically located communities, thereby frequently investigating **dialect** change and variation. Wave three studies focus on the *social meaning* of **variables**, with variation not simply reflecting but actually constructing social categories and social meaning. Third wave studies also often focus on variation within one speaker (intra-speaker variation or stylistic variation), and with the various and overlapping constructions of identities within the individual. More details will be added to this big picture with a detailed discussion of the characteristics of sociolinguistic research into identity that follows.

INDEXICALITY

The process by which language comes to be associated with specific locally or contextually significant social characteristics is referred to as the **indexicality** of language, and it is crucial to a discussion of language and identity. A whole language or just one linguistic form can become an index of, or a pointer to, a speaker's social identity, as well as of typical activities of that speaker (Milroy 2000). Thus indexicality entails an association of a language or a linguistic form with some sort of socially meaningful characteristic. This is seen most obviously in code-switching situations, where speakers shift between different languages that have different social meaning in their community. For example, Dubois and Horvath (2000) demonstrate how French, once used as a symbol of identity for Cajun people in Louisiana, is being replaced in the speech of young Cajun people with French-accented English, as many of them do not speak French. As these young people are unable to use French to signal their Cajun identity, they are using what linguistic resources they do have, thus speaking French-accented English (see Chapter 9).

The indexicality of language, however, may sometimes work against the speaker, where the speaker's dialect is perceived and evaluated negatively by interlocutors. A listener may ascribe social characteristics to a speaker that the speaker might want to resist. In an extract from *Bella*, a British women's magazine, Milroy (2000: 24) quotes a young woman from the north of England, working in London, who complains, 'People can't see further than my voice and assume I'm aggressive and common. They think I should own pigeons and have an outside toilet.' As Milroy explains:

> Helen experiences difficulty when people hear her voice because they attribute to that voice undesirable qualities imagined to be characteristic of working class speakers, such as aggressiveness and commonness.
>
> (Milroy 2000: 24)

Helen's comment clearly illustrates the fact that listeners sometimes associate a particular dialect with a corresponding set of social characteristics. Where speakers have access to more than one language or dialect, language can also be used to resist other-imposed identities. In Bailey's (2000) work in New York, Wilson, a speaker of Dominican English, Dominican Spanish, African American English and hispanicized English, successfully uses Spanish to resist hegemonic forms of ascription (classification based on phenotype as African American). Bailey (2000: 578) therefore states that 'language has the constitutive power to overcome what are seen by many as static natural boundaries'. In both Milroy and Bailey's examples, we can see that identity is a function of both self and other ascription.

IDENTITY AS A SOCIAL CATEGORY

Labov's (1966) study and subsequent replications (e.g. Trudgill 1974a) were founded on a **correlational approach** to language and identity. As Mendoza Denton (2002) states, in this way, sociolinguistic researchers in the early days of the discipline assigned identity by social category membership. Identity was viewed as researcher-designated broad, fixed social categories such as social class, age, sex and ethnicity. This kind of research was important however because it not only revealed the range of variation in a community, it also highlighted which types of people used particular **variants**.

Among others, Johnstone and Bean (1997: 222) have pointed out that correlational studies are descriptive rather than explanatory, and that while 'social facts bear heavily on linguistic ones, social facts are not determinants of linguistic facts'. Mendoza Denton (2002: 475) similarly states that early variationist research provided no explanation at all, being 'a statistically motivated observation-cum-speculative-description'. Yet such essentialization was generally how identity was perceived at this time. Social psychologists, such as Tajfel (1974), follow this view, defining social identity as:

> that part of an individual's self concept which derives from his [sic] knowledge of his membership of a social group (or groups) together with the emotional significance attached to that membership.
>
> (Tajfel 1974: 69)

103

Individuals were therefore viewed 'as occupying particular social identities throughout their lives by virtue of their position in the social structure' (Bucholtz 1999: 209). In other words, a speaker's identity viewed through language was seen as fixed and as a product of certain social factors. Speakers were therefore also considered largely agentless, viewed as the products of a particular social structure, which they in turn would reproduce through their language.

IDENTITY AS A CONTACT PHENOMENON

After the earliest large-scale surveys of language variation, some researchers working within this paradigm sought a more nuanced explanation of variation by going beyond a view of identity defined by social category. Methods of data collection, analysis and interpretation also reflected the attempt to understand in more detail how variation may be more locally situated. Ethnographic methods embedded researchers in their communities so that their analytical principles and interpretations reflected the perspectives of the speakers of those communities.

One groundbreaking approach was the study of language through **social networks** in Belfast (Milroy and Milroy 1978; Milroy 1980; see Chapter 10). Social and geographical mobility in terms of who a speaker mixed and identified with, as well as macro social factors, were shown to be important in understanding variation. Individual speaker variation might also be explained in terms of the speaker's network connections. The Milroys' study also acknowledged contact with others as being highly important in terms of the influences on a speaker's linguistic identity. Thus network theory acknowledged the importance of contact in language variation and was used 'to explain individual behaviour of various kinds which cannot be accounted for in terms of corporate group membership' (Milroy 1980: 135).

SPEECH ACCOMMODATION THEORY AND ACTS OF IDENTITY

Giles's (1977) **Speech Accommodation Theory** (SAT) in social psychology, and the work of Le Page and Tabouret-Keller (1985) on acts of identity were highly influential in shaping later views of identity within sociolinguistics. Giles's SAT was founded on the idea that speakers could change their speech while in interactions in order to align themselves or distance themselves from their interlocutors (see Chapters 11 and 13). The work of Le Page and Tabouret-Keller (1985) on **creole** languages has been particularly important in laying foundational theories for sociolinguistic study of identity, because it acknowledges that a speaker is not merely a passive voice-piece of his or her social position in society, but rather makes sometimes conscious choices as to how to speak. In this model, speakers are viewed as actively exploiting linguistic resources available to them in order to project differing identities for different contexts. Such a choice itself represents an act of identity:

An individual creates for himself [*sic*] the patterns of his linguistic behaviour so as to resemble those of the group or groups with which from time to time he wishes to be identified.

(Le Page and Tabouret-Keller 1985: 181)

This research emphasizes both the **agency** of speakers in their ability to manipulate linguistic resources available to them and the ability to actively project different identities through language with various interlocutors. This model further importantly acknowledges that speakers, by actively exploiting the linguistic resources in their repertoires, are not simply products of a social structure reproducing that same social structure, but rather can create the identity they wish to project in an interaction. Identity is thus viewed not as a fixed but as a dynamic phenomenon.

Reconceptualizations of identity employed in other academic disciplines, most importantly in sociology, were also gradually adopted in later sociolinguistic work (see Bucholtz 1999 and Norton 2000). Sociolinguists have begun to envision the speaker as more than just a product of his or her social context, and more an agent with the ability to select linguistic resources available in the community repertoire. This post-structuralist conception of identity places more emphasis on the individual and less on the community, and views identity as complex, contradictory, multifaceted and dynamic across time and place.

IDENTITY AS PRACTICE

Much sociolinguistic work from the late 1980s to the present day bears signs of the influence of the above theoretical insights of Giles and Le Page and Tabouret-Keller, perhaps particularly in the prominent role that has been accorded to identity. The research discussed in this section represents the third wave of sociolinguistic study of variation, being concerned with how groups of speakers come together and develop distinct ways of speaking around their joint enterprises. Many studies have been conducted investigating **communities of practice** (CofP), see Chapter 10.

Eckert's (1989, 2000) study of adolescent peer groups investigated language variation at a Detroit high school. She found that speakers were actively exploiting and manipulating a range of variants in their community repertoire as a resource to mark peer group membership, in effect as a form of identity *practice*. Students defined themselves through language either as Jocks (college-bound students oriented to middle-class values) or Burnouts (underachieving students bound for the workplace rather than college), and their distinct use of language reflected their own self-conceptualization. Eckert and McConnell-Ginet (1995) revealed that the most innovative variants of the variables under study (the backing of (uh) as in the word *fun*) from /ʌ/ to /ɔ/ and the raising of (ay) as in the word *file* from /aɪ/ to /ɔɪ/) were being used by the 'Burned-out Burnout girls' (those with the strongest affiliation to Burnout values), in order to distinguish themselves from the more 'jocky' Burnout girls. The researchers explained this phenomenon as the girls using language as a means to appear tough, since it was not appropriate for girls to be physically aggressive as it was for their male counterparts. The study again suggested that social categories imposed by the researcher, such as social class or gender, may not always be the salient ones for the population under study, and that the researcher has to understand the community in order to be able to interpret the variation found therein. As Eckert (1989: 246) states, understanding the community under study and focusing more on 'the relation of language use to the everyday practice that constitutes speakers' class-based social participation and identity in the community' yields complex interpretations, because an individual speaker is unlikely to index only one aspect of their identity on any one occasion. According to Eckert, it is this complex interaction between social phenomena in the construction of identity that motivates a speaker's choice of variants at any given time. Eckert's work thus illustrates a major change in the way variation can be viewed by sociolinguists. Variation may also be the result of a speaker exercising a sometimes conscious choice over particular variants available to him or her in the community's linguistic repertoire. Language is considered to be *constitutive* of social identity (in other words, a speaker can actively manipulate linguistic resources to create identities), and is not merely a *reflection* of one's general social position in the world, as some earlier studies had assumed.

Bucholtz's (1999) CofP study of the language of a group of high-school students that self-identified as 'nerds' examined the speech of these students at phonological, syntactic, lexical and discoursal levels. Bucholtz identified linguistic features that members of this CofP exploited to construct their group identity. Bucholtz argues that a CofP model enables researchers to access identities that are rooted in actions or practice, and can reveal that a speaker may have multiple identities, and can take part in multiple identity practices, being one minute nerd, another minute daughter, and so on. This approach to identity is clearly different from earlier ones, in the belief that distinct **styles** of speech are sometimes consciously manipulated by individuals to signal group membership.

DIALECT CONTACT CONTEXTS

In this section, a recent approach to studying identity and social variation within a **dialect contact** context is described. These recent works use a language ideology framework to inform the analysis and interpretation of phonological data (Irvine and Gal 2000; Ochs 1992; Silverstein 1992). The issue in these studies is the use of similar variants by speakers within a community but with apparently different social meaning. Let us now therefore return to indexicality.

A justified criticism of much sociolinguistic work particularly from linguistic anthropologists is that sociolinguists assume a direct correlation between a linguistic feature and a social characteristic. Silverstein (1992: 316) refers to this correlation as *first-order indexicality* (that is, one person uses form X, while another uses form Y). But it is important to understand exactly what is behind this indexing of linguistic features with social characteristics. Silverstein suggests a model by which the overt or covert noticing, discussion and rationalization of first-order indexicality offers a means of identifying ideology, and as such may be operationalized to provide a means of tapping into speakers' beliefs and feelings about other groups. That is, speakers' reactions to language, evident both in language behaviour (**hypercorrection**, style shifting) and in overt comment about language and other social phenomena, can also be viewed as manifestations of ideological stances. These ideological stances can provide a means of making sense of the indexicality inherent in language, i.e. how language forms index speakers' social identities.

Dyer's (2000, 2002) and Wassink and Dyer's (2004) studies of communities in Corby, UK, and Kingston, Jamaica, utilize this language ideology model in two very different dialect contact contexts. Dyer's (2000) study of Corby investigated changes occurring in the local English dialect due to the inmigration of large numbers of Scots to work in a newly built steelworks in the town. (Corby is around 100 miles north of London and 300 miles south of Glasgow, Scotland.) A major point of study was the social significance or meaning of the identity projected by young Corby people who sounded Scottish but had no Scottish ancestry. This promised to be especially interesting, since Scottish, and more particularly Glaswegian English (from whence many of the Corby migrants hailed) is often viewed as a **stigmatized** variety (Macaulay 1977). Wassink and Dyer (2004) further examined how phonological features in Kingston and Corby, considered stigmatized by some speakers because of their association with either a rural Jamaican or a Scottish background, were apparently being used as symbols of local pride by the younger generations.

A variationist analysis of the data from these studies might have concluded that speakers were indexing a Scottish identity in using Scottish variants, or a rural identity in the use of traditionally rural variants in the Jamaican context. However, an analysis of speaker ideologies showed that the salient social categories for speakers had changed over time. The opposition between Scottish and English that was salient for the oldest speakers in the Corby study had apparently been replaced by an opposition between Corby and the neighbouring town of Kettering for the youngest speakers. The historically Scottish variants were in use because younger speakers perceived them as markers of a specifically Corby identity. Similarly, in the Kingston data, younger speakers are apparently using **basilectal** or formally stigmatized forms (e.g. **palatalization** before /a/ as in [gʲarlic] for *garlic*) without being judged as rural speakers.

Apart from uncovering distinct meanings for the same phonological features used by different generations in the same communities, studies using a language ideology framework have also been able to explain the meaning of the projection of apparently contradictory identities through the use of features that index different social characteristics. Dyer's (2002) work shows that young people in Corby are able to choose between features that have been adopted over a wide geographical area, termed **levelled** or supra-local features, to index an outward-looking identity, or more local (i.e. historically Scottish) ones to signal affiliation with their town community.

NEW DIRECTIONS IN THE STUDY OF LANGUAGE AND IDENTITY

The exploration of identity within sociolinguistics has come a long way from the statistical correlation of linguistic and **social variables**, with researchers employing many different and varied frameworks of analysis and interpretation informed both by their own discipline, and others such as social psychology, sociology and anthropology. In contrast to the earliest sociolinguistic studies, sociolinguistic research now considers identity as a primary focus of investigation. Work on both social and stylistic variation in terms of speaker identity is flourishing. An important growing body of research within linguistic anthropology that we have left aside in this chapter is concerned with how identities are constructed interactionally in conversation. (See Mendoza Denton 2002, Bucholtz and Hall 2004 and 2005, for excellent overviews of this research that is mostly analysed through discourse.)

The perception of identity that sociolinguists have now is undoubtedly more complex than at the outset of our discipline, but also undoubtedly more satisfying and more explanatory of variation. In short, there is acknowledgement now that identity is realized through language in sometimes apparently oppositional ways.

> Any given construction of identity may be in part deliberate and intentional, in part habitual and hence often less than fully conscious, in part an outcome of others' perceptions and representations, and in part an effect of larger ideological processes and material structures that may become relevant to interaction.
>
> (Bucholtz and Hall 2004: 376)

FURTHER READING

Bucholtz, M. and Hall, K. (2004) 'Language and identity', in A. Duranti (ed.) *A Companion to Linguistic Anthropology*, Oxford: Blackwell, pp. 369–94.

Eckert, P. (2000) *Linguistic Variation as Social Practice*, Oxford: Blackwell.

Le Page, R.B. and Tabouret-Keller, A. (1985) *Acts of Identity: Creole-based Approaches to Language and Ethnicity*, Cambridge: Cambridge University Press.

Mendoza Denton, N. (2002) 'Language and identity', in J.K. Chambers, P. Trudgill and N. Schilling-Estes (eds) *The Handbook of Language Variation and Change*, Oxford: Blackwell, pp. 475–99.

13
MOBILITY, CONTACT AND ACCOMMODATION

PETER AUER

The term **accommodation** is used in two different ways in sociolinguistics. On the one hand, it refers to *interpersonal* accommodation, i.e. the **convergence** of two or more interactants' way of speaking within an interactional episode. Models for the analysis of interpersonal convergence (or **divergence**) have their sources in social psychology, particularly in the work of Howard Giles (such as Giles 1973). It is a matter of debate whether this type of accommodation, which is temporary and has as its domain a bounded interactional encounter, can lead to **language change** on the community level (see Auer and Hinskens 2005 for a discussion). I will not be concerned with this meaning of 'accommodation' here. The second way in which the term is used refers to what is sometimes called *long-term dialect accommodation*, the convergence which may occur in (groups of) speakers who change their place of living more or less permanently within the same language area. This type of 'internal' migration and the subsequent **dialect contact** between the brought-along **variety** and the one spoken in the receiving area can lead to a durable change in speech habits of the immigrant group.

A few comments are necessary on the delimitation of the topic of this chapter. First, as the term *long-term dialect accommodation* suggests, the convergence has to last beyond an interactional episode. Whether frequent interpersonal convergence (short-term accommodation) is the basis and therefore the driving force behind long-term accommodation will be discussed below. It cannot be taken for granted that the social psychological model which explains interpersonal accommodation can be expanded to explain long-term dialect accommodation as well.

Second, the term also suggests a difference between **language contact** and dialect contact. It is not normally used in studies on **bilingualism** due to migration. Intuitively this seems justified, since convergence between structurally distant language systems can lead to **code switching**, **code mixing**, lexical borrowing, language loss, etc., whereas dialect contact is rather associated with more gradual, often **quantitative** changes in the realization of certain **variables** in **morphology** and **phonology**. At a closer look, the difference is difficult to pinpoint, however, particularly when it comes to structurally closely related languages and structurally very distinct **dialects**. Borrowing and code mixing can occur between dialects just as between languages, even though the structural regularities by which they are constrained may be somewhat different. Also, language contact may lead to processes of gradual structural convergence, for instance in syntax. As a rule of thumb, it may be said though that the greater the structural distance between the **varieties** in contact the easier it is to establish a dichotomic contrast between them in speech. On the other hand, closely related contact varieties will tend to lead to non-dichotomic surface contrasts and more gradual differences (but see Auer in press a, for the limits of this rule of thumb). Studies on long-term dialect accommodation have mostly been concerned with the quantitative analysis of these gradual differences, not with, for example, code mixing patterns although such a type of convergence occurs and may index accommodation as well.

Third, in studies on accommodation as a consequence of migration, the focus is on changes in the language behaviour of the migrants. It is not impossible though that the receiving group may accommodate to the immigrants and change their speaking habits, or that the immigration has a more indirect but still permanent impact on the local varieties. For instance, it has been argued that the large-scale immigration of speakers of Brabant (particularly Antwerp) into the Hague–Amsterdam area, as it occurred in consequence of the fall of Antwerp to the Spanish in 1585, led to a massive Brabantish influence on the Amsterdam dialect (see Paardekooper 2001 for details).

Last, accommodation as a consequence of migration should be distinguished from **koine** ('new dialect') formation, as it often occurs when immigrants from a variety of dialect areas migrate into an area which was not or only sparsely inhabited before, or in which they formed a segregated speech community. It also has to be distinguished from **pidgin** and **creole** formation. (Koine formation is described in Chapter 22, and pidgin and creole formation in Chapter 21 of this *Companion*.) Again, the line is not always easy to draw. Koine formation seems to imply accommodation, but in the prototypical case, all speakers accommodate to each other, such that a new variety can emerge. As soon as the koine has stabilized, new arrivals in the immigrant area will accommodate it (see Auer in press b for an example). Segregated communities with a distinct variety (koine, pidgin, creole) may start to converge with the surrounding community after some time (see the discussion of Afro-American English in isolated rural communities in North America, in Mallinson and Wolfram 2002 and Wolfram 2003).

SOME BASIC DISTINCTIONS

Within the field of (long-term dialect) accommodation, some further distinctions are necessary. First of all, it goes without saying the repertoires of the migrants and the receiving society can be of various types. The most important constellations seem to be the following.

1 The immigrants share a standard variety with the receiving area, but additionally use a regional variety (dialect) which differs (more or less) from that of the receiving area (see Bortoni-Ricardo 1985; Matter and Ziberi 2000; Payne 1980; Werlen *et al.* 2002). For instance (an example to which we will come back below), speakers of the Upper Saxonian Vernacular spoken in the east of Germany (formerly GDR) migrated into

various western (formerly FRG) states around 1990. They shared with the receiving communities standard German as the H-variety, but brought along regional **vernaculars** distinct from those of the receiving area (Auer *et al.* 1998, 2000; Barden and Großkopf 1998).

2 The immigrants use a different standard variety from the receiving community (and often also different regional varieties). This is the case of migration from the United Kingdom into the United States or vice versa, from francophone Canada into France and vice versa, from Germany into Switzerland and vice versa, etc. (See Chambers 1992 on Canadian/British English, Trudgill 1983 on British pop singers using American/ Afro-American English features and Trudgill 1986: 11–38 on British/American English in general).

3 The immigrants use a dialect, while in the receiving area a variety is spoken which is close(r) to the standard variety. This is often the case with immigration into the capital (for instance, into Oslo by speakers of western Norwegian dialects, into Helsinki by Finnish dialect speakers (see Nuolijärvi 1994), into Paris by French dialect speakers or into Copenhagen by Danish dialect speakers). Depending on the **prestige** of the standard variety, and particularly the prestige of the brought-along regional varieties, the pressure to accommodate to the standard-near variety of the capital may be high.

4 The immigrants speak only dialect and the receiving area has a more complex repertoire including a different dialect and an overarching standard. A case in point is remigration of extraterritorial groups of speakers 'under the roof' of the relevant standard variety (such as in dialect speakers from the (former) German language enclaves in East Europe or in the former Soviet Union who remigrate into Germany every few hundred years; see Berend 1998).

Depending on the situation, different processes of accommodation may set in. In the simplest case (2), the loss of the brought-along features implies the acquisition of those of the receiving areas. All other cases are more complex. In (3) and (4), the immigrants face the task of acquiring the standard variety, which may or may not lead to the loss of the brought-along dialect. Only in (4) may they additionally acquire the local vernacular (L-variety). Finally, in (1) the features of the brought-along variety may be given up in favour of the standard or a more standardized way of speaking and/or the features of the local vernacular of the receiving area may be acquired. It is essential to distinguish between the *acquisition* of a new variety (or some of its features: *positive accommodation*) and the *loss* (or *non-usage*) of a brought-along variety (or some of its features: *negative* accommodation), since the two processes follow different regularities. In situations in which a common standard variety overarches the regional ways of speaking, it is also useful to distinguish direct accommodation of the dialect of the receiving area from indirect accommodation: that is, the increasing use of the neutral standard forms at the expense of the regional/dialectal forms.

METHODS FOR THE INVESTIGATION OF ACCOMMODATION

Most investigations into long-term dialect accommodation follow a **real-time** methodology (panel investigation): a group of migrants is observed over a period of time (such as one or two years). However, long-term dialect accommodation has also been reconstructed using **apparent-time** methodology; in this case, larger periods of time such as one or more decades have been studied making use of the standard techniques of **variationist sociolinguistics**.

It should be kept in mind that almost all studies on long-term dialect accommodation have been concerned with **phonology** and **phonetics**. Particularly studies on syntax are lacking.

External factors influencing accommodation

Internal migration is a suitable testing ground for the relevance of weak and strong **social network** ties for linguistic accommodation since it is essentially linked to social network formation. Migrants are almost always in a situation in which old networks break down and new ones must be constructed. On the other hand, they are confronted with strong local networks. It is therefore not surprising that studies on long-term dialect accommodation have often resorted to network theory in order to explain the amount of accommodation found in the informants. In its simplest version, the network-based approach assumes that the amount and duration of exposure to the new linguistic environment determine the degree of accommodation of the varieties spoken in the receiving area. Indeed, segregation (in the sense of strong network contacts within the migrant group and little interaction with the receiving society) has been shown to favour maintenance of the brought-along repertoire; it can prevent accommodation from taking place (see Bortoni-Ricardo 1985). However, there is no direct link between frequency of contact with the receiving community and convergence to its way of speaking. For instance, Bortoni-Ricardo (1985) found a strong interaction with **gender**, with female migrants being dependent on their grown-up children for access to the receiving city's variety. Although their networks were restricted to the family, they none the less showed a strong negative accommodation (loss of Caipira features) in some variables than men who had more extensive networks. Nuolijärvi (1994), in a study of migration into Helsinki, also found a strong effect of gender (women accommodating more strongly than men), but also of the prestige of the dialect of origin on negative accommodation to the Helsinki vernacular. Speakers of Finnish with an Ostrobothnian dialect background found it easier than those of the more negatively evaluated Savo dialects to maintain their dialect after migration. In her study, speakers who had to do with a large number of people professionally adapted less to the Helsinki vernacular (standard) than those who lived in more restricted networks.

It is therefore plausible to assume that subjective factors such as loyalty to the dialect of origin, the prestige of the varieties concerned, as well as general satisfaction with post-migration life play a role. In a study on internal migration in Germany (Saxonians to the west German cities of Saarbrücken and Constance), Auer *et al*. (1998) distinguished three main integration types:

1 Immigrants who join networks with other immigrants from the same background, erecting a dense social structure around them which provides shelter against the new social environment and mutal help to survive socially in relative autonomy. Contacts with local members are restricted to a minimum. Linguistic accommodation is not required and does not take place. Rather, linguistic developments in the group are suppressed, sometimes more than in the society from which the migrant group has originated. This case of segregated but strong networks was not observed among the Saxon immigrants.

2 Immigrants who join the local networks and become members of a densely structured social aggregate in which the locals are dominant (these are the Type A group in Table 13.1). These Saxons were highly satisfied with their new social environment; contacts with Saxon compatriots no longer played an important role in their new life.

3 Immigrants who did not succeed, or were not interested, in establishing strong network ties with any – local or migrant – network; instead, they were engaged in open networks, with unstable, rapidly changing and often superficial contacts. Three subtypes were distinguished according to subjective parameters:

   (a) Migrants who were satisfied with this situation (the B group in Table 13.1).
   (b) Migrants who were unhappy with this situation, and who attempted to change their situation (although unsuccessfully); in doing so, and in experiencing failure, they developed a strong disliking for the receiving region and for West Germany in general. Their attitudinal and factual orientation was backwards towards Saxony (the C group in Table 13.1).
   (c) Finally, migrants who were also unhappy with this situation and made an effort to change it (again without much success) but had no orientation towards Saxony; rather, they tried to make their way in the West (the D group in Table 13.1).

Table 13.1 Levels of accommodation across integration type (%)

Integration type	A	B	C	D
Loss of Saxon features	38	27	−29	45
Adoption of local features	Yes	No	No	Yes

According to a frequency-based model of the link between network contacts and accommodation, informants with weak ties with members of the local community would not be expected to accommodate the local dialect features or give up their own vernacular.

The overall results of the **longitudinal study** which spanned a period of two years are summarized in Table 13.1; they refer to the relative loss of Upper Saxon features (average of all thirteen phonological variables investigated), that is, *negative* accommodation, and to accommodation of the local regiolect (*positive* accommodation). As the overall results show, successful integration into the local community (A) leads as expected to positive and negative accommodation. However, the effect is even stronger among migrants with weak networks but a strong attitudinal orientation towards the receiving area and away from the area of origin (D). Auer *et al*. (2000) show that individuals who change their attitudinal orientation also change their accommodation pattern.

Another external factor influencing the amount of accommodation is **age**. Children and adolescents are better dialect learners than adults (Bortoni-Ricardo 1985). However, this statement needs to be refined, since different types of variables are subject to this age effect to different degrees. Payne (1980), in a study on internal US migration, finds evidence that children of immigrants into Philadelphia older than 7 cannot fully acquire lexicalized phonological variables.

Internal (linguistic) factors influencing accommodation

An important question is whether certain linguistic variables lend themselves more easily to negative and/or positive dialect accommodation than others. Often, the notion of 'salience' is invoked to identify linguistic features which are given up and/ or acquired fast (drawing on Schirmunski 1928/29; see Trudgill 1986, Auer *et al*. 1998 and Kerswill and Williams 2002 for a discussion). Arguably, features with a high degree of linguistic awareness, which can be controlled consciously, are better candidates for negative and/or positive accommodation than those which are used unconsciously and are hard to control. However, awareness and control are only necessary conditions for early loss/acquisition. It is also necessary that the attitudinal pattern is favourable for accommodation (neutral or negative evaluation of the brought-along features, neutral or positive evaluation of those of the receiving area). Acquisition may be blocked even then when the feature is radically stereotypical (such as AmE [æ] for BE [a] in *dance*, etc.). There may also be structural reasons for which dialect acquisition is delayed. For instance, there is evidence that mergers are better acquired than splits, and that lexicalized rules present a particular obstacle to acquisition (Payne 1980). Shockey (1984), however, shows that the unmerging of the AmE **intervocalic tap** /ɾ/ into /d/ and /t/ by American immigrants in England is successful (presumably because it is supported by orthography), although it leads to an opposition /ɾ ~ t/ instead of BE/d ~ t/. Attempts to predict the sociolinguistic salience of a phonological feature on the basis of its structural characteristics (such as phonemicity, articulatory distance) have not proved to be successful.

FURTHER READING

Auer, P., Barden, B. and Großkopf, B.E. (1998) 'Subjective and objective parameters determining "salience" in long-term dialect accommodation', *Journal of Sociolinguistics* 2 (2): 163–87.

Chambers, J.K. (1992) 'Dialect acquisition', *Language* 68: 673–705.

Payne, A.C. (1980) 'Factors controlling the acquisition of the Philadelphia dialect by out-of-state children', in W. Labov (ed.), *Locating Language in Time and Space*, New York: Academic Press, pp. 143–78.

14

LANGUAGE ATTITUDES

PETER GARRETT

In his seminal work on linguistic variation, Labov argued a significant role in sociolinguistics for the study of **language attitudes**. **Sociolinguistic variables**, he maintained, gained social meaning from their distributional patterns. His 'subjective reaction test' was one technique for gathering such data – for example, finding that New Yorkers associated **rhoticity** with high-ranking occupations (Labov 1972b). This concept of **prestige** has been an enduring aspect of language attitudes findings. Since then, much pioneering language attitudes work has been conducted at an interface between social psychology, where attitudes hold a place of central prominence for understanding social behaviour and thought, and sociolinguistics, with its focus on social aspects of language specifically. This chapter first reviews some of this work and then considers some of the main current issues and developments.

As a psychological construct, attitude is not easily defined, but there is broad acceptance of Sarnoff's definition: 'a disposition to react favourably or unfavourably to a class of objects' (see Bradac *et al.* 2001). Attitudes are generally seen as learned through human socialization, with those acquired early in the life span – like many language attitudes (Day 1982) – less amenable to change in later life (Sears 1983). Attitudes are commonly viewed as comprising three types of components: cognitive (beliefs and stereotypes), affective (evaluations) and behavioural, although how behaviour relates to the other two components is not clear-cut (see Garrett *et al.* 2003: 7 ff.). Attitudes are also attributed various functions: for example, (negative and positive) stereotypes are employed to provide order to our social world and, in particular, to explain intergroup relations (Tajfel 1981).

Because attitudes are a mental construct, there can be uncertainty whether our research data truly represent the respondents' attitudes. This concern generates much methodological debate. There are essentially three research approaches, usually termed the *societal treatment approach*, the *direct approach* and the *indirect approach*. The first of these is a broad category that typically includes observational (e.g. **ethnographic**) studies, or the analysis of various sources within the public domain – for example, the discourse of government or educational policy documents, employment and consumer advertisements, novels, television programmes, cartoons, style and etiquette books (see Garrett *et al.* 2003: 15). It is fair to say that studies in this category, which often delve deeper into the socio-cultural and political backdrop to attitudes, have tended to receive insufficient foregrounding in contemporary mainstream reviews of language attitudes research.

The direct approach involves simply asking people to report self-analytically what their attitudes are, and is much used in larger-scale surveys, for example of attitudes to the promotion of minority languages (O'Raigain 1993) or of attitudes in second language learning (Gardner and Lambert 1972). But attitudes researchers are always wary of response biases: in particular, 'acquiescence bias' (where people may give the responses they feel the researchers are looking for) and 'socially desirable responses' (where people voice the attitudes they think they ought to have, rather than the ones they actually hold). In Montreal in the 1950s, Lambert and his colleagues (Lambert *et al.* 1960), sceptical of local people's overt responses as a true representation of their privately held inter-ethnic views, developed an indirect method known as the **matched-guise technique** (MGT). It relies upon vocal 'guises', where typically researchers record a single speaker (occasionally a professional actor) who commands or can imitate the required **speech styles** (e.g. **accent**), and deceive listeners into thinking they are listening to different speakers saying similar things, or reading the same text aloud in their different accents. The rationale is that all speech features apart from the one under investigation (accent) are controlled out, so that any differences in listener evaluations must be because they judge accents differently. This elegant experimental technique has been a dominant method since then. Some studies have made modifications, such as using several speakers producing their own varieties, aiming to gain 'authenticity', but at the expense of intrusive idiosyncratic voice properties. For example, in Bayard *et al.*'s (2001) study of international Englishes, where they found evidence of US English replacing **Received Pronunciation** (RP) as the prestige **variety**, eight different speakers were used: one male and one female speaker of each variety. The MGT has allowed the manipulation of a range of variables, including language, dialect and accent variables in various **speech communities**, levels of accentedness, speech rate, lexical intensity, lexical formality, **age** and speech **accommodation** (see Garrett *et al.* 2003 for a methodology-focused review).

The use of attitude-rating scales in this indirect approach allows some sophisticated statistical analysis. One well established finding from such analysis has been that respondents generally judge and differentiate language along three primary dimensions: superiority (characteristics such as prestige, intelligence, competence), social attractiveness (e.g. friendliness, trustworthiness) and dynamism (e.g. enthusiasm, liveliness) (Zahn and Hopper 1985). For example, speakers of lower-class, minority or '**non-standard**' varieties tend to enjoy more favourable evaluations in terms of social attractiveness but fare less favourably on perceived competence and intelligence compared with **standard** varieties, which are associated with more **social status** but have often been found to project less social attractiveness. 'Regional standard varieties' have also been identified in some contexts. These attract higher competence and prestige ratings than other regional varieties but without losing ground on social attractiveness. In Canada, Edwards and Jacobsen (1987) found that Nova Scotian English operated as a regional standard (see also Garrett *et al.* 2003 on Wales).

Apart from studies of accent, Bradac *et al.* (1988) have found that low levels of lexical diversity lead to judgements of low speaker status and competence in some contexts. And Street *et al.* (1984) found that speaking faster was associated with increased competence. (Reviews of such findings include Cargile *et al.* 1994; Bradac *et al.* 2001.) This experimental approach to studying attitudes has also allowed comparison of the relative effects of different levels of language on evaluative reactions. For example, Levin *et al.*'s (1994) study comparing lexical formality and accent, and Giles and Sassoon's (1983) study comparing accent and lexical diversity, both found accent to be more potent overall.

Studies using similar approaches have produced some striking findings in applied fields. In **forensic linguistics** in Australia, Seggie (1983) found a relationship between attributions of guilt and a suspect's accent. Where a suspect was accused of white-collar crime, more guilt was attributed to RP than other accents, while a broad Australian accent attracted higher guilt ratings in cases of assault. Dixon *et al.* (2002) found a Birmingham (UK) accent attracted higher guilt ratings than RP, in particular where the suspect was also described as black and the crime-type was armed robbery. In an employment interview context, Kalin *et al.* (1980) found significant effects of accent on evaluations of job candidates, for example, with **English English**-speakers judged more suitable for the higher-status job (foreman), and West Indian English-speakers associated more with the low-status job (cleaner). Parton *et al.* (2002), examining the effects of 'powerful' and 'powerless' **speech styles** in job interviews, found that a powerless speech style (with more frequent use of **hedges** and hesitations) resulted in negative attributions of employability and competence. In contrast, the powerful speech style attracted higher evaluations of competence but not of social attractiveness. In the educational context, Seligman *et al.* (1972) showed Canadian teachers combinations of audio recordings, schoolwork and pictures of students, and students' speech style was shown to have important effects on their assessment. Granger *et al.* (1977) showed US teachers differing combinations of pictures and speech samples of school students, and asked them to rate the speech performance of the students. **Ethnicity** and **social class** were found to be the significant variables influencing their assessments, with black speakers rated lower that white speakers overall. Garrett *et al.* (2003), researching judgements of school success among regional English dialect-speakers in Wales, found school students to be much more differentiating than the teachers. Students seemed to see school success partly in terms of an English–Welsh dimension, with the more anglicized Welsh English dialects clustering separately from those regarded as more Welsh and less associated with scholastic success.

Health communication research has included work on the speech features in conversations between patients and doctors. Fielding and Evered (1980), for example, found that patients' accent can affect the way they are diagnosed: a middle-class-accented patient was more likely to be diagnosed in psychiatric terms, compared with the physical terms of the diagnosis for the lower-class accented patient reporting the same symptoms. Gould and Dixon (1997) studied reactions to linguistic adaptations (e.g. careful intonation, simple and repeated sentence structures) used by a health professional to enhance a patient's comprehension and recall. While respondents were found to prefer these sorts of accommodative speech features aimed at increasing memory performance, they tended to react negatively to the doctors producing them, viewing them as patronizing. Hence in terms of doctor–patient relations and their implications for patients' compliance with doctors' instructions, the adaptive speech style was not necessarily as helpful as one might assume. Studies of the effects of evaluative reactions to language and communication in these sorts of applied settings highlight the crucial impacts that attitudes can have on people's life opportunities.

Although the indirectness of using verbal guises can help inhibit (for example) socially desirable responses from masking private attitudes, direct approaches also feature large. Indeed, Giles (1970) used both approaches and found little difference in the results, suggesting that not all contexts share the highly charged sensitivities that Lambert and colleagues felt in Montreal in the 1950s. The 1990s saw interest grow in folklinguistic and **perceptual dialectological** studies of attitudes, generally direct in approach and most notably promoted by Preston (1996, 1999). Various techniques are used. In some, respondents receive blank maps of countries on which to draw in what they perceive as the main dialect regions, and then characterize those regions in their own words. Such folklinguistic comment on varieties and speakers reflects a considerable range of sociocultural background. Preston has found that the notion of language correctness is a major source of comment in the United States on regional varieties of US English, to the point where many regard anything that is not correct as not really language: '*Ain't* ain't a word, is it?' (Preston 1996: 55).

The above gives an impression of the vast amount of illuminating research conducted in this area from the 1970s. Inevitably, it has always attracted essential critical discussion. Reservations are voiced about the authenticity of the accents produced for matched-guise studies, for example, and whether reading a passage aloud on audio-tape constitutes language use that is too decontextualized for studying people's attitudes (see Garrett *et al*. 2003: 57 ff.). And Edwards (1999: 105) has argued for more 'bridging' between social psychology and sociolinguistics in order to find out more about which specific speech features give rise to particular types of evaluative reactions. To exemplify, he points to Charles Boberg's work on how foreign words spelt with <a> are nativized in English. Boberg (1997) concludes that, although British and US English often nativize similarly, the British default tends to be /æ/, whereas /ɑ:/ is becoming increasingly the US default in the belief that it is paradoxically more British and correct (e.g. in 'macho' and 'pasta').

Arguments are also heard for greater use of **qualitative** approaches, for example, involving interviews and **discourse analysis**, rather than relying so much on stimulus tapes and rating scales. Indeed, Potter and Wetherell (1987) take the view that attitudes do not have sufficient demonstrable permanence to be investigated as stable and durable 'psychological states'. They propose a form of discourse analysis where 'attitudes' are sought in speakers' accounts in conversational contexts. Exemplifying through semi-structured interviews with New Zealanders on the topic of Maoris, they paint a picture of a range of evaluative stances emerging in social interaction, showing considerable variability and volatility. Potter and Wetherell present an important argument giving emphasis to how we do social evaluation in face-to-face interaction. But it can be argued that our assumptions and expectations also form part of the context of our social interaction, and these are cognitive in nature, and language attitudes can be comparatively stable stereo-typed responses to community-level phenomena (such as dialects and discourse styles). Coupland and Jaworski (2004) emphasize that, while it is the case that larger-scale survey-based attitude research risks pre-specifying the dimensions of people's value judgements, there is, in the study of evaluations emerging in situated social interaction, a corresponding risk that overgeneralization will occur from interpretations of local occurrences in rather small amounts of data.

To this end, there may be benefits in exploring the compatibility of ethnographic, discourse analytical approaches with surveys across larger populations, and how far these approaches can be combined into individual studies. Garrett *et al.* (2003) report a series of studies into attitudes towards Welsh English dialects. They collected data from teachers and teenagers all over Wales, using a combination of semi-structured interviews and questionnaires which included attitude-rating scales, perceptual dialectological map-filling tasks and short qualitative responses, such as labels and characterizations, and other short, immediate written reactions. They were able to show some generalizable patterns in their **quantitative** data: for example, distinguishing dialect communities in terms of prestige, pleasantness and Welshness. Against this backdrop, the qualitative data captured more depth, reflecting, for example, the respondents' social and cultural positions as teachers and teenagers, and giving insights into the teenagers' inter-group relationships and identity negotiation. RP speakers, for example, were quantitatively rated as prestigious by both teachers and teenagers, but the qualitative data showed that they were strongly outgrouped by the teenagers. For them, RP was 'the voice of success' but certainly 'not our voice'.

Finally, and relatedly, the emerging interest in 'language ideology' (see Chapter 16) in sociolinguistics reflects a contemporary motivation for a more critical examining of our sociocultural evaluations and assumptions, their histories and links with struggles for power. Some of these recent developments in language attitudes research also arguably reflect a move towards further exploring such ideological and critical perspectives in the study of social meanings of language.

FURTHER READING

Garrett, P., Coupland, N. and Williams, A. (2003) *Investigating Language Attitudes: Social Meanings of Dialect, Ethnicity and Performance*, Cardiff: University of Wales Press.

Giles, H. and Coupland, N. (1991) *Language: Contexts and Consequences*, Milton Keynes: Open University Press.

Kristiansen, T., Garrett, P. and Coupland, N. (eds) (2005) *Subjective Processes in Language Variation and Change.* Special issue of *Acta Linguistica Hafniensia* 37.

Lippi-Green, R. (1997) *English with an Accent: Language, Ideology, and Discrimination in the United States*, London and New York: Routledge.

Niedzielski, N. and Preston, D. (1999) *Folk Linguistics*, Berlin: Mouton de Gruyter.

15

POLITENESS AND POWER

SANDRA HARRIS

It is over three decades since Robin Lakoff (1973) wrote her article on the logic of **politeness**, which for many linguists marks the beginning of the now burgeoning field of research into linguistic politeness carried out primarily within the fields of sociolinguistics and **pragmatics**. During those decades linguistic politeness has developed as a significant and challenging field of research, much of which is cross-cultural and involving researchers on a global scale. The work of Brown and Levinson (1978, 1987) on politeness universals, which focuses on the notion of **face** and **face-threatening acts** and is strongly influenced by Goffman, has stimulated a large amount of research, exercised immense influence and is still the canonical model against which much of the literature on linguistic politeness defines itself. Although Brown and Levinson's model, involving concepts of **negative face** and **positive face** and the consequent generation of a series of **negative politeness** and **positive politeness** strategies, has been widely criticized, it is only recently that their basic paradigm has been seriously challenged. An important aspect of that challenge has centred on the relationship between politeness and **power**.

Until relatively recently the majority of work on politeness has been focused on interpersonal and informal contexts, with a resultant emphasis on the volition of individual speakers. Indeed, Brown and Levinson's own work makes little attempt to deal with different discourse types, although it is based on empirical evidence from three widely divergent languages and cultures. In fairness, Brown and Levinson (1987) do include power as a crucial component of their well known formula for computing the weightiness of face-threatening acts, and much of the empirical work generated by their theories addresses the issue of 'power' in some way, particularly in conjunction with the **speech act** of requesting. But again, it was Robin Lakoff (1989) who first argued explicitly well over a decade ago not only that politeness and power are closely related but that the relationship between them could be insightfully clarified if theories of politeness were extended to include professional and institutional contexts, which force us to see politeness from a different perspective, since many of these contexts involve a built-in asymmetry of power and **social status**. A number of studies have attempted to do this (see Linde 1988 on flight crews; Perez de Ayala 2001 and Harris 2001 on political discourse; Aronsson and Rundstrom 1989 and Spiers 1998 on medical discourse; Penman1990 on courtroom discourse, and so on), but few of these address in detail the relationship between politeness and power.

In addition, a considerable number of writers have explored the relationship between power and verbal interaction from various perspectives (see Wartenberg 1990, Ng and Bradac 1993, Diamond 1996 and, particularly, those linguists working within **Critical Discourse Analysis**; see McKenna 2004 for an assessment of recent work). However, it is significant that none of these, including Fairclough (2001) in his edition of *Language and Power* and Thornborrow (2002) in her *Power Talk*, foreground the role of politeness even in the context of data taken from a range of institutional settings, though both Fairclough and Thornborrow analyse perceptively the relationship between power and discursive roles as they are manifest in such settings.

DEFINING THE FIELD

Given the large literature and the huge theoretical baggage which has accumulated around both 'power' and 'politeness', perhaps it is not so surprising that their conjunction has proved problematic. It is well beyond the scope of this chapter to attempt to offer a conclusive definition of either term. Instead, I shall first of all present, very briefly and in summary form, Brown and Levinson's model of politeness and power, followed by a review of how recent work challenges that paradigm in relation to certain important issues being debated in the field.

Brown and Levinson (1987: 76) propose a specific formula for assessing the weightiness (W) of a face-threatening act, which involves three essential components: power (P), social distance (D) and the rating of impositions to the extent that they interfere with an individual's face wants within a particular culture/society (R):

$Wx = D (S, H) + P (H, S) + Rx$

(S = speaker, H = hearer).

Brown and Levinson maintain that, as a consequence, these three 'dimensions' (D, P, R) contribute to the seriousness of a face-threatening act (FTA), and thus to a determination of the level of politeness with which, other things being equal, an FTA will be communicated (Brown and Levinson 1987: 76).

Thus the greater the social distance and the power hierarchy between speaker and hearer the more weight becomes attached to a face-threatening act, particularly one which also involves a relatively high level of imposition (for example, many requests, accusations, some offers, and so on). Brown and Levinson further argue that these dimensions subsume all other relevant factors in any particular context and, importantly, that their formula thus predicts further that individuals will choose a higher level of linguistic mitigation as the weightiness of an FTA increases proportionately.

Brown and Levinson (1987: 77) conceptualize power (P) as 'an asymmetric social dimension of relative power', i.e. 'P (H, S) is the degree to which H [hearer] can impose his [*sic*] own plans and his self-evaluation (face) at the expense of S's [speaker] plans and self-evaluation'. This definition thus views power primarily as an individual attribute, vested in the hearer: it is the hearer's 'power' relative to his/her own which the speaker must take into account when uttering a potentially face-threatening act. The purpose of Brown and Levinson's formula is thus to enable us to predict (both as interactants and researchers) the scale and number of redressive strategies and mitigating linguistic forms a speaker is likely to use in particular interactions by calculating the variability of the social distance and relative power of the participants along with the weightiness of the imposition. Thus one of the important aspects of Brown and Levinson's work is, for them, its predictive power. The formula would seem to apply most obviously to 'requests' (nearly all Brown and Levinson's own examples of its application involve 'requests'), predicting that the greater the power (and distance) between speaker and hearer the more redressive strategies will be used by the less powerful inter-actant, particularly when making a weighty request of a more powerful one. (For specific criticisms of Brown and Levinson's formula see Coupland *et al*. 1988; Spiers 1998; Harris 2003; Mills 2003; Watts 2003.)

REVIEW OF RECENT WORK: SOME CURRENT ISSUES

Politeness research has now become a wide-ranging and multi-disciplinary field of study, and only a relatively small amount of literature can be reviewed in this brief space. Moreover, the issues raised are complex ones which often draw on concepts and understandings in other disciplines. Nevertheless, it is significant that a number of books (mainly in series on sociolinguistics) have been published within the past four or five years which are of particular interest to research on politeness and power, and I shall concentrate primarily on these books: Eelen (2001), Holmes and Stubbe (2003), Watts (2003), Locher (2004) and Mills (2003), with some reference also to recent journal articles. That this number of recently published books can be seen to explore certain common aspects of linguistic politeness suggests its continuing high level of interest as a research field. (A glance at the hundreds of internet entries under 'politeness' also suggests a continuing high level of popular interest and its perceived relevance to everyday life.)

Conceptualizing power

All recent writers on politeness and power seek to conceptualize power not as a static component of particular interactive situations or as an inherent attribute which certain individuals possess but rather as a complex, multi-faceted and dynamic force. Power is 'something people *do* to each other' (Eelen 2001: 224); 'our focus is workplace discourse and we examine how people *do* power and politeness throughout the day in their talk at work' (Holmes and Stubbe 2003: 1). Drawing on Bourdieu's work on **symbolic power**, Eelen goes on to argue that:

> the subordinate pays deference to the superordinate because the superordinate is in a position to *demand* deference from the subordinate. Although power is still

associated with specific socio-structural positions, which convey power to their occupants, it is no longer an objective external force but becomes relative to how it is *used* by those occupants. So instead of determining behaviour, power becomes relative to behaviour – or better: is itself a form of behaviour.

(Eelen 2001: 114)

Watts (2003) also stresses the nature of power as a process, a social practice, in his concept of emergent networks, whereby interactants continually act out and negotiate relationships, including those of power and dominance, through their interactions in particular contexts.

Perhaps the most explicit discussion of the nature of power in interaction is Locher (2004). Locher does not attempt to define power as such but rather offers a 'checklist' for understanding the nature and exercise of power. Her concept of power as relational, dynamic and contestable not only enables us to perceive conflicts and clashes of interests which might be latent but is also 'meant as a tool for the analysis of power using a **qualitative** approach to linguistic data' (Locher 2004: 40). Thus the issue of conceptualizing power in research concerned with linguistic politeness has centred on attempting to find a way to do justice to the theoretical complexity and multi-faceted nature of power as a form of social practice while at the same time providing a version of power which can act as a credible and useful analytical tool and will enable us 'to operationalize the concept and identify the exercise of power in naturalistic linguistic data' (Locher 2004: 321). These versions of power are markedly different from Brown and Levinson's, and are designed, among other things, to be applicable to longer stretches of verbal analysis as well as to make use of and illuminate radically different discourse types.

Conceptualizing politeness as contestable rather than predominantly normative

Politeness has proved as hard to define as power, and, as with power, more recent work has tended to regard politeness as a 'contested concept' rather than as one which is predominantly normative. Making use of Bourdieu's notion of **habitus**, Eelen (2001) argues that politeness is most productively analysed not as a system or a normative set of prescripts but, once again, as a social practice which is both dynamic and interactive, with variability seen as a positive component that builds into human communication a capacity for social and cultural negotiation and change rather than as an inconvenience which must be argued away or concealed by statistics in a **quantitative** analysis. One of the consequences of this way of approaching politeness is to reject Brown and Levinson's notion that certain speech acts (such as requests, orders, offers, accusations, and so on) are inherently face-threatening and, in consequence, the primary motivation of a speaker is to select both strategies and linguistic forms which serve to mitigate the face threat, particularly when the hearer is more powerful than the speaker. Indeed, Watts (2003: 98) argues that:

participants in verbal interaction are polite (or not, as the case may be), that they assess their own behaviour and the behaviour of others as (im)polite, and that (im)politeness does not reside in a language or in the individual structures of a language.

This is a radically different view of politeness from those many studies, including Brown and Levinson's, which seek to link polite linguistic behaviour with particular normative structures and forms within specific languages and cultures.

There are several consequences of taking such a view. First of all, as most recent writers would maintain, the emphasis of most research in past decades has been on linguistic politeness rather than **impoliteness**, which has been studied far less often. Impoliteness can no longer be seen merely as the polar opposite of politeness, and the relationship between them is a much less straightforward one. Brown and Levinson spend relatively little time analysing impoliteness, but it is perhaps implicit in their model that impoliteness mainly constitutes an attack on face. Mills (2003: 122) argues rather that 'impoliteness has to be seen as an assessment of someone's behaviour rather than a quality intrinsic to an utterance'. Thus both politeness and impoliteness most crucially involve judgements and interpretations of hearers which can be argued about and disputed. A form which may be deemed polite in one context (even such forms as are conventionally associated with politeness such as 'please' and 'thank you') may be interpreted differently in another.

Second, a version of politeness as social practice places particular emphasis on the interactive context, and most recent work on politeness and power involves a version of context which applies at a number of different levels of analysis, including the type of speech event, the immediate physical context, the topic being discussed, social and cultural expectations of the participants, **gender**, **age**, education, status and power differences, distance and affect between interactants, personal histories, and so on. Mills (2004) suggests that the notion of **communities of practice** is a particularly useful one, especially in view of the difficulty of defining a culture or a society, if we add 'a wider notion of the social and an awareness of the pressure that institutions can exert on communities and individuals' (Mills 2004: 197).

Negotiation of status and identity

Locher (2004) suggests that in both informal social situations and more formal discourse contexts (her examples of the latter are a university staff meeting, a political radio interview, extracts from a US Supreme Court hearing and a televised presidential debate), the exercise of power and politeness often tends to involve the negotiation of status and, more generally, **identity**. Clearly, the degree of negotiation is constrained, especially in institutional contexts, by interactants' formal positions of power (or powerlessness), but Locher demonstrates that, even in the case of the radio interview which involves the US President, there is a surprising amount of negotiation of both power and identity. Harris (2003) likewise argues that relatively powerful people such as magistrates, doctors and police officers, even in institutional contexts where their power is built into hierarchical structures, are often 'polite' and make extensive use of redressive strategies and mitigating forms, something which Brown and Levinson's model previously quoted would not predict. In the workplace, where once again power hierarchies tend to be structural, Holmes and Stubbe (2003: 163) conclude that 'power and politeness consistently emerge as important dimensions constraining the ways in which participants negotiate and resolve miscommunication and problematic issues at work', particularly where there is a difference in relative status between the interactants. Identity and status are discursively negotiable, though not without constraints and boundaries, even in situations where power is explicitly exercised and 'politeness' is a crucial component of this process of negotiation.

Some methodological implications

There are a number of methodological implications which are raised by recent work on the interface between politeness and power. Perhaps the most significant is the willingness of researchers to draw on other disciplines and the focus on qualitative rather than quantitative methods. Locher (2004: 30) argues conclusively that 'power is thus a concept that needs a qualitative analysis of data in order to become sufficiently identifiable for discussion', though her own work does make use of a relatively limited amount of quantitative data, mainly to support her fine-grained qualitative analyses of lengthy stretches of discourse. All the other writers (Holmes and Stubbe, Mills, Watts, and Eelen) also focus strongly on qualitative analysis, with Eelen (2001: 141) and Mills (2003: 43) in different ways defending this position most explicitly. A further important trend is the emphasis on the collection of natural language data as evidence (and away from the use of questionnaires except as supplementary to the primary data) and on interactive spoken language. Moreover, the extracts used in recent research as evidence are often fairly lengthy ones, and taken from a variety of discourse types and situations even when the focus is on a single context (such as the workplace, as in Holmes and Stubbe). The extracts then provide the data for the detailed analyses and close readings which all these writers engage in. (Although Brown and Levinson also use natural language data as evidence, their extracts tend to be brief, with the emphasis on speaker utterances consisting often of single speech acts.) The importance of analysing such extracts as situated discourse, and the crucial significance of contextual features both in the immediate and wider sense is paramount in recent work. Lastly, all these writers point to the importance of recording interactive discourse which becomes a site of 'dispute' or 'struggle' as being particularly interesting and revealing in enabling us to understand in greater depth how power is exercised and its relation to politeness.

Conclusion

Both Eelen (2001) and Watts (2003) make quite large claims for the shift to a perspective of politeness where the main characteristics of the theory are 'argued to be variability, evaluativity, argumentativity, and discursiveness' (Eelen 2001: 240) and which represents 'a radical departure from the theories of linguistic politeness currently available' (Watts 2003: 262). Certainly, viewing politeness as an area of discursive struggle in social practice is a far cry from the popular non-linguistic view of politeness as good manners or etiquette. Clearly, the high level of interest in politeness and power which both the quantity and, more important, the quality of recent research represent is to be welcomed, along with the challenging nature of much of that research and its proposal of new paradigms.

However, perhaps a tentative note of caution should be voiced as well. Watts (2003) argues that:

> The goal of a theory of linguistic politeness which takes (im)politeness as its starting point should not be to explain *why* speakers say what they say and to predict the possible effects of utterances on addressees. It should aim to explain how all the interactants engaged in an ongoing verbal interaction negotiate the development of emergent networks and evaluate their own position and the positions of others within those networks. (Im)politeness then becomes part of the discursive social practice through which we create, reproduce and change our social worlds.
>
> (Watts 2003: 255)

While it is certainly true that politeness research has been dominated too long by the 'face'-oriented model of Brown and Levinson, the great strength of that model, and probably one of the main reasons for its dominance for such a lengthy period, is its coherence, level of detail and testability, supported by cross-cultural empirical evidence. In fact, the vast amount of criticism directed at Brown and Levinson, particularly from speakers of Asian languages, has proved extremely insightful and productive in creating a large literature on a wide range of issues (negative versus positive politeness, individualism versus collectivism, deference versus volition, universalism versus cultural relativity, and so on) as well as raising some searching questions which new theories have begun to address. In addition, it seems to me that perhaps we shouldn't quite so conclusively write off concepts such as 'predictability' or 'normativity', particularly when everyday popular versions of politeness still take them very seriously. Also, although the emphasis on qualitative methodology in the examination of politeness and power is clearly justified, there is still room, in my view, for quantitative data to make a useful, if supportive, contribution. There is no doubt, however, that, given the limitations of Brown and Levinson's model, research on linguistic politeness did and does need to move in significantly new directions and that the recent work referred to in this chapter represents such a move in exciting and challenging ways. It also seems that a clearer and more comprehensive understanding of the complex relationship between politeness and power will play an essential part in establishing both the degree of applicability and the explanatory power of new theories of linguistic politeness in a more general sense.

FURTHER READING

Brown, P. and Levinson, S. (1987) *Politeness: Some Universals in Language Usage*, Cambridge: Cambridge University Press.

Eelen, G. (2001) *A Critique of Politeness Theories*, Manchester: St Jerome.

Harris, S. (2003) 'Politeness and power: making and responding to "requests" in institutional settings', *Text* 23 (1): 27–52.

Locher, M. (2004) *Power and Politeness in Action: Disagreements in Oral Communication*, Berlin: Mouton de Gruyter.

Part IV
SOCIO-POLITICAL FACTORS

16

THE IDEOLOGY OF THE STANDARD LANGUAGE

JAMES MILROY

INTRODUCTION: THE PRINCIPLE OF UNIFORMITY

Many widely used languages, such as English, French and Spanish, are regarded as each possessing a **standard** variety, and this affects the manner in which speakers think about their own language and about language in general. We may say that speakers of such widely used languages, unlike speakers of some less well known languages, live in **standard language cultures**. In such cultures, **language attitudes** are dominated by powerful ideological positions that are largely based on the supposed existence of this standard form, and these, taken together, can be said to constitute the **standard language ideology** or 'ideology of the standard language'. Speakers are not usually conscious that they are conditioned by these ideological positions: they usually believe their attitudes to language to be common sense and assume that virtually everyone agrees with them. We shall discuss this further below: first, we need an outline of the process that is involved in the **standardization** of a language.

Standardization applies to many things besides language: it applies to weights and measures, for example, and to many kinds of object, such as electrical plugs and fittings and factory-made objects generally. In these instances it is desirable for functional reasons that the exact value of each measure should be agreed among users, and that each relevant object should be exactly the same as all the others of its kind. Thus, as a process, standardization consists of the imposition of uniformity upon a class of objects, and so the most important structural property of a standard variety of a language is uniformity or invariance. This means – ideally – that every sound should be pronounced in the same way by every speaker, and that all speakers should use the same grammatical forms and vocabulary items in exactly the same way. (It also implies that the language should not undergo change.) In principle, therefore, when there are two or more variants of some linguistic form, only one of them is admitted into a standard variety. For example, although the expressions *you were* and *you was* are both used in English, only one of them is considered to be the standard form. To fulfil the requirements of standardization alone it would not matter which of these **variants** were the one accepted: standardization merely requires that one, *and only one*, of them should be accepted. In practice, however, the choice of one over the other is affected by factors outside the standardization process itself, and these factors, taken together, are what constitute the standard ideology.

The ideal of absolute uniformity is never achieved in practice. Although language standardization discourages variability, no language is ever completely invariant. In written language, uniform practice is quite close to being achieved – particularly in printed usage – but spoken language is less amenable to standardization. The pronunciation of English, for example, varies tremendously in the geographical and social dimensions, and it can change quite rapidly. A standard language, therefore, is an idealization – an idea in the mind rather than a fully achieved reality, and the varieties that we call **Standard English**, Standard French, etc., are not in fact completely invariant or totally immune to change.

The ideal of the standard always requires active maintenance, and to the extent that various factors (such as the educational system) contribute to maintenance, the presence of a standard variety may slow down the process of **language change**. The availability of a standard variety is in fact highly functional in human affairs, just as standardized weights and measures are so obviously functional. Standard varieties are comprehensible much more widely than localized **dialects** are. Furthermore, **elaboration** of function is one of the characteristics of a standard language: it can be used in a wide variety of different spheres of activity. Indeed, elaboration of function can be seen as one of the driving forces that encourage standardization. As the language becomes used in a greater and greater variety of functions, it becomes more and more important that a near-uniform variety should be available to fulfil all these functions. Just as the proliferation of varying coinages or weights and measures is dysfunctional, so a proliferation of different forms of the language would be highly undesirable in a society that requires widespread communications.

In history, the progressive standardization of weights and measures went hand in hand with the rise of capitalism and expansion of large-scale commercial activity, and something similar seems to have happened in language standardization. Medieval (pre-standard) varieties of language were highly divergent and variable. Although linguistic uniformity is particularly desirable in the case of legal, commercial and official written documents (as these require clarity and lack of ambiguity), the progress of standardization over the centuries has been broadly parallel to economic and technological progress. One of the consequences of this long-term drive towards uniformity in language use has been the spread of the standard ideology among speakers. We now turn to this, with attention to a number of interrelated and overlapping characteristics – the notion of **correctness**, the importance of **authority**, the relevance of **prestige**, and the idea of legitimacy.

CORRECTNESS AND AUTHORITY

An important consequence of language standardization has been the development of consciousness among speakers of a 'correct', or canonical, form of language. In standard-language cultures, virtually everyone subscribes to the idea of correctness. Some forms are believed to be right and others wrong, and this is generally taken for granted as common sense. Although rules of correctness are actually superimposed upon the language from outside, they are considered by speakers to be rules inherent in the language itself. In this view, the utterance *I seen it*, for example, is *obviously* wrong, and *I saw it* is – equally obviously – correct. For the vast majority in a standard language culture, including very highly intelligent and educated people, this is just how it is: correctness rules are thought to be rules of language (not of society), and no justification is needed for rejecting *I seen it*. Sometimes a justification *is* given, e.g. that *seen* is the participle, not the past tense, but when this happens it is a rationalization after the fact. There is no rule inherent in language that restricts *seen* to the past participle and forbids it as a past tense form: the 'correctness' of *I saw it* depends solely on the fact that it has become the standard form of the past tense. In purely linguistic terms, the choice of one usage over another is entirely arbitrary. That is to say that if the standard variety had preferred *seen*, *I seen it* would be considered correct.

This arbitrariness is clearest in rules of spelling. Spelling is the most successfully standardized level of language, and variation in spelling is not normally tolerated. The spelling *sope*, for example, is considered wrong and the spelling *soap* right. Yet there is no reason why it should not be the other way round (in the eighteenth century, Dr Samuel Johnson's dictionary accepted both spellings: similarly, *choak* and *choke*). In a standard language culture, however, the choice is not arbitrary: it is believed to be a *linguistic* fact that one is right and the other wrong. Everybody is supposed to know this – it is part of general knowledge to know it, and in a standard language culture it is your own fault if you cannot spell or if you speak incorrectly. It is believed to be open to everyone to learn what the correct forms are; therefore, it is thought to be quite proper to discriminate – in employment, for example – against people who use **non-standard** forms. Although it is now unacceptable to discriminate openly against someone for reasons of **ethnic** group, **social class**, religion or **gender**, it is still acceptable to discriminate openly on linguistic grounds. Unfortunately, people do not usually realize that language stands proxy for these other social categories. As a person who uses non-standard linguistic forms will often be from a minority ethnic group or a lower social class, the effect of language discrimination is to discriminate against ethnic minorities and lower social class groups.

The belief in correctness is an extremely important factor in what we have called the maintenance of a standard language, or, more precisely, maintenance of the consciousness of a standard, and this belief leads to a popular view that is directly contrary to what most linguistic theorists teach. Theorists generally teach that language is the possession of every native speaker – that it is primarily an internal development within the speaker's mind, and that it is therefore essentially a cognitive phenomenon. In a standard language culture, however, a language is – by implication – the possession of only a few persons (usually not clearly specified) who have the authority to impose the rules of language on everyone else. This ideological position is already clear in the work of the writer Jonathan Swift (1712), who believed that a group of persons should be appointed to 'fix' the English language as a permanent uniform structure: 'what I have most at heart', he wrote 'is, that some Method should be thought on for *ascertaining* and *fixing* our language for ever [. . .] For I am of Opinion, that it is better a language should not be wholly perfect, than that it should be perpetually changing.' Underlying Swift's assumptions is the view that language is a cultural phenomenon – embedded in social affairs rather than an outgrowth of an individual's cognitive faculties – and this is in fact the popular view in any standard-language culture. Language is from this point of view analogous to cultural products such as art, law and religion, and it is felt to have an overarching presence outside the speaker and his/her immediate surroundings. For all these reasons, it makes perfect sense in such a culture to pass judgement on good and bad, right and wrong, beautiful and ugly in language.

The educational system becomes a crucial factor in spreading the knowledge of the standard language. Indeed, people find it reasonable to say that children go to school to 'learn English', when in fact in pre-school years they have already acquired the basis of spoken English grammar and phonology naturally and without explicit instruction. At school the child learns in particular to read and write, and **literacy** is acquired in the standard language. Thus, children are believed to be taught their native language at school through the agency of authorities who have privileged access to its mysteries, and of course it is knowledge of the standard written form that children acquire. It is characteristic of the standard ideology for people to believe that this uniform standard variety with all its superimposed rules of correctness is actually the language itself.

The maintenance of a standard language clearly depends on obedience to authority. For this purpose it is desirable that the standard language should be **codified**. Standard English, unlike most other varieties of English, has been codi-fied over the centuries in the form of dictionaries, grammar books, pronunciation guides and manuals of usage, and these are routinely consulted as authorities on correctness. Although many of the handbooks on usage can be useful, particularly for writers of English, some of them (often glorying in titles such as *Improve your English!*) are ill informed, and their authors may even boast that they are scientists or engineers who are not qualified as linguistic experts. Frequently, they advocate usages that are out of date and condemn usages that are normal spoken English, such as 'It's me' and 'Who do you think you're talking to?' In some coun-tries, overarching authority is enshrined in a national academy, such as the Académie française, which may have some legislative power (see Chapter 20). Such authorities commonly make pronouncements as to what is acceptable in the language concerned, but their most prominent activity is to condemn new usages that have entered the language, particularly words that are **borrowed** from another language. Thus, they are concerned not only with maintaining uniformity, but also with keeping the language 'pure'.

PRESTIGE

It was noted above that in selecting one usage out of two or more alternatives, the standardization process is indifferent as to which form is selected, and that in practice other factors are involved in the process of selection. One of these is authority; another is **prestige**, to which we now turn. Most people will consider that one of the following sentences is in some sense 'better' than the other:

(1) He was a man what didn't believe nothing.
(2) He was a man who didn't believe anything.

It may be said that (2) has higher prestige than (1). It may further be claimed that the (standard) 'dialect' of (2) has higher prestige than the (non-standard) dialect of (1). It should be noted, however, that prestige is not primarily a property of a linguistic form or variety – it is a property of speakers, or groups of speakers, some of whom are accorded higher social prestige than others, and this is very clearly related to varying social class or social status. Thus, prestige is conferred on language varieties by speakers, and speakers tend to confer prestige on usages that are considered to be those of the higher social classes. At this point we also become involved with authority: some social groups have more authority than others. What is clear is that the selection process is highly sensitive to social and socio-political factors.

The converse of prestige is **stigma**. Linguistic forms that are favoured by the lower social classes tend to be stigmatized in the wider community, and these are typically the forms that are rejected in the educational system. Indeed, sometimes urban dialects are so heavily stigmatized that it is even claimed that their speakers do not know 'their own language'. The following comments by a school inspector in 1925 are an extreme example of the effects and workings of the standard ideology:

> Come into a London elementary school and . . . [y]ou will notice that the boys and girls are almost inarticulate. They can make noises, but they cannot speak . . . listen to them as they 'play at schools'; you can barely recognise your native language.

Prestige, is, however, a slippery concept, as individuals may differ in assigning prestige to particular groups and hence to particular uses of language. In particular, it is not necessarily true that the dialect of the very highest social group is the main contributor to a standard variety. On the contrary, sociolinguistic inquiries suggest strongly that the dialects of small elite groups are generally recessive. In Britain, for example, the speech of the heir to the throne seems to be rather old-fashioned, and younger members of the royal family are more in tune with current middle-class speech. In the United States, the upper classes of Boston and New York had no effect whatever on what became the American 'Network Standard' pronunciation. What becomes the standard appears to be determined largely by those who depend for their livelihood on communicating widely in society; for example, business people, lawyers, journalists. The relative prestige of certain such groups may play a part in determining what becomes standard, and some of these people may possibly model their speech on a social group that they perceive to be above them, but a standard language is not the direct product of the language of the highest social groups, such as the very rich or the aristocracy.

LEGITIMACY

The establishment of the idea of a standard variety, the diffusion of knowledge of this variety, its codification in widely used grammar books and dictionaries, and its promotion in a wide range of functions – all lead to the devaluing of other varieties. The standard form becomes the legitimate form, and other forms become, in the popular mind, illegitimate. They are commonly referred to as non-standard or even sub-standard. Historical linguists have been prominent in establishing this legitimacy, because it is important that a standard language, being the language of a nation state, and sometimes a great empire, should share in the (glorious) history of that nation state. Indeed, the language is commonly seen as part of the identity of the nation state. In the 1920s the influential language historian H.C. Wyld regarded the standard variety as the most important 'dialect' and based his history of English on it. He claimed that other dialects were irrelevant except in so far as they had contributed to the history of the standard. To that extent, these dialects had a degree of legitimacy: Victorian dialectologists had demonstrated that these rural forms might be useful in reconstructing early stages of English. These dialects, therefore, had *histories*. With urban vernaculars, however, it was quite otherwise.

Urban forms of English, although probably used by a majority of the population at that time, were not considered to be 'dialects' at all: they were seen by Wyld (doubtless in agreement with general opinion) as vulgar and ignorant attempts to adopt or imitate the standard. Thus, they were thought to have no independent histories and were therefore illegitimate offspring. Since then, written histories of English from around 1500 have until quite recently usually been designed as histories of the internal structure of only one variety – standard English. This is seen as also including the language of literature, as the work of great authors also helps to confer legitimacy (and prestige) on the language. (If we can say that English is 'the language of Shakespeare', we are conferring additional honour upon it.) Histories of English are largely *codifications* of the history of the standard language, and these codifications are themselves part of the process of the legitimization of the standard language in its function as the language of the nation state and its colonies and ex-colonies. The historicization of the language requires that it should possess a continuous unbroken history, a respectable and legitimate ancestry and a long pedigree, and historical linguists have certainly conferred these things on English – but chiefly, as we have seen, on its standard variety.

We can conclude by noting that all standard languages have to be given some form of legitimacy, and all have to be maintained and protected through authority and doctrines of correctness. There is usually also a tradition of popular complaint about language, bewailing the low quality of general usage and claiming that the language is degenerating. This too contributes to keeping the standard ideology prominent in the public mind. In standard language cultures, the alternative to all this is too terrible to contemplate: it is believed that if these efforts at maintenance are neglected, the language will be subject to corruption and decay, and will ultimately disintegrate. The future of the language, it is claimed, cannot be left to the millions of fluent native speakers who use it every day: if it is not taken care of by privileged authorities, it will inevitably decline.

FURTHER READING

Bex, T. and Watts, R. (eds) (1999) *Standard English: The Widening Debate*, London: Routledge.

Cameron, D. (1995) *Verbal Hygiene*, London: Routledge.

Foley, W.A. (1997) *Anthropological Linguistics*, Oxford: Blackwell.

Milroy, J. and Milroy, L. (1997b) *Authority in Language: Investigating Standard English* (third edition), London: Routledge.

17

THE INFLUENCE OF THE MEDIA

JANE STUART-SMITH

Sociolinguistics appears to be at an impasse. Whilst experts ignore or dismiss television as a set of social factors, speakers across the globe equip themselves with ever more possibilities for watching more and more television; they also believe, unlike most linguists, that watching television affects the way they speak. The advent of television represents one of the most significant social phenomena of the twentieth century, and yet, oddly, whether television might influence language – or not – is a neglected area of sociolinguistic research.

This chapter will concentrate on a specific and controversial topic for sociolinguistics, namely the potential impact of television on what are seen as core systems of language, pronunciation and grammar. The following sections will briefly outline current views on television and language, consider possible insights from media effects research and conclude by reviewing results from the handful of studies which exist to date, including some new results from a recent project specifically investigating the relationship between television and **accent** change.

MEDIA AND MYTH IN LANGUAGE CHANGE

The 'traditional' sociolinguists' response to the potential impact of the television on language is found clearly formulated in the work of the distinguished socio-linguist Peter Trudgill. Trudgill (1986, 1988) argues that a key process of **language change** is **diffusion**, or the spreading of linguistic innovations across geographical regions. Diffusion is assumed to take place through linguistic **accommodation**, whereby speakers may alter their speech in response to those with whom they are talking. Thus diffusion is the transmission of linguistic features as a result of socio-psychological processes that take place during face-to-face interaction between speakers. Television fits awkwardly with such a model: whilst we watch television, and may even talk to it, it is argued that we cannot interact with characters on television in such a way that accommodation is likely to take place, and so television may not be directly involved in processes of diffusion. Trudgill admits that television may act as a source for new **lexis** and **idioms**, or as a model for speakers of a **dialect** to acquire the core **phonology** and **syntax** of the **standard variety** of a language (or indeed across languages), but here such changes require conscious motivation by speakers to orientate towards, and imitate, such a model.

Nevertheless, it is still possible to find linguistic changes taking place which are difficult to explain by diffusion. Trudgill himself deals with exactly this when discussing the appearance of [f] for /th/ in e.g. *think* (and also [v] for /dh/ in e.g.

brother), so-called TH-**fronting**, a feature usually associated with London accents, in relatively non-mobile working-class speakers in Norwich. He suggests that the change is the result of a combination of factors working together, including less overt opportunities for contact between Norwich speakers and those from London, but he also speculates about the potential role of television programmes based in London in promoting positive attitudes towards London dialect features: 'television may be part of a "softening-up" process leading to the adoption of the merger [of /f/ with /th/], but it does not cause it' (Trudgill 1986: 55).

According to the traditional view, then, television may be able to influence systemic language change, but indirectly through changes in attitudes towards linguistic varieties. It has also been claimed (Milroy and Milroy 1985), drawing on the results from sociological research into the diffusion of innovations more generally (Rogers 1995), that while television may increase speakers' awareness of innovations, it is less likely to promote their adoption. This could then explain how dialect speakers of **English English**, for example, have gained greater awareness of standard varieties of English through television broadcasting, but without actually adopting features of the standard.

However, the persistence of the problematic spread of TH-fronting across urban accents of English English, and particularly its continued emergence in less mobile youngsters, has led to suggestions for a more important role for television. Williams and Kerswill (1999) wonder about the potential impact of youth-oriented broadcast media increasing the exposure of this, and other features, as a set of 'youth norms' (after Foulkes and Docherty 2000). Foulkes and Docherty (2002) speculate that passive exposure to varieties, assuming a degree of linguistic similarity in patterning of pre-existing features, may perhaps act as a 'catalyst, enabling speakers to redeploy resources already available to them'. And Kerswill (2002: 680–1) considers the usefulness of Peter Auer's (1998) 'identity projection model'. This allows speakers to shift their speech not only towards conversational partners who are physically present, but also towards linguistic stereotypes of socially attractive speakers which exist in the mind of the speaker (see also Bell's 1992 outgroup referee design), and information about which may be drawn from sources such as television (Carvalho 2004: 141–2).

At the same time, it would be misleading to suggest that all linguists have been so sceptical about the potential impact of television on language. Interestingly, German sociolinguists have been, and continue to be, far more outspoken. For example, Brandt (1984: 1672) writes that it is simply without argument (*unumstritten*) that the broadcast media affect their audience – including their language; rather what is difficult is to quantify and qualify the influence exerted. Muhr (2003) makes strong claims for exposure to **German German** television as a key factor in current lexical, and grammatical, changes underway in Austrian German. Exposure is even explicitly cited as an agent in language change by Lameli (2003), whose **variationist** study into post-war **standardization** of German dialects argues for the importance of the introduction of radio broadcasting in German households. If we assume, as Androustopoulos (2001: 4), that media language forms 'part of the global sociolinguistic condition of a speech community', we might expect this to be reflected in contemporary speech patterns. Working with similar assumptions, German scholars, and in particular Werner Holly and his colleagues, are leading research into 'communicative appropriation' (*kommunikativer Aneigung*), or the ways that speakers may incorporate linguistic features from models offered by television programmes into their own discourse (Holly 2001). Work of this kind largely considers chunks of speech lifted intact from media discourse, and so might perhaps be thought to fall outside the scope of the specific problem of media influence on core language systems. However, speakers do also seem to be able to lift specific features, including pronunciation, and manipulate these creatively and productively (Androustopoulos 2001; Branner 2002).

To sum up, the possible influence of television has become another 'language myth' (see Chambers 1998). Leaving aside more recent German scholarship, the majority of linguists seem to view any possible influence of television as very weak, possibly providing information about linguistic variation, presenting alternative linguistic models, and affecting attitudes to existing varieties. The consensus seems to be that since we cannot interact with television characters in the same way as with our friends, neighbours and workmates, represented television dialects are unlikely to affect our own speech. At the same time, and perhaps surprisingly for an area of linguistics which is grounded in empirical research, evidence is rarely discussed. Indeed, there is a question as what may count as evidence in such a debate. Even sociolinguistic opinions of the impact of media on language tend to rely on personal, anecdotal and/or circumstantial evidence. For example, linguists working on American English dialects point to the continued diversity of American dialects as clear evidence that television is not promoting linguistic change (that is, any kind of standardization); see Chambers (2004). While the same generalization can equally – and correctly – be applied to **British English** dialects, it cannot be used to argue that television may not ever influence language. The difficulty is that systematic evidence is lacking.

LOOKING OVER THE WALL: INSIGHTS FROM MEDIA EFFECTS RESEARCH

The problem for sociolinguists is simply that so many people watch television, that the numerous and complex bundles of factors that television now represents can no longer be ignored. However, we should not only be challenged into action by the sheer prevalence and social importance of television in the everyday lives of ordinary people. We have at our disposal a wealth of methods and results from research into the general sociological effects of the media, carried out under the many guises of mass communication theory. It appears that the media, including television, are assumed to affect social behaviour (McQuail 2005: 424 f.), though caution is advised.

Relatively early in media effects research it was recognized that 'mass communication ordinarily does not serve as a necessary and sufficient cause of audience effects, but rather functions among and through a nexus of mediating factors and influences' (Klapper 1960: 8). In other words, television may only be expected to act as a contributory factor, working with other factors. Furthermore, the role of viewers as active interpreters of media texts, who decode and negotiate meanings, is increasingly emphasized (see Buckingham 1987), though this does not necessarily mean that the audience can always resist (Philo 1999). Media effects research has also, and for some time, highlighted the possibility of vicarious relationships between viewers and media characters, 'para-social interaction' (McQuail 2005: 406). We also learn from another area of communications research, into the diffusion of innovations, which models the flow of innovations through social systems, that whilst media channels are generally important at the information stage for most people, a few individuals (early adopters) respond more readily to media channels (Rogers 1995: 197).

If we translate these insights into terms appropriate for sociolinguistics, we could speculate as follows: television may be a contributory factor in language change, but, if so, probably only for certain (or a few?) individuals, under specific circumstances, possibly those who show evidence of para-social interaction with the television. But we emphasize that without satisfactory evidence such a set of assumptions must be treated as entirely speculative.

AT THE FRONTIERS: RESEARCHING THE INFLUENCE OF TELEVISION ON LANGUAGE

Only a very few **quantitative** sociolinguistic studies have included factors to do with television as extralinguistic **variables** to be correlated with linguistic features. The results have been contradictory.

Whilst examining syntactic changes towards the standard in Brazilian Portuguese, Naro (1981) found a link between a variable which captures following *novelas* (soap operas representing middle-class life and values) and higher use of the standard construction. Naro's interpretation of these data is interesting, since from the outset he redefines the television variable into one which represents 'the speaker's degree of penetration into the culture of the surrounding higher socio-economic levels' (Naro 1981: 86), effectively sidestepping the issue of direct causality. In a later study on the same variety which shows further significant correlations but with a more complex media variable, Naro and Scherre (1996) again refuse a causal interpretation. By contrast, Saladino (1990) found no statistical evidence to support the assumption that watching standard Italian on television was leading to standardization in the phonology of a south Italian dialect. Carvalho (2004) also failed to find significant correlations between exposure to television (showing Brazilian Portuguese) and the Brazilian Portuguese feature of **palatalization** which she observed to be spreading among her Uruguayan Portuguese informants. However, her interviews with these speakers demonstrate that for some individuals television plays an important – and overt – role in this change, since not only do they admire the Brazilian Portuguese shown on the television, but they also state explicitly that they want to emulate and imitate televised language.

These studies share a sociolinguistic characteristic in that, in each case, change is taking place from a potentially less socially desirable dialect towards one which is recognized to be more attractive. Whilst Naro's results do not reveal whether the changes accord with speakers wanting to shift towards the speech of the *novelas*, Carvalho's findings show clear evidence of conscious orientation towards televised models. But note that this kind of voluntary shifting via imitation is precisely what Trudgill anticipates as the exceptional circumstances which would allow television to influence core linguistic systems.

A study carried out in Glasgow allows us to return to the original problem. Here we have another instance of non-mobile working-class adolescents showing increasing use of apparently southern English English features such as TH-fronting (Stuart-Smith 1999). The media themselves were swift to blame watching television, and in particular dramas set in London, such as the exceptionally popular soap, *EastEnders*. But evidence, for or against, the influence of television in these changes did not exist.

The findings motivated a three-year project enquiring into the potential influence of television on accent variation and change, which combined methods from sociolinguistics and media effects (Gunter 2000) to allow us to work with thirty-six working-class adolescents from Glasgow over two years. Early results from the television/language experiment indicate some differences in linguistic patterning according to the dialect of the televised stimulus, with more response to the London programmes for certain speakers. Preliminary results from a large-scale multi-factorial model using multiple regression confirm that television variables which capture engagement with *EastEnders* show significant correlations with the linguistic variables analysed to date, namely (th) and (dh).

It is important to resist the temptation to over-interpret these findings at this stage. First, the correlation results simply indicate that there are links between television variables and linguistic variables; causality may operate in either direction. They allow us to acknowledge that such variables have a place in our statistical – and descriptive – model, but not necessarily our explanatory one. **Longitudinal** correlations are necessary to establish causality, and these may be difficult to achieve. Second, further detailed analysis of the particular components of the study, and how they interrelate, is necessary. For us to move towards an interpretation of a causal relationship, we would presumably want to find consistency across a range of linguistic variables, across the various parts of the study, and within individuals participating in the study. Note that our approach is thoroughly sceptical, and always attempts to maintain an appreciation of the complexity of the issues and data involved.

We also investigated two other claims about television and language made by sociolinguists, and we present brief results here.

Could watching television be responsible for a 'softening up' process in these changes?

We interpreted Trudgill's speculation in terms of the potential relationship between watching television and attitudes elicited towards tape-recorded excerpts of the same passage read by similarly aged female speakers of different British urban accents, including working-class London. In a later part of the questionnaire we elicited attitudes towards London as a mental concept. Attitudes towards London accents, both real and conceptual, were varied, but on average tended to be less positive than towards other urban accents (see Figure 17.1).

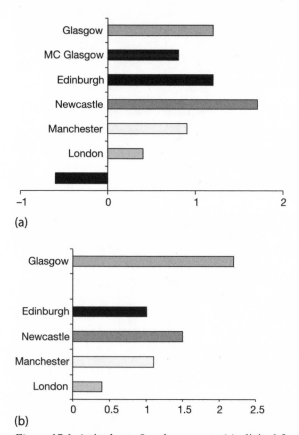

Figure 17.1 Attitudes to London accents (a) elicited from listening to a recording and (b) in response to the question 'What do you think of the accent of London?' Average scores are shown for thirty-six working-class Glaswegian informants

Using linear regression we tested three different dependent variables:

1 Attitude towards the London recording.
2 Mental image of a London accent.
3 Feelings towards London as a place.

with the following independent variables:

1 Correct identification of the London recording.
2 Having relatives in the south of England.
3 Naming *EastEnders* as favourite television programme.
4 Watching *EastEnders*.
5 Visiting London.

The only **dependent variable** to yield results was the attitudinal response towards
the London recording (see Table 17.1). The only significant result was a negative
link with watching *EastEnders*. Most of the children watch *EastEnders*, but
the majority did not like listening to the London speaker. Subsequent testing
with variables which captured degrees of engagement with *EastEnders*, as opposed
to just exposure, did not change the result. For these speakers at least, we do not
have evidence that watching – or engaging – with *EastEnders* promotes positive
attitudes towards a London accent.

Table 17.1 Results of linear regression for the dependent variable (attitude towards
London recording)

	Unstandardized coefficients		Standardized coefficients		
	B	Std error	Beta	t	Sig.
(Constant)	2.61	0.91		2.85	0.01
Place identification (London)	0.01	0.15	0.01	0.05	0.96
Relatives in south England	0.89	0.54	0.26	1.66	0.11
Favourite TV programme is *EastEnders*	–0.08	0.56	–0.02	–0.15	0.88
How often do you watch *EastEnders*?	–1.04	0.33	–0.54	–3.21	0.00
How often have you been to London?	0.12	0.26	0.07	0.45	0.65

Note: $n = 35$; $r^2 = 0.201$; $F = 2.756$; $p = 0.037$

Does watching television promote awareness of linguistic innovations?

We were interested here in assessing whether watching television programmes set
in London resulted in an awareness of London accent features, and in particular
of those features which are being incorporated into Glaswegian. We investigated
this claim through an informal imitation task carried out with the boys in the study

(see Preston 1992). Each boy was first asked to name objects/ideas from a set of pictures in his own accent. He was then shown a picture of a leading actor from *EastEnders*, and asked to name the objects again in the accent of the character, and to discuss the accent.

All the boys thought that the character's accent was different from their own, and most identified it as English, with some thinking that it was posh, and one thinking it was 'more tough'. Most linguistic comments referred to **pitch** (deeper voice) and voice quality, for example: 'It's like a sore throat accent . . . or . . . they took his tonsils out or something,' which is quite appropriate for this particular character. Very little was said about segments, though one boy said, 'He changes the letters, if it was "f " he'd use "v",' which indicates some awareness, but some confusion too.

Our initial impression was that the boys had changed little in their imitations, but close auditory analysis revealed that most had made at least slight alterations in response to the task, though not necessarily in the direction of our expected London target, and we therefore renamed their performance 'phonetic alteration' (Figure 17.2). **Suprasegmental** differences included lowering pitch, lengthening syllables and using whispery, sometimes harsh, ventricular voice. Segmental changes were variable. Few English English vowel qualities were attempted. Consonants were as likely to be realized with their standard pronunciation, so [th] for /th/, as non-standard [f] or Scottish [h], with a high degree of variability within and across speakers.

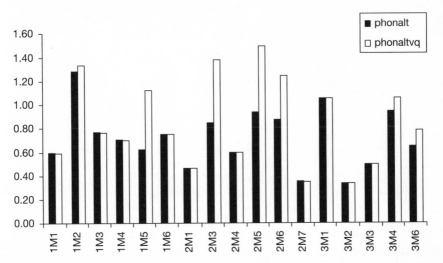

Figure 17.2 Indices of phonetic alteration in response to the informal imitation task, derived from narrow auditory transcription. Dark bars indicate the total number of observed differences between own accent elicitation and character accent imitation, normalized according to the number of pairs elicited per speaker. Light bars show the same but include scores for alteration in voice quality

The results of this task showed that our informants were certainly aware that this character's accent was different from their own. Moreover some imitations were remarkably faithful to features of voice quality exhibited by this particular character. But we did not find any evidence for awareness of the specific segmental features of London English that we expected.

CONCLUSION

Sociolinguists are unlikely ever to receive a definitive answer as to whether television does – or does not – affect core systems of language. Projects like the Glasgow project mentioned briefly here help us to move slightly closer to a better appreciation of the direction and complexity of these relationships. But what emerges is the social significance of television and television programmes for individuals. And as long as this persists, the potential impact of television will continue to be a controversial and challenging issue for sociolinguists.

FURTHER READING

Carvalho, A.M. (2004) 'I speak like the guys on TV: palatalization and the urbanization of Uruguayan Portuguese', *Language Variation and Change* 16: 127–51.

Chambers, J. (1998) 'TV makes people sound the same', in L. Bauer and P. Trudgill (eds), *Language Myths*, New York: Penguin, pp. 123–31.

Muhr, R. (2003) 'Language change via satellite: the influence of German television broadcasting on Austrian German', *Journal of Historical Pragmatics* 4: 103–27.

Trudgill, P. (1986) *Dialects in Contact*, Oxford: Blackwell.

18

MULTILINGUALISM

SUSAN GAL

Multilingualism is the use of more than one language by a single individual or community. In the popular imagination and in linguistic theory, multilingualism is often assumed to be an anomalous, exceptional practice. The knowledge and use of a single language – **monolingualism** – has been taken as the natural human condition. Yet, both historically and currently, most of the world's communities and a majority of speakers are multilingual to a greater or lesser extent. The privileging of monolingualism as against multilingualism is due to the dominance of the European nation state, which has been legitimated by a monolingualist language ideology. This ideology – now taken for granted throughout the world – presumes that each ethnic group has a language of its own and by virtue of this difference deserves political autonomy. It imagines such exclusive groups, each with its own language and culture, to be distributed over the landscape in separate territories like pieces in a jigsaw puzzle. Linguistic knowledge, in this view, is an emblem of political belonging and thus multilingualism implies political unreliability or mixed loyalty. The biblical story of Babel suggests a much older distrust of multilingualism in the Western tradition. A single, universal language was seen as the gift of paradise, while **linguistic diversity** and hence the need for multilingualism were presented as divine punishment for human arrogance.

In the contemporary world, however, increasing flows of migrants, tighter economic ties across the globe and the formation of multinational units such as the European Union undermine the nation state and its legitimating ideologies. As a result, and despite the legacy of the Babel story, there is increasing recognition of the high incidence and practical advantages of multilingualism. This recognition extends to the significance of multilingualism historically, before the rise of nation states and in the centuries since. Linguists and linguistic anthropologists have gathered an impressive amount of evidence from all over the world documenting the diverse cultural principles (ideologies) concerning language in general and especially the many forms of multilingualism in individuals and communities. This evidence constitutes a challenge to linguistic approaches that start from an assumption of monolingualism. The result has been a profound shift in linguistic and sociolinguistic theory, indeed a reconsideration of what we call 'language' and the ways to study it. A brief **ethnographic** survey of some classic cases of multilingualism will demonstrate that the nation-state ideology is only one among many possible conceptualizations of language. It is not general enough to form the basis of linguistic theory. I then discuss the theoretical innovations in the study of language that have resulted from the close examination of multilingualism.

A TOUR OF MULTILINGUAL PRACTICES: BEYOND EUROCENTRISM

Native South America is a good place to start for studying the relations between language, territory and culture/ethnicity. In the Vaupés area of the north-west Amazon, between Colombia and Brazil, the indigenous population live in long-houses that shelter four to eight nuclear families and are located several hours' distance from each other over rough rainforest terrain. According to anthropologist Jean Jackson (1974), in the 1970s the native population of 10,000 was divided into over twenty mutually exclusive groups, each with a distinct name and a distinct language that was not mutually intelligible with the others (such as Tukanoan, Arawak and some from the Carib family). Every native person belongs to one such group from birth. Most important, every person *must* marry outside his/her language group. Whatever their language group, all Vaupés Indians share the same cultural practices and live within a single territory. Women go to live in the long-house of their husband, so longhouses include speakers of as many as four different languages, often more. Most communication occurs not within a linguistic group but across groups, and is enabled by the fact that all Vaupés Indians speak at least three languages fluently, many speak four or five, and some understand as many as ten. Any two residents of a longhouse may well have quite different arrays of languages in their **linguistic repertoire**. No language is considered superior or ranked higher than any other. Choice of language for an interaction depends on many situational factors, including the 'father language' of the longhouse in which the interaction takes place, the purpose of the interaction and the languages known by the interactants. This case illustrates a general principle: that social groups are each identified with a single language need not be a sign of hostility, social cleavage or even cultural difference between the groups. Far from being a cause of strife, in the context of Vaupés language ideology, multilingualism creates **solidarity** among speakers of different languages by bringing them together in the intimate relation of marriage. It is a way of organizing the whole society.

A similar role is played by multilingualism at our next stop, Aboriginal Australia, but assumptions about the relation between language and territory are different. It is not uncommon for one person to speak four or five languages in north Queensland, even in areas where languages differ greatly in vocabulary and grammar. Routine multilingualism has long been bolstered by the practice of obtaining spouses from faraway places. Unlike in the Vaupés, however, languages in native Australia are culturally associated with tracts of land, often discontinuous territories. As anthropologists Alan Rumsey (1993) and John Haviland (1996) report, native Australians think of languages as having been directly placed in the landscape by the founding acts of Dreamtime heroes. The link between a person and a language is only a secondary effect of the connection of both person and language to the same landscape. Language, like the land itself, is something one normally inherits from one's father. The language that people inherit in this way and therefore 'own' is often one they cannot speak. Nor need one live on the territory associated with one's language. Those who share one language are unlikely to have the same overall linguistic repertoire. Nor do they live together, though they may maintain regular contact. But the converse also occurs: speakers of a particular language may belong to geographically and politically distinct **social networks**, and have little contact with each other.

Throughout Australia and among the Vaupés, anthropologists have found a high respect for linguistic diversity, even while speakers value their own language(s) as ideal for communication. In New Guinea too, historians have documented this pattern of 'egalitarian multilingualism' in the pre-colonial era. More recent reports, however, document a cultural ranking and hierarchy among languages. In the Buang-speaking villages of the lowlands near the city of Lae almost everyone is also fluent in Tok Pisin, the English-based **lingua franca**. Many also know another New Guinean language, Yabem, spoken by missionaries. Colonialism and missionizing produced the current form of **trilingualism** in which Yabem is used for religious schooling, Buang for informal circumstances or traditional ritual practices, and Tok Pisin for strangers and political affairs. As Gillian Sankoff's (1980) ethnography shows, speakers of Tok Pisin are ranked higher than others because, in a culture that considers the 'foreign' to be a source of knowledge and power, Tok Pisin is the language that points to a speaker's contact with strangers, the government and the wider world. Villagers value multilingualism even more than Tok Pisin: the more languages a man knows the more he demonstrates his political prowess. Switching between Tok Pisin, Buang and Yabem in a single speech is recognized as the most prestigious and effective form of public speaking, a skill expected to be part of the linguistic repertoire of village leaders and powerful entrepreneurs.

This respect for the foreign and for artful alternation among languages is diametrically opposed to current European ideals that equate a single language with a single ethnic group, value **purism** and **correctness** of linguistic form in leaders, and consider language to be the expression of the group's spirit, ethos or **identity**. But there are many historical examples from Europe that would be familiar to New Guinea speakers. In the eighteenth and nineteenth centuries the Balkan merchants of the Ottoman Empire spoke Greek as the language of business, Ottoman Turkish for administrative contacts and, depending on their origins, a Slavic or Romance language for family affairs. Indeed, many a merchant wrote his accounts in Bulgarian with Greek letters and Turkish numbers. Before the advent of the current regime of nation states, the aristocratic houses of continental Europe engaged multiple governesses to assure the breadth of their sons' linguistic repertoires, and Latin education ensured **bilingualism** for those who aspired to scholarship or the higher echelons of the Roman Catholic Church. A good example is Count Széchenyi István (1791–1860), often called the 'Greatest Hungarian' for his many contributions to the modernization of Hungarian politics and economy. Unlike leaders in New Guinea, Széchenyi was taught to keep his languages separate and 'pure'. But like them – and like current leaders of the European Union – he thought of each as suited to different tasks: he wrote his diaries in German, corresponded in English with British friends and in French with ladies of his own circle. He learned Hungarian as a young adult and spoke Latin, as necessary, when participating in Hungarian politics.

Even within current nation states, and current nation-state language ideology, there are diverse cultural conceptions about the relation between language and a speaker's identity. A good example is the village of Kupwar, located in Maharashtra province, near the Mysore border in contemporary India. In this region, Marathi is the main language of government, trade and schooling. But in Kupwar, with a population of 3,000 (in the 1960s), there are four languages: the landowners and craftsmen are Kannada-speaking, a Moslem minority speak Urdu. A small group of landless labourers are Marathi-speakers; rope makers speak Telugu. All local men are bi- or multilingual; many women are not. Linguists identify the four languages of the village as originating from two distinct language families (Dravidian, Indo-Aryan) and their standard forms are mutually unintelligible. But they have coexisted in this village for some 400 years. Speakers use the language of their own group when interacting with family in their own domestic compounds. The medium of inter-group communication is Marathi, which is considered ethnically neutral. Switching between languages is common. But as long as the ethnic separateness of home life is valued, and distinct language remains a signal of ethnic separateness in the local language ideology, multilingualism will be maintained. As a result of adaptation over time by multilingual speakers, however, the four languages have converged into a single grammatical system, as linguists John Gumperz and Robert Wilson (1971) discovered. Only lexical differences remain, marking all utterances as belonging to one or another language.

Kupwar's language ideology and the village's repertoire are the result of socio-linguistic change on the Indian subcontinent that has been quite different from that in Europe. In both world regions over the last two millennia there have been local **vernaculars** as well as languages of wider distribution (e.g. Sanskrit and Latin, respectively). But as historian Sheldon Pollock (1993, 2003) has noted, only in Europe did political centralization entail the denigration and elimination of local linguistic practices. As empires became nation states, powerful efforts were made – in England, France, Spain, among others – to create monolingual populations, in accordance with nation-state ideology. Benedict Anderson's (1983) influential book on 'imagined communities' details how centralized education, general conscription, press capitalism and national labour markets contributed to creating **standard languages** that aspired to be homogeneous across national territory. But this ideal was never realized as a sociolinguistic reality. Regional minorities have dwindled through **language shift**, but many continue to use their language, often in addition to the national language that is needed for social mobility. The minority languages are rarely valued as highly as **national languages**, however. Often, only revival efforts can convince minority speakers that their languages are adequate to 'high' cultural uses such as government, art and education.

Since the Second World War labour migrants have further complicated the picture. They have brought to west Europe the languages of former colonies and of east Europe. The prevalence of return migration ensures the maintenance of many migrant languages, which are also reinforced through ethnic schooling, used in religious observance and in specially targeted mass media. Yet multilingual migrants are often denigrated for their multilingualism. For most of Europe's population the **hegemony** of nation-state ideology has made monolingualism a symbol of 'modernity'. Only very recently, with the rise of English as a global language of business, scholarship and diplomacy, has a new value emerged: in many contexts, knowledge of English along with some other language has come to seem 'modern'. Like migrants, multilingual speakers of regional languages are often stigmatized – and denigrate themselves – for being 'traditional' or insufficiently modern, and for the practice of **code switching** between languages, a practice which is considered insufficiently 'pure'.

From the perspective of European nation states, linguistic purity and schools espousing linguistic correctness are both defences against foreign influence. Yet purity has always been undermined by what linguists know as 'language continua'. All over Europe (as also elsewhere in the world), when one travels in the countryside, the linguistic forms of neighbouring villages are often mutually intelligible, even across national boundaries. One such continuum, known as West Romance, stretches from the coast of Portugal to the centre of Belgium, and from there to the south of Italy. Another, known as West Germanic, reaches from the Netherlands to eastern Austria. Varieties spoken in Vienna and Ostend (or Paris and Madrid) are not mutually intelligible, but they are linked by a chain of mutual intelligibility in the villages between. In such continua, linguistic similarity is a matter of gradients. Standard national languages are superimposed on these linguistic continua. The location of the boundary between German and Dutch, or between French and Spanish, is not a linguistic but a political matter. A village's language is 'a form of French' not mainly because of its linguistic features but because village inhabitants orientate to French schooling, politics and French labour markets.

To summarize the results of our tour: (1) There is no necessary relationship between territory, ethnic/cultural identity and language. These relationships are formulated by language ideologies, as part of social institutions. (2) Local language ideologies mediate between socio-political arrangements, identity and linguistic practice. Australian Aborigines can 'own' a language without speaking it. Széchenyi was passionately Hungarian – by his own account – although he learned Hungarian only relatively late in life. (3) What is valued in language is also a matter of cultural principles, as these interact with political regimes. The desire for access to resources motivates the learning of languages in Kupwar and also among linguistic minorities in contemporary Europe; among the Vaupés the goal is marriage. (4) Everywhere, cultural conceptions and institutional arrangements define how speakers allocate languages to social circumstances – which language(s) for politics, for intimacy, scholarship or prayer; how much switching is appropriate and what social meaning it conveys. Cultural principles also define what counts as exemplary and prestigious, what counts as only proficient or inadequate knowledge of linguistic forms.

THEORETICAL IMPLICATIONS OF STUDYING MULTILINGUALISM

We now know that there is logic and regularity in the allocation of languages to social uses, and there is systematic cross-cultural variation in language ideologies. These are significant advances in research on multilingualism. Another is the notion of linguistic repertoire, because unlike 'native speaker' or 'mother tongue' it makes no unwarranted assumptions about order of acquisition and linguistic ability. Thus, even if some language is the first learned, it need not be the one used most effectively for all purposes, or the most significant emotionally. A Balkan merchant may have spoken a Slavic language in his natal family, but it was in Turkish that he could most effectively speak to Ottoman tax collectors, while feeling a sense of belonging to Greek because it identified his most important station in life, that of merchant. Villages or larger social groupings can also be described as having a linguistic repertoire that includes all the forms any member speaks, with whatever proficiency, by local criteria. A community's repertoire will not be the same as any individual repertoire. Much fine work has been done on the basis of these insights that reject Eurocentric starting points for analysis.

The study of multilingualism also has more radical implications. Most important, it has demonstrated that the viewpoint of the linguist is not sufficient for understanding the form and organization of linguistic practices. This goes against the principles introduced by Ferdinand de Saussure, the founder of modern structuralist linguistics. He proposed that languages are internally structured units that can be studied separately from their social contexts and the cultures of their speakers. Yet, in Kupwar and in European language continua, the different parts of a 'language' did not hold together, as structural analysis would lead us to expect. Further, linguistic analysis alone cannot predict what aspects of language – **lexicon**, **phonology**, **morphosyntax**, **pragmatics** – will be taken by speakers as socially significant in marking language boundaries. Even mutual intelligibility depends on sociocultural factors: it can be enhanced by the belief that linguistic forms are shared, and – as among the Vaupés – by shared cultural expectations about what is to be said and when. In all our examples, the judgements and presuppositions of speakers about their own linguistic practices – their language ideologies – played a crucial role in defining what counts as separate languages and what practices are adequate, acceptable or outstanding exemplars. Such judgements are indispensable starting points for any kind of linguistic analysis.

In short, even if we are interested only in linguistic regularities – let alone in sociolinguistic ones – we must acknowledge that languages are not natural objects that scholars merely find, observe, describe and count. Rather, they are products of social and cultural processes. To include speakers' reflexive, meta-communicative knowledge in our analyses, sociolinguistic research starts with a conceptual distinction between **language community** and **speech community**. These focus on two different aspects of linguistic phenomena. As members of *speech* communities, people orientate to patterns of usage; to the norms of who speaks what language or linguistic **variety** to whom on what occasions, and with what social significance. The same people, when acting as members of *language* communities have different concerns: they jointly orientate towards particular named languages and the linguistic rules for making propositions about the world in the lexically distinctive and grammatically regular ways identified with those named forms. As linguist Michael Silverstein (1996) has stressed, in studying language communities the focus is first on linguistic structures themselves, and then on the relative orientation of speakers towards the institutional norms that regiment and sustain those means of predication and the correctness of forms.

The intersections of these two analytically distinct kinds of communities are of great interest for sociolinguistic analysis. Only rarely is there the full overlap between speech community and language community that would allow the norms of social allocation and the norms of denotational code to be prescribed and maintained by the same institutions. For example, those who live in Buang-speaking villages are members of a *speech* community that displays regularity in the alternation among Buang, Yabem and Tok Pisin. Even those who do not understand propositions in Tok Pisin or Yabem know that leaders are adding to their **prestige** and **power** by mixing the three. But if we focus only on those who know Tok Pisin, we see that they display, in addition, a different kind of orientation to the *language* community of Tok Pisin. Village leaders who are Tok Pisin speakers attend to the ideals of correctness in grammar and lexicon that are salient among Tok Pisin speakers everywhere, including those from cities who espouse educated norms. Village leaders are members of a far-flung Tok Pisin language community in which their locally admired ability to switch with grace and ease among languages is not what gains them prestige. In the language community of Tok Pisin they can gain respect only through their ability to display correct usage of Tok Pisin as defined by monolinguals.

There are often heated debates in multilingual speech communities between those who support the purity of each language and those who champion the many practices common to such communities that juxtapose and combine languages. Switching among languages according to interlocutor and situation is one such practice, as is code switching within a single sentence. Phonological and syntactic interference, interlingual puns and massive **borrowing** are also practices in which speakers simultaneously recognize the contrast between languages and also juxtapose or mix those languages, thereby picking out and often increasing their similarities. Kathryn Woolard (1999) has termed many of these practices *bivalent* because the resulting linguistic forms could equally belong in both languages. Those who argue for the legitimacy of bivalent practices are often supporting the peaceful coexistence of two or more language communities within a single speech community. Depending on the language ideologies presupposed, however, arguments for (or against) bivalent practices can also carry more complicated political messages. The most general point is that, as Gal and Irvine (1995) have argued, both differentiation and convergence of languages can result from contact, coexistence and discursive struggle.

The distinction between language communities and speech communities echoes a contrast introduced by the Russian literary scholar Mikhael Bakhtin in his arguments against Saussure. Bakhtin proposed that *heteroglossia* – diversity of linguistic form – is produced by two opposed sociocultural forces operating simultaneously. A centripetal force creates unification, standardization and regimentation; an opposing centrifugal force creates differentiation and variation in linguistic practices. Saussure studied the unified linguistic structures that resulted from centripetal force. By contrast, Bakhtin was interested in the difference between medical discourse and legal talk, between intimate chat and bureaucratic pronouncements, between sacred prayer and secular gossip, between the speech of the working class and that of the elite. These differences would now be called **registers** in a single language. They consist of linguistic forms that signal changes in the role relations between speakers, their professional identities, their distinct ideologies or social locations.

The languages of a multilingual speech community commonly stand in the same relation of functional contrast to each other as do registers in monolingual speech communities. When this happens, switch in language and switch in register signal the same kinds of social differences. They both signal changing alignments between speakers in the event of speaking and changes in stance towards the objects of discussion. Once we acknowledge 'language' as a social product, with boundaries actively created by processes such as **standardization** and cultural differentiation, monolingual and multilingual speech communities can be seen, rightly, as more similar than they are different. The insights about language ideology, linguistic repertoires and allocation of forms to different functions gained through the close study of multilingualism hold for all speech communities.

FURTHER READING

Bakhtin, M. (1983) 'Discourse in the novel', in *The Dialogic Imagination*, Austin, TX: University of Texas Press, pp. 259–420.

Gal, S. and Irvine, I. (1995) 'The boundaries of languages and disciplines: how ideologies construct difference', *Social Research* 62 (4): 967–1001.

Gumperz, J.J. (1982) *Discourse Strategies*, New York: Cambridge University Press.

Woolard, K. (1999) 'Simultaneity and bivalency as strategies in bilingualism', *Journal of Linguistic Anthropology* 8 (1): 3–29.

19

LANGUAGE AND EDUCATION

JANET MAYBIN

In its broadest sense, the relationship between language and learning begins long before children go to school. At the same time as they acquire their first language, they are learning how to use it in socially approved ways and they become exposed, through talk, print and the media to the beliefs and values of their community. Children who grow up in a **multilingual** environment also learn at an early age how to draw on their different languages in various ways, depending on the context and who they are talking to. Anthropologists have shown how young children in different communities are being continually socialized through dialogues with parents and others, the talk and stories they hear around them, and the ways in which they learn to engage with different kinds of writing and images in their environment (see Chapter 18).

At the same time as learning to become an active member of their community through language, children also learn to use it for their own individual purposes: to get other people to do things for them, to express affection or anger and to struggle to make sense of the world around them. Talk is always multifunctional, simultaneously expressing ideas or putting a point of view and conveying something about the relationship between the speakers. It also in some way expresses the speaker's sense of who they are as a person, through the feelings and emotions being expressed, the value position they are taking up, or the language **variety** they choose to use. When considering the role of language in education, it is important to remember that language in schools and colleges is not only a vehicle for academic teaching and learning, but is also simultaneously involved in expressing or challenging particular kinds of relationships, value positions and identities.

In this chapter I look first at the ways in which language has been seen as closely connected with learning in formal educational contexts. I then consider the implications of this for students from different **speech communities** and mention some of the ways in which sociolinguistic insights have informed educational practice.

TALK AND LITERACY IN THE CLASSROOM

Most classroom business, whether to do with teaching the curriculum or managing groups of students, is mediated through dialogue. There tends to be a distinctive pattern of **turn-taking**, referred to as the *Initiation–Response–Feedback* (IRF) or Initiation–Response–Evaluation (IRE) sequence (see Sinclair and Coulthard 1975 for the original study; also Stubbs 1983, 1986). Typically, the teacher initiates the sequence by asking students a question. A student then responds and the teacher evaluates and follows up the response, often also initiating the next sequence. This **turn-taking** pattern positions the teacher as the speaker with institutional authority who selects and organizes the knowledge to be conveyed to students. While some classrooms may involve small-group work, and teachers sometimes draw on the expertise of an individual student, the IRE sequence is a ubiquitous feature of most teacher–student dialogues.

Researchers have shown how knowledge between teachers and students is constructed through these asymmetric dialogues. Whether the discussion is focused on the results of a science experiment, or a poem students have just read, or an explanation of a historical event, teachers direct students' attention to particular dimensions or features of whatever is under discussion, selectively repeat and reformulate the responses students give to their questions and recapitulate previous classroom discussion. In this way, teachers and students construct a body of shared knowledge about the topic. While some critics have argued that the dominance of the IRE pattern in classroom dialogue seriously limits the role of students in their learning, others have pointed out that teacher questions can be used in many different ways: to elicit explanations, to probe students about their reasons for holding particular opinions or to ask them to reflect on their own understanding. Through questions, students can be coaxed to consider alternative possibilities, perceive new connections and reach insights in ways which they could not have managed on their own.

The Russian psychologist Lev Vygotsky (1962) saw language as both a cultural tool, which inducts children into the shared knowledge and understandings of their society, and also a psychological tool, which extends their learning and development. He argued that dialogue with teachers or more capable peers can stretch children so they are able to extend through what he terms their 'zone of proximal development', that is, the difference between what a child can manage to do independently on its own, and what it is able to achieve when given intellectual guidance and support from others. This support has been termed 'scaffolding' (Bruner 1990), where the teacher does not simply help a learner but provides cues and prompts so that they can find answers for themselves, and can internalize how to do this independently in the future. In other words, scaffolding is about teaching children how to learn (what questions to ask, what features to focus on) as well as how to solve a specific problem. Sociocultural theories of teaching and learning, which build on Vygotsky's work (such as Leont'ev 1981 and Newman *et al.* 1989), see education as taking place through dialogue, with classroom discourse reflecting the history, cultural values and social practices of children's schools and communities.

One of the social dimensions of talk in the classroom which has interested sociolinguists is the relation between language and **gender**. Research has documented differences and inequalities in girls' and boys' language behaviour, suggesting that boys are competitive rather than collaborative and that they dominate classroom interaction and the use of classroom computers. Books and other resources tend to be chosen to reflect their interests and activities. Against this, recent trends towards more uses of collaborative talk in the classroom may be seen as a feminization of classroom discourse. The notions of what counts as 'competitive' or 'collaborative' talk have now been problematized, but it is clear that children's motivation to learn, and the ways in which they take part in classroom talk and **literacy** activities, are shaped by their sense of gender (or **social class**, or **ethnic**) identity and the ways in which they feel positioned within classroom discourse (see, for example, Crawford 1995; Coates 1998, 2004; Holmes and Meyerhoff 2003; see also Chapter 7).

In addition to learning how to take part in classroom conversations, pupils are also introduced to the technical vocabularies and ways of viewing the world which are connected with specific school subjects. And, right from the beginning of schooling, students are shifted by teachers towards using more literate forms of language. Psychologists like David Olson have argued that the acquisition of literacy is enormously important for children and for society in general, because it leads to more abstract, explicit, rational, scientific thinking. Anthropologists and sociolinguistics, however, have suggested that it is not the acquisition of literacy itself which produces what Olson calls 'a literate mode of thought', but engagement in particular kinds of literacy practices, and the ways of thinking associated with them (see Olson *et al.* 1996; Olson and Torrance 2001).

The anthropologist Brian Street (1984, 1995) argues that the literacy taught in schools is not simply a neutral collection of technical skills, but a particular culturally valued 'essayist' literacy. People learn other kinds of literacies in the other domains of their lives, but these may not be equally valued by educationalists. For instance, a student may produce poor essays at school but demonstrate high levels of IT literacy at home playing video and computer games. He/she is seen as a failure at school but as an expert among friends. As well as involving skills and competences, literacies have social meanings and impact on people's identities. Research with non-traditional students in higher education confirms that academic uses of language and literacy are not neutral skills but can be associated with particular stereotypes and a 'posh academic' identity which some students find alienating, and may not want to acquire. Researchers in the New Literacy Studies who focus on the social and ideological dimensions of literacy advocate more recognition in the classroom of students' out-of-school or vernacular literacy practices (see Barton 1994; Gee 1996; Street 1995).

LANGUAGE IN AND OUT OF SCHOOL

Many children experience striking differences between language and literacy practices at home and school. In multilingual communities they may be educated through a second or third language, and many **monolingual** children also find that the language variety they speak, and the ways in which they use language, do not fit well with expectations in the classroom.

In the 1960s and 1970s the British sociologist Basil Bernstein (1971, 1977, see also 1996) suggested that the reason why so many working-class children were failing in the British educational system was that they grew up learning what he called a **restricted code**, in contrast to the **elaborated code** also acquired by middle-class children. These different codes provided contrasting ways of taking meaning from the world. Bernstein describes how working-class children learn a restricted code in position-oriented families where social control is exercised through the authority of parents and fixed-role relationships. There is an emphasis on solidarity and shared communal meanings, and children learn to use language in relatively implicit ways, with short sentences containing few adjectives and adverbs, linked by repetitive conjunctions like 'and' or 'then'. In contrast, in middle-class, person-oriented families, communication is more open and roles are less fixed. Social control is exercised through explanation and appeals to the child as a person, and children are encouraged to express their own ideas and viewpoints. Children brought up with an elaborated code, Bernstein argued, are used to drawing on a wider range of syntactic and semantic linguistic forms and are able to use language explicitly, organize experience conceptually and articulate decontextualized ideas much more easily than children from working-class homes (see Chapter 6).

Bernstein's ideas about the restricted and elaborated code were taken up by some educationalists to argue that working-class and minority children suffered from language deprivation. In the United States, compensatory education programmes were advocated for African American children speaking African American Vernacular English (AAVE). Sociolinguists at the time argued strongly against the idea that children from communities speaking **non-standard** varieties of English were linguistically deprived, and the American sociolinguist William Labov (1969b) famously explained how AAVE was as grammatically logical as **Standard English**. Sociolinguists argued that the problems some children experienced in school stemmed not from language *deficit* but from language *difference*. Some suggested that rather than trying to change the child to fit the school, schools should recognize, value and build on the languages and language **varieties** which children brought with them. The debate about the status of AAVE and its role in schooling simmers on, surfacing in the late 1990s in arguments about whether Ebonics (AAVE) should be recognized as a separate language from Standard English, and used in school as an initial medium of instruction (see Lippi-Green 1997 and Baugh 2000).

Over the last thirty years, anthropologists and sociolinguists in the United States have documented how children from various different ethnic and social class groups may face unfamiliar language practices at school. For instance, studies of Native American children who were reluctant to talk in class found that, at home, these children were expected to learn through silent watching and listening, and privately practising skills before demonstrating them in front of others. They therefore felt uncomfortable about answering questions in class, which meant making mistakes and demonstrating their ignorance publicly. In addition, community social activities tended to be communally organized, rather than hierarchically, as in school. For these children it was a matter not simply of learning new vocabulary or question-and-answer routines, but of being faced with language practices which were at odds with their community beliefs about the nature of learning and how people should relate to each other.

In a long-term study of young children in three local communities, the American anthropologist Shirley Brice Heath (1982, 1983) found that children in black and white middle class families in the urban Maintown learnt through interactions with carers, for instance in bedtime stories, how to give the reasoned explanations, explicit verbal commentaries and personal reactions to stories which would be expected by their teachers at school. In the nearby white working-class community Roadville, where religious practice included an emphasis on written scripture, children came to school with experience of alphabet and number books and real-life stories about children like themselves, but they tended to see texts as inflexible records of the truth. Finally, children growing up in the black working-class community of Trackton were unfamiliar with story books but skilled in oral story-telling, making metaphorical connections in stories and performing for an audience.

In school, the Maintown children were successful and Roadville children performed well initially but fell back when asked to relate imaginatively to ideas in a story, or apply knowledge from one context to another. The most serious mismatch was for Tracktown children, who were faced with unfamiliar stories and questions asking them to supply labels, attributes and discrete features of objects and events in a decontextualized way. Their ability to link situations metaphorically and recreate scenes was not valued in infant school, where there was an emphasis on basic skills, and many Trackton children failed to pick up the school composition and comprehension skills which could have helped them translate their abilities into an acceptable channel.

Sociolinguists have always argued that language use is naturally diverse, and that different languages and language varieties should be equally valued. The recognition that children come to school with diverse language repertoires and practices has influenced educational programmes aimed at valuing and building on children's out-of-school knowledge and practices. These programmes have often emphasized 'appropriate' rather than 'correct' uses of language and tried to draw on community language practices as an educational resource. The educational pendulum in the United States and United Kingdom swung back in the 1990s towards a sharper emphasis on standard language and curriculum regulation, but the debate about how far education should start with and build on the diversity of language practices children bring to school, and how far schools should concentrate more on teaching them the socially powerful forms of academic language and literacy, continues.

Proponents of the Australian genre approach, for instance, which builds on Halliday's (1985) functional theory of language as 'social semiotic', warn against basing the curriculum too much on students' own language experience, which could leave them 'stranded in their own words'. Instead, they argue, all children, especially students who are educationally disadvantaged or for whom English is a second language, need to be explicitly taught the important genres – for example, report, explanation, argument – which are the key to disciplinary knowledge and social advancement. This involves training students to recognize and reproduce the abstract and condensed linguistic forms used in writing (see Kress and van Leeuwen 2001; Jewitt and Kress 2003).

The genre approach has been criticized for its association with a transmission style of teaching which encourages writing structured in a set number of dominant genres encoding specific views of the world and particular ways of thinking and acting. Critics argue that it could produce unreflective conformity in students rather than critical independent thought. In many domains of life, genres are not structured simply, and speech and writing involve genre mixing and hybridity. In response, genre teachers argue that students need to become proficient in a range of important genres before they can reflect critically on the ways in which texts represent the world. More recently the explicit and systematic analysis of texts has been combined with efforts to immerse students in a range of literacy practices, and encouragement to critically examine the texts they are reading, writing and designing.

A recognition of the changing nature of communicative technologies in society has emphasized the multimodal nature of all texts which may combine words, gestures, still or moving images, typefaces, sound effects, hypertextual links and so on in various different ways to produce meaning in oral, print and electronic texts. On the one hand, many children are acquiring language experience and competence with computers and mobile phones which may not be sufficiently acknowledged or used as a resource for learning in school, and on the other hand educationalists are beginning to explore how they can best prepare children for the **multiliteracies** and **multimodality** of communication in the twenty-first century (Jewitt and Kress 2003).

The twenty-first century also sees the increasing use of English as a global language, and continuing patterns of migration which mean that many students are receiving education through a second language. **Bilingual** and **multilingual** children quickly acquire the **communicative competence** to use their different languages appropriately, often experiencing these as connected with different aspects of their identity. The language medium for education, however, is dictated by political and economic concerns and many children, whether in multilingual societies or in migrant communities, have to make the transition to a societally dominant language.

It is generally believed best for children to receive their initial education in their first language, although many parents want their children to be educated in the most prestigious language. The Canadian sociolinguist James Cummins (1996) argued that it takes around five years for a child to develop a new language to the level needed for school academic purposes (the 'threshold' hypothesis), but that concepts developed in their first language can be easily transferred to a second language as it develops. In practice, resources are not always available for bilingual education, especially if the number of children speaking a particular language makes special provision financially impractical. Political policy also shapes the possibilities available. Where the emphasis is on the integration of minority groups, their languages are not supported in school. In England, where educational policy is strongly monolingual, bilingual children may attend community-run schools to receive additional education in their other languages. In the United States, the 'English Only' lobby is strongly associated with an anti-immigration position. In Wales, on the other hand, political pressure has led to the establishment of some state-sponsored bilingual education, and in the new democratic South Africa parents and communities were able to democratically decide on which of the eleven **official languages** should be used as the medium of education in their schools. (Most chose to go straight for English, from Grade 1.)

Sociolinguistic research has influenced the teaching of English as a second language (**ESL**), shifting methods away from oral drill and towards the immersion and interactive strategies believed to develop learners' communicative competence, i.e. the ability to use language appropriately and effectively in different situations and for different purposes and audiences. Researchers have also, however, pointed out the importance of the kinds of identity which the learner is offered as an English speaker, and how these impact on their motivation and progress in the language. Some learners may welcome English as a vehicle for developing a new kind of identity, but many ESL students resent that their competences in other areas of the curriculum, or, in the case of adults, the skills and training they have received in their first language, are often not recognized or valued and they are 'deskilled' in the English-speaking environment. Within the international teaching context, sociolinguists have argued that inequalities between anglophone communities and second language learners are encoded within the discourse of ESL teaching and textbooks. The very specific ways in which language and literacy are seen as connected with learning and are used within educational contexts, and the social and ideological implications of these practices for all children, are highlighted in multilingual contexts.

FURTHER READING

Cope, B. and Kalantzis, M. (eds) (2000) *Multiliteracies: Literacy Learning and the Design of Social Futures*, London: Routledge.

Mercer, N. (2000) *Words and Minds: How We Use Language to Think Together*, London: Routledge.

Norton, B. (2000) *Identity and Language Learning: Gender, Ethnicity and Educational Change*, London: Longman.

Pennycook, A. (1998) *English and the Discourses of Colonialism*, London: Routledge.

20

LANGUAGE POLICY AND LANGUAGE PLANNING

SUE WRIGHT

Language is one of the key elements in the construction of human groups. All children are socialized into their respective language groups, and adults, striving to maintain comprehensibility within the group, teach children the structures and lexis used by the group, and correct them as they learn. Thus all human beings police, protect and promote language to a degree, and forms of **language policy** and **language planning** (LPLP) occur in all societies.

However, there is one type of political setting in which LPLP has been undertaken in a particularly rigorous and systematic way. Nationalism, with its ideal of a culturally and linguistically homogeneous people differentiated from neighbours, has led to more conscious and consistent top-down LPLP than any other form of governance. This chapter considers the role of LPLP in nation building and then reflects on efforts to try and influence language practices in an increasingly post-national age.

TRADITIONAL LPLP: STATUS, CORPUS AND ACQUISITION PLANNING

Many, perhaps most, histories of LPLP present it as a discipline which 'blossom(ed) during the 1970s' (Bratt-Paulston and Tucker 2003: 409) and discussions of the conscious human management of language often claim that 'traditional research first emerged in the 1960s and 1970s in order to aid programmes of "modernization" in "developing" countries' (Tollefson 2005: 42).

This period was indeed a time of intense LPLP activity, as the governing classes of newly independent states considered how to manage language matters in the new polities and Western-trained linguists proposed themselves as researchers and consultants. The excitement generated by the flurry of activity in LPLP in the 1960s and 1970s prompted scholars who followed to try and systematize ideas and devise classifications and typologies of the various theories and interventions (Neustupny 1983; Nahir 1984; and see Hornberger 2005 for an overview). This reflection led to the classic division of LPLP into **status planning**, **corpus planning** and **acquisition planning** (Cooper 1989, building on earlier work by Kloss 1969):

> Status planning is the decision to confirm a language in its functions and its domains or to introduce a new language into these functions and domains. Such decisions are

often made at the highest levels of a polity and enshrined in law. This is the case when a language is formally adopted as a **national language**.

Corpus planning is an attempt to change the forms and structures of the language itself. This task is often undertaken by national language planning agencies, whose role differs according to the situation. Where a spoken language is being adopted for official use there will need to be **codification** and **standardization** to create a written form. For a language which is already written, the agency may be asked to elaborate new terms for new technologies and domains in order to avoid borrowing from other languages.

Acquisition planning concerns the implementation of status and corpus policy. Once it has been decided that a certain language will play a certain role in public life, and once the form of that language has been decided, educationists organise how it will be acquired.

(Cooper 1989: 1)

However, both as an activity undertaken by governments and as a domain of scholarly enquiry, status, corpus and acquisition planning can be traced much further back, to the very beginning of nation-state building.

LPLP IN THE SERVICE OF NATION BUILDING IN EUROPE

LPLP in state nations

European LPLP starts in the early modern period with the **standardization** and spread of Western European **vernaculars**. The first state nations appeared as France, Spain, Britain, Sweden, and the Netherlands emerged from feudalism. The ruling dynasties in each country overcame the challenge to their power from their aristocracies, and secured stable state boundaries. The era of strong central government that followed ensured that the dialect of the capital and court would take precedence over the other dialects and languages on state territory, and would be used by the civil service which administered the country for the monarch. Early examples of status planning came when the use of the vernacular became a legal requirement. The Edict of Villers-Cotterêts (1539) in France ensured that, as the use of Latin declined in official, contractual and legal settings, it was the language of the king that replaced it, and no other. The Act of Union (1536) in Britain decreed that only those Welsh who had learnt English could hold public office.

Scholars contributed to establishing vernacular usage. The Accademia della Crusca in Florence and the Académie française in Paris are two early instances of the state turning to linguists for corpus planning. Where there was no official corpus planning institute, as in Britain, individual scholars, such as Samuel Johnson, undertook the work of elaborating grammars and dictionaries.

Acquisition planning came a little later. Before the nineteenth century the great majority of people remained on the land in small groups using local dialects, as they had for centuries. Absolute monarchs made no attempt to alter this state of affairs, since they saw no need to interact with their subjects. However, once subjects became citizens and voters they needed to participate in public life. The new political philosophy which made the people sovereign in the state eventually brought with it universal education and was one reason for linguistic **convergence**.

LPLP in nation states

The philosophy of nationalism spread across Europe, and by the mid-nineteenth century most of the continent had been touched by the ideology. Fired by the nationalist ideal, elites sharing similarities of language and culture claimed a territorial base, and a new kind of nation state came into being. German and Italian unity resulted from complex political and social developments, but the community of language and culture was a central organizing principle.

Throughout the nineteenth century and in every part of the continent various movements for national self-determination appeared. From the Greeks in the south-east to the Irish in the north-west, language was central to the case for independence. To be a 'nation', a group felt it had to be both cohesive and distinct. A single 'national' language could demonstrate this. Independence movements used their linguists to develop the distinct language needed for the nation's claim to sovereignty (Smith 1991; Gellner 1983). Since the languages of Europe are, in their vast majority, not discrete languages but **dialect continua** that change gradually across space, a flurry of corpus planning had to take place to create distinction.

When national self-determination was achieved, the ideal of perfect congruence of polity and a linguistically homogenous nation still remained a chimera. In the highly complex patterns of European settlement, few areas actually contained a linguistically homogeneous population. Newly independent 'nations' included minority populations from completely distinct linguistic groups as well as speakers of allied but divergent dialects. Thus, after independence, acquisition planning took place in an attempt to weld together disparate groups.

DEGREES OF SUCCESS IN TOP-DOWN LPLP

To a large degree planners achieved their twin goals of linguistic convergence and minimal variation within the state and maximal linguistic differentiation from neighbours (Haugen 1966). A traveller crossing the political borders of Europe in the early to mid-twentieth century would have been very conscious that national borders were also linguistic borders. The linguistic balkanization of the continent was never complete but overt LPLP in education services and centralized administrations and LPLP as a side effect of other policies such as general conscription promoted internal cohesion and erected language borders in the continua.

It is quite remarkable the degree to which nineteenth and early twentieth-century Europeans accepted the imposition of national languages. The reasons are multiple, but some key factors seem indisputable: nationalist ideology put people under pressure to use the national language as part of the extreme and exclusive loyalty demanded by the nation state; the democratization of the political process seemed to require that all citizens belong to a single community of communication; a positivist scientific perspective and structuralist linguistics made LPLP seem theoretically possible; universal education made it practically possible. Finally, all these phenomena occurred alongside industrialization, which drew individuals into the linguistic melting pots of towns where the national language became the **lingua franca** (Gellner 1983). The very fact that minority language populations became a political issue from the nineteenth century onwards testifies to the triumph of convergence policies in creating majorities.

LPLP in nineteenth and early twentieth-century Europe was far more successful than in the states that gained their independence from the European colonial powers in the second half of the twentieth century. Few postcolonial governments attained the nationalist ideal of congruence of language, people and territory to the degree that it was achieved in some European states. Even in Indonesia and Tanzania, two countries where LPLP was pursued vigorously, the national languages have not spread throughout the whole population or become the media for all public domains.

As LPLP in its organized form has clear links with nation building and nationalism, is it fading as an activity, in what is arguably a post-national era? Interestingly, this does not seem to be the case. The new political paradigm is producing LPLP action and reaction among social actors, and LPLP is growing in importance in the universities (see Ricento 2005). Many linguists seem, however, to have moved from being supportive of governmental LPLP to take a largely critical and oppositional stance.

GLOBALIZATION AND LPLP

Before discussing what post-national LPLP is like, we must first agree that we are moving into post-national times. I would argue that there is evidence that the sovereign nation state with its impermeable borders, protected domestic market, self-reliance in defence and single public culture and language is evolving if not disappearing. Since World War II much sovereignty has been relinquished as elements of political, economic and judicial control have shifted to institutions, authorities and corporations that operate transnationally and supranationally. National self-reliance has waned, with the regimes, networks, flows and inter-actions of globalization. The imagined community of the nation that Anderson (1983) saw as deriving from common cultural practices is diluted as people interact across borders to a far greater degree than ever before.

All these aspects of globalization have had linguistic effects. New patterns of association have emerged among elite groups as governance becomes interstate rather than intrastate. This means that actors with competence in different national languages require a means of communication. The circulation of ideas and information through the medium of new technologies encourages transnational civil society and worldwide virtual communities (wherever people can afford the hardware). The solution to the communication needs of a globalizing world is, at least for the moment, greater use of English as a lingua franca.

The spread of English has prompted a variety of LPLP reactions. In the last decades policy makers in many states have been concerned to limit the incursions of English. In some situations the attempt has been to stop English replacing another language in the lingua franca role. Thus the French government, elite and intellectuals have fought a long rearguard action to preserve French as a language for international forums (Ager 1996). In other situations the struggle has been to maintain the national language in all the domains in which it was traditionally used. Thus, for example, the Swedes have acted to protect the use of their national language in scientific research and higher education, where English is now often the medium (Oakes 2001).

LPLP to limit the spread of English as the lingua franca in a particular area or **domain** seems to have had little effect. Where people have seen it to be to their advantage to learn and use English they have done so. Top-down policy making has not found widespread acceptance among those it hoped to influence. For example, the European Union tried to promote diversity in foreign language learning through programmes such as Lingua, but schools have largely ignored policies for diversity and provided the English classes that parents demanded (Wright 2004).

LPLP scholars are divided on the globalization issue. Some see a common language as a common good (Crystal 2003; van Parijs 2004). Others see the spread of English as a new imperialism and as hegemonic and exploitative in the Gramscian sense (Phillipson 1992; Tollefson 2005; Skuttnab-Kangas 2000). These latter argue that non-native speakers of English learn the language because they feel they cannot afford not to. However, by ensuring their individual advantage these learners guarantee their disadvantage as a collective. Non-native speakers will always be disadvantaged in linguistic settings where native speakers dominate.

The oppositional stance to English can be problematic, since it is made in English and exemplifies how the language gives access to a wide audience or readership as well as being a medium of exclusion and control. Aware of this, a number of scholars have developed the concept of *performativity*. Canagarajah (1999) points out that language should not be reified; it exists only in its speakers. Those who acquire and use a language make it their own. As speakers 'appropriate' English the language no longer 'belongs' solely to **mother-tongue** speakers, and British and American norms become just two examples of **World Englishes** (Kachru 1986a).

The new research culture has challenged the modernist and structuralist epistemology that underpinned traditional LPLP research. Instead of examining how governments and elites used language to confirm their power and construct national groups, the relationship is turned on its head and LPLP investigates how language, **discourse** and culture shape ideology and the organization of the world

(Pennycook 2005). Within the framework of the growing importance of **discourse analysis**, Pennycook and others have led a move to a micro level of investigation. The approach is to focus on how 'we perform identity with words (rather than reflect identities in language)' (Pennycook 2005: 71).

Interest in how individuals experience the language ideologies that affect them and how they respond in terms of **identity** has sparked both specific **ethnographic** studies (such as Heller 1999) and general theory-building work (Joseph 2004).

DEVOLUTION OF POWER AND LPLP

However, this postmodern strand in the discipline has not completely obscured traditional LPLP. There is still a lot of nation building around and, where it is to be found, old-style LPLP is there too.

As the state has weakened with the relocation of power to the supranational level, many of the groups that were incorporated into the 'nation' have shown how little they were assimilated. Demands for devolved powers or independence have been made as soon as the political climate made them possible.

Groups that seek political autonomy or independence usually demand language rights as part of their struggle, and once they achieve their goals mostly set about LPLP in the old positivist, technicist manner. Thus, after the Spanish constitution (1978) devolved power to Catalonia, the Basque Country and Galicia, each Autonomy began status, corpus and acquisition planning. Both before and after 1997 devolution, the Welsh brought their language back into the public space to a considerable degree, employing traditional status and acquisition strategies. The countries which have formed on the territory of the former Soviet Union and Yugoslavia have all undertaken classic nation building, including LPLP. In these and other settings there are still politicians engaged in status planning and numerous linguists working on corpus and acquisition planning.

One sometimes finds odd alliances in LPLP circles, as these classic nation builders join ranks with the postmodernists and critical theorists, often in the name of linguistic *diversity*. This umbrella term needs careful unpicking because it can mean promotion of a state **standard** as much as commitment to protection of all the world's languages.

DIVERSITY, RIGHTS AND THE DISAPPEARANCE OF LANGUAGES

Another group of scholars who take an oppositional position are those who work to preserve and protect languages with a very small (and often dwindling) number of speakers and where pressures and enticements to shift to another language, often the 'national' language, are having an effect. This could be seen as a poacher-turned-gamekeeper development, since LPLP linguists often helped engineer the **language shifts** and convergence that caused language minorities and **language death** in the first place.

Support for **minority languages** reflects a new moral and legal environment. Since 1948 and the Universal Declaration of Human Rights there has been growing awareness of and respect for human rights, including the right to use one's own language. This is, of course, an individual right. The only guarantee is that speakers will not be persecuted for using their language. They are not assured use of it outside the private sphere.

The minority language rights movement is working, however, for group rights, such as the adoption of minority languages in politics, education, the media and administration. Learning from the legitimization and institutionalization of 'national' languages, and the process by which other languages were minoritized, academics and activists are clear that mere tolerance will not be enough for minority language survival. **Diglossic** arrangements in which minority languages are encouraged in the private sphere but not employed in public are as likely to lead to language shift in the long run as prohibition (May 2005).

So LPLP strategies for the maintenance and **revitalization** of minority languages draw from the status, corpus and acquisition planning paradigm once again. Edwards (1992) suggests, in a predictive typology, thirty-three elements that favour **language maintenance**. There are a number of variables in this list that no amount of state support or group effort could affect (geographical settings and religious practices that ensure the group remain together), but the bulk of the protection strategies replicate LPLP in nation building. Fishman's two influential books (1991, 2001) on the necessary conditions for language maintenance and revitalization confirm these parallels between minority language protection and 'national' language promotion. As Brutt-Griffler (2002) states, minority language rights are essentially normative. Activists promote internal convergence and maintain external difference through corpus planning, and seek institutionalization of the language, in particular in education.

International agencies such as the Council of Europe take the same view. The CoE Charter for Regional or Minority Languages relies on traditional nation-building strategies, promoting the use of a language in relations between the citizen and state institutions and as the medium of education and the media to preserve or revitalize it. There is no confidence that a language will survive unless it has these public roles.

However, as there are perhaps 6,000+ languages in the world (Grimes 2000), depending on how we define a language, simple arithmetic makes it clear that they are not all going to be employed in the governance of the 200+ states that exist in the world today. Fewer than 4 per cent are languages with any kind of official status in the countries where they are spoken. The vast majority of languages are unwritten, not recognized officially, restricted to local communities, used only in the home and with a small number of speakers (Romaine 2002).

Some suggest that there is no need to try. Steiner (1998) argues that languages have always died out as their speakers were constrained by political or economic pressure to shift to other languages, but that diversity remains, because new varieties develop from new patterns of association. The situation has, however, never been quite as it is today. Krauss (1992) suggests that unless something remarkable happens there may be as few as 600 languages at the end of the twenty-first century.

Many linguistic human rights activists see this withering of diversity as an unmitigated disaster for humanity. In one analysis (Skutnabb-Kangas 2000) the disappearance of a language amounts to **linguicide** or **linguistic genocide**. Such terms suggest that some scholars believe that **agency** is involved and that LPLP could counteract shift and death. A closely allied group of **ecolinguists** are equally dismayed. They argue that there are parallels between language diversity and bio-diversity and that any language that disappears is a calamity, since its loss entails the disappearance of the world view associated with it. They too believe that intervention may stem language loss (Fill and Mühlhäusler 2001).

However, at present, it is difficult to see how the linguistic rights and the eco-linguistic activists will succeed. There is no agreed approach to the preservation of languages that is not nation building on a smaller scale and little successful LPLP outside that framework. There is also no agreement on who has the right to intervene in minority linguistic matters.

Conclusion

LPLP is an extremely interesting research field today with many conundrums. Top-down policies conceived in accordance with the intellectual traditions of nationalism, structuralism and positivism were immensely successful in affecting language practices. They continue in many guises today, particularly where groups gain political independence and set up institutions and state networks. However, in other settings language practices seem to have become ungovernable. In the context of globalization the agency for change is diffuse (Swaan 2001) and is not easily influenced by traditional LPLP.

LPLP scholars were traditionally members of the establishment. In the early period of nationalism every would-be national group needed its linguists to elaborate a particular national language differentiated from the languages adjacent on the dialect continuum, to be codified and standardized. Wherever governing elites wished to impose the ideal of one language, one people and one territory, they relied on linguists and language teachers to translate policy into practice. In post-national settings, many LPLP scholars have become critical of the way language is managed in state formation and power relations. New research directions in LPLP scholarship seek to discover how discourse and cultural practices reproduce and maintain power and spread ideologies. An oppositional LPLP has come into being which is active in minority language maintenance, rights and diversity on the one hand and resistance to the **hegemony** of a global lingua franca on the other.

FURTHER READING

Anderson, B. (1983) *Imagined Communities*, London: Verso.

Ricento, T. (ed.) (2005) *An Introduction to Language Policy*, Oxford: Blackwell.

Swaan, A. de (2001) *Words of the World*, Cambridge: Polity Press.

Part V
LANGUAGE CHANGE

21

CREOLES AND PIDGINS

SALIKOKO S. MUFWENE

Creoles and **pidgins** have attracted more and more attention among linguists since the 1970s. The number of research questions has increased from what kinds of restructuring processes account best for their emergence to whether the processes that explain these evolutions are unique to these new language varieties. While there have also been more studies of especially **morphosyntactic** features, debates have intensified about whether creoles in particular form a unique type of languages, with structural peculiarities that set them apart from (other) natural languages. Linguists have indeed been ambivalent about whether creoles are natural languages and whether the restructuring processes that have produced them are non-ordinary, unusual, or abnormal.

One of the recent debates has also been over whether creoles (and pidgins) are not genetically related to their **lexifiers**, the languages from which they have evolved, or whether they constitute some sort of parentless languages, from the point of view of genetic linguistics. (The term 'lexifier' is used here even though it innacurately suggests that only the vocabulary was selected from the colonial European language from which it evolved.) This is tied to the question of whether they are really separate languages or **dialects** of their lexifiers, in the same capacity as other colonial, non-creole **vernaculars** (such as North American English and French dialects) which evolved around the same time, in the seventeenth and eighteenth centuries, from primarily colonial **non-standard** varieties of the same European languages. These questions are tied to the **ideology** of language **purity**, akin to that of racial purity, inherited from the nineteenth-century European societies, which treated people 'of mixed races' as 'unnatural,' 'anomalies', or 'inferior,' and 'mixed languages' as aberrations, at best as children out of wedlock. All this was consistent with the notion of 'species', with which that of 'race' was then synonymous in biology. As membership in the same species is predicated on the potential for particular organisms to breed among themselves, cross-species organisms were considered as less natural, if not as less fit.

Other research about creoles has focused on societal and inter-individual variation. Since DeCamp's (1971) seminal paper on this phenomenon in Jamaican Creole it has been designated as the **(post-)creole speech continuum**, thus associated, unjustifiably, with **decreolization** *qua* debasilectalization. The latter terms designate a process by which the **basilect**, the variety that is structurally the most different from those of the local standard (the **acrolect**), approximates structures of the latter. History suggests that the continuum, which obtains in any **language community**, must have been inherent in creole **speech communities**

175

since their beginnings. An interesting question (arising especially from Lalla and D'Costa 1990, Chaudenson 2001 and Mufwene 2001) is also whether the acrolect is a separate language from the creole, commonly identified primarily with the basilect. Due to space constraints, I can cover in this chapter only a subset of the above questions, especially that of their emergence. I start by explaining what kinds of languages are called *creoles* and *pidgins*.

DEFINING AND DESCRIBING CREOLES AND PIDGINS

As best characterized by the first two of Robert Chaudenson's (2001) 'unities of time, place, and action', creoles are new vernaculars that emerged during the seventeenth and eighteenth centuries from non-standard varieties of European languages in (sub)tropical plantation settlement colonies around the Atlantic, in the Indian Ocean, and in the Pacific. These are generally settings where Europeans came to settle new homes and the colonial, European languages were always used as vernaculars, the case of Hawaii being somewhat atypical (see below). The non-European populations who appropriated them and modified them into creoles were also not indigenous to the colonies (characterized by Chaudenson as *exogenous*) and became the overwhelming majorities quite early, while the Natives were marginalized, driven out of their ancestral land, and/or killed by the new European rulers. (Hawaii is also partly atypical in this case, as its indigenous population has survived to some extent.) The relevant colonies were typically insular or coastal, associated with the cultivation of sugar cane (the case of the majority, such as Surinam, Jamaica, Guyana, Haiti, Hawaii, Louisiana, Martinique, and Mauritius) or rice (coastal South Carolina and Georgia, in the United States). Coffee cultivation also became an important industry in the Caribbean and the Indian Ocean. These agricultural industries generated particular population structures in which non-Europeans quickly became overwhelming majorities. The segregation that ensued fostered the **divergence** of the new, non-European varieties of the colonial languages into creoles, under variable **substrate** influence.

However, the above characterization reflects only the way these colonial vernaculars have been studied to date. There is a long list of exceptions. For instance, Brazil, the first colony to have exploited sugar cane industrially, did not produce a creole; neither did Cuba or the present Dominican Republic, which are also insular. On the other hand, Cape Verde and Curaçao produced creoles, although they developed no agricultural industries. And there are other creole-speaking territories like Guinea Bissau and Sierra Leone, whose creoles were originally imported from other places (Cape Verde in the former case and primarily Jamaica in the second), although they have undergone further evolutions triggered by the new ecologies of their usage. The latter two are not plantation settlement colonies either. These differential evolutions of European languages in the colonies should make us cautious about generalizing too hastily regarding the particular conditions under which creoles evolved and the specific restructuring mechanisms involved in the process.

A careful, ecological approach to creoles and pidgins (based largely on historical, economic and social consideration of colonization) will also show that, contrary to the received doctrine, pidgins are not the ancestors of creoles. The map in Figure 21.1 reveals a geographical complementary distribution of places around the world where creoles and pidgins lexified by European languages emerged. Although Hawai'i appears to be an exception, note that its pidgins evolved on the plantations, in which, unlike in the New World and the Indian Ocean, the contract labourers lived in houses that were segregated **ethnolinguistically**. Thus, the members of each group (Chinese, Japanese, Portuguese, Korean, and Filipino) socialized primarily among themselves and used the pidgin they developed literally for minimal interactions with members of the other groups. This is indeed the explanation for the survival of traditional ethnic distinctions among the descendants of former contract labourers in Hawai'i. In the New World and the Indian Ocean, ethnic mixing since the *homestead* phase (homesteads, called *habitations* in French, were farm-size dwellings, without a major agricultural industry in place) led to the obliteration of such ancestral distinctions.

Also, the first variety to be called *pidgin* emerged in Canton, in the late eighteenth century, lexified primarily by English (Baker and Mühlhäusler 1990; Bolton 2000). According to the received doctrine, the term evolved from the Cantonese pronunciation of *business* in *business English*, which some sources then recorded derisively as *pigeon English*. According to Smith and Matthews (1996), a more probable etymology would be the Cantonese phrase *bei chin* 'pay money', which makes sense if one factors in the fact that Chinese Pidgin English emerged in a trade setting and Cantonese has a voicing alternation **phonological** rule affecting **obstruents**.

Unlike creoles, pidgins have typically been associated with trade colonies, settings which Europeans initially did not intend to settle permanently and in which their languages, or some indigenous languages (especially in the Americas), functioned only as **lingua francas**. The populations in contact spoke their native vernaculars within their respective groups. Pidgins have often been derided as **broken languages**, because their structures are very much reduced compared with those of their lexifiers. This state of affairs is a function of the naturalistic conditions of the learners' attempts to appropriate the target language without tutoring or sufficient exposure to it, and only for minimal communication. In the case of European languages, contacts between fluent speakers and learners were sporadic, aside from the fact that the targets were non-standard varieties and the model speakers did not always have native competence. For instance, according to Huber (1999), a Portuguese pidgin seems to have functioned as a generalized trade language on the West African coast until about the early nineteenth century.

Both creoles and pidgins seem to have evolved gradually from close approximations of the lexifier to basilectal varieties. Critical in this evolutionary process is the role of *interpreters* in spreading the target language. In the case of creole vernaculars, these interpreters were the *creole slaves*, those who were locally born

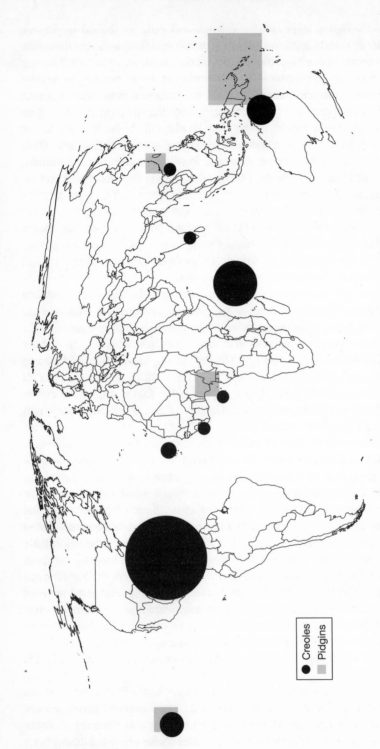

Figure 21.1 Geographical distribution of creoles and pidgins 'lexified' by Western European languages

and spoke closer approximations of the colonial languages during the homestead phase of the development of the colonies, in the seventeenth century. During the late seventeenth and eighteenth centuries, as the colonies shifted into the *plantation* phase (marked by the emergence of large plantations as the primary economic industry), the slave populations quickly became the overwhelming majorities. Eventually, the *bozal slaves* (freshly brought from Africa) also became more numerous than their creole counterparts. The varieties of the colonial languages to which they were exposed diverged more and more significantly from the varieties spoken during the homestead phase (see below). This basilectalization process, which produced modern creoles, is thus simply divergence evolution under the selective influence of the languages previously spoken by the bozal slaves. This has been identified as substrate influence.

In the case of pidgins, history informs us that the initial contacts of Europeans with the indigenous populations with whom they traded were mediated by interpreters. The latter learned closer approximations of the European lingua francas. As trade increased and increasing numbers of Natives interacted directly with the traders, more and more Natives attempted to use what they had heard the interpreters speak. This evolution in language practice was bound to restructure the target away from its original form, under the selective substrate influence. As in the case of creoles, the significance of this influence can be expected to have increased once the European language was used as a lingua franca also among the Natives themselves. The more typologically similar the substrate languages were, the more they could influence the new language variety away from its lexifier, as is evident from the Melanesian pidgins (see, for example, Keesing 1988). This factor may have fostered the myth that the lexifier did not make a significant grammatical contribution to the structures of its creole and pidgin offspring.

The term *pidgin* has been extended to structurally and functionally reduced varieties of some non-European languages whose emergence is also associated with trade, such as Chinook Jargon (in the American north-west), Delaware Jargon (in the north-eastern part of the United States), Mobilian Jargon (in the American south-east), and Lingua Geral (in south-eastern Brazil). Although some have also been identified in Asia and Africa (the early stages of Baba and Bahasa Malay in the Strait of Malacca, and those of Kikongo-Kituba, Lingala, and Sango in central Africa, for example), it is noteworthy that no pidgins lexified by European languages can be identified in the Americas. Could it mean that in these particular cases the Europeans adopted a variety that was already functioning as a trade language among the Natives themselves? Like most other questions, future research may answer this one conclusively.

To date, most of these pidgins have died, for instance the Portuguese lingua franca used by European traders and the indigenous pidgins of the Americas. Changes in the socio-economic ecologies of the relevant territories made them useless. Others adapted to these changes differently and evolved into more complex varieties called **expanded pidgins**, which now function primarily as urban vernaculars, for instance, Tok Pisin (in Papua New Guinea), and Nigerian and

Cameroon pidgin Englishes. Only Tok Pisin is associated with plantation exploitation colonization (in territories which Europeans dominated politically and exploited economically from the mid-1800s to the mid-1900s in the primary interest of the relevant metropoles but did not settle as new homes).

Expanded pidgins are all as complex as creoles, which does not necessarily entail that creoles are nativized or vernacularized pidgins, contrary to the received doctrine. From an evolutionary perspective, the evolution means that the structural complexity of a language is partly a function of the diversity of its domains of usage. All speakers, adults and children, natives and non-natives, are involved in the complexification process, as a language evolves through the cumulation of exaptations (accidental adaptations sometimes unrelated to the original function) which speakers make during their communicative acts. Such exaptations include substrate influence and other processes identified as innovations, (including the now popular process of **grammaticization**, the evolution of new grammatical functions from current lexical items).

A factor that has typically been overlooked in studies of the development of creoles is the role played by interpreters in the initial stages of the colonial human contacts. It bears on the question of whether, as claimed in most of the genetic creolistics literature, there was a break in the transmission of the lexifier. It also bears on the question of whether creoles and pidgins emerged abruptly, like biological gene mutations, or evolved gradually, like non-mutant biological populations. In the case of pidgins lexified by European languages, colonial history reveals that communication between the European traders and the Natives was facilitated by interpreters who, at the onset of colonization, had learned the target in Europe, in the case of Portuguese, or locally from missionaries, in the case of English in China and Hawaii in the late eighteenth and early nineteenth centuries respectively. That is, the original trade languages consisted of closer approximations of target languages, which diverged away structurally, with a reduced morphosyntax, once trade intensified, there were too few interpreters, and more and more Natives traded directly with the Europeans. This account suggests that modern West African English pidgins may have emerged only in the nineteenth century, after the abolition of the slave trade, as the latter practice would have discouraged the kind of interactions nurturing the widespread usage of a European language among Africans. Earlier English varieties used during the slave trade and reported by, for instance, Hancock (1980) need not have been pidgins.

In the case of creoles, the interpreters of the homestead phase were creole slaves, who acquired the colonial languages natively and who eventually served as language models to, and *seasoned* (roughly 'enculturated'), the *bozal* slaves. Once the latter grew demographically superior, more and more of them were seasoned by non-creole slaves who had simply arrived earlier. This ecological change favoured the basilectalization of the colonial vernacular among the slaves. History suggests that, since the transmission of the European language did not have to depend on regular contacts between Europeans and non-Europeans, the interpreters assured continuity in the spread of the trade language or colonial vernacular even at a time when settlement colonies became racially segregated.

THE DEVELOPMENT OF CREOLES

Quite a few hypotheses have been proposed since the late 1970s on the development of creoles. They mark a shift away from the concern in the 1960s over whether these varieties emerged from the same Mediterranean or West African proto-pidgin, or whether they developed independently but resemble each other structurally because of other structural and ecological factors. Creolists such as Taylor (1960), Thompson (1961), and Whinnom (1965) defended a **monogenesis** hypothesis, arguing that modern creoles and pidgins had all evolved either from the Mediterranean lingua franca used for trade since the Middle Ages or from the Portuguese lingua franca used on the West African coast from the sixteenth century to the nineteenth (the original **relexification** hypothesis). By the 1970s the consensus was on **polygenesis** (separate developments). It was then also assumed quite unanimously (at least since Schuchardt 1914 and Bloomfield 1933) that creoles had emerged from pidgins by **nativization** – the acquisition of the pidgins as mother tongues and vernaculars – and the ensuing complexification and stabilization of their structures.

Today, the main competing accounts are the **substrate hypothesis** (invoking substrate influence as the primary explanation for the structural peculiarities of creoles), the **superstrate hypothesis** (emphasizing the origin of the individual structural peculiarities in the non-standard varieties of the lexifier), the language **bioprogram** hypothesis (invoking the agency of children to account for structural similarities among the new vernaculars), and imperfect second language learning/ acquisition (which has not been dubbed a particular name). Many creolists interested in the origins issue support hybrid positions.

The substrate hypothesis (lately defended especially by Alleyne 1980, Holm 1988 and Keesing 1988) is about as old as genetic creolistics itself, going back to late nineteenth-century French philologists such as Adam (1883), Vinson (1882), and Baissac (1880), who attributed the structural divergence of creoles from their lexifiers to features of the non-European languages previously spoken by their learners. The only difference is that modern substratists do not consider the substrate languages as inferior or their speakers as anatomically and mentally ill-equipped to learn the sophisticated structures of the European languages.

The strong modern version of the substratist account is known as the relexification hypothesis. According to its proponents (chiefly Lefebvre 1998), Haitian Creole (about which the hypothesis, incorrectly also associated with Sylvain 1936, has been developed) is Ewe-Fon spoken with a French vocabulary. Obviously, any variety that is a by-product of the naturalistic appropriation of a language by a non-native group of speakers will normally be influenced by the languages previously spoken by its new speakers. However, to date, research on second language acquisition has identified no learners who have modified a target language in the way claimed by relexificationists. Otherwise, substrate influence is not mutually exclusive with any other account of creoles' structural features, provided there is a principled explanation of the specific structural and/or language-external conditions under which specific features from particular (groups of) languages are selected into the creoles' structures.

The superstrate hypothesis is a misnomer, because creolists such as Chaudenson (2001) and Mufwene (2001), to whom the position is attributed, do not deny substrate influence on the structures of creoles. Assuming that creoles' structural features originate in the lexifier, which was targeted by the learner, does not entail that the features were integrated intact in the emergent vernacular. As with the substrate hypothesis, one must account in a principled way for the selection of particular variants of the lexifier's features, sometimes from different dialects, into creoles' structures. Since language appropriation does not entail faithful replication, allowance must be made for some features to have been modified and a few others to have been introduced selectively, under specific language-external conditions. This is indeed a useful way of invoking influence from substrate languages on features of the lexifier which were selected and restructured into creoles' systems. This modification-cum-integration of both the substratist and superstratist positions is known as the **complementary hypothesis** (Mufwene 1986, 2001). Part of the debate remains over whether creoles are genetic offspring of their lexifiers or should be denied this connection, as claimed by creolists such as Thomason (2001).

The language bioprogram hypothesis (Bickerton 1981, 1984, 1999) can also be related to the same late nineteenth-century philologists who also claimed that creoles' structures reflect the mental inferiority of the minds that produced them, minds in their most natural and pristine states unaffected by artefacts of the 'more evolved' European cultures. Bickerton assumes that the pidgins that allegedly preceded the creoles were syntaxless. The children who appropriated these lingua francas of their parents as vernaculars would have assigned them a grammar inspired by Universal Grammar, which he calls the *bioprogram*. This common kind of genesis would account for structural similarities among creoles, a fact that typological diversity among the substrate languages cannot account for.

However, even creoles that have evolved from the same lexifier also differ among themselves in respect to some structural features. The bioprogram is not the only factor that can account for their family resemblance, because, as observed by Chaudenson (2001), the structures of the non-standard varieties of the relevant European languages are also very similar. Moreover, the different combinations of substrate languages that came in contact with them were very similar from one colony to another. Parallel modifications of more or less the same target structures under similar substrate influence would yield similar structural outputs. The proposed reinvention of a language from scratch seems cognitively costly and has no parallel in any other setting of language 'transmission'. In addition, while the structures of pidgins may reveal more internal variation than any other language, owing largely to differences in substrate influence on its different **idiolects**, this state of affairs does not entail absence of syntax.

The imperfect-second-language-learning hypothesis as proposed by especially Sankoff (1979) and Thomason and Kaufman (1988) is an attempt to reconcile the non-relexificationist substrate hypothesis and the language bioprogram hypothesis, invoking universal principles of second language acquisition, acknowledging substrate influence through interference from the learner's mother tongue, and making allowance for adults, putatively the primary agents of the divergence of creoles' structures from those of their lexifiers, to have access to the language bioprogram. One must, however, recognize that substrate features would not have been selected into creoles' structures if children acquiring language in those settings where the lexifier itself was available had not picked up the divergent features from the adult populations and made them available to those to whom they served as model speakers (DeGraff 1999).

A more significant problem is the exclusive association, by Thomason and Kaufman, of imperfect language learning with creoles and the like. All language 'acquisition' is imperfect replication, which explains why languages change. The changes reflect modification of the local ecological conditions, including novel communicative challenges, even when the relevant community of speakers has not been in contact with other communities (Mufwene 2001). Claiming that changes are more extensive under contact conditions sheds no light on the distinction between the restructuring which results in a creole and that which does not, especially since there are no change-inducing processes, or a particular combination thereof, that are specific to creoles. Nor is there a yardstick that enables linguists to measure the threshold of changes undergone by a particular language in order to identify it as a creole.

Mufwene (2001) and DeGraff (2003) have assumed a uniformitarian position, arguing that creoles have evolved by the same restructuring processes observable in the evolution of other languages. What makes them peculiar is perhaps the triggering ecological changes that have been claimed to be specific to them. However, every language has evolved more or less singularly, according to specific ecological changes affecting its ancestor. Genetic creolistics seems to be inviting linguists loud and clear to rethink the practice of genetic linguistics, including historical dialectology, focusing on the role of both the internal and external ecologies of a language in its evolution. The latter term applies to all sorts of changes, including structural and pragmatic, language speciation/diversification, and developments resulting in the gradual birth of new varieties or death of some of the current ones (see Chapters 14 and 24).

FURTHER READING

Chaudenson, R. (2001) *Creolization of Language and Culture*, London: Routledge.
DeGraff, M. (ed.) (1999) *Language Creation and Language Change: Creolization, Diachrony, and Development*, Cambridge, MA: MIT Press.
Holm, J. (1989) *Pidgins and Creoles* Vol. II, *Reference Survey*. Cambridge: Cambridge University Press.

Kouwenberg, S. and Singler, J.V. (eds) (2005) *The Handbook of Pidgin and Creole Studies*, Malden, MA: Blackwell.

Mufwene, S.S. (2001) *The Ecology of Language Evolution*, Cambridge: Cambridge University Press.

22

KOINEIZATION

DONALD N. TUTEN

The term **koineization** refers to a process of **mixing** of **dialects** (or mutually intelligible **varieties** of language) which leads to the rapid formation of a new dialect or **koine**, characterized by mixing, **levelling** and **simplification** of features found in the dialects which formed part of the original mix. Koineization generally occurs over the course of three generations (including first-generation adults during the 'pre-koine') and is often found in new towns, frontier regions and colonies which have seen sudden in-migration followed by the establishment of a permanent community. This chapter discusses the origins of the terms and concepts *koine* and *koineization*, typical types of linguistic change associated with koine formation, the social conditions and speaker behaviour which lead to those changes, and the time scale of koineization, or focusing.

FROM KOINE TO KOINES AND KOINEIZATION

Originally, Koine (*meaning* 'common, shared') was a variety of ancient Greek that first arose during the expansion of the Athenian empire in the fifth century BCE and which came to be the primary variety of Greek used throughout the eastern Mediterranean following the conquests of Alexander the Great in the fourth century BCE. It developed from older dialects such as the Attic dialect of Athens and the Ionic dialects of Asia Minor, and showed mixing and simplification of features from these dialects.

In the twentieth century, scholars often employed the term *koine* to refer to any common or widely shared variety of language. More recently sociolinguists have come to use the term rather more specifically: to refer to a variety of a language, normally showing mixing, levelling and simplification, which develops as a result of rapid population movement and mixing of speakers of different dialects in a new community. Koineization is a model which seeks to describe and explain the processes which lead to the formation of a koine. In recent years, such processes have drawn growing attention as it has become clear that immigration and dialect mixing leading to koine formation have occurred at many times in many languages.

The developments of certain language varieties have been closely studied as examples of koineization, and their developments have, in turn, been important in outlining the basic processes of koineization. These studies include the following:

1 The local dialect of the town of Høyanger in Norway, which saw a large and rapid increase in its population between 1916 and 1920, with mixing of eastern and western dialects of Norwegian (Omdal 1977).

2 The speech of the new town of Milton Keynes in England (see Kerswill and Williams 2000a, b), which was founded in 1967 and populated by a mix of persons of varied dialectal backgrounds.

3 Varieties of overseas Hindi-Bhojpuri (Barz and Siegel 1988), which developed in the nineteenth century when groups of Indian workers of varied dialectal origin were moved to English colonies such as Fiji, Guyana, and South Africa.

4 The English dialects of former British colonies such as Australia and New Zealand (Trudgill 1986, 2004).

5 European and colonial varieties of Spanish (Penny 2000; Tuten 2003), which developed over centuries of expansion and settlement.

These regions and language varieties represent highly prototypical cases of koineization, but the model of koineization is also likely to be of value in explaining the development of the speech of any city or region which receives large rapid inflows of immigrants speaking a variety of dialects.

THE LINGUISTIC CHANGES OF KOINEIZATION

There are several types of linguistic change which have occurred regularly in cases of koineization, including mixing, levelling, **reallocation**, simplification, and **interdialect**.

Mixing, levelling, reallocation

These terms are used to refer in different ways to the effects of what is essentially a process of selection of forms. Mixing highlights the selection and incorporation of linguistic features from the different pre-existing dialects which contribute to the pre-koine linguistic pool (the language used by the first generation of immigrants). Levelling, on the other hand, emphasizes the **reduction** or elimination of marked or minority **variants** and the selection of high-frequency or majority variants found in the pre-koine. So, for example, the Fiji Hindi pre-koine, which showed mixture from a variety of Bhojpuri-Hindi dialects, almost certainly included the competing forms /kja:/ and /ka:/ (meaning 'what') as well as the competing forms /ke/ and /kaun/ (meaning 'who'). However, it was the forms used with greatest absolute frequency – whatever dialect they were from – that survived in Fiji Hindi: /ka:/ for 'what' and /kaun/ for 'who' (Trudgill 1986: 101).

Such levelling is sometimes incomplete, with more than one dialectal variant surviving but each with a different function, generally social or stylistic. Thus, in Fiji Hindi, there exist two forms of the third person possessive, /okar/ from the Bhojpuri dialects and /uske/ from the Hindi varieties; the Hindi form has become the unmarked norm in Fiji Hindi, while the Bhojpuri form is considered rustic (Siegel 1997: 127).

Simplification and interdialect

Not all features of a koine can be found in pre-existing contributing dialects. These features generally arise through the process of speech **accommodation** with 'imperfect' dialect acquisition (see below), in which speaker-learners create new forms by altering existing dialect features in their own speech. A common way in which speaker-learners generate new forms and features is by replacing irregular forms with easy-to-generate regular or transparent forms (such forms may also exist in some contributing dialects, making their adoption even more likely). This process, known as simplification, can be defined as an increase in regularity or transparency, or as a general reduction in units and rules (particularly in **phonology** and **morphology**; phonemic mergers, for example, are one frequent outcome).

Many clear examples of simplification can be found in Spanish, a variety of Romance which has undergone several periods of koineization during its development. During the Middle Ages, irregular past tense (preterite) forms of most Spanish verbs were simplified: irregular *escrise* 'I wrote' became *escribí*, which is more easily generated and transparently related to the infinitive form *escribir*; similarly, *mise* 'I put (in)' was replaced by *metí*, clearly related to the infinitive *meter* (Penny 2000: 52). Simplification is particularly favoured when several irregular forms from different dialects enter into competition during koineization. For example, the conservative dialects which led to the formation of early Spanish all used contractions of prepositions and articles. This can be seen in the case of the preposition *en* 'in, on' and the feminine singular article *la* 'the', which were fused in different ways in different dialects: *enna, ena, na*. Such forms had to be memorized by speaker-learners (as is the case in the modern French contraction of *de* 'of' and *le* 'the' in *du* 'of the'), but during koineization these competing irregular forms were simplified to the transparent, regular and easily reproduced sequence *en la* 'in the' (Tuten 2003: 119).

Other features of koines, known as **interdialectalisms**, show a special kind of mixing, which results when speaker-learners reanalyse or rearrange forms and features of the contributing dialects. In their efforts to avoid marked variants, they may produce intermediate or 'fudged' phonetic realizations, as has been shown to be the case in Milton Keynes (Kerswill and Williams 2000a: 85). They may also pair forms and functions in novel ways, as can be seen in reallocation. They may mix parts of forms together to create new hybrid forms, such as when speakers in Høyanger mixed the dialectal forms *myra, myrar, myrer* 'songs' and created the novel *myre* (Trudgill 1986: 103). And, of course, speaker-learners often use a feature or form with greater frequency than it is used in any contributing dialect (statistical **hypercorrection**), and it is this phenomenon which underlies the general tendency for majority (or salient) variants to grow yet more frequent and become selected in the resultant koine.

CONDITIONS OF SPEAKER ACTIVITY: SOCIAL NETWORKS, ACCOMMODATION AND ACQUISITION

Understanding the linguistic changes which lead to the development of a new koine requires an understanding of the changing social conditions which affect the linguistic activity of speakers, which, of course, is what leads to the changes in the linguistic system. Prototypical koineization is always characterized by geographical movement of speakers of different dialects into a new town or region which is relatively unpopulated (or where the original population has been removed). Such speakers generally leave behind the more established **social networks** of their home communities and move to a new community where weak social ties and loose-knit social networks predominate, at least at first. As has been made abundantly clear in sociolinguistic research, stable close-knit social networks are conservative norm-enforcement mechanisms which impede change of all types. Conversely, the loose-knit social networks and weak social ties which characterize a koineizing community favour the introduction and adoption of innovations. At the same time, speakers enter into contact with speakers of other dialects, who are also removed from the constraints of their home communities. Thus, in the koineizing community, all speakers become innovators *vis-à-vis* speakers of other dialects, and variation *peaks* at the very time that the strength of norm-enforcement mechanisms *declines* to a minimum.

How do speakers respond in such a situation? According to British sociolinguist Peter Trudgill (1986), adult speakers attempt to accommodate to other speakers. As they work to develop new social networks, they change the way they speak so as to minimize differences. The easiest way for adult speakers to do this is by eliminating marked features of their speech (often sociolinguistic stereotypes which are likely to be noticed and even commented upon by others). However, they may also attempt to learn features used by other speakers, particularly those which they perceive to be frequent, salient, or socially valuable in some way. (For this reason it is helpful to conceive of language users as 'speaker-learners'.) Such accommodation and limited acquisition by adult speakers initiate the processes of mixing, levelling and simplification which characterize koineization.

Still, research by the British sociolinguist Paul Kerswill (1996) has shown that the most important accommodation between speakers probably takes place not among the first generation of adult immigrants but rather among their children and grandchildren. In part, this may be so because children are more capable learners of languages and dialects. But that cannot be the main reason, for it is not the youngest children who lead such changes, but rather older children (ages 6–12) and adolescents. This is because the youngest children are focused on their primary caregiver(s) and model their speech on those persons, while older children tend to switch their psychosocial orientation to their peers. In doing so they make great efforts to accommodate to and acquire the speech of their peers, in a process that leads to the negotiation of new norms.

If speaker-learners tend to accommodate to and learn features of others' speech, which features do they accommodate to? First and foremost, it seems that they accommodate to and acquire the features used with greatest frequency by original members of the pre-koine **speech community**. The primary exception to this is the tendency to use more regular and transparent forms and features, which are generated as speaker-learners eliminate marked features of their own speech, or when they are presented with so many variant irregular forms that they find it difficult to learn any one. In other words, inconsistency of use by adults and other children makes it more difficult for speaker-learners to learn a particular form or rule, and thus favours overgeneralization of more frequent or regular forms and rules by succeeding generations of children. In general, accommodation to and overgeneralization of high-frequency forms leads to the levelling of majority forms, while overgeneralization of regular or transparent forms/features by speaker-learners leads to simplification in the linguistic system. Such over-generalization is quite obviously favoured by lack of consistent input and lack of strong norm-enforcement mechanisms.

There are two significant exceptions to these generalizations, however. First, although speaker-learners do tend to accommodate to and overgeneralize high-frequency forms, it has been shown that at least some features are selected even though they are not majority items in the pre-koine linguistic pool. We must assume then that some forms and features tend to be perceived by speaker-learners as 'salient', that is, they are more noticed and may be reproduced with sufficient frequency to become a feature in the new koine. It is not entirely clear what makes a form or feature 'salient', although high frequency certainly helps. It has been claimed that stressed items and items coming at the beginning of syllables, words and phrases tend to be cognitively prominent, and are thus more likely to be noticed and learned, but generalizations such as this have not been consistently useful in explaining which features become salient to speaker-learners. Indeed, it has become increasingly clear that forms and features, even if cognitively prominent in some way, must acquire salience through social and cultural conditioning (see Kerswill and Williams 2002). How this happens is not well understood, but it may be that research in **perceptual dialectology** will add to our understanding.

The other important exception to the above generalizations stems from the fact that many speaker-learners sometimes misanalyse – or reanalyse – the linguistic input, and therefore introduce entirely novel forms or features. In general, such reanalyses remain as minority variants in the linguistic pool, and are eliminated in the process of levelling. However, on occasion they do survive if enough speaker-learners make the same reanalysis. Examples of this are not frequent in the literature on koineization, but one dramatic example comes from the development of *leísmo*, found today in the Spanish of central northern Spain. It seems that medieval koineization led to an unusual extension of the indirect object pronoun *le* ('to him/her/it') to use as a masculine singular direct object pronoun (normally *lo*). This seems to have occurred because, at the time of koineization, both *le* and *lo* (or its precursor) suffered vowel deletion, with both reduced to /l/. However, deletion of final /-e/ was a far more frequent phenomenon than deletion of any other vowel, and speaker-learners in the koineizing context hypercorrected, interpreting direct object /l/ as a short form of *le*, and from there began to use *le* as a direct object (see Tuten 2003: 198). This reanalysis introduced an apparently anomalous change into the system, though from the perspective of speaker-learners it was probably a simplifying change. This example is also useful because it shows – contrary to popular belief – that koineization does not consist merely of reduction to a 'lowest common denominator'. Koines are indeed compromise varieties, but they may contain quite novel features.

THE TIMESCALE OF KOINEIZATION

How long does it take for new linguistic norms to focus or stabilize in a new koine? Most scholars now agree that focusing will normally take place over the course of three generations: the first generation of (adult) in-migrants, the second generation (children of the first generation) and the third generation (children of the second). While the adults of the first generation probably do make some accommodations, it is not strictly speaking necessary for them to alter their speech in any way, for the most important accommodation and acquisition will take place among the older children and adolescents of the second and third generations.

Of course, this three-generation model is merely prototypical. Focusing of new norms may reach near completion by the second generation (as appears to be the case in Milton Keynes), or it may take much longer than three generations, in which case the researcher will have to explain why koineization was retarded. In every case, certain factors must be present for focusing to occur. Speakers must interact freely and form new social networks, and, most important, they must develop a common identity which is marked linguistically. Some scholars also believe that the degree of lexical and structural similarity between the contributing dialects can increase the rate of focusing, but this is probably secondary to the development of new social ties and a common identity.

CONCLUSION

Ultimately, any study of koineization will aim to study not just linguistic outcomes or the conditions of speaker activity, but rather the links between the two. Indeed, it is the study of these links that makes the study of koineization so valuable, for it has become a means by which scholars can respond to the **actuation problem**, or the fundamental question of how and why linguistic changes occur when and where they do.

FURTHER READING

Kerswill, P. and Trudgill, P. (2005) 'The birth of new dialects', in P. Auer, F. Hinskens and P. Kerswill (eds) *Dialect Change: Convergence and Divergence in European Languages*, Cambridge: Cambridge University Press.

Kerswill, P. and Williams, A. (2000a) 'Creating a new town koine: children and language change in Milton Keynes', *Language and Society* 29: 65–115.

Trudgill, P. (1986) *Dialects in Contact*, Oxford: Blackwell.

Trudgill, P. (2004) *New Dialect Formation: The Inevitability of Colonial Englishes*, Edinburgh: Edinburgh University Press.

Tuten, D.N. (2003) *Koineization in Medieval Spanish*, Berlin and New York: Mouton de Gruyter.

23

COLONIAL AND POSTCOLONIAL VARIETIES

BARBARA A. FENNELL

The topic of language, colonialism and postcolonialism is very broad and takes the linguistic observer in the West at least as far back as the Greek and Roman empires. It can be approached from a variety of angles, starting with an examination of the macro-social and political function of language in colonial, imperial and post-colonial situations, considering for example the different ways that colonial and imperial powers exerted their **hegemony** through language. This might include the overt banning of the use of (an) indigenous language(s) (as in Stalinist Russia), or more indirect inculcation of colonial or imperial values and ideologies through education in the colonial language, which features the programmatic use of cultural icons and economic models.

On the linguistic level, one might examine how language changes when it is separated from the core and transplanted to new and often both literally and meta-phorically distant physical, social, cultural and political contexts. As well as looking at and for processes and significant features of language variation and change, one would need to consider the impact on an individual(s) and on (a) language(s) of contact with other indigenous or immigrant **dialects** and languages, which in turn would engender questions about patterns of **multilingual** communication, language choice and **identity** issues. Here, again, there are significant differences between colonial contexts where there is one dominant colonial language affording or requiring direct contact with native speakers of indigenous languages, and those contexts in which contact with the prestige language is restricted, possibly leading to the development of (stable) pidgins and creoles, such as those that developed in the Caribbean and the American South.

At the beginning of the twenty-first century it is accepted that English is a world language and that part of the reason for its spread is that it has been used as a language by colonizers for hundreds of years: indeed, since the twelfth century. Given the status and extent of English across the globe, particularly since the end of World War II, it is also possible to examine language, colonialism and post-colonialism from the point of view of the development of the English language, enquiring how external **varieties** of English (New Zealand English, Canadian English, South African English, for example) emerged in the colonial, imperial and Commonwealth eras, and how they have evolved and function in postcolonial times. This also entails consideration of the 'new Englishes' which have emerged in countries such as Malaysia, where English was never spoken as a native lan-guage by any significant portion of the population but where its use is regarded as crucial for scientific, economic, political and cultural competitiveness and advancement.

Finally, in providing such a (necessarily brief) overview of language, colonialism and postcolonialism, one must always take into account that besides English there have been numerous other important colonial and imperial languages, some of the best documented being Greek, Latin, Spanish, Portuguese and French in the West, while languages such as Russian, Japanese and Chinese also have a long and fascinating colonial and imperial linguistic history (see Comrie 1981; Phillipson 1992).

At the macro level it is important to bear in mind that each colonial power, whether, for example, Britain, France, Rome, China or Russia, organized and administered its territories differently, depending on the ideology of the rulers and the particular circumstances of the individual colony or territory under its control. Consequently, language performed a different array of functions under different regimes. While the colonial masters all used language more or less consciously as a political tool, they used it in different ways, depending on the political systems they were propagating. France, for example, usually pursued a policy of direct rule, under which an idealized version of (Île-de-France) French was imposed upon its subjects. Education from primary school on aimed to cultivate individual citizens who were perfectly **monolingual** in Standard French, thereby continuing the policy of suppressing **minority languages** that had been operative within France itself. As a consequence, the use of local languages was not allowed in school at all, even in the playground. One result of this francophone preoccupation was that **literacy** was brought to certain parts of Africa where there had been none before French rule and this is reflected in the fact that in postcolonial Africa there are still a number of countries that retain French as an **official language** (Morocco, Algeria, Congo). In other words, the policy of linking the requirement for French with the attainment of citizenship and the privileges it afforded individuals had important consequences for the spread of French within a particular colonial context, and for the linguistic legacy it left in the postcolonial era.

Britain, on the other hand, usually pursued a policy of indirect rule, preferring to impose forms of government exerted by local hierarchies, who therefore needed to learn English for communication 'upwards', while using the local language(s) in interaction with those they ruled, thus establishing a stratified diffusion of English, with only those in positions of authority needing to learn and use English with any native or near-native competence. English was the language of administration and tertiary education, cementing the empire at a supranational level, and an individual needed to learn English only if he or she strove (opportunity permitting) for social, economic and/or political advancement. This kind of system, institutionalized in India for example in legal and civil service examinations that had to be taken in English, meant that language performed a kind of gatekeeping function, leaving huge sections of the population unable to gain access to a model of Standard English that they could acquire. This consequently led in

India to the development of what Kachru (1986b) referred to as a 'cline' of **bilingualism**, with speakers at the top of the hierarchy almost perfectly fluent in English and one (or more) native national language(s), with those further down the social scale more dependent on their local language(s), acquiring levels of proficiency, if any, in English that fell short of fluency and could constitute as little as a few words or phrases. Adopting terms from **pidgin** and **creole** linguistics, one could state that only the elite in India typically acquired **acrolectal**, or near-native, English, while the character of the English spoken further down the social order was progressively more pidgin-like or **basilectal**. Again, such policies have important consequences for **World English** and for the postcolonial legacy in countries previously under British rule.

It is inevitable in colonial situations that colonizer and colonized come into contact with new and alien phenomena, including contact with foreign languages and dialects. **Language contact** between indigenous and immigrant varieties can be the cause of linguistic change, but the exact outcomes of contact are entirely dependent on the peculiar circumstances of the contact. In some instances, language contact can lead to the complete loss of one or more languages, to the benefit of another or others. The colonizers might impose their language on the colonized, forcing them to become monolingual in the colonizing language (as with most Native Americans, Australian Aborigines); or they may eschew their own language in favour of the indigenous language or languages (or dialects) they encounter.

Most often, most transparently, and perhaps most trivially, language contact in colonial situations leads to lexical change, though the likelihood of grammatical, as well as lexical, influence increases, and there is also greater chance of mutual influence, where contact between languages is stable and prolonged (see McMahon 1994: 24).

Features of American English may be used to illustrate lexical change on encountering new flora, fauna, cultural concepts and geographical features, or when new socio-political structures develop. The standard processes are as follows: **borrowing**; semantic shift or extension from the original meaning of a word or words; **calquing** or loan translation; coining new words or deriving new words from old ones; and descriptive compounding. Locally established animal and plant names, place names and river names are often borrowed by colonizers from indigenous or established languages: for example, *skunk*, *squash*, *sumac*, *Milwaukee* and *Potomac* are typical loans from Native American languages, while *prairie*, *levee* and *bayou* are loans from the French, who were established in North America before the English-speakers and had their own terms for these new phenomena. *Corn*, *oak*, *bee* and *robin* are examples of semantic extension, since they are used in American English to refer to different flora and fauna from those they originally designated in British English. *Prairie dog* and *bullfrog* are examples of new compounds from the existing word stock. *Gubernatorial*, *caucus*, *presidential*, *senate*, *assembly* and *primary* are illustrations of common words that have developed as an independent American political system emerged. Differences between British and American spelling (e.g. *honour–honor, fibre–fiber, tyre–tire,* *cheque–check*), promulgated in the early nineteenth century by Noah Webster, reflect an attempt to assert linguistic independence from Britain and are significant in the development of a separate, endocentric, American standard.

Beyond providing the opportunity for borrowing words for new concepts (such as *pizza*, *piazza* and *mezzanine* from contact with Italian) encounters between colonial dialect speakers and immigrant learners of **English as a second language** can lead to **dialect levelling** and the emergence of a relatively uniform variety. There will be more on this in the discussion of New Zealand English below, but here we can point out that historians of the English language have frequently pointed to the uniform schooling of non-native speakers and the prevalence of Webster's *Blue Book Speller* in American schools as contributors to the relative unity of American English, which was often remarked on by early travellers (see Fennell 2000, for further discussion of the development of American English).

Montgomery (2004) provides us with excellent insights into the way colonial varieties are affected by contact on the grammatical level, when he considers the role of Ulster Scots in the formation of the Midland dialect of American English. While there is certainly lexical evidence for this, the syntactic evidence is less overt, and precisely for that reason, perhaps, resistant to change. Features such as combining *all* with interrogative pronouns ('What all is he doing?'); *want* + preposition (*want in*, *want out*); *whenever* meaning 'at the time that' for a single event in the past ('He wasn't born whenever we moved off') persist in modern Ulster and in the American midland today, and are, along with several other features, persuasively indicative of Ulster (Scots) influence on the dialect (Montgomery 2004: 318, and see Hickey 2004).

Depriving individuals of access to an adequate model of the dominant language can in extreme cases lead to the development of (stable) pidgins and creoles (see Chapter 21). Work by AAVE specialists has suggested that plantation culture and in particular isolation from whites were crucial to the **creolization** of English in the southern United States. (See Wolfram and Schilling-Estes 1999 and Edwards 2004 for further discussion.) What is typical for AAVE, Jamaican Creole and other creole varieties is that more egalitarian social structures and access to the **standard** lead to creole shifts towards the standard again. (See Fennell 1997 for a discussion of this process.)

Since the end of World War II, Britain and the other Western colonial and imperial powers have almost completely relinquished their dependencies and this has led to a variety of models of language use in the postcolonial era. It is ironic that, with the development of political independence from Britain (and to some extent the United States), the English language has developed into a true *Weltsprache*. Kachru (1985: 12) described the way English has spread around the world as a series of three concentric circles, where English primary language speakers (from the United States, the United Kingdom, Australia, Canada, Ireland and New Zealand) constitute the *inner circle*, countries such as India, Singapore, Guam and Liberia, which use English as an important second language in a multilingual setting, constitute the *outer circle*, and countries where English is used primarily as an **international language** (such as Russia, China, Japan) constitute the *expanding circle*. Much of this expansion has to do with the centrality of the English language to political, economic and intellectual enterprise on a world scale: much of that centrality has developed as a direct result of the colonial spread of English.

A recent twist in studies of colonial and postcolonial language is the great interest within English sociolinguistics in new dialect formation, which is the study of dialects that have been exported to colonial contexts and for which we have a significant amount of information regarding patterns of settlement and original dialect sources. A major aim of these studies, which concentrate on Australian, New Zealand and South African English, is to ascertain what processes are involved in the development of the expatriate variety and which factors are important in its development. This kind of study is concerned with processes of dialect levelling, **accommodation** and the emergence of 'compromise' dialects that are clearly different from Standard English in Britain but are clearly typologically very close to it.

In a collection of excellent papers on the legacies of colonial English edited by Hickey (2004) the focus is on three major issues:

1 What *input* went into which overseas variety.
2 The impact of dialect **mixing** and/or language contact on the structure of overseas varieties.
3 Evaluating different reasons for why extraterritorial varieties have the particular features they show.

(Hickey 2004: 1)

Hickey goes on to list a series of factors that shape colonial varieties:

1 Dialect input and the survival of features from a mainland source or sources.
2 Independent developments within the overseas communities, including realignments of features in the dialect input.
3 Contact phenomena where English speakers coexisted with those of other languages.
4 An indirect influence through the educational system in those countries in which English arose without significant numbers of native-speaker settlers.
5 Creolization in those situations where there was no linguistic continuity and where virtually the only input was a pidgin, based on English, from the preceding generation.

(Hickey 2004: 1–2).

In a related discussion Trudgill (2004: 1 ff.) proposes a combination of six main factors that may explain how colonial Englishes came to be different from the English of Britain, from which they stemmed. For the purpose of brevity, I generalize Trudgill's six factors here, though he himself takes American English as his point of departure and extrapolates from the American situation to other colonial varieties:

1 Colonial English adapts to topographical and biological features unknown in Britain.
2 Linguistic changes subsequently occur in English in Britain that do not occur in the colonial varieties.
3 Linguistic changes develop in the colonial varieties that do not occur in Britain.
4 The colonial varieties experience contact with different indigenous languages that English in Britain does not.
5 The colonial varieties may experience contact with European languages that Britain does not.
6 Processes of dialect contact influence the development of English in colonial situations differently from the way they influence British English, so that each develops from 'a unique blend of British types of speech' (Kurath 1949: 1).

(Trudgill 2004: 1–2)

With a few known exceptions (Newfoundland English, Rural Falkland Islands English, Cape Breton English) colonial Englishes developed as a result of dialect mixing as well as language contact and the other factors in Trudgill's list. Trudgill discounts **monogenetic** theories proposed for colonial varieties of English (with the exceptions above) and other languages. In particular he does not agree with Hammarström's (1980) claim that Australian English is transplanted Cockney, or Bauer's (2000) assertion that New Zealand English derives from a variety of English spoken in the south-east of England.

Though the emphasis in language histories has until recently been on *languages* in contact, *dialect* mixing is important in the development both of colonial varieties and of standard languages; indeed, this was certainly the case for English in the British Isles. It is also true of the development of Standard German, which emerged as an amalgam of a number of regional standard forms, given Germany's highly regionalized status, with the Saxon chancery standard eventually developing the greatest influence, itself deriving from a complex series of dialects, including those compromise dialects developed by colonial Germans in the east (see Keller 1978; Barbour and Stephenson 1999).

When we talk about dialect mixing in the context of the development of colonial varieties, we are referring not only to regional but also to social **accents** and dialects. As Trudgill points out, for example, in the continuum of New Zealand English, accents tend to become progressively 'broader' and further from Standard British English the lower the speaker is on the social scale. Both lexical and grammatical features reflect regional and social differences, with past participle forms as past tenses (e.g. 'I done that'; 'she seen him') and variation in subject–verb agreement ('it were raining'; 'we was robbed') illustrative of this point (Trudgill 2004: 14–15). Trudgill claims (2004: 20–3) that the similarity between Australian, New Zealand, South African and some Falkland Island English is likely to stem from the fact that these varieties developed from similar dialect mixtures.

The research of Trudgill and others on New Zealand English (Gordon *et al.* 2004) suggests that it takes about fifty years for a new unitary dialect to emerge from a dialect mixture situation (again, allowing for individual variation). This assertion also implies the importance of first and second-generation settlers in the development of colonial dialects. Trudgill argues that, given that colonial dialects develop in what he calls a '*tabula rasa*' situation (in a context where there were no speakers of the colonial language originally), it is possible to predict how colonial dialects will develop. That is, he argues for a certain amount of determinism in the emergence of colonial dialects (p. 28). This '*tabula rasa*' situation is, he argues, both crucial and unique to colonial situations and is not present for example in the development of new-town dialects (see Kerswill 1994). Trudgill (2004: 27) argues that it is second-generation speakers who generate a new pronunciation out of the mixture that their parents' generation represents. What is remarkable here is that they do not simply continue to speak their parents' varieties, part of the reason for which appears to be the need to 'talk like others talk' and therefore accommodate one's language to that of their peers. This would appear to be part of a universal tendency for speakers young and old to develop 'behavioural co-ordination' (Trudgill 2004: 28). Furthermore, children, who are the crucial force in developing a unified linguistic variety, are generally not yet sensitive to social factors such as **status** and **prestige**, which leads them to promote uniformity with those with whom they interact and to minimize difference.

Trudgill develops the argument that what renders the four southern hemisphere varieties of English different from the English of Britain is that they inherited the results of language changes that had occurred so far in Britain and then continued them after separation. With time, they continued to evolve in a similar variation after separation because of what Trudgill (2004) calls *drift*, which 'involves propensities to linguistic changes resulting from structural properties which varieties inherit'. This can even happen with features that are not present in the mother dialect before it is imported, allowing the colonial variety to develop in ways consistent with the typology of the language but differently from the source.

From this necessarily selective and condensed discussion, we can see that consideration of language, colonialism and postcolonialism entails far-reaching insights into the macro and micro issues of language variation and change. There are further consequences, of course, for language imposition and **language death** (see Chapter 24), and for **language policy** and **language planning** (see Chapter 20), which have implications for educational policy (see Chapter 19) as well.

FURTHER READING

Görlach, M. (1991) *Englishes: Studies in Varieties of English 1984–1988*, Amsterdam: Benjamins.

Görlach, M. (1998) *Even More Englishes: Studies 1996–1997*, Amsterdam: Benjamins.

Greenbaum, S. (1996) *Comparing English Worldwide: The International Corpus of English*, Oxford: Clarendon Press.

Jenkins, J. (2003) *World Englishes: A Resource Book for Students*, London: Routledge.

Prakash, G. (ed.) (1985) *After Colonialism: Imperial Histories and Postcolonial Displacements*, Princeton, NJ: Princeton University Press.

24

LANGUAGE DEATH

DIANE NELSON

Many of us are aware of the issue of 'biodiversity' in biology. In nature, ecosystems host a wide variety of plants, animals and microbes which rely on each other in complex ways to survive. Because of human activity, many species are now becoming endangered or extinct. If many extinctions happen at the same time in an ecosystem, biologists and ecologists worry that the whole system will be thrown out of balance, causing further extinctions. When plants and animals are threatened with extinction, biodiversity campaigners try to raise public awareness and funds to protect such species, for example the Sumatran tiger, the mountain gorilla and the whooping crane. At the moment, so many species are becoming endangered that biologists talk of a 'biodiversity crisis' in progress.

However, what many don't realize is that a similar crisis is happening in linguistic diversity, and that the scale of the crisis is even greater. The statistics are astonishing. At the moment, linguists believe, around 6,000 languages are spoken around the world. Michael Krauss, a linguist who works on **endangered languages**, has predicted that by the end of this century 90 per cent of languages currently spoken will be extinct (see Hale *et al*. 1992). The Foundation for Endangered Languages estimates that half the world's languages are moribund, which means that they are no longer being passed on to younger generations. The linguist David Crystal (2000, 2003) calculates that a language dies every two weeks. In Australia alone, out of the 260 aboriginal languages originally spoken, 100 are already extinct, 100 are nearly extinct and only around twenty are being passed on to children.

Before we look at the causes of the current extinctions, it is important to define what we mean by **endangered languages** and the notion of 'threats' to languages. Anyone who reads the letters to the editor in most UK newspapers might be under the impression that English is a 'threatened language'. Every week someone complains that bad spelling, sloppy usage or **borrowing** from other languages is causing the death of English. Similar sentiments can be found in France, Japan, Iceland or just about anywhere that prints newspapers. However, none of these languages is endangered in any real sense; they are simply undergoing natural processes of language change. Any language that has official national status and is used by the legal system, education and the media is not going to disappear any time soon.

Other speakers who often feel their language is under threat live in immigrant communities. For grandparents who speak Finnish in Canada or Hungarian in

Argentina it can be heartbreaking to see grandchildren growing up without speaking a word of the ancestral language. In many of these communities, projects are under way to keep the languages in use. In some towns in Massachusetts, for example, Armenian American children can study Armenian at school. The question is, are these endangered languages? The answer would have to be no, because even if a language dies within an immigrant community, there are still plenty of speakers back home. The vast majority of truly endangered languages are spoken by indigenous peoples who have lived in their region for many generations.

We might then consider using numbers of speakers as a way to decide if a language is endangered. Michael Krauss argues that, for a language to survive, it needs at least 100,000 speakers (see Hale *et al.* 1992). However, this turns out to be more complicated than it seems. For example, L.R. Storto (2003) notes that there are only 185 speakers of Karitiana in Brazil, but out of a total community population of 191. Although 185 seems like a very small number, Karitiana-speakers still make up 96 per cent of the population of their community. At the other extreme, Yiddish, with around 3 million speakers, is considered by many to be an endangered language. Unlike the Karitiana community, most speakers of Yiddish are elderly and very few are children. This means that the language is not being passed on to the next generation, and so is under threat of extinction. Simply counting the number of speakers, then, is not the best way to decide if a language will survive. Instead, the viability of a language depends on how well it is being passed on to children.

The next question we may ask is, why do languages die? We can identify three different types of **language death**. The first may be seen as 'death through change'. To most people the term 'dead language' means an ancient language, such as Latin, Ancient Greek or Old English. We know about them because speakers of these languages left behind written documents, but it is certain that thousands of other ancient languages died without a trace because they were never written down. These languages are technically extinct because they have no native speakers and are no longer being passed on to children. On the other hand, the three languages all 'died' because they gradually developed into new languages: Latin became the modern Romance language family, including French, Portuguese and Italian; Ancient Greek became Modern Greek; Old English became Modern English. This kind of 'death' can be seen as part of an inevitable process for all languages.

Another, more radical type of language extinction is linked with the sudden death or scattering of an entire community of speakers. Sometimes this is due to natural disasters. For example, in 1998 an earthquake off the coast of Papua New Guinea killed and displaced thousands of speakers of Arup, Malol, Sissano and Warupu. In other cases, genocide or invasion is the cause of language death. After the arrival of Christopher Columbus in 1492 the Spanish rounded up the entire Taino population of the Bahamas and sold them into slavery. No indigenous Caribbean languages survive today. British settlers in Australia hunted down the aborigines of Tasmania in the nineteenth century; their languages are all now extinct. In 1835 Maori warriors from New Zealand sailed eastward to the Chatham Islands and killed the men of the Moriori tribe. The Morioris went into decline and the last full-blooded member of the tribe died in 1933, along with their language.

Today, the most common cause of language death is not population death, but **language shift**. This happens when speakers of a language do not pass it on to their children. Instead, the children acquire a different language from the parents, and gradually the language of the entire community 'shifts'. Unlike the extinction of an animal species, the people don't die, only their language does. According to sociolinguist Joshua Fishman (1991), a typical case of language shift can happen over three generations. First, a generation of speakers of language X, the grandparents, do not pass their language on to their children and encourage them to speak another language, Y. The next generation, the parents, grow up with only a passive knowledge of X but as fluent speakers of Y. The household is **bilingual** in both languages. Their children grow up as full speakers of Y, knowing a few words of X at the most and perhaps wishing they knew more of their ancestral language. If this process of shift happens in most of the families in a community, a language may die in only three generations.

This raises an important question: why would parents decide *not* to pass on their own language to their children in the first place? In looking at this issue, some linguists use the metaphors **language murder** and **language suicide**. According to this view, language 'murder' happens when governments or other institutions try to 'kill off' **minority languages** by passing laws or punishing speakers; this puts pressure on speakers from the outside. Language 'suicide' happens when people in a community feel they would be better off economically, politically or socially if they spoke a different language; this means that pressure comes from the inside to stop using their 'worthless' language and adopt a new 'useful' one. Other linguists, such as Daniel Nettle and Suzanne Romaine (2000), see 'murder' and 'suicide' as two sides of the same coin. They argue that speakers of a minority language do not suddenly decide that their language is worthless out of the blue. Instead, these feelings are often the result of generations of political and social disadvantage forced on them by speakers of the 'majority' or **national language**. To explain how this situation came to be so widespread around the world, we need to go back deep into prehistory to find out why speakers of some languages clearly have more power and resources than others.

Jared Diamond (1997), an evolutionary biologist, historian and biogeographer, explores this question. Travelling around the world in the current century, it is clear that people in the West have more wealth and power than people in the developing world, particularly Africa, South America and parts of Asia. Many of the **official languages** in the world, such as English, French and Spanish, come from Europe. Clearly this is related to the fact that Western European nations colonized much of the world up to the twentieth century. But why did the Spanish arrive on the shores of Latin America, instead of the Latin Americans arriving on the shores of Spain? Diamond argues that the roots of the current imbalance in the world's wealth and power can be traced back to the origins of farming. People living in

Europe and Asia 12,000 years ago had access to plants and animals that could be easily domesticated. This led to the beginning of farming, which allowed people to produce more food than they actually needed to survive. Towns emerged, along with complex societies with classes of artisans, priests and soldiers, and then trade and commerce, and then colonialism and large-scale wars. On the other hand, people who lived in other parts of the world 12,000 years ago were unlucky in the plants and animals they had access to. Because these species were difficult to domesticate, the people remained hunter-gatherers and lived in small, egalitarian groups. When the Spanish conquistadors stepped off their ships in the Bahamas, the indigenous people had no chance against them. And because farmers of Europe and Asia had been living at close quarters with their livestock animals for thousands of years, the settlers carried diseases such as smallpox, measles, tuberculosis and influenza. Indigenous peoples on other continents had no resistance to these infections and died in their millions as they came into contact with Europeans.

Linguists Daniel Nettle and Suzanne Romaine (2000) believe that the current wave of language deaths is directly related to this revolution in farming thousands of years ago. Most of the areas of the world where languages are dying the fastest are the areas where indigenous peoples lived as hunter-gatherers or nomads until recently, including the Americas, southern Africa, Siberia and Australia. With the spread of European farming techniques and capitalism in the past few hundred years, land has became a precious resource, and small tribes of nomadic people have been stripped of their land, pushed farther and farther to the margins, and deprived of economic and political power. As a result, the languages spoken by these people have become stigmatized. Nettle and Romaine distinguish between *metropolitan* languages and societies, where wealth and power are concentrated, and *peripheral* languages and societies, which are on the margin.

How does this process of marginalization happen? Language endangerment and death are not always the result of a policy or deliberate goal by metropolitan powers. As in the cases of the Spanish in the Bahamas and the British in Tasmania, indigenous people have been removed from their land because they stood in the way of European settlement. The death of their languages happened as a by-product of the death or displacement of the people. However, there are also cases where governments go out of their way to target minority languages in order to force language shift. In some countries, minority languages are seen as politically dangerous and subversive, and a threat to national unity. The 1536 Act of Union (Wales) legally barred Welsh-speakers from being judges or holding office. In Stalin's Soviet Union, children from ethnic minority villages were sent to Russian-language boarding schools to 'Russify' them. And until 2002 in Turkey it was illegal to speak Kurdish in a public place, and Kurdish names were not recognized. Many Kurds were imprisoned under these laws.

Language shift can also be hastened in less official ways. Some missionary groups have discouraged minority languages as part of their evangelical message. Nora Marks Dauenhauer and Richard Dauenhauer (1998), who work on the native languages of Alaska, see this as a problem in a deeply religious community. Certain churches still describe the Tlingit language as 'demonic', and send out the message that God doesn't like native Alaskan languages. Instead, the Bible is taught exclusively in English. In the same community, children were punished or humiliated in school for speaking their native language until quite recently. One middle-aged man commented, 'Whenever I speak Tlingit, I can still taste the soap.' In the United Kingdom, the Welsh Not was used in schools until the twentieth century. When a child in a Welsh school was heard speaking Welsh he or she was given the wooden Not to hold. At the end of the day, the child holding the Welsh Not was given a beating.

We have seen how speakers of minority groups are under different kinds of pressure to give up their languages. Yet it is also true that they may feel drawn just as powerfully *towards* metropolitan languages, because this is seen as the route to access to education, law, politics, and most of all, economic success. If you want to move to the city in Brazil you must speak Portuguese, or Bahasa Indonesian in Indonesia. For people in many developing countries, the only escape from poverty seems to be to lose the indigenous language and start speaking a more 'useful' one. Linguist Peter Ladefoged (1992) notes that in Kenya, for example, it is a source of pride in some families when young people speak Swahili instead of Dahalo, because it means that they can move to the city and become successful. Ladefoged concludes that language shift is not always a bad thing, and that it should be up to individual choice which language to speak. But others dispute this view. Daniel Nettle and Suzanne Romaine ask: what choice do these people actually have, after so many years of being marginalized in the schools, churches and law?

This brings us to another important question. What difference does it make if a language dies? In 1995 Bogon, the last speaker of Kasabe, died in Cameroon. What died with him and why should anyone care? First of all, for linguists, the loss of a language is a loss for science. In the same way that biologists hate to lose an animal or plant species, linguists hate to lose languages. Like all scientific disciplines, linguistics works by formulating hypotheses and then testing them against the available evidence. In this way, linguists try to work out what is or is not a possible structure or system for human language, and this in turn has important consequences for what we know about the human brain and human societies. In many cases, endangered languages show us the possible 'limits' of language. English has around forty discrete sounds, including both **vowels** and **consonants**. The language with the most sounds is !Xu, with 141, spoken by about 8,000 people in Namibia and Botswana. Many of these sounds are **click** consonants, which are found only in languages of southern Africa. The language with the fewest sounds is Rotokas, with eleven, spoken by about 4,000 people in New Guinea. Linguists see both languages as equally valuable.

The people who tend to care most about losing languages, however, are the speakers themselves. As Nora Marks Dauenhauer and Richard Dauenhauer (1998: 71) explain, 'Facing the loss of language or culture involves the same stages of grief that one experiences in the process of death and dying.' Each language contains a sound system, words, and rules for putting words together, but it is also a keystone of cultural **identity**. Languages are where we store our names, jokes, puns, stories, songs, myths and information about the plants, animals and land around us. Language also offers a glimpse into the world view of the people who speak it. Central Pomo, for example, has five different verbs which translate as 'sit' in English, including different verbs for birds sitting on a wire, a person sitting on the ground, and an object sitting on a surface. On the other hand, it has only one verb which might translate as 'carry something in a bag', 'pull a bucket out of a well' or 'string beads'. Central Pomo is nearly extinct, and once it dies its unique way of categorizing objects and processes will be lost for ever. Just as biologists believe that biodiversity is good for the planet, linguists believe that linguistic diversity is good for human societies.

The statistics of language death are certainly depressing. However, in many communities, efforts are being made toward **revitalization** of endangered languages and reversing language shift. Many international organizations are now involved in documenting and funding threatened languages, including UNESCO, the European Union and the Foundation for Endangered Languages. For a revitalization effort to be successful, the main motivation has to come from the community of language speakers themselves. Linguists can also work with speakers to come up with a writing system if the language is unwritten, write grammars and descriptions of the language, and eventually help to prepare teaching materials for schools. Since transmission of the language to the next generation is the key to preserving it, children are the focus of many revitalization programmes. For example, children in Hawaii may spend their days in **language nests** with total immersion in the Hawaiian language. Some of these programmes have managed to turn back the process of language death. In 1970 Mohawk was introduced in local Quebec schools for just fifteen minutes a day, then thirty. By 1994 total immersion was available for Mohawk children from nursery to Grade 4. Today, around half the parents in the community choose to send their children to Mohawk-language schools. Other languages remain in danger. In Finnish Lapland only about 250 speakers of Inari Saami are left, despite attempts to introduce the language in schools and nursery groups. In order to reverse language shift on a global scale, it is clear that much more public awareness is needed if a catastrophe is going to be avoided.

FURTHER READING

Crystal, D. (2000) *Language Death*, Cambridge: Cambridge University Press.

Dalby, A. (2003) *Language in Danger*, London: Penguin.

Dixon, R.M.W. (1997) *The Rise and Fall of Languages*, Cambridge: Cambridge University Press.

Grenoble, L. and Whaley, L. (eds) (1998) *Endangered Languages: Language Loss and Community Response*, Cambridge: Cambridge University Press.

Nettle, D. and Romaine, S. (2000) *Vanishing Voices*, Oxford: Oxford University Press.

GLOSSARY

Those glossary items which appear in the preceding chapters are indicated with a cross-reference at the end of the definition (as Chapters 9, 22, for example). Other terms which are used as part of the definition are presented in **bold**. All items in the glossary are included in the index.

accent The characteristic pronunciation patterns of a **variety** of speech. A speaker's accent can often identify their **social class**, **age**, **gender**, geographical origins, ethnicity and even their political affiliations. Accent can be technically described by **phonemes** and **intonation** patterns. Chapters 1, 6, 8, 11, 12, 14, 17, 20, 23.

acceptance In **language planning**, when **speech communities** agree to take on a particular **variety** of language suggested, engineered or imposed by the authorities. Chapter 20.

accommodation The phenomenon in which speakers change the manner in which they speak, depending upon who they are interacting with, the investigation of which is referred to as **Speech Accommodation Theory**. Two key facets of the theory are **convergence** and **divergence**. Convergence refers to the phenomenon of speakers adopting the speech strategies of their fellow interlocutors, often thought to signal **solidarity**. Conversely, divergence refers to instances where speakers deliberately change features of their speech, commonly thought to act as a social distancing device. Accommodation can occur at any linguistic level, from **accent** features right through to discourse features. Chapters 11, 12, 13, 14, 17, 22.

acoustic analysis In **phonetics**, the analysis of the physical properties of speech sounds. Chapters 1, 3.

acquisition planning In **language planning**, once **corpus planning** and **status planning** decisions have taken place, **acquisition planning** refers to the role of educationists in deciding how a variety will be acquired. Chapter 20.

acrolect In a **post-creolization** situation, the **acrolect** is the variety spoken mostly by those at the top of the social hierarchy or with the greatest educational status. This variety is closer to the **lexifier** language than the **mesolectal** or **basilectal** forms. Chapters 21, 23.

actuation problem The problem that sociolinguists have in providing an explanation for the initial trigger of **language change**. Chapter 22.

address terms The forms that individuals use to refer directly to one another which encode the level of solidarity–social distance between them. Address terms are often analysed to examine power relations between interlocutors, as well as to examine linguistic practices in particular cultures. Many languages also use the **T-V pronoun system** in order to denote levels of solidarity–social distance through second person pronouns. Address terms are often studied as part of linguistic **politeness**. Chapter 15.

adjacency pairs Used in **conversation analysis** to refer to a sequence of two utterances, spoken by different interlocutors, where the first part demands that the second part be given, such as a question and answer. The second pair part must be uttered in order for an adjacency pair sequence to be successfully completed.

affricate A **manner of articulation** description of a **consonant** sound whereby two articulators are completely closed and then slowly released, creating turbulence, resulting in audible friction, such as [tʃ] and [dʒ].

age A **social variable** utilized by sociolinguists in order to assess language variation and change. Chapters 4, 6, 7, 8, 9, 12, 13, 14, 15, 20.

age grading The process when **language change** occurs within an individual speaker as he/she progresses through life. Chapter 8.

agency A social science term which refers to one's ability to be able to act. It is contrasted with the constraints imposed by social and political **structure**. Chapters 9, 10, 12, 16, 20, 21.

allophone The realization of **variants** of a **phoneme**.

alveolar A **place of articulation** description of a **consonant** sound whereby the tip or blade of the tongue touches the **alveolar ridge**.

alveolar ridge The ridge that is positioned at the front part of the roof of the mouth, in between the back of the teeth and the hard palate.

anti-language Refers to the language variety of a marginalized group or 'non-conventional' group. Anti-languages should be viewed in opposition to **standard languages**.

apparent-time studies A technique used to assess **language change** by comparing the speech of younger speakers and older speakers within the same **speech community** at the same time. Chapters 2, 8, 13. Compare with **real time studies**.

approximant A **manner of articulation** whereby consonant sounds are produced by the turbulence created by two articulators being close together, such as /l/ or /w/. Chapter 1.

artificial language A language that has been deliberately created for particular purposes, such as Esperanto, created in the late nineteenth century as an attempt to devise an **international language**.

aspiration The noise made by the friction created by air moving quickly through the vocal tract when a **stop** is released.

Audience Design An approach to assessing stylistic variation in language use, whereby individual speakers change their **speech style** in direct response to their audience. The term was coined by Bell (1984) during his investigations of speaker style on New Zealand radio stations. Chapter 11.

auditorial The technique in **phonetic** analysis which involves listening to recorded data. Chapter 3.

authority The amount of power that institutions have in terms of implementing and maintaining a **standard language**. Chapter 16.

autonomy The level of independence a **variety** has when compared with other varieties. It is a term often used in relation to a **dialect continuum**.

back-channelling Used in **conversation** and **discourse analysis** to refer to the supportive verbal noises and gestures that a hearer makes, such as 'mhm' or 'yeah'. Backchannels are sometimes referred to as **minimal responses**. Chapter 5.

basilect In a **post-creolization** situation the basilect is the variety spoken mostly by those at the bottom of the social hierarchy or with the least educational status. This variety is furthest away from the **lexifier** language and is often regarded as the most 'authentic' form of the **creole**. Chapters 12, 21, 23.

bidialectalism This term refers to a speaker's ability to use two or more **dialects**, and to know how to **code-switch** appropriately between these different varieties.

bilabial A **place of articulation** description of a **consonant** sound produced with both lips, such as /p/ and /b/.

bilingualism The ability of a speaker or group to speak two or more languages. It is important to emphasize two *or more* here, as, whilst the term is used by some sociolinguists to describe speaking two languages, it is often used to refer to those who can speak many languages. Bilingualism can be further split into **coordinate bilinguals**, referring to speakers who have learnt two languages from birth. This contrasts with **compound bilinguals**, who have learnt their native language and then another language later in life. Chapters 11, 18, 19, 23, 24. See also **multilingualism**.

bioprogram In reference to the origins of **pidgins** and **creoles**, the view that the **agency** of children can account for structural similarities among new creoles. Based on the premise that pidgins are syntaxless, the hypothesis argues that, as children have an in-built ability to learn language, when they appropriate the **lingua francas** of their parents as **vernaculars** they assign them a grammar called the *bioprogram*. This then accounts for the grammatical similarities between creoles. Chapter 21.

boosters An expression of certainty by a speaker, which increases the overall force of an utterance, such as use of the phrase 'of course'. Often used in investigations of linguistic **politeness**. See also **hedges**, **modality**.

borrowing When bilingual speakers transfer lexical items from one language to another. Chapters 13, 16, 18, 20, 23, 24.

British English The English spoken in Britain as opposed to just England. See Chapters 1, 2, 6, 8, 13, 17, 23. See also **English English**.

broken language Pejorative term referring to the simplification of language varieties. Often used to denigrate speakers of **pidgins**. Chapter 21.

calquing A form of **borrowing** whereby expressions from one language are translated into another language. Chapter 23.

cardinal vowels A system designed to categorize vowel quality. Cardinal vowels operate on scales ranging from front to back, and open to close, roughly corresponding to the positioning of the tongue when a vowel sound is made. The term 'cardinal' refers to the cardinal points on a compass. See **close vowel**, **fronting**, **open vowel**.

centralization When a vowel sound shifts and is made in the centre of the tongue. This can be as a result of **language change**.

change from above Linguistic changes of which speakers are consciously aware ('above' the level of consciousness). See also **language change**.

change from below Linguistic changes of which speakers are not consciously aware ('below' the level of consciousness). See also **language change**.

child-directed speech (CDS) The speech that adults use when talking to children. Chapter 8.

circularity A methodological problem where a part of the sampling method is flawed, as when a linguistic feature is used to define a group of people that the study will then go on to analyse linguistically. In order to avoid circularity, researchers need to use other criteria to determine their analytical categorizations. Chapter 10. See also **circularity**.

class Chapters 6, 20. See **social class**.

classical language A language which no longer has native speakers but has been **standardized** and still has **prestige**, such as Latin.

click A consonant sound which is produced when air flow begins by a closure of the back of the tongue on the velum. Chapter 24.

close vowel Refers to the positioning of the tongue as high in the mouth when a vowel sound is produced. See also **cardinal vowels**.

code A neutral term used in a very general sense to cover any form of communication. Its usage avoids the political and social evaluations that are reflected in terms such as language, **dialect** and **register**.

code mixing When speakers engage in **code switching** within sentences, also known as **intra-sentential** code switching. Mixing often makes it difficult to decipher which language is being spoken at any one time. Chapter 13.

code switching When speakers switch between different codes in the course of a single interaction. Often used to refer to **bilingual** or **multilingual** speakers. Researchers investigate the motivations as to why code switching takes place. Code switching can be split into two further components, **situational code switching**, where a change in the physical situation brings about a switch, and **metaphorical code switching**, where the situation remains the same but switching can be brought about by, for example, a change in topic. Chapters 9, 16, 11, 12, 18.

codification During the process of **standardization**, when a variety becomes fixed through the publication of resources such as dictionaries and grammar books. Chapters 12, 16, 20. See also **language planning**.

coherence In **discourse analysis**, the manner in which a text links together semantically.

cohesion   In **discourse analysis**, the specific lexical and grammatical language features which link a text together.

communicative competence   Often associated with the **ethnography of communication**, this refers to the level of skills and knowledge that are required in order to be able to communicate in an appropriate and effective manner in a **speech community**. Chapters 8, 19.

community of practice   In contrast with **speech communities** and **social networks**, there is a focus on examining language as a form of practice. Eckert and McConnell-Ginet (1992: 464) define it as 'an aggregate of people who come together around mutual engagement in an endeavor. Ways of doing things, ways of talking, beliefs, values, power relations – in short – practices – emerge in the course of this mutual endeavor.' Chapters 2, 10, 12, 15.

complementary hypothesis   In reference to the origins of **creoles** and **pidgins**, the complementary hypothesis refers to the position whereby the **substrate hypothesis** and **superstrate hypothesis** are integrated. Chapter 21.

compound bilingual   See **bilingualism**.

conflict model   Based on a Marxist interpretation of society, whereby social classes are in conflict with one another owing to the unequal distribution of **power** in society. Chapters 6, 10. Contrast with **consensus model**.

consensus model   Based on a functionalist view of society, whereby relationships between social classes are thought to be harmonious. A social theory that is in direct opposition with the **conflict model**. Chapter 10.

consonant   A category of speech sound which is further distinguished by its **place of articulation**, **manner of articulation** and whether it is **voiced** or **voiceless**. Chapters 1, 17, 24.

convergence   Chapters 11, 13, 20. See **accommodation**.

Conversation Analysis (CA)   Derived from **ethnomethodology**, the analysis of the sequential nature of face-to-face interaction by the application of systematic analytical frameworks such as the **turn-taking system**. Chapter 5.

conversational implicature   Grice's (1975) term to explain how hearers look beyond the literal meaning of utterances and instead look for implied meaning in specific contexts. For example, the implicature of B's saying *I was out all evening* in response to A's question *Did you see that Neil Connery film last night?* is that B did not see the film, although the possibility is not precluded. (B could, for instance, have seen the film at a friend's house.) Grice uses the flouting of **conversational maxims** to assess when **implicature** has taken place. See also **co-operative principle**.

conversational maxims   To explain **conversational implicature**, Grice (1975) devised four maxims, *quantity*, *quality*, *relation* and *manner*, which underlie the **co-operative principle**. Quantity refers to uttering the right amount of information, quality refers to stating something you believe to be true or for which you have evidence, relation refers to being relevant, and manner refers to being brief and orderly, as well as avoiding obscurity and ambiguity.

conversationalization   A term used in **Critical Discourse Analysis**, associated with Fairclough (1995), to describe the process of social change whereby speech strategies commonly associated with informal, private spheres have permeated their way into the public sphere, in order to make power relations between speakers more covert. See also **hegemony**.

co-operative principle Coined by Grice (1975), the view that when engaging in interaction, speakers co-operate with one another by ensuring that they make appropriate contributions at appropriate points in an appropriate manner. See also **conversational maxims**.

coordinate bilingual See **bilingualism**.

copula The verb 'to be', which often serves a central social function in many varieties and has been a particular feature for sociolinguistic investigation. Chapters 4, 9.

corpus planning In **language planning**, corpus planning refers to attempts to change the forms and structures of the language itself. This task is often undertaken by national language planning agencies. Chapter 20.

correctness When **standardization** has taken place, speakers develop evaluative views as to the 'correct' way in which language should be used. Often these notions are based on nothing more than folklinguistic beliefs embedded with social prejudice which serve to perpetuate negative stereotyping of social groups with less political and economic **power**. Chapters 16, 18. See also **folk-linguistics, standard language ideology**.

correlational approach Used to describe the work of sociolinguists where **linguistic variables** are correlated with **social variables** such as **age, sex** and **social class** in order to assess **language variation** and **language change**. Chapter 12.

covert prestige When speakers will use a **non-standard** variety more frequently as an in-group identity marker. Often associated with **masculinity**. Chapters 6, 7, 9.

creoles New vernaculars that emerged during the seventeenth and eighteenth centuries from **non-standard** varieties of European languages in (sub)tropical plantation settlement colonies around the Atlantic, in the Indian Ocean and in the Pacific. Chapters 12, 13, 21, 23.

creolization Based on the theory that **creoles** are derived from **pidgins**, this term refers to the process by which the language system of a pidgin becomes more complex and turns into a creole when a new generation of users learn it as their native language. Chapter 23. See also **creole, pidgin, post-creole continuum**.

Critical Discourse Analysis (CDA) An approach devised by Fairclough (1989) which differs from other forms of discourse analysis by having the clear political aim of attempting to reveal connections of hidden relationships encoded in language that may not be immediately evident, in order to bring about social change. Critical discourse analysts often conduct research on disadvantaged groups such as ethnic minorities. **Discourse** in CDA is defined broadly as a form of social practice. CDA can be carried out at any linguistic level (phonological, lexical grammatical or discoursal), and it can be used to analyse both spoken and written texts. Chapters 5, 15.

cross-cultural communication Often focused on in **discourse analysis** and the **ethnography of communication**, the study of communication that takes place when those who belong to different cultural groupings interact with one another. Chapter 5.

crossing Rampton's (1995) term to signify when a speaker/group of speakers use fragments of languages which they do not speak themselves. It can be viewed as a type of **code switching**. Chapter 11.

cultural capital Bourdieu's (1991) term used to signify the advantages that the dominant class accrues for itself by gaining prestigious cultural knowledge that is imbued with social, political and economic power. Chapter 6.

debasilectalization Chapter 21. See **post-creole speech continuum**.

decreolization Chapter 21. See **post-creole speech continuum**.

deficit approach In language and **gender** research, the perspective that women's language is deficient due to the linguistic practices that are associated with men's speech being the norm. Women's language is thus negatively evaluated as weak and powerless. Chapter 7. See also **dominance approach**, **difference approach**, **social constructionist approach**.

deixis Those aspects of language which serve to anchor the speaker personally and socially and which are specific to them and their situation. The deictics of person (*I*, *you*), place (*here*, *there*), time (*now*, *then*) and social setting (including **modality**, **address terms** and **register**) shift, depending on who is speaking.

dental A **place of articulation** whereby consonants are produced by the tip or blade of the tongue as it touches the front teeth, such as /θ/ or /ð/.

dependent variable In statistical terms, a linguistic feature specifically selected by the researcher for investigation which can be correlated by examining it in conjunction with other factors, known as **independent variables**. Chapters 1, 9, 17.

depidginization A process by which a **pidgin** becomes more complex and acquires a more complicated language system. See also **expansion**.

devoicing When the reduction of vocal fold vibration takes place. Chapter 1.

diachronic Used to describe studies where the same language situation is assessed to monitor how it develops through a period of time.

diacritics Marks that are added to written symbols in order to signify how a sound should be pronounced.

dialect The pronunciation, **lexis** and grammar of a language variety, associated with a particular geographical area or social group. Chapters 1, 2, 3, 4, 6, 8, 9, 10, 11, 12, 13, 16, 17, 20, 21, 22, 23. See also **sociolect**.

dialect boundary See **isogloss**.

dialect chain Chapter 20. See **dialect continuum**.

dialect contact Chapters 12, 13. See **language contact**.

dialect continuum A set of dialects whereby there is gradual change that occurs between varieties. There tends to be mutual intelligibility between those speakers who are at different points along the continuum but who live adjacent to one another, but it does depend upon amount of contact (see **language contact**) and also speakers' attitudes to one another (see **accommodation**). The further away speakers get from each other along the continuum the more difficult it becomes for them to understand each other. Sometimes referred to as **dialect chains**.

dialect levelling Chapters 22, 23. See **levelling**.

dialectology The scientific study of **dialects**. As this field of investigation has developed, further categorizations have been made between **traditional dialectology** and **urban dialectology**. Chapter 21. See also **perceptual dialectology**.

difference approach In language and gender research, an approach which interprets the linguistic differences between women and men as a consequence of differences in the language that girls and boys learn during the socialization process. This can lead to miscommunication in later life. Chapter 7. See also **deficit approach**, **dominance approach**, **social constructionist approach**.

diffusion A process of **language change** whereby linguistic forms and innovations are spread from one geographical area to another. *Relocation* diffusion involves innovations being carried by speakers migrating to new locations. *Expansion* diffusion involves innovations being passed on through day-to-day contact between speakers who have adopted the innovation and those who have not. Chapter 17.

diglossia Two distinct forms of a language that exist with clear functional separation in a socially stable situation. They are categorized as a 'high' variety and a 'low' variety. The high variety is the prestigious form used in formal situations, whereas the low variety is the informal form used in everyday talk. Speakers are conscious of the switch from high to low varieties. Chapter 20.

diphthong A vowel that changes quality within a single syllable. Chapter 9.

directives A **speech act** whereby a speaker attempts to get the hearer to do something. Directives are sometimes known as commands. Chapter 7.

discourse(s) Traditionally used to mean language above the level of a sentence, though it can be used in a post-structuralist sense, following Foucault (1972: 49), whereby discourses are seen as 'practices that systematically form the objects of which they speak'. Frequently used in this latter manner in **critical discourse analysis** and recent language and **gender** studies. Another use of discourse is as a general categorization device for language used in a particular social setting, such as 'business discourse'. Chapters 1, 2, 5, 6, 20.

Discourse Analysis Used as a broad term to refer to the investigations of spoken or written language in any of the different senses that the term **discourse** is defined within sociolinguistics. Also sometimes used as an overarching term to include **conversation analysis**, though such usage is frowned upon by many conversation analysts. Chapters 5, 14, 16, 20.

discourse marker Words or phrases which identify and signal the structure of the discourse, such as the use of 'right' as a marker to signal that you wish to take the conversational **floor**. Chapter 4.

discourse variation When discourse features are used for comparative purposes in order to assess language variation and change. Chapter 1.

divergence Chapters 6, 11, 13, 21, 22. See **accommodation**.

domains Particular settings where the choice of **code** and **code switching** between different varieties can be observed, for example, 'family' and 'religion'. Chapter 20.

dominance approach In language and gender research, an approach which interprets linguistic differences in women's and men's speech in terms of men's dominance and women's subordination. Dominance is reflected in linguistic practice. Chapter 7. See also **deficit approach**, **difference approach**, **social constructionist approach**.

EAP English for Academic Purposes.

ecolinguistics Chapter 20. See **ecology of language**.

ecology of language The study of language in relation to its broader environment. Work in this area is sometimes called **ecolinguistics**. Chapter 5.

EFL English as a Foreign Language. See also **TEFL**.

elaborated code A term coined by Bernstein (1971) in his work on educational disadvantage. An explicit 'superior' code that can be communicated by not gesturing to the immediate context. Chapters 6, 19. Contrast with **restricted code.**

elaboration In reference to the process of **standardization**, when a language is used in a greater and greater variety of functions, and thus the need for a near-uniform variety becomes more salient. Chapter 16.

elicitation tests Tests set up for the specific purpose of being able to obtain linguistic data from **informants**. Chapter 2.

ELT English Language Teaching, used in a general sense as an overarching reference term.

endangered language A language that is in danger of becoming extinct, often due to younger generations no longer learning particular varieties. Chapter 24. See also **language death**.

English English The English spoken in England, as opposed to the English spoken in other English-speaking countries, such as Scotland, New Zealand or Australia. Chapters 1, 14, 17. Compare with **British English**.

ESL English as a Second Language. Places where English is not a native language but where it does have an official role. Chapters 19, 24.

ESP English for Specific Purposes.

ethnicity A social identity variable utilized by sociolinguists in order to assess **language variation**. Chapters 1, 5, 6, 7, 8, 9, 11, 12, 14, 16, 19.

ethnography The study of particular individuals or groups over a prolonged period of time by directly observing them, often using the techniques of **participant observation**. Chapters 2, 8, 10, 12, 14, 16, 18, 20. See also **ethnography of communication**.

ethnography of communication A sociolinguistic subdiscipline which uses **ethnography** to investigate the interplay of communication and language **codes**. Chapters 5, 10.

ethnolinguistics The investigation of language and culture. This term overlaps extensively with the **ethnography of communication**. Chapters 9, 21.

ethnomethodology The sociological discipline from where **Conversation Analysis** derives. From a language perspective, ethnomethodologists are generally interested in examining the content of talk.

expanded pidgins Chapter 24. See **expansion**.

expansion A process synonymous with **depidiginization** whereby a **pidgin** evolves into a far more complex variety and becomes used in a far wider range of functions.

eye dialect The use of **non-standard** spelling, rather than phonetic notation, in order to signify how language is being pronounced.

face A term coined by Goffman (1967), referring to the public self image that individuals have when interacting with one another. Brown and Levinson (1987) split face into **positive face** and **negative face** as part of their politeness universals theory.

face-threatening act (FTA) Brown and Levinson's (1987) term to describe a situation when a demand or an intrusion is made upon a person's **face**. When an FTA is performed, interlocutors have a choice: whether to use strategies of linguistic politeness in order to mitigate the FTA, or whether to deliver it 'baldly' without mitigation. Chapter 15. See also **face**, **politeness**.

felicity condition In **speech act** theory, the conditions that need to be fulfilled by both participants and the specific context in order for a speech act to be assessed as being carried out successfully.

femininity/femininities Originally thought to be an attribute that speakers have that is reflected through their speech, more recent language and **gender** research from a **social constructionist** perspective has pluralized this concept, demonstrating how different types of femininities exist. This helps researchers move away from the problematic view that all women are a homogeneous group, as well as enabling more sophisticated models of societal **power** relations to be developed. Chapter 7. See also **masculinity/ masculinities**.

field A category within Halliday's (1978) systemic analysis which refers to the social setting or purpose of an interaction. Chapter 5.

floor In **Conversation Analysis**, the term is used to refer to the conversational **turn-taking** system which speakers use when interacting with one another. To 'hold the floor' means that you are taking a turn in the conversation. See **turn-taking**.

folklinguistics The everyday, popular conceptions about language use in society. These often draw on stereotypes about language use and language users. Chapters 6, 7, 16.

Forensic Linguistics A subdiscipline where linguistic analyses are used to examine crime in order to help aid members of the legal profession. From a sociolinguistic perspective, researchers have been involved in activities such as analysing **accent** and **dialect** features to help with suspect identification. Chapters 1, 14.

fossilization   When the meaning of particular language forms becomes fixed. Chapter 9.

fricative   A **manner of articulation** whereby a consonant sound is produced by forcing air through a narrow constriction which creates turbulence, such as /f/ and /v/. Chapter 1.

fronting   Sounds produced further forward than their usual position, at the front of the tongue and/or mouth.

gender   A term used to indicate **social construction** as opposed to biological **sex**. Chapters 1, 5, 6, 7, 8, 9, 10, 11, 13, 15, 19. Also used in a technical linguistic sense as a grammatical noun categorization device.

German German   The German spoken in Germany, as opposed to the German spoken in Austria, etc.

glide   In reference to **approximant consonants**, movement of the articulators during the production of a sound, such as with /j/ and /w/. Sometimes called *semivowels*. Chapter 3. See also **liquids**.

glottal stop   A **plosive consonant**, symbolized [ʔ], which is articulated by adducting the vocal folds such that they meet along their entire length. Chapter 7.

glottalization   The name given to the habit of using glottalized forms of /p t k/ in words like *sip*, *sit* and *sick*. In some accents (e.g. that of Tyneside) **intervocalic** glottalization of /p t k/ in words such as *supper*, *sitter*, or *sicker* is also extremely common. Chapter 3.

glottalized stop   A **stop consonant** such as [p] or [k] which is preceded, followed or accompanied simultaneously by the glottal stop [ʔ]. Chapter 8.

grammaticalization   In reference to **language change**, the evolution of new grammatical functions from current lexical items. Chapters 9, 21.

graphization   The act of devising an orthography for a previously unwritten language.

H-dropping   /h/, if absent from words such as *hot*, *happy*, etc., is said to have been 'dropped' in some English and Welsh accents of English. Note that the absence of /h/ in function words like *him*, *herself*, *have*, etc., is a regular feature of virtually all **accents** of English, including **standard** ones, and is not usually classified as H-dropping. Chapters 1, 3.

habitus   Bourdieu's (1991) term used to refer to the set of dispositions that incline individuals to act and react in certain ways. Habitus is developed during socialization, and it provides us with a sense of how to act in everyday situations. From a sociolinguistic perspective, language is seen as one practice in which habitus embeds itself. Chapters 10, 15.

hedges   An expression of uncertainty on behalf of the speaker which reduces the overall force of an **utterance**, such as use of the phrase 'sort of'. Often used in investigations of linguistic **politeness**. Chapters 7, 14. See also **boosters, modality**.

hegemony A notion coined by Gramsci (1971) as part of his theory of societal power. Power is enacted by gaining the consent of people, held in place by **ideologies** implemented by social institutions which favour the dominant social class. Often used in **Critical Discourse Analysis**. Chapters 18, 20, 23.

heteronomy A variety that is not considered to be independent of a **standard variety**, and which has not undergone the process of **standardization**. Compare with **autonomy**.

high rising terminal An intonation pattern characteristic of many varieties of contemporary spoken English, which involves the use of a high-rising contour on statements. Also known as Australian Question(ing) Intonation and 'uptalk', it has been frequently associated with Australian and New Zealand English, but is also common in North American English, and increasingly in **British English**. Chapter 7.

historicity When language users view their **code** as having a sense of longevity.

hypercorrection The overgeneralization of linguistic forms which carry overt social **prestige** often through the misapplication of rules (e.g. the pronunciation of [h] in a word such as *honour*). Also applied to the higher frequency use of prestige forms by members of lower social groups than members of higher social groups in a formal **speech style**. Chapters 12, 22.

identity Broadly speaking, a category that refers to the sense of who we are as individuals or groups. It can be very roughly split into social and regional identity. Aspects of our social and regional identities, such as **social class**, **age**, **ethnicity** and geographical origin are correlated with **linguistic variables** in studies of **language variation**. Identity is therefore seen as a fixed cateogry. More recently, from a **social constructionist** perspective, identity is conversely seen as a fluid and dynamic concept, something that we actively do/perform when engaging in language production. Chapters 5, 8, 9, 10, 11, 12, 14, 18, 20, 23.

ideology Used in two different ways, first to refer to the beliefs that individuals or groups have about the world, and second from a Marxist-influenced perspective, to refer to the system of commonsense assumptions that we have about the world which hide authority and hierarchy and treat it as natural. The second definition is commonly used in **critical discourse analysis**. Chapters 9, 20. See also **hegemony**.

idiolect The linguistic system used by an individual speaker (including features of pronunciation, grammar, lexical items and **pragmatics**). Such similar but not identical idiolects make up the **sociolect**. Chapter 21.

idiom A fixed expression whose meaning cannot be worked out from its constituent parts, such as *to kick the bucket* (to die). Chapter 17.

immersion Education programmes in which students are taught a second or foreign language through its constant use.

impoliteness Chapter 15. See **politeness**.

independent variable A term from statistics denoting a factor with a value varying independently of another, **dependent variable**. For example, **social class** is an independent variable whose value may be determined and controlled by the researcher (e.g. by making the choice to group individual speakers in the sample by income bracket rather than, say, occupation). Independent variables are also known as predictor variables. Chapters 1, 9, 11, 17. See also **dependent variable**.

indexicality The process by which an association is formed between a language or a linguistic form and a socially meaningful characteristic. A linguistic form can therefore become indexical of a speaker's social identity. Chapter 12.

indicator A **linguistic variable** which does not carry any social significance for speakers. Chapter 1. See also **marker** and **stereotype**.

informant An individual whose speech and/or language is observed, recorded or sampled by a linguistic researcher, generally interactively but sometimes anonymously or even posthumously. Other terms such as *interviewee, subject* and *speaker* are also used in sociolinguistic studies. Chapter 5.

instrumental analysis The use of scientific instruments (now typically electronic) and computer software to perform **acoustic analysis** of speech, vocal tract imaging, measurements of airflow, aspects of speech articulation, etc. Chapters 1, 3.

interdental fricatives The consonants /θ/ (as in *thin*) and /ð/ (as in *then*), which are articulated with the tongue tip and/or blade positioned between the upper and lower teeth such that air exits noisily from the mouth. Chapter 9.

interdialectism A type of linguistic restructuring that occurs in a **language contact** situation. Through this restructuring, speakers may reanalyse or rearrange forms and features of the contributing **dialects**, and they may produce intermediate or 'fudged' phonetic realizations that originally occurred in neither the source nor the target language variety. Chapters 9, 22.

international language A language used, or intended for use, for communication across national boundaries by speakers not sharing a common language, such as *Esperanto*. Chapter 23.

International Phonetic Alphabet (IPA) A system of symbols based on the Roman and Greek alphabets first published by the International Phonetic Association in 1888 in order to represent human speech sounds unambiguously and in detail. The alphabet is periodically revised so as to incorporate newly discovered sounds in previously undescribed languages or **dialects**.

interruption In reference to the **turn-taking** system, an interruption occurs when a disruptive violation of another speaker's turn takes place. Interruptions need to be distinguished from instances of **supportive simultaneous talk**, where speakers talk at the same time in order to engage in the process of the joint production of discourse. Chapter 5.

intersentential switch In reference to **code switching**, when switching takes place at sentence boundary. Compare with **intrasentential switch**.

217

intervocalic Appearing between two vowels, as the /t/ of *water*. Chapters 1, 11, 13.

intervocalic tap The **voiced alveolar consonant** [ɾ] where it appears as a positional allophone of /t/ between vowels, as in [sɪɾɪ] *city*. This phenomenon is often referred to as *flapping*, and is particularly common in American, Canadian and Australian English. In some varieties (e.g. Scottish English) there is a tendency to use [ɾ] as an allophone of /r/ in **intervocalic** contexts, e.g. in *very, pour out*, etc. Chapter 16.

intonation Variations in the **pitch** of a speaker's voice that are used to signal linguistic contrasts (e.g. a question versus a statement) and emotional/affective state (e.g. surprise, scepticism, refusal, boredom). Chapters 1, 7, 14.

intrasentential switch In reference to code switching, this refers to when switching takes place within a sentence. See also **code mixing**.

intrusive /r/ In non-**rhotic accents** of English, a type of /r/ in which a rhotic **consonant** is inserted in contexts in which there is no historical or orthographic motivation to do so, such as in 'saw up' or 'sawing' (compare *soar up*, where the /r/ that is inserted is described as **linking /r/**, because its insertion is historically and orthographically justified). Chapter 1.

isogloss A term used in **dialectology** to refer to an imaginary line dividing two geographical areas to indicate some linguistic discontinuity (e.g. with respect to languages, **dialects/accents**, or one or more individual linguistic features). Where isoglosses for several different linguistic features 'bundle', a **dialect boundary** may be interpreted. Such dialect boundaries are not often clear-cut, however, and isoglosses often criss-cross. The term derives from the Greek for 'same tongue', and is therefore perhaps less appropriate for the concept than the related term *heterogloss* 'different tongue'. Chapter 1.

jargon Technical or specialist vocabulary most commonly associated with a professional or special interest group. Such vocabulary may not be understood by people outside these groups. The vocabulary can therefore be used to mark group membership.

judgement sample A sample of a population in which the researcher has known in advance the type of **informant** required for the study (that is, the social or **independent variables** of interest) and has sought out informants who fulfil certain criteria to fill certain quotas. Chapter 2. See also **random sample**.

koine In a broad sense the term refers to any common or widely shared variety of language. A narrower definition, commonly used in recent years, is to refer to a variety of a language, normally showing **mixing, levelling** and **simplification**, which develops as a result of rapid population movement and mixing of speakers of different **dialects** in a new community. Chapters 13, 22.

koineization An approach which aims to describe and explain the processes that lead to koine formation. Chapter 22.

labiodental A **place of articulation** of a **consonant** sound involving the lower lip and upper incisor teeth such as /f/ and /v/.

labiodental approximant This sound, symbolized [ʋ], is increasingly commonly used in **British English** as a pronunciation of /r/, despite its earlier associations with infantile, impaired or affected upper-class speech. Chapter 1.

language attitudes Study of how people judge and evaluate themselves and others based upon usage of different varieties. Chapters 2, 14, 16.

language change One of the facts about language is that it is continuously changing. Change occurs when use of a particular **variant** increases and gradually ousts the previous norm. It can occur on a phonological level, a grammatical level or a lexical level, and can be overt or covert. Observing variation in language is vital for understanding language change, as, although not all variability in language structure involves change, all change involves **language variation**. Chapters 8, 10, 13, 16, 23.

language contact A situation in which more than one language exists in a given area or **speech community** which may lead to speakers of one language deliberately or subconsciously introducing into their own language features of the other language. Can be equally applied to dialects, known as **dialect contact**. Chapters 9, 13, 23.

language death When a **speech community** shifts to another language, or when the last speakers of a language die. Chapters 20, 23, 24.

language loyalty Where language users have positive attitudes towards a **variety** and feel an affinity towards its use. See also **language attitudes**.

language maintenance Refers to the situation whereby a language (often a transplanted **minority language**) is retained and used by speakers alongside, or instead of, a more dominant language. Chapters 5, 20.

language murder When governments or other institutions try to 'kill off' minority languages by passing laws or punishing speakers; this puts pressure on speakers from the outside. In more extreme cases, it can also be used to refer to when a language dies out owing to all of its speakers being murdered, sometimes called **linguicide**. Chapter 24. See also **language death**.

language nests From Māori *te kohanga reo* 'the language nest'. These groups, first started in New Zealand with the aim of maintaining spoken Māori, involve exposing children to a lesser-user or endangered community language by leaving them in the care of older native speakers who converse with them only in the language they are seeking to preserve. Chapter 24.

language planning The role that governments or institutions play in planning which varieties are acceptable in a given **speech community**. Chapters 20, 23. See also **acquisition planning**, **corpus planning**, **language policy**, **status planning**.

language policy Used generally to refer to the aims of language planners, though it can be used as a synonym for **language planning**. Chapter 20.

language shift When the language of a population changes from one variety to another. Chapters 20, 24. See also **language death**, **language murder**, **language suicide**.

language suicide When people in a **speech community** feel they would be better off economically, politically or socially if they spoke a different language. Pressure for change therefore comes from the inside to stop using a 'worthless' variety and adopt a new 'useful' one instead. Chapter 24. See also **language death**.

language variation Chapters 8, 9, 12. See **variationist sociolinguistics**.

lateral Describes an airstream which is directed to one or both sides of an obstruction in the oral tract, as in the articulation of [l], [ʎ] or [ɬ].

levelling A process of **language change** which involves the loss of locally or socially marked variants of particular phonological, morphological or lexical variables in a **variety** which often follows social or geographical mobility and resultant **dialect contact**. Chapters 9, 12, 22.

lexicon The inventory of words in a language. Also used as an alternative to *dictionary*. Chapter 18.

lexifier In **pidgin** and **creole** situations, the language (often a colonizing European language) which largely provides the base of the creole is known as the lexifier language. It inaccurately suggests that only the vocabulary of the colonizing language is selected. Chapter 21.

lexis The words of a language, usually not distinguished from the **vocabulary** of an individual speaker. Chapters 5, 17, 18.

lingua franca A variety used as a form of communication between two or more different speakers or groups of speakers who do not share a common language. Chapters 18, 20, 21.

linguistic capital A term associated with Bourdieu (1991), linguistic capital is embodied by socially highly valued language forms, such as (in England) **Standard English** and **Received Pronunciation**. See also **cultural capital**, **prestige**.

linguistic diversity The linguistic diversity of a country or region depends on the number of languages spoken within it, as well as on how closely they are related to one another. (The diversity index is higher if the languages come from a range of language families, rather than from just one family.) As with biological diversity, the equatorial zones are especially diverse linguistically; notable are New Guinea (some 750 languages) and Nigeria (about 470 languages). The field of the **ecology of language** makes much of this connection. Chapters 18, 24.

linguistic genocide Chapter 20. See **language murder**.

linguicide Chapter 20. See **language suicide**.

linguistic market Derives from Bourdieu's (1991) work where society comprises a range of overlapping and interrelated markets. In the linguistic market, linguistic competence (like any other cultural competence) functions as a form of capital. Different varieties are evaluated in different ways, and the **varieties** which have the most value or **prestige** are associated with the dominant class. Chapters 8, 10.

linguistic repertoire Refers to the set of linguistic varieties that a person uses. Chapter 18.

linguistic variable   In sociolinguistics, a descriptive and analytical unit used to describe and quantify patterns of variation in speech and writing. Variables are categories containing two or more distinguishable **variants**, the distribution of which is often non-random and can be shown to be dependent upon and constrained by other linguistic or non-linguistic factors, such as a sound's position within a syllable, or the **age** of the speaker, or the formality of the situation in which an utterance occurs. Chapters 1, 3, 4, 9, 10, 11, 12.

linking /r/   In non-rhotic accents of English, a type of /r/ in which a **rhotic consonant** is pronounced at the end of a word containing a historically attested /r/, such as *soar* if it is followed by a vowel-initial word, as in the sequence *soar away*. See **intrusive /r/**. Chapter 1.

liquid   Reference to **approximant consonants** other than **glides** such as /j/ and /w/. The liquid consonants of English are /l/ and /r/ (strictly speaking just [ɹ], since /r/ can be realized as a non-liquid **tap** or trill in many varieties of English). Chapter 3.

literacy   Broadly, the ability to read and write, though some writers prefer to talk about *literacies* as sets of competences, and **multiliteracies** to recognize that competence is expected in different forms of reading and writing . Functional literacy is defined in relation to the norms of the society in question, rather than being an absolute global standard. Chapters 19, 23.

loan word   A word which may have been introduced into a language from another language. See also **borrowing**.

longitudinal study   A study that collects data and information from a particular speaker or group of speakers over a period of time in order to track processes of **language change**. Chapter 13. See also **real time**.

manner of articulation   The way in which a speech sound is articulated, rather than the place in the vocal tract at which it is articulated. The notion of degree of stricture (i.e. the magnitude of the obstruction to the airflow during a sound's production) is central.

marker   A **linguistic variable** which does carry social significance for speakers, generally if they are discussing their own language variety. Chapter 1.

masculinity/masculinities   Originally thought to be an attribute that speakers have that is reflected through their speech, more recent language and gender research from a **social constructionist** perspective has pluralized this concept, demonstrating how different types of masculini*ties* exist. This helps researchers move away from the problematic view that all men are a homogeneous group, as well as enabling more sophisticated models of societal power relations to be developed. Chapter 7.

matched-guise test   A technique using vocal 'guises' associated with studies of **language attitudes**. Typically, a single speaker is recorded who can imitate the required **speech styles**, such as different **accents**, and deceive listeners into thinking they are listening to different speakers saying similar things, or reading aloud the same text in their different accents. The rationale is that all speech features apart from the one under investigation are controlled, so any differences in listener evaluations must be because they judge the speech styles differently. Chapter 14.

mesolect   In a post-creolization situation, the **variety** spoken mostly by those in the middle of the social hierarchy. Mesolectal varieties form a continuum between the **acrolect** and the **basilect**.

metafunction   In the systemic analysis of linguistics of Halliday (1978), there are three overarching metafunctions of language: the *textual*, the *ideational* and the *interpersonal*.

metaphorical code-switching   See **code switching**.

minimal pair   A pair of meaningful words that differ in only one **phoneme**, such as *fan* and *van*, *cheese* and *seize* or *thought* and *thawed*. The existence of at least one **minimal pair** demonstrates the phonemic status of the sounds by which the two words in the pair are distinguished. Chapter 11.

minimal responses   Brief utterances such as 'mhm' or 'yeah' which listeners make in response to a speaker. They can be either supportive or disruptive. Supportive minimal responses, sometimes called **back-channels**, are the most frequent, and show active and collaborative listenership. Disruptive minimal responses can be where a string of minimal responses are used to attempt to gain the **floor**, or when minimal responses are delayed, thus indicating a lack of interest in the current speaker. Chapters 2, 7.

minority language   A language spoken as a **mother tongue** by a small number of speakers relative to the population of a region or country as a whole which has a different language as its **national language**. Some minority languages have strong **vitality**, such as Basque in Spain, while others are moribund or **endangered languages**, such as Gaelic in Scotland. Chapters 20, 23, 24.

mixing   In reference to **koineization**, mixing highlights the selection and incorporation of linguistic features from different pre-existing **dialects** which contribute to the language used by the first generation of immigrants. Chapters 22, 23.

modality   In general, the features of language which are used to express a speaker's attitude or commitment to a proposition. Specifically, modality has been used to refer to modal verbs and auxiliaries, and modal adverbial phrases. Chapter 4.

mode   A category within Halliday's (1978) systemic analysis which refers to the medium of communication used, for example, whether it is written or spoken. Chapter 5.

monogenesis hypothesis   In reference to the origin of **creoles** and **pidgins**, the view that all modern creoles and pidgins had evolved either from the Mediterranean **lingua franca** used for trade since the Middle Ages, or from the Portuguese lingua franca called Sabir, used on the West African coast from the sixteenth century to the nineteenth. Monogenesis is the original **relexification hypothesis**. Chapters 21, 23.

monolingualism The ability of a speaker or group to speak one language. Chapters 9, 11, 18, 19, 23. Contrast with **bilingualism** and **multilingualism**.

monophthong A vowel with only one discernible quality. Chapter 9. Compare with **diphthong**.

morphology The branch of theoretical linguistics which deals with the internal structure of words. Words are made up of smaller grammatical units called morphemes. Morphology is traditionally divided into two areas: *inflection*, which considers variation in form of a word for grammatical purposes, such as *make, makes*, and *word formation* (or *derivation*) – the construction of a new word from an existing word, such as *quick, quickly*. Chapter 13.

morphosyntax The part of morphology that covers the relationship between syntax and morphology. It deals with *inflection* and paradigms (which are defined by the requirements of syntactic rules), but not with *word formation* or compounding. See **morphology**. Chapters 4, 18.

mother tongue The language used by an individual from birth (also referred to as *first language, L1, primary language, home language*). It is usually also the language of the home and the community, but this may not be the case in **bilingual** or **multilingual** situations. Chapter 20.

multilingualism The ability of a speaker or group to speak three or more languages, though some sociolinguists use it interchangeably with **bilingualism**. Others argue that multilingualism should be used only as an overarching term in reference to societies and not individual speakers. Chapters 5, 11, 18, 19, 23.

multiliteracies Chapter 19. See **literacy**.

multimodality Refers to the multiple nature of modern communication, with text, symbol and image interacting in ways that modern technology has allowed. Chapter 19.

multiple negation Stretches of language where more than one instance of a negative form is used, such as 'I *don't* do that *never*'. Associated with **non-standard** varieties. Chapters 7, 9.

narrative Early definitions focus on the structuralist approach of Labov and Walesky (1967) where a narrative is any sequence where two or more clauses have a temporal ordering. Later work has also examined narrative content, and how narrative can be used as a lens through which **identity** performance can be observed. Chapter 5.

nasal A **place of articulation** description of a sound produced when the soft palate is lowered so the air escapes through the nose. The **consonants** /m/, /n/ and /ŋ/ are nasal, and /i/ is often nasalized in the context of these consonants. Chapters 3, 9.

national language A language which is associated with a particular country. The language may also be seen as a symbol of national identity. In some countries more than one national language may be recognized, such as Switzerland, in which German, French, Italian and Romansh are all national languages. Chapters 18, 20, 24. See also **official language**.

native speaker A speaker who acquires a language from birth as a native or first language. The acquisition is achieved through interaction with family and community members and not through formal instruction. In **bilingual** or **multilingual** contexts, people can be native speakers of more than one language, but everyone is a native speaker of at least one language. Chapter 20. See also **mother tongue**.

nativization In reference to the origins of **creoles** and **pidgins**, nativization refers to the acquisition of pidgins as **mother tongues** and **vernaculars**, which has led to the theory that a pidgin becomes a creole when a first generation of new speakers acquires the variety as a mother tongue. Chapter 21.

negative concord Chapter 4. See **multiple negation**.

negative face Part of Brown and Levinson's (1987) politeness theory, referring to a person's desire not to be imposed upon. Chapter 15. See also **positive face**, **negative politeness**.

negative politeness In Brown and Levinson's (1987) model, the tactics that speakers use in order to appeal to the addressee's **negative face**, using strategies that minimize the imposition being made upon the hearer's autonomy. Chapter 15. See also **politeness**.

non-standard Descriptive of a linguistic form different from that found in a **standard** variety, or of a variety other than the institutionally approved one. Liverpool English is a non-standard variety of British English, and the use of /uː/ rather than /ʊ/ in words such as *hook*, *cook*, *look*, etc., by its speakers is a non-standard pronunciation. Chapters 1, 4, 5, 9, 10, 14, 16.

observer's paradox The fact that the presence of a researcher will change the language data that are produced in the context being observed. Chapter 2.

obstruent A **consonant**, the articulation of which involves significant obstruction to the airstream. **Stops/plosives**, **affricates** and **fricatives** are all **obstruents**. Chapter 21.

official language An institutionally approved language for communication within and across national borders. Typically, a country will have a small number of official languages: Nigeria, in which about 470 languages are spoken, has only one official language (English). South Africa, on the other hand, has eleven official languages (English, Afrikaans, Zulu, Swati, Ndebele, Southern Sotho, Northern Sotho, Tsonga, Tsawa, Venda and Xhosa). Chapters 19, 23, 24. See also **national language**.

open vowel A vowel produced with maximal tongue and jaw lowering, such as /a/ and /ɑ/.

orality Primary oral cultures, or those that do not have a system of writing. A second orality can also be identified as one which is dominated by electronic modes of communication, such as television and telephones.

overlaps In the **turn-taking** system, when an instance of slight over-anticipation occurs by a speaker taking the conversational **floor** a little too early, resulting in slight cross-over between their initial **utterance** and the final utterance of the current speaker. Chapter 5.

overt prestige   Chapters 6, 7, 9. See **prestige**.

palatal   A **place of articulation** at which sounds are produced by raising the front of the tongue towards the hard palate so as to touch or approximate it. /j/ is a palatal **approximant**, while /tʃ/ and /dʒ/ are sometimes described as palatal **affricates**. /i/ is sometimes described as a palatal **vowel**. Chapters 12, 17.

participant observation   A technique of data collection in which the sociolinguist either becomes a member of the group being investigated or is already a member of that group. Chapters 2, 10.

patois   A term used to refer to a **non-standard** spoken **variety**. For some, the term can carry the negative connotation of 'uneducated', and so is rarely used in sociolinguistics. The term is found without negative connotation among some **speech communities**, however (e.g. the term *Patwa* is used by speakers of Jamaican Creole to refer to their variety).

perceptual dialectology   An area of sociolinguistics and dialectology which investigates metalinguistic attitudes and **folklinguistics**. Various techniques can be used such as giving respondents blank maps of countries on which to draw in what they perceive to be the main dialect regions, and then characterize those regions in their own words. Chapters 14, 22.

phatics   Those elements of speech which serve mainly a social function rather than a content function, such as 'Good morning,' 'How's it going?' 'Pleasure to have met you,' and so on. Phatic tokens are typically used to open and close conversations, and **repair** broken-down conversations.

phoneme   A class of speech sounds constituting a contrastive phonological element. /l/ is a phoneme of English which contrasts with other consonants (e.g. /g/ in *gate* versus *late*, or /d/ in *feed* versus *feel*) and which has two contextually conditioned **allophones**, [l] and [ɫ], in many **accents** of English such as **Received Pronunciation**.

phonetic(s)   Pertaining to human speech sounds. Phonetics is that branch of science devoted to the description and analysis of speech articulation, acoustics and audition. Chapters 1, 2, 3, 4, 6.

phonology   The branch of theoretical linguistics which deals with the organization of sound systems in the languages of the world, by attempting to account for the membership and geometry of a language's speech sound inventory, systematic alternations and processes in speech production, rules governing the ways in which speech sounds may combine into well formed syllables and words, and the interface between abstract sound systems and actual speech sounds on the one hand and the language's morphological rules on the other. Chapters 1, 3, 4, 5, 11, 13, 17, 18, 22.

pidgin   A language variety which functions as a **lingua franca**. Originally thought to derive from the Cantonese phrase *bei chin* 'pay money', pidgins are typically associated with trade colonies. Chapters 13, 21, 23.

pitch   In the description of pronunciation, pitch refers to qualities of **intonation** and tone. Chapters 5, 17.

place of articulation One dimension of the description of a speech sound, the place of articulation specifies where in the vocal tract a sound is produced mechanically: for example, **velar** sounds such as /g/ and /k/, **dentals** such as /t/ and /d/, **bilabials** such as /p/ and /b/, and so on.

plosive In describing pronunciation, plosives are those consonants in which the air flow is stopped and then released suddenly such as /b/ and /g/. See also **stop**.

politeness Broadly speaking, an analysis of linguistic forms which shows adherence to an accepted set of social and cultural principles emphasizing solidarity and social distance. Within **pragmatics**, politeness theory has become a key area of interest, and various theories and models have developed. The most well known politeness theory is Brown and Levinson's (1987) model, based on the notion of **face**. In recent years researchers have begun to examine the previously neglected concept of **impoliteness**, often thought to highlight the norms and conventions of politeness more effectively, as interactants tend to notice more when interlocutors are being *impolite* as opposed to polite. Chapter 15.

polygenesis hypothesis In reference to the origins of **creoles** and **pidgins**, the polygenesis hypothesis posits that creoles and pidgins developed separately from one another. Chapter 21. Contrast with **monogenesis hypothesis**.

positive face Part of Brown and Levinson's (1987) politeness theory, referring to a person's need to be wanted, liked and/or admired. See also **negative face**, **positive politeness**.

positive politeness In Brown and Levinson's (1987) **politeness** theory, the tactics that speakers use in order to appeal to the addressee's **positive face**, using friendliness and appreciation. Chapter 15. See also **negative politeness**.

post-creole speech continuum In a situation in which a **creole** has become established, the **lexifier** or other powerful language often exerts pressure towards its own **standardization**. A continuum often emerges, with an **acrolectal** variety of the creole close to the interfering language, through various **mesolectal** varieties, down to the **basilectal** or fully-fledged creole. Chapter 21.

post-national A recognition of the linguistic effects of globalization, such that languages such as English no longer correspond with national boundaries. Chapter 20.

postvocalic 'r' The /r/ in words like *farm* and *car*, pronunciation of which defines a **rhotic** accent (such as most North American, Irish and Scottish accents). The term 'non-prevocalic /r/' is sometimes used for the same feature; this is more precise, since the /r/ in 'parrot' is postvocalic but does not indicate rhoticity as it is not non-prevocalic. Chapters 1, 6.

power A key notion in **discourse analysis**, determining the institutional or individual ability to control or influence social or linguistic patterns. Chapters 6, 7, 9, 15.

pragmatics The study of meaning with regard given not only to the semantic content of **utterances** but also their social setting in context. Chapters 4, 15.

prescriptivism The tendency to argue for desired patterns in language rather than describing linguistic phenomena.

prestige Social value ascribed to a pattern of language use. Chapters 1, 6, 14, 16.

purity/purification The sense that a community has of its own language variety being unaffected by foreign varieties; and the desire to purge 'foreignisms' from the language. Chapters 18, 21.

qualitative Studies which are qualitative tend to emphasize the individual or detailed uses of language in unique or very particular and unreplicable settings. Chapters 8, 10, 11, 14, 15, 16. Compare with **quantitative**.

quantitative Studies which are quantitative tend to deploy analytical techniques based on statistical investigation, and are therefore typically reliant on large amounts of data for their reliability. Chapters 4, 7, 8, 10, 11, 12, 13, 14, 15, 17. Compare with **qualitative**.

queer linguistics The investigation of language and **sexuality** which focuses on lesbian, gay and bisexual language. The term 'queer' has been reappropriated by researchers in this area to have positive connotations, in contrast with the negative associations which have traditionally accompanied it, which include its use as an expression of abuse. Chapter 7.

quotative The reporting clause indicating direct speech, such as 'he said . . .', 'so I goes . . .', 'and I'm like . . .'. Chapters 4, 7.

random sample Selection of informants in a study based on chance rather than **judgement**. Chapter 2.

reallocation In **koineization**, when a process of **levelling** is incomplete, two forms from different source **varieties** might be used to refer to the same thing, so the different forms are reallocated with distinct functions. Chapter 22.

real-time studies Sociolinguistic investigations often of a **longitudinal** nature which follow real change over time. Chapters 2, 8, 13. Compare with **apparent time studies**.

Received Pronunciation (RP) An **accent** of **British English** with high **prestige** but a small **speech community** (around 3 per cent of the UK population), commonly thought of as the pronunciation of traditional or conservative BBC announcers. Though it is broadly a southern British accent, it tends to be spoken by educated speakers regardless of geographical origin. Chapters 1, 6, 11, 13, 14.

reduction In **koineization**, part of the process of **levelling** involves the elimination of certain minority **variants** where another linguistic option already exists. Chapter 22.

register Broadly, the combination of lexicogrammatical choices appropriate to the social setting and context. In **systemic linguistics**, register can be described by **field**, **tenor** and **mode**.

relexification hypothesis In theories of **creole** origin, the assertion that the vocabulary of a new language is heavily **borrowed** to 'fill out' the grammar of a source language. Chapter 21. See also **substrate hypothesis**.

repair In **conversation analysis**, the strategy by which a speaker re-initiates a dialogue which has stalled or broken down, often involving **phatics**. Chapter 5.

restricted code A term coined by Bernstein (1971) in his work on educational disadvantage. A code characterized by linguistic choices where meaning is implicit and needs interlocutors to be familiar with one another and to share a local context. Chapters 6, 19.

retroflex In the description of pronunciation, /r/ is retroflex when the tongue is curled back towards the roof of the mouth.

revitalization The expansion of a language's **speech community**, either by natural population increase or by deliberate **language planning**. Chapters 5, 20, 24.

rhotic/rhoticity An **accent** is said to be rhotic if the speaker systematically pronounces **postvocalic /r/**, as in 'farm', 'car' and 'oar'. Most Irish, Scottish and American accents are rhotic. Chapters 1, 3, 14.

rounding In describing pronunciation, **vowels** can be pronounced with lips more or less spread or rounded, changing the vowel quality.

S-curve model A structure or template associated with the temporal diffusion of innovations in language. The S-curve has been observed in diffusions of all kinds and illustrates the speed of diffusions which begin slowly as early adopters make use of the innovatory form. A period of rapid acceleration follows during which the change catches hold and begins to be used by the majority of speakers in the **speech community**. Finally the trajectory of the spread tails off as the change approaches categoricity. 'S-curve' refers to the shape of the line when the number of speakers (vertical axis) is plotted against time (horizontal axis). The vertical axis could also represent the number of words or texts affected.

sample frame A means of delimiting the boundaries for a set of data, such as 'names on the electoral register'. Chapter 2.

sampling universe A means of delimiting the setting for selecting a set of data (such as a city or neighbourhood). Chapter 2.

semantics The study of meaning, usually restricted to formal and referential dimensions of the sentence. Chapter 4.

semantic differential scales A means of eliciting informants' perceptions, using a bipolar scale, such as *attractive–unattractive, prestigious–stigmatized*, upon which informants mark their perceptions. Chapter 2.

sex In sociolinguistic research, sex refers to biological sex in order to make a distinction with the social constructionist term **gender**. Chapters 4, 6, 7, 12.

sexuality A dimension of study particularly in **queer linguistics**, sexuality can be seen as a social identity factor which influences language use. Chapter 7.

shibboleth A pronunciation which is strongly **stereotyped** to a particular **speech community**, serving to identify that speaker very readily, often with **prescriptivist** overtones. The term is biblical in origin (see Judges 12: 1–15).

sibilant In the description of pronunciation, a sibilant is produced when the tongue partially restricts the airflow (as in /s/ and /ʒ/).

sign language A fully realized language performed with the hands and upper body expressions, often combining both alphabetic and lexical sign symbols.

simplification A process in **koineization** and **creolization** in which morphological complexities and semantic functions are reduced or eliminated. Chapter 22.

situational code switching See **code switching**.

slang Informal vocabulary, usually **stigmatized**, that often serves to mark out a **subculture**.

social class Traditionally, a group is defined by their relationship to the economic control of production; more recently in sociolinguistics, class has also been measured by wealth, occupation, education and self-perception, and used as a significant **social variable**. Chapters 1, 5, 6, 7, 8, 9, 11, 12, 14, 16, 19.

social constructionist approach A theoretical perspective which sees social categories such as **gender** as fluid notions which are constructed in discourse practices. Chapter 7.

social dialectology An alternative term for **urban dialectology**, mainly founded in **variationist sociolinguistics**, to distinguish it from traditional, geographically based **dialectology**. Chapter 6.

social network A framework which measures the strength of individuals' social ties. Strong social networks are seen to act as (linguistic) norm-reinforcement mechanisms. Chapters 1, 9, 10, 12, 13, 18, 22.

social status The sense that **power**, privilege and respect accrue to particular people sharing certain valued social positions, such as of **social class**, or education. Chapters 9, 14, 15.

social stratification Usually referring to **social class** hierarchy, stratification is typically categorized in bands such as 'lower working class', 'middle middle class', or by other socio-economic scores. Chapter 10.

social variable In **variationist sociolinguistics**, the aspect of a speaker's social identity (such as **social class**, **age** or **gender**), which can then be correlated with **linguistic variables** to reveal the principles behind usage. Social variables are **independent variables** in statistical terms. Chapters 2, 7, 8, 9, 12.

socialization The process by which individuals are trained both informally and institutionally to conform to a community or **subculture**. Chapter 20.

sociolect An alternative term for **register**, to differentiate variation on the basis of the context of use from **dialect**.

sociolinguistic competence By analogy with **communicative competence**, the ability to interpret and manipulate structured variation in language. Chapter 8.

sociolinguistic interview An **elicitation** technique involving a question-and-answer session, often guided by a questionnaire or other protocols. Chapters 5, 6.

sociolinguistic variable A feature of language that varies systematically according to social context. Chapters 1, 3, 8, 14.

solidarity   The sense that an individual has of belonging to a social group.

spectrogram   A computer display or print-out showing the wave patterns of pronunciation. Chapters 1, 3.

Speech Accommodation Theory   Chapters 11, 12. See **accommodation**.

speech act   In **pragmatics**, the notion that an **utterance** is a performance and has a social force as well as a semantic content (such as *threatening*, *promising*, *questioning*, and so on). Chapters 5, 15.

speech community   A community defined or strongly identified by its shared linguistic practices. Chapters 5, 6, 7, 8, 9, 10, 11, 14, 18, 19, 21, 22.

speech repertoire   The set of verbal **varieties** available to either a speech community or an individual to use.

speech style   Chapters 6, 10, 14. See **style**.

Standard English   The **prestige dialect** of **British English**, prescribed in official and formal settings and sanctioned for writing in the education system. Chapters 4, 6, 9, 16, 19, 23, 24.

standard (language/variety)   The **variety** of a language (usually a historically significant **dialect**) which has been officially elevated to prestige status and is preferred in official documents, media, public and formal speech. Chapters 4, 10, 11, 13, 14, 16, 17, 18, 19, 23.

standard language cultures   Groups of speakers of powerful standardized languages such as English, French, Spanish, Mandarin, and others. Chapter 16.

standard language ideology   The perspective that insists upon the rightness of standardization, often with an associated moral injunction to use the standard form in all settings. Chapter 16. See **prescriptivism**.

standardization   The process, often imposed by institutions or through the education system, of marking out a language variety as the approved and sanctioned form. Chapters 8, 16, 17, 18, 20.

status planning   In **language planning**, status planning refers to the decision to confirm a language in its functions and its domains or to introduce a new language into these functions and domains. Chapter 20.

stereotype   A **linguistic variable** which speakers are highly aware of as being sociolinguistically significant. Chapter 1. See also **indicators** and **markers**.

stigma/stigmatization   The sense that a linguistic feature (and, by extension, its users) is socially inferior, faulty or proscribed. Chapters 12, 16.

stop   In the description of pronunciation, the air flow is stopped before being released in **plosives** such as /b/, /k/ and /d/.

stress   In the description of pronunciation, stress refers to the articulatory force placed on certain syllables, which gives an **accent** its characteristic rhythm and timing. In **pragmatics**, it is also used to indicate items (typically words) emphasized for particular meaningful contrastive effect.

structure   A social science term referring to the essential role that the social structure plays in enacting societal power, rather than focusing on the power of the individual to act. It is frequently used in **Critical Discourse Analysis**. Chapter 10. Compare with **agency**.

style In general, a describable and systematic pattern of linguistic usage. In sociolinguistics, style has been used to indicate the perceived formality of the context of situation. Chapters 11, 12.

subculture A group that is seen or sees itself as contained within a dominant culture or even marginal to it. Alienation in the subculture often results in a *counter-culture*. Chapter 7.

subjective reaction test When subjects are asked to evaluate speakers based upon listening to a recording of their speech. An example would be the **matched-guise test**. Chapter 2.

substrate In a **bilingual** or **multilingual** setting, the least dominant language is the substrate. The term is particularly useful in describing **creoles** where the historically dominant language (the **superstrate**) continues to mould the new variety. Creole grammars are often traceable to the substrate language. Chapters 9, 21.

substrate hypothesis In reference to the origins of **pidgins** and **creoles**, the substrate hypothesis posits that substrate influence should be seen as the primary explanation for the structural peculiarities of **creoles**. Chapter 21. See also **relexification hypothesis**.

superstrate In a **bilingual** or **multilingual** setting, the most influential language is the superstrate. **Creole lexis** is often enriched from the superstrate. Chapter 21.

superstrate hypothesis In reference to the origins of **pidgins** and **creoles**, the superstrate hypothesis emphasizes the origin of the individual structural peculiarities in the **non-standard** varieties of the **lexifier**.

supportive simultaneous talk Instances where two or more speakers talk at the same time in a supportive manner in order to engage in the joint production of discourse.

suprasegmentals Aspects of pronunciation at the level of **intonation**, tone and **pitch**. Chapters 1, 17.

symbolic power Associated with Bourdieu (1991), the ability of certain discourse practices to signify and construct **power**, such that power is enacted as a linguistic behaviour. Chapter 15.

synchronic In sociolinguistics, a study which is undertaken as a 'snapshot' of a moment in time. Contrast with **diachronic**.

syntax The study of the sequencing principles of sentences and utterances. Chapters 13, 17.

systemic analysis In Halliday's (1978) systemic functional linguistics, grammar is explained as a categorized system based around the metafunctions of *textuality*, *interpersonality* and *ideation*; this weight given to social and contextual matters has made it a popular tool in sociolinguistics. Chapter 5.

T–V pronoun system A linguistic differentiation between, basically, singular (T) and plural (V) *you* forms. The distinction is often used also to signify intimacy, **politeness**, respect, authority, **prestige** and formality, as well as simple number.

taboo language Areas of language usage which a society has marked off as prohibited or requiring of euphemism or mitigation (typically sex, death and religious transgression). Chapter 7.

tag question A pragmatic invitation to register solidarity by adding an empathetic question to an **utterance**, such as 'you know what I mean' or 'isn't it'. Chapters 1, 7.

tag switching When a speaker switches to another **code** (language, **accent** or other **variety**) simultaneous with the use of a clause tagged on to the end of the **utterance**, such as '. . . you know' or '. . . innit?' See also **code switching**.

tags Appended phrases in **utterances**, often with vague referents, typically serving as **solidarity** or **politeness** markers (such as 'you know', 'you get me', 'and that'). Chapter 1.

tap In describing pronunciation, the movement in which the tip of the tongue is flicked against the ridge behind the teeth, producing a 'tapped /r/' rather than a **retroflex /r/**. Chapters 1, 13.

TEFL Teaching English as a Foreign Language.

tenor In Halliday's (1978) systemic linguistic description of **register**, *tenor* refers to the relations between participants in the discourse. Chapter 5.

TESOL Teaching English to Speakers of Other Languages.

TH-fronting An **accent** feature in which the 'th' in, for example, 'thick' or 'brother' is pronounced with a /f/ or /v/. Chapter 17.

topic In discourse, *topic* is the subject of the conversation. It is often grammatically realized by being made prominent at the beginning of **utterances**. Chapters 5, 11.

trade language A language used in trade or contact situations; either an existing language used as a **lingua franca** or a new **variety** with the potential to form a **pidgin**.

traditional dialectology The study of **dialect** variation largely on the basis of geographical location. Chapter 2. Contrast with **urban dialectology**.

transcription The representation of speech in written notational form. Different conventions for transcribing reflect different levels of analysis. Chapter 5.

trilingualism The phenomenon in which an individual speaks three languages, often in a community which recognizes a functional (*triglossic*) or social use for each variety. Chapter 18.

turn-taking The phenomenon in conversation whereby speakers tend to avoid simultaneous speech and allow interactants to 'hold the floor'. The **turn** has been treated as the unit of spoken discourse, analogous to the clause as the unit of semantics. Chapters 1, 5, 7, 19.

underlexicalized The situation in which a language variety has only a few words for an item, usually indicating a cultural lack of interest in the phenomenon, by contrast with overlexicalized items (such as British words for types of rain or drug abusers' terms for their substances).

uptalk See **high rising terminal**.

urban dialectology A means of studying **language variation** not so much by wide geographical spread as in relation to other **social variables**.

utterance A string of speech equivalent to the unit of the sentence in writing; used in **pragmatics** to indicate the social context as well as the semantic proposition. Chapter 4.

uvular fricative In describing pronunciation, a sound produced by the uvula (the hanging tissue at the back of the mouth) partially restricting the airflow. Chapter 1.

variable A feature of language which shows variation in different social contexts. Chapters 2, 4, 6, 9, 13, 17. See also **dependent variable**, **independent variable**, **linguistic variable**, **social variable**.

variable rule A linguistic pattern which depends on a predicted frequency of its realization, rather than occurring on every occasion of use. Chapters 1, 14.

variant Linguistically equivalent but socially distinct choices in language, such as the variants *man, bloke, fellah, gadgie, chap*. Chapters 1, 2, 3, 4, 7, 8, 10, 12, 16, 21, 22.

variationist (sociolinguistics) A major approach within sociolinguistics which investigates the systematic causes and principles of variation in language against **social variables** such as **social class**, **age**, **ethnicity**, and so on. Chapters 1, 6, 8, 13, 17.

variety A systematic pattern of language use, such as a language, a **dialect**, an **accent**, a **sociolect**, and so on. Chapters 1, 4, 8, 9, 11, 12, 13, 14, 16, 17, 18, 19, 21, 22, 23.

velar Velar sounds are those produced at the velum or soft palate such as /g/ and /k/.

vernacular Traditionally regarded as the **mother tongue** of a speaker, the **vernacular** has been used to refer to **non-standard** varieties often perceived to stand in contrast with the **standard** variety. Chapters 6, 9, 18, 20, 21.

vernacular culture A **community of practice** in which group identity is strongly bound up with linguistic norms. Chapter 8.

vitality The sense that a community of speakers have of their own speech being a living language with a strong extensive **speech community**.

vocalization Where a sound, such as /l/ is pronounced as a **vowel** such as [o]. Chapter 3.

voiced Chapter 3. See **voicing**.

voiceless Chapter 3. See **voicing**.

voicing Altering sound by engaging the larynx, for example, voiceless /p/ is voiced as /b/. Chapters 3, 11.

voicing bar A dark band of frequencies in a **spectrogram** which measures whether a sound is voiced or voiceless. Chapter 3. See also **voicing**.

voiceless stop **Consonant** sounds produced by obstructing and releasing the air without the larynx being engaged, such as /k/, /p/ and /t/. Chapter 3.

vowel A sound produced by unobstructed airflow over the tongue, such as /a/, /o/, and /i/. Chapters 1, 3, 6, 9, 17.

World Englishes Any language variety of English including those developed by communities in which English was not indigenous in modern history. Chapters 20, 23.

REFERENCES

Adam, L. (1883) *Les Idiomes négro-aryens et malayo aryens: essai d'hybridologie linguistique*, Paris: Maisonneuve.

Adank, P., Van Heuven, V. and van Hout, R. (1999) 'Speaker normalization preserving regional accent differences in vowel quality', in J.J. Ohala, Y. Hasegawa, M. Ohala, D. Granville and A.C. Bailey (eds) *Proceedings of the XIV International Congress of Phonetic Sciences*, Berkeley, CA: Department of Linguistics, University of California.

Adger, D. and Smith, J. (2005) 'Variation and the minimalist program', in L. Cornips and K. Corrigan (eds) *Syntax and Variation: Reconciling the Biological and the Social*, Amsterdam: Benjamins, pp. 149–78.

Ager, D. (1996) *Francophonie in the 1990s: Problems and Opportunities*, Clevedon: Multilingual Matters.

Alleyne, M.C. (1980) *Comparative Afro-American*, Ann Arbor, MI: Karoma.

Altendorf, U. and Watt, D. (2005) 'The dialects in the south of England: phonology', in E.W. Schneider, K. Burridge, B. Kortmann, R. Mesthrie and C. Upton (eds) *A Handbook of Varieties of English: A Multimedia Reference Tool* I, *Phonology*, Berlin: Mouton de Gruyter, pp. 178–203.

Anderson, B. (1983) *Imagined Communities: Reflections on the Origins and Spread of Nationalism*, London: Verso.

Anderson, B. and Milroy, L. (1999) 'Southern changes and the Detroit AAVE vowel system', paper presented at NWAV 28, Toronto.

Androutsopoulos, J. (2001) 'From the streets to the screens and back again: on the mediated diffusion of ethnolectal patterns in contemporary German', in *Series A: General and Theoretical Papers*, Essen: University of Essen.

Androutsopoulos, J.K. (ed.) (2003) *Discourse Constructions of Youth Identities*, Philadelphia, PA: Benjamins.

Anttila, A. and Cho, Y.Y. (1998) 'Variation and change in optimality theory', *Lingua* 104: 31–56.

Argyle, M. (1994) *The Psychology of Social Class*, London: Routledge.

Aronsson, K. and Rundstrom, B. (1989) 'Cats, dogs and sweets in the clinical negotiation of reality: on politeness and coherence in pediatric discourse', *Language in Society* 18: 483–504.

Ash, S. (1997) 'The vocalization of intervocalic /l/ in Philadelphia', in H.B. Allen and M.D. Linn (eds) *Dialect and Language Variation*, Orlando, FL: Academic Press, pp. 25–53.

Ash, S. (2002) 'Social class', in J.K. Chambers, P. Trudgill and N. Schilling-Estes (eds) *The Handbook of Language Variation and Change*, Oxford: Blackwell, pp. 402–22.

Ashmore, A. and Reed, D. (2000) 'Innocence and nostalgia in conversation analysis: the dynamic relations of tape and transcript', *Forum: Qualitative Social Research* 1 (3): 1–17.

Atkinson, R. (1998) *The Life Story Interview*, Thousand Oaks, CA: Sage.

Auer, P. (1998) 'Structural convergence and interpersonal accommodation in a theory of language change', paper given at European Science Foundation Network on *The Convergence and Divergence of Dialects in a Changing Europe*, Reading: University of Reading.

Auer, P. (in press, a) 'The monolingual bias in bilingualism research – or: why bilingual talk is (still) a challenge for linguistics', in M. Heller (ed.) *Bilingualism*, London: Palgrave.

Auer, P. (in press, b) 'A(nother) scenario for new dialect formation: the German koiné in Rio Grande do Sul (Brazil)', to appear in a *Festschrift*.

Auer, P., Barden, B. and Großkopf, B.E. (1998) 'Subjective and objective parameters determining "salience" in long-term dialect accommodation', *Journal of Sociolinguistics* 2 (2): 163–87.

Auer, P. and Hinskens, F. (2005) 'The role of interpersonal accommodation in a theory of language change', in P. Auer, F. Hinskens and P. Kerswill (eds), *Dialect Change*, Cambridge: Cambridge University Press.

Auer, P., Barden, B. and Großkopf, B.E. (2000) 'Long-term linguistic accommodation and its sociolinguistic interpretation: evidence from the inner-German migration after the *Wende*', in K. Mattheier (ed.), *Dialect and Migration in a Changing Europe*, Frankfurt: Peter Lang, pp. 79–98.

Bailey, B. (2000) 'Language and negotiation of ethnic/racial identity among Dominican Americans', *Language in Society* 29: 555–82.

Bailey, G. (2002) 'Real and apparent time', in J.K. Chambers, P. Trudgill and N. Schilling-Estes (eds) *The Handbook of Language Variation and Change*, Oxford: Blackwell, pp. 312–32.

Baissac, C. (1880) *Etude sur le patois créole mauricien*, Nancy: Berger-Levrault.

Baker, P. and Mühlhäusler, P. (1990) 'From business to pidgin', *Journal of Asian Pacific Communication* 1: 87–115.

Bakhtin, M.M. (1981) *The Dialogic Imagination*, Austin, TX: University of Texas Press.

Bakhtin, M. (1983) 'Discourse in the novel', in *The Dialogic Imagination*, Austin, TX: University of Texas Press, pp. 259–420.

Baranowski, M. (2006) 'Doing the Charleston (South Carolina)', in W. Wolfram and B. Ward (eds) *American Voices: How Dialects Differ from Coast to Coast*, Malden, MA: Blackwell, pp. 29–35.

Barbour, S. and Stephenson, P. (1999) *Variation in German: A Critical Approach to German Sociolinguistics*, Cambridge: Cambridge University Press.

Barden, B. and Großkopf, B. (1998) *Sprachliche Akkommodation und soziale Integration*, Tübingen: Niemeyer.

Barrett, R. (1999) 'Indexing polyphonous identity in the speech of African American drag queens', in M. Bucholtz, A.C. Liang and L. Sutton (eds) *Reinventing Identities: the Gendered Self in Discourse*, Oxford: Oxford University Press, pp. 313–31.

Barthes, R. (1966) 'Introduction to the structural analysis of narratives', in S. Sontag (ed.) *A Barthes Reader*, London: Vintage, pp. 1–13.

Barton, D. (1994) *Literacy: An Introduction to the Ecology of Written Language*, Oxford: Blackwell.

Barz, R.K. and Siegel, J. (eds) (1988) *Language Transplanted: The Development of Overseas Hindi*, Wiesbaden: Harrassowitz.

Bauer, L. (2000) 'The dialectal origins of New Zealand English', in A. Bell and K. Kuiper (eds), *New Zealand English*, Wellington: Victoria University Press, pp. 40–52.

Baugh, J. (2000) *Beyond Ebonics: Linguistic Pride and Racial Prejudice*, New York: Oxford University Press.

Bayard, D., Weatherall, A., Gallois, C. and Pittam, J. (2001) '*Pax Americana?* Accent attitudinal evaluations in New Zealand, Australia and America', *Journal of Sociolinguistics* 5: 22–49.

Bayley, R. (2002) 'The quantitative paradigm', in J.K. Chambers, P. Trudgill and N. Schilling-Estes (eds) *The Handbook of Language Variation and Change*, Oxford: Blackwell, pp. 117–41.

Beal, J. (1997) 'Syntax and morphology', in C. Jones (ed.) *The Edinburgh History of the Scots Language*, Edinburgh: Edinburgh University Press, pp. 335–77.

Beal, J., Corrigan, K. and Moisl, H. (forthcoming) *Using Unconventional Digital Language Corpora* I, *Synchronic Corpora;* II, *Diachronic Corpora*. Basingstoke: Palgrave Macmillan.

Bedisti, E. (2004) *The Influence of Social Class on the Language of School Children in Greece*. PhD thesis, University of Reading.

Bell, A. (1984) 'Language style as audience design', *Language in Society* 13: 145–204.

Bell, A. (1991) *The Language of News Media*, Oxford: Blackwell.

Bell, A. (1992) 'Hit and miss: referee design in the dialects of New Zealand television advertisements', *Language and Communication* 12: 327–40.

Bell, A. (1997) 'The phonetics of fish and chips in New Zealand: marking national and ethnic identities', *English World Wide* 18: 243–70.

Bell, A. (1999) 'Styling the other to define the self: a study in New Zealand identity making', *Journal of Sociolinguistics* 3: 523–41.

Bell, A. (2000) 'Maori and Pakeha English: a case study', in A. Bell and K. Kuiper (eds) *New Zealand English*, Wellington: Victoria University Press, pp. 221–48.

Bell, A. (2001) 'Back in style: re-working Audience Design', in P. Eckert and J.R. Rickford (eds) *Style and Sociolinguistic Variation*, New York: Cambridge University Press, pp. 139–69.

Berend, N. (1998) *Sprachliche Anpassung. Eine soziolinguistisch-dialektologische Untersuchung zum Russlanddeutschen*, Tübingen: Niemeyer.

Bernstein, B. (1971) *Class, Codes and Control* I, London: Routledge.

Bernstein, B. (1977) *Class, Codes and Control* III, London: Routledge.

Bernstein, B. (1996) *Pedagogy, Symbolic Control and Identity: Theory, Research, Critique*, London: Taylor and Francis.

Bex, T. and Watts, R. (eds) (1999) *Standard English: The Widening Debate*, London: Routledge.

Bickerton, D. (1981) *Roots of Language*, Ann Arbor, MI: Karoma.

Bickerton, D. (1984) 'The language bioprogram hypothesis', *Behavioral and Brain Sciences* 7: 173–221.

Bickerton, D. (1999) 'How to acquire language without positive evidence: what acquisitionists can learn from creoles', in M. DeGraff (ed.) *Language Creation and Language Change: Creolization, Diachrony, and Development*, Cambridge, MA: MIT Press, pp. 49–74.

Blom, J.-P. and Gumperz, J.J. (1972) 'Social meaning in linguistic structure: code-switching in Norway', in J.J. Gumperz and D. Hymes (eds) *Directions in Sociolinguistics*, New York: Holt, Rinehart and Winston, pp. 407–34.

Bloomfield, L. (1933) *Language*, New York: Holt, Rinehart and Winston.

Boberg, C. (1997) *Variation and Change in the Nativization of Foreign (a) in English*. PhD thesis, University of Pennsylvania.

Bolton, K. (2000). 'Language and hybridization: pidgin tales from the China coast', *Interventions* 5: 35–52.

Bortoni-Ricardo, S.M. (1985) *The Urbanization of Rural Dialect Speakers*, Cambridge: Cambridge University Press.

Bourdieu, P. (1991) *Language and Symbolic Power*, Cambridge: Polity Press.

Bradac, J., Cargile, A. and Hallett, J. (2001) 'Language attitudes: retrospect, conspect, and prospect', in P. Robinson and H. Giles (eds) *The New Handbook of Language and Social Psychology*, Chichester: Wiley, pp. 137–55.

Bradac, J.J., Mulac, A. and House, A. (1988) 'Lexical diversity and magnitude of convergent versus divergent style-shifting: perceptual and evaluative consequences', *Language and Communication* 8: 213–28.

Brandt, W. (1984) 'Hörfunk und Fernsehen in ihrer Bedeutung für die jüngste Geschichte des Deutschen', in W. Besch, O. Reichmann and S. Sonderegger (eds), *Sprachgeschichte* II, Berlin: de Gruyter, pp. 1669–78.

Branner, R. (2002) 'Zitate aus der Medienwelt. Zu Form und Funktion von Werbezitaten in natürlichen Gesprächen', *Muttersprache* 4: 337–59.

Bratt-Paulston, C. and Tucker R. (2003) *Sociolinguistics: The Essential Readings*, Oxford: Blackwell.

Britain, D. (1998) 'Linguistic change in intonation: the use of high-rising terminals in New Zealand English', in P. Trudgill and J. Cheshire (eds) *The Sociolinguistics Reader* I, *Multilingualism and Variation*, London: Arnold, pp. 213–39.

Britain, D. (1999) 'As far as analysing grammatical variation and change in New Zealand English <is concerned/ø>', in A. Bell and K. Kuiper (eds) *New Zealand English*, Amsterdam: Benjamins, pp. 198–220.

Britain, D. and Matsumoto, K. (2005) 'Languages, communities, networks and practices', in M.J. Ball (ed.) *Clinical Sociolinguistics*, Oxford: Blackwell, pp. 3–14.

Brown, P. and Levinson, S. (1978) 'Universals in language usage: politeness phenomena', in E. Goody (ed.) *Questions and Politeness*, Cambridge: Cambridge University Press, pp. 256–311.

Brown, P. and Levinson, S. (1987) *Politeness: Some Universals in Language Usage*, Cambridge: Cambridge University Press.

Bruner, J. (1990) *Acts of Meaning*, Cambridge, MA: Harvard University Press.

Brutt-Griffler, J. (2002) *World English: A Study of its Development*, Clevedon: Multilingual Matters.

Bucholtz, M. (1999) ' "Why be normal?": language and identity practices in a community of nerd girls', *Language in Society* 28: 203–23.

Bucholtz, M. and Hall, K. (2004) 'Language and identity', in A. Duranti (ed.) *The Blackwell Companion to Linguistic Anthropology*, Oxford: Blackwell, pp. 369–94.

Bucholtz, M. and Hall, K. (2005) 'Identity and interaction: a sociocultural approach', *Discourse Studies* 7: 585–614.

Buckingham, D. (1987) *Public Secrets: EastEnders and its Audience*, London: British Film Institute.

Cameron, D. (1995) *Verbal Hygiene*, London: Routledge.

Cameron, D. (1996) 'The language–gender interface: challenging co-optation', in V. Bergvall, J. Bing and A. Freed (eds) *Rethinking Language and Gender Research: Theory and Practice*, London: Longman, pp. 31–53.

Cameron, D. (1997) 'Performing gender identity: young men's talk and the construction of heterosexual masculinity', in S. Johnson and U.H. Meinhof (eds) *Language and Masculinity*, Oxford: Blackwell, pp. 47–64.

Cameron, D. and Kulick, D. (2003) *Language and Sexuality*, Cambridge: Cambridge University Press.

Canagarajah, S. (1999) *Resisting Linguistic Imperialism in English Language Teaching*, Oxford: Oxford University Press.

Cannadine, D. (1998) *Class in Britain*, London: Penguin.

Cargile, A., Giles, H., Ryan, E.B. and Bradac, J. (1994) 'Language attitudes as a social process: a conceptual model and new directions', *Language and Communication* 14: 211–36.

Carter, P. and Local, J. (2003) 'Modelling change in the liquid system in Tyneside English', *Proceedings of the XV International Congress of Phonetic Sciences*, Barcelona, August, pp. 1193–6.

Carvalho, A.M. (2004) 'I speak like the guys on TV: palatalization and the urbanization of Uruguayan Portuguese', *Language Variation and Change* 16: 127–51.

Cedergren, H. and Sankoff, D. (1974) 'Variable rules: performance as a statistical reflection of competence', *Language* 50 (2): 333–55.

Chambers, J.K. (1991) 'Canada', in J. Cheshire (ed.) *English Around the World: Sociolinguistic Perspectives*, Cambridge: Cambridge University Press, pp. 89–107.

Chambers, J.K. (1992) 'Dialect acquisition', *Language* 68: 673–705.

Chambers, J.K. (1995) *Sociolinguistic Theory: Linguistic Variation and its Social Significance*, Oxford: Blackwell.

Chambers, J.K. (1998) 'TV makes people sound the same', in L. Bauer and P. Trudgill (eds) *Language Myths*, New York: Penguin, pp. 123–31.

Chambers, J.K. (2003) *Sociolinguistic Theory: Linguistic Variation and its Social Significance* (2nd edn), Oxford: Blackwell.

Chambers, J.K. (2004) 'TV and your language', *Do you speak American?* Website for McNeil-Lehrer Productions <http://www.york.ac.uk/depts/lang/Jack_Chambers/>, accessed December 2005.

Chambers, J.K. and Trudgill, P. (1998) *Dialectology* (2nd edn), Cambridge: Cambridge University Press.

Chaudenson, R. (2001) *Creolization of Language and Culture*, London: Routledge.

Cheshire, J. (1982) *Variation in an English Dialect: A Sociolinguistic Study*, Cambridge: Cambridge University Press.

Cheshire, J. (1987) 'Syntactic variation, the linguistic variable and sociolinguistic theory', *Linguistics* 25 (2): 257–82.

Cheshire, J. (2002) 'Sex and gender in variationist research', in J.K. Chambers, P. Trudgill and N. Schilling-Estes (eds) *The Handbook of Language Variation and Change*, Oxford: Blackwell, pp. 423–43.

Cheshire, J. (2005a) 'Syntactic variation and beyond: gender and social class variation in the use of discourse – new markers', *Journal of Sociolinguistics* 9 (4): 479–508.

Cheshire, J. (2005b) 'Syntactic variation and spoken language', in L. Cornips and

K. Corrigan (eds) *Syntax and Variation: Reconciling the Biological and the Social*, Amsterdam: Benjamins, pp. 81–106.

Cheshire, J., Edwards, V. and Whittle, P. (1989) 'Urban British dialect grammar: the question of dialect levelling', *English World Wide* 10 (2): 185–225.

Cheshire, J., Kerswill, P. and Williams, A. (2005) 'On the non-convergence of phonology, grammar and discourse', in P. Auer, F. Hinskens and P. Kerswill (eds) *Dialect Change: Convergence and Divergence in European Languages*, Cambridge: Cambridge University Press, pp. 135–67.

Chomsky, N. (1986) *Knowledge of Language: Its Nature, Origin and Use*, New York: Praeger.

Coates, J. (ed.) (1998) *Language and Gender: A Reader*, Oxford: Blackwell.

Coates, J. (2004) *Women, Men and Language* (3rd edn), London: Longman.

Coates, J. (in press) '"Everyone was convinced that we were closet fags": the role of heterosexuality in the construction of hegemonic masculinity', in S. Kyratzis and H. Sauntson (eds) *Language, Sexualities and Desires: Cross-cultural Perspectives*, London: Palgrave.

Comrie, B. (1981) *The Languages of the Soviet Union*, Cambridge: Cambridge University Press.

Connell, R.W. (1995) *Masculinities*, Cambridge: Polity Press.

Cooper, R. (1989) *Language Planning and Social Change*, Cambridge: Cambridge University Press.

Cope, B. and Kalantzis, M. (eds) (2000) *Multiliteracies: Literacy Learning and the Design of Social Futures*, London, Routledge.

Corrigan K.P. (1997) 'The acquisition and properties of a contact vernacular grammar', in A. Ahlqvist and V. Capková (eds) *Dán Do Oide: Essays in Memory of Conn R. Ó Cleirigh*, Dublin: Linguistics Institute of Ireland, pp. 75–93.

Cortazzi, M. (1999) 'Narrative analysis', in A. Bryman and R. Burgess (eds) *Methods of Qualitative Research* II, Thousand Oaks, CA: Sage, pp. 246–58.

Coulmas, F. (2005) *Sociolinguistics: The Study of Speakers' Choices*, Cambridge: Cambridge University Press.

Couper-Kuhlen, E. and Selting, M. (eds) (2001) *Studies in Interactional Linguistics*, Amsterdam: Benjamins.

Coupland, N. (1984) 'Accommodation at work: some phonological data and their implications', *International Journal of the Sociology of Language* 46: 49–70.

Coupland, N. (2001a) 'Age in social and sociolinguistic theory', in N. Coupland, S. Sarangi and C. Candlin (eds) *Sociolinguistics and Social Theory*, Harlow: Pearson, pp. 185–211.

Coupland, N. (2001b) 'Language, situation, and the relational self: theorizing dialect style in sociolinguistics', in P. Eckert and J.R. Rickford (eds) *Style and Sociolinguistic Variation*, New York: Cambridge University Press, pp. 185–210.

Coupland, N. and Jaworski, A. (2004) 'Sociolinguistic perspectives on metalanguage: reflexivity, evaluation and ideology', in A. Jaworski, N. Coupland and D. Galasiński (eds) *Metalanguage: Social and Ideological Perspectives*, The Hague: Mouton, pp. 15–51.

Coupland, N., Coupland, J. and Giles, H. (1991) *Language, Society and the Elderly: Discourse, Identity and Ageing*, Oxford: Blackwell.

Coupland, N., Grainger, K. and Coupland, J. (1988) 'Politeness in context: intergenerational issues', *Language in Society* 17: 253–62.

Crawford, F. (2002) 'Entering the community: fieldwork', in J.K. Chambers, P. Trudgill and N. Schilling-Estes (eds) *The Handbook of Language Variation and Change*, Oxford: Blackwell, pp. 20–39.

Crawford, M. (1995) *Talking Difference: On Gender and Language*, London: Sage.

Crystal, D. (1999) *The Cambridge Encyclopedia of the English Language* (2nd edn), Cambridge: Cambridge University Press.

Crystal, D. (2000) *Language Death*, Cambridge: Cambridge University Press.

Crystal, D. (2003) *English as a Global Language* (2nd edn), Cambridge: Cambridge University Press.

Cummins, J. (1996) *Negotiating Identities: Education for Empowerment in a Diverse Society*, Ontario, CA: California Association for Bilingual Education.

Czarniawska, B. (1997) *A Narrative Approach to Organization Studies*, Thousand Oaks, CA: Sage.

Daiute, C. and Lightfoot, C. (eds) (2004) *Narrative Analysis: Studying the Development of Individuals in Society*, Thousand Oaks, CA: Sage.

Dalby, A. (2003) *Language in Danger*, London: Penguin.

Dauenhauer, N.M. and Dauenhauer, R. (1998) 'Technical, emotional, and ideological issues in reversing language shift: examples from south-east Alaska', in L. Grenoble and L. Whaley (eds) *Endangered Languages: Language Loss and Community Response*, Cambridge: Cambridge University Press, pp. 57–98.

Day, R. (1982) 'Children's attitudes toward language', in E.B. Ryan and H. Giles (eds) *Attitudes towards Language Variation*, London: Arnold, pp. 116–31.

de Fina, A. (2003) *Identity in Narrative: A Study of Immigrant Discourse*, Amsterdam: Benjamins.

DeCamp, D. (1971) 'Toward a generative analysis of a post-creole speech continuum', in D. Hymes (ed.) *Pidginization and Creolization of Languages*, Cambridge: Cambridge University Press, pp. 349–70.

DeGraff, M. (1999) 'Creolization, language change, and language acquisition: a prolegomenon', in *Language Creation and Language Change: Creolization, Diachrony, and Development*, Cambridge, MA: MIT Press, pp. 1–46.

DeGraff, M. (2003) 'Against creole exceptionalism', *Language* 79: 391–410.

Diamond, J. (1996) *Status and Power in Verbal Interaction: A Study of Discourse in a Close-knit Social Network*, Amsterdam: Benjamins.

Diamond, J. (1997) *Guns, Germs and Steel: The Fate of Human Societies*, New York: Random House.

Dixon, J., Mahoney, B. and Cocks, R. (2002) 'Accents of guilt? Effects of regional accent, race, and crime type on attributions of guilt', *Journal of Language and Social Psychology* 21: 162–8.

Dixon, R.M.W. (1997) *The Rise and Fall of Languages*, Cambridge: Cambridge University Press.

Docherty, G.J. and Foulkes, P. (1999) 'Derby and Newcastle: instrumental phonetics and variationist studies', in P. Foulkes and G. Docherty (eds) *Urban Voices*, London: Arnold, pp. 47–71.

Docherty, G.J. and Foulkes, P. (2001) 'Variability in (r) production: instrumental perspectives', in H. Van de Velde and R. van Hout (eds) *'r-atics: Sociolinguistic, Phonetic and Phonological Characteristics of /r/*, Brussels: IVLP, pp. 173–84.

Docherty, G.J., Foulkes, P., Milroy, J., Milroy, L. and Walshaw, D. (1997) 'Descriptive adequacy in phonology: a variationist perspective', *Journal of Linguistics* 33: 275–31.

Drew, P., Chatwin, J. and Collins, S. (2001) 'Conversation analysis: a method for research into interactions between patients and health-care professionals', *Health Expectations* 4: 58–70.

Dubois, S. and Horvath, B. (1998a) 'From accent to marker in Cajun English: a study of dialect formation in progress', *English World Wide* 19: 161–88.

Dubois, S. and Horvath, B. (1998b) 'Let's tink about dat: interdental fricatives in Cajun English', *Language Variation and Change* 10: 245–61.

Dubois, S. and Horvath. B. (1999) 'When the music changes, you change too: gender and language change in Cajun English', *Language Variation and Change* 11: 287–313.

Dyer, J. (2000) *Language and Identity in a Scottish-English Community: A Phonological and Discoursal Analysis*. PhD thesis. Ann Arbor, MI: University of Michigan.

Dyer, J. (2002) ' "We all speak the same round here": dialect levelling in a Scottish-English community', *Journal of Sociolinguistics* 6 (1): 99–116.

Eckert, P. (1989) *Jocks and Burnouts: Social Categories and Identity in the High School*, New York: Columbia University Teachers' College.

Eckert, P. (1997) 'Gender and sociolinguistic variation', in J. Coates (ed.) *Language and Gender: A Reader*, Oxford: Blackwell, pp. 64–75.

Eckert, P. (1998) 'Age as a sociolinguistic variable', in F. Coulmas (ed.) *The Handbook of Sociolinguistics*, Oxford: Blackwell, pp. 151–67.

Eckert, P. (2000) *Linguistic Variation as Social Practice: The Linguistic Construction of Identity in Belten High*, Oxford: Blackwell.

Eckert, P. (2002) 'Constructing meaning in sociolinguistic variation', paper presented at the annual meeting of the American Anthropological Association, New Orleans, November.

Eckert, P. and McConnell-Ginet, S. (1992) 'Think practically and look locally: language and gender as community-based practice', *Annual Review of Anthropology* 21: 461–90.

Eckert, P. and McConnell-Ginet, S. (1995) 'Constructing meaning, constructing selves: snapshots of language, gender and class from Belten High', in K. Hall and M. Bucholtz (eds) *Gender Articulated: Language and the Socially Constructed Self*, London: Routledge, pp. 469–507.

Eckert, P. and McConnell-Ginet, S. (1999) 'New generalizations and explanations in language and gender research', *Language in Society* 28 (2): 185–201.

Eckert, P. and Rickford, J.R. (eds) (2001) *Style and Sociolinguistic Variation*, New York: Cambridge University Press.

Edwards, D. (1997) *Multilingualism*, Harmondsworth: Penguin.

Edwards, J. (1992) 'Sociopolitical aspects of language maintenance and loss: towards a typology of minority language situations', in W. Fase, K. Jaspaert and S. Kroon (eds) *Maintenance and Loss of Minority Languages*, Amsterdam: Benjamins, pp. 37–54.

Edwards, J. (1995) *Multilingualism*, Harmondsworth: Penguin.

Edwards, J. (1999) 'Refining our understanding of language attitudes', *Journal of Language and Social Psychology* 18: 101–10.

Edwards, J. and Jacobsen, M. (1987) 'Standard and regional standard speech: distinctions and similarities', *Language in Society* 16: 369–80.

Edwards, V. (2004) *Multilingualism in the English-speaking World*, Oxford: Blackwell.

Eelen, G. (2001) *A Critique of Politeness Theories*, Manchester: St Jerome.

Eggins, S. and Slade, D. (2004) *Analysing Casual Conversation*, London: Equinox.

Eisikovits, E. (1987) 'Variation in the lexical verb in inner-Sydney English', *Australian Journal of Linguistics* 7: 1–24.

Eisikovits, E. (1998) 'Girl-talk/boy-talk: sex differences in adolescent speech', in J. Coates (ed.) *Language and Gender: A Reader*, Oxford: Blackwell, pp. 42–54.

Fairclough, N. (1989) *Language and Power*, London: Longman.

Fairclough, N. (1995) *Critical Discourse Analysis*, London: Longman.

Fairclough, N. (2001) *Language and Power* (2nd edn), London: Longman.

Fairclough, N. (2003) *Analysing Discourse: Textual Analysis for Social Research*, London: Routledge.

Feagin, C.L. (1979) *Tense Marking in Black English: a Linguistic and Social Analysis*, Arlington, VA: Center for Applied Linguistics.

Fennell, B.A. (1997) *Language, Literature and the Negotiation of Identity: Foreign Worker German in the Federal Republic of Germany*, Chapel Hill, NC: University of North Carolina Press.

Fennell, B.A. (2000) *A History of English: A Sociolinguistic Approach*, Oxford: Blackwell.

Fennell, B.A. and Butters, R.R. (1996) 'Historical and contemporary distribution of double modals in English' in. E.W. Schneider (ed.) *Focus on the USA*, Varieties of English around the World 16, Amsterdam: Benjamins, pp. 265–88.

Fielding, G. and Evered, C. (1980) 'The influence of patients' speech upon doctors: the diagnostic interview', in R. St Clair and H. Giles (eds) *The Social and Psychological Contexts of Language*, Hillsdale, NJ: Erlbaum, pp. 51–72.

Fill, A. and Mühlhäusler, P. (eds) (2001) *The Ecolinguistics Reader: Language, Ecology and Environment*, London: Continuum.

Fishman, J. (1972) 'Domains and the relationship between micro- and macro-sociolinguistics', in J.J. Gumperz and D. Hymes (eds) *Directions in Sociolinguistics*, New York: Holt, Rinehart and Winston, pp. 235–53.

Fishman, J. (1991) *Reversing Language Shift*, Clevedon: Multilingual Matters.

Fishman, J. (ed.) (1999) *Handbook of Language and Ethnic Identity*, Oxford: Oxford University Press.

Fishman, J. (2001) *Can Threatened Languages be Saved?* Clevedon: Multilingual Matters.

Foley, W.A. (1997) *Anthropological Linguistics*, Oxford: Blackwell.

Fordham, S. and Ogbu, J. (1986) 'Black students' school success: coping with the burden of "acting white"', *Urban Review* 18: 176–206.

Foucault, M. (1972) *The Archaeology of Knowledge*, London: Routledge.

Fought, C. (2002) 'Ethnicity', in J.K. Chambers, P. Trudgill and N. Schilling-Estes (eds) *Handbook of Language Variation and Change*, Oxford: Blackwell, pp. 444–72.

Fought, C. (2003) *Chicano English in Context*, Basingstoke: Palgrave Macmillan.

Fought, C. (2006) *Language and Ethnicity*, Cambridge: Cambridge University Press.

Foulkes, P. and Docherty, G.J. (eds) (1999), *Urban Voices: Accent Studies in the British Isles*, London: Arnold.

Foulkes, P. and Docherty, G.J. (2000) 'Another chapter in the story of /r/: "labiodental" variants in British English', *Journal of Sociolinguistics* 4 (1): 30–59.

Foulkes, P. and Docherty, G.J. (2001) 'Variation and change in British English /r/', in H. Van de Velde and R. van Hout (eds) *'r-atics: Sociolinguistic, Phonetic and Phonological Characteristics of /r/*, Brussels: IVPL, pp. 27–44.

Foulkes, P. and French, J.P. (1999) 'Forensic phonetics and sociolinguistics', in R. Mesthrie (ed.) *The Concise Encyclopaedia of Sociolinguistics*, Amsterdam: Pergamon, pp. 329–32.

Foulkes, P., Docherty, G.J. and Watt, D. (1999) 'Tracking the emergence of structured variation: realisations of (t) by Newcastle children', *Leeds Working Papers in Linguistics and Phonetics* 7: 1–25.

Foulkes, P., Docherty, G.J. and Watt, D. (2005) 'Phonological variation in child-directed speech', *Language* 81 (1): 177–206.

Freed, A. (1996) 'Language and gender in an experimental setting', in V. Bergvall, J. Bing and A. Freed (eds) *Rethinking Language and Gender Research: Theory and Practice*, New York: Longman, pp. 54–76.

Fridland, V. (1999) 'The southern shift in Memphis, Tennessee', *Language Variation and Change* 11: 267–85.

Frosh, S., Phoenix, A. and Pattman, R. (2002) *Young Masculinities*, London: Palgrave.

Gal, S. and Irvine, I. (1995) 'The boundaries of languages and disciplines: how ideologies construct difference', *Social Research* 62 (4): 967–1001.

Gardner, R.C. and Lambert, W.E. (1972) *Attitudes and Motivation in Second Language Learning*, Rowley, MA: Newbury House.

Garner, M. (2004) *Language: An Ecological View*, Oxford: Peter Lang.

Garrett, P., Coupland, N. and Williams, A. (2003) *Investigating Language Attitudes: Social Meanings of Dialect, Ethnicity and Performance*, Cardiff: University of Wales Press.

Garside, R., Leech, G. and McEnery, A. (eds) (1997) *Corpus Annotation: Linguistic Information from Computer Text Corpora*, London: Longman.

Gee, J.P. (1996) *Social Linguistics and Literacies: Ideology in Discourses* (2nd edn), London: Taylor and Francis.

Gellner, E. (1983) *Nations and Nationalism*, Oxford: Blackwell.

Giddens, A. (2001) *Sociology* (4th edn), Cambridge: Polity Press.

Giles, H. (1970) 'Evaluative reactions to accents', *Educational Review* 22: 211–27.

Giles, H. (1973) 'Accent mobility: a model and some data', *Anthropological Linguistics* 15: 87–105.

Giles, H. (1977) *Language, Ethnicity and Intergroup Relations*, New York: Academic Press.

Giles, H. (1979) 'Ethnicity markers in speech', in K. Scherer and H. Giles (eds) *Social Markers in Speech*, London: Cambridge University Press, pp. 251–89.

Giles, H. and Coupland, N. (1991) *Language: Contexts and Consequences*, Milton Keynes: Open University Press.

Giles, H. and Powesland, P.F. (1975) *Speech Style and Social Evaluation*, London: Academic Press.

Giles, H. and Sassoon, C. (1983) 'The effect of speaker's accent, social class background and message style on British listeners' social judgements', *Language and Communication* 3: 305–13.

Glauser, B. (1991) 'Transition areas versus focal areas in English dialectology', *English World-Wide* 12: 1–24.

Glauser, B. (2000) 'The Scottish/English border in hindsight', *International Journal of the Sociology of Language* 145: 65–78.

Godfrey, E. and Tagliamonte, S. (1999) 'Another piece for the verbal -s story: evidence from Devon in southwest England', *Language Variation and Change* 11 (1): 87–121.

Goffman, E. (1967) *Interaction Ritual*, New York: Anchor Books.

Gold, D.L. (1981) 'The speech and writing of Jews', in C.A. Ferguson and S.B. Heath (eds) *Language in the USA*, New York: Cambridge University Press, pp. 273–92.

Gordon, E., Campbell, L., Hay, J., MacLagan, M., Sudbury, A. and Trudgill, P. (2004)

New Zealand English: Its Origins and Revolution, Cambridge: Cambridge University Press.

Gordon, M.J. (2001) *Small-Town Values and Big-City Vowels: A Study of the Northern Cities Shift in Michigan*, Durham, NC: Duke University Press.

Görlach, M. (1991) *Englishes: Studies in Varieties of English 1984–1988*, Amsterdam: Benjamins.

Görlach, M. (1998) *Even More Englishes: Studies 1996–1997*, Amsterdam: Benjamins.

Gould, O. and Dixon, R. (1997) 'Recall of medication instructions by young and elderly adult women: is overaccommodative speech helpful?' *Journal of Language and Social Psychology* 16: 50–69.

Grabe, E., Post, B., Nolan, F.J. and Farrar, K. (2000) 'Pitch accent realization in four varieties of British English', *Journal of Phonetics* 28: 161–85.

Gramsci, A. (1971) *Selections from the Prison Notebooks* (trans. Q. Hoare and G. Nowell-Smith), New York: Lawrence and Wishart.

Granger, R., Mathews, M., Quay, L. and Verner, R. (1977) 'Teacher judgements of the communication effectiveness of children using different speech patterns', *Journal of Educational Psychology* 69: 793–6.

Greenbaum, S. (1996) *Comparing English Worldwide: The International Corpus of English*, Oxford: Clarendon Press.

Grenoble, L. and Whaley, L. (eds) (1998) *Endangered Languages: Language Loss and Community Response*, Cambridge: Cambridge University Press.

Grice, H.P. (1975) 'Logic and conversation', in P. Cole and J. Morgan (eds) *Syntax and Semantics* III, *Speech Acts*, New York: Academic Press, pp. 45–65.

Gries, S.T. (2005) *Multifactorial Analysis in Corpus Linguistics*, London: Continuum.

Grimes, B. (ed.) (2000) *Ethnologue: Languages of the World*, Dallas, TX: Summer Institute of Linguistics.

Gumperz, J.J. (1982) *Discourse Strategies*, New York: Cambridge University Press.

Gumperz, J.J. and Wilson, R. (1971) 'Convergence and creolization: a case from the Indo-Aryan/Dravidian border', in D. Hymes (ed.) *Pidginization and Creolization of Languages*, New York: Cambridge University Press, pp. 151–68.

Gunter, B. (2000) *Media Research Methods: Measuring Audiences, Reactions and Impact*, London: Sage.

Guy, G. (1980) 'Variation in the group and the individual: the case of final stop deletion', in W. Labov (ed.) *Locating Language in Time and Space*, New York: Academic Press, pp. 1–36.

Guy, G. (1993) 'The quantitative analysis of linguistic variation', in D. Preston (ed.) *American Dialect Research*, Amsterdam and Philadelphia: Benjamins, pp. 223–49.

Guy, G. (1997) 'Competence, performance and the generative grammar of variation', in F. Hinskens, R. van Hout and L. Wetzels (eds) *Variation, Change and Phonological Theory*, Amsterdam: Benjamins, pp. 125–43.

Hale, K., Krauss, M., Watahomigie, L.J., Yamamoto, A.Y., Craig, C., Jeanne, L.M. and England, N.C. (1992) 'Endangered languages', *Language* 68: 1–42.

Hall, K. (1997) '"Go suck your husband's sugarcane!" Hijras and the use of sexual insult', in A. Livia and K. Hall (eds) *Queerly Phrased: Language, Gender and Sexuality*, New York: Oxford University Press, pp. 430–60.

Hall, K. (2003) 'Exceptional speakers: contested and problematised gender identities', in J. Holmes and M. Meyerhoff (eds) *The Handbook of Language and Gender*, Oxford: Blackwell, pp. 353–80.

Halliday, M.A.K. (1978) *Language as Social Semiotic*, London: Arnold.

Halliday, M.A.K. (1985) *An Introduction to Functional Grammar*, London: Arnold.

Halliday, M.A.K. (1994) *An Introduction to Functional Grammar*, (2nd edn), London: Arnold.

Halliday, M.A.K. and Hasan, R. (1985) *Language, Context, and Text*, Oxford: Oxford University Press.

Hammerström, G. (1980) *Australian English: its Origin and Status*, Hamburg: Buske.

Hancock, I.F. (1986) 'The domestic hypothesis, diffusion, and componentiality: an account of Atlantic anglophone creole origins', in P. Muysken and N. Smith (eds) *Substrata versus Universals in Creole Genesis*, Amsterdam: Benjamins, pp. 71–102.

Harris, S. (2001) 'Being politically impolite: extending politeness theory to adversarial political discourse', *Discourse and Society* 12 (4): 451–72.

Harris, S. (2003) 'Politeness and power: making and responding to "requests" in institutional settings', *Text* 23 (1): 27–52.

Haugen, E. (1966) 'Dialect, language, nation', *American Anthropologist* 68 (4): 922–35.

Haugen, E. (1972) *The Ecology of Language*, Stanford, CA: Stanford University Press.

Have, P. ten (1999) *Doing Conversation Analysis: A Practical Guide*, London: Sage.

Haviland, J.B. (1996) 'Owners versus Bubu Gujin: land rights and getting the language right in Guugu Yimithirr country', *Journal of Linguistic Anthropology* 6 (2): 145–60.

Heath, S.B. (1982) 'What no bedtime story means: narrative skills at home and school', *Language and Society* 11: 49–76.

Heath, S.B. (1983) *Ways with Words: Language, Life and Work in Communities and Classrooms*, Cambridge: Cambridge University Press.

Heller, M. (1999) *Linguistic Minorities and Modernity: A Sociolinguistic Ethnography*, London: Longman.

Henry, A. (2002) 'Variation and syntactic theory', in J.K. Chambers, P. Trudgill and N. Schilling-Estes (eds) *The Handbook of Language Variation and Change*, Oxford: Blackwell, pp. 262–82.

Henry, A. (2005) 'Idiolectal variation and syntactic theory', in L. Cornips and K. Corrigan (eds) *Syntax and Variation: Reconciling the Biological and the Social*, Amsterdam: Benjamins, pp. 109–22.

Hickey, R. (2004) *Legacies of Colonial English: Studies in Transported Dialects*, Cambridge: Cambridge University Press.

Holborn, M. and Haralambos, M. (2000) *Sociology: Themes and Perspectives*, London: Collins.

Hollien, H. (1987) '"Old Voices": what do we really know about them?' *Journal of Voice* 1 (1): 2–17.

Holly, W. (2001) *Der sprechende Zushauer. Wie wir uns Fernsehen Kommunikativ Aneigen*, Wiesbaden: WV.

Holm, J. (1988) *Pidgins and Creoles*, I, *Theory and Structure*, Cambridge: Cambridge University Press.

Holm, J. (1989) *Pidgins and Creoles* II, *Reference Survey*, Cambridge: Cambridge University Press.

Holmes, J. (1992) *An Introduction to Sociolinguistics*, Harlow: Addison Wesley Longman.

Holmes, J. and Marra, M. (2002) 'Having a laugh at work: how humour contributes to workplace culture', *Journal of Pragmatics* 34: 1683–710.

Holmes, J. and Meyerhoff, M. (1999) 'The community of practice: theories and methodologies in language and gender research', *Language in Society* 28 (2): 173–83.

Holmes, J. and Meyerhoff, M. (eds) (2003) *The Handbook of Language and Gender*, Oxford: Blackwell.

Holmes, J. and Stubbe, M. (2003) *Power and Politeness in the Workplace: A Sociolinguistic Analysis of Talk at Work*, London: Longman.

Hornberger, N. (2005) 'Frameworks and models in language policy and planning', in T. Ricento (ed.) *An Introduction to Language Policy*, Oxford: Blackwell, pp. 24–41.

Houck, C.L. (1968) 'Methodology of an urban speech survey', *Leeds Studies in English* 11: 115–28.

Howe, D. and Walker, J.A. (1995) 'Negation and the History of African American English', paper presented at the Symposium on Objectivity and Commitment in the Study of Early Black English, NWAVE 26, Université Laval, Quebec.

Howe, D. and Walker, J. (2000) 'Negation and the creole-origins hypothesis: evidence from early African American English', in S. Poplack (ed.) *The English History of African American English*, Oxford: Blackwell, pp. 109–40.

Hubbell, A.F. (1950) *The Pronunciation of English in New York City*, New York: Columbia University Press.

Huber, M. (1999) 'Atlantic creoles and the Lower Guinea coast: a case against Afrogenesis', in M. Huber and M. Parkvall (eds) *Spreading the Word: The Issue of Diffusion among the Atlantic Creoles*, London: University of Westminster Press, pp. 81–110.

Hudson, R.A. (1996) *Sociolinguistics* (2nd edn), Cambridge: Cambridge University Press.

Huffines, M.L. (2006) 'Fading future for ferhoodled English', in W. Wolfram and B. Ward (eds) *American Voices: How Dialects Differ from Coast to Coast*, Oxford: Blackwell, pp. 258–63.

Hughes, A., Trudgill, P. and Watt, D. (2005) *English Accents and Dialects: An Introduction to Social and Regional Varieties of English in the British Isles* (4th edn), London: Hodder Arnold.

Humm, M. (1989) *The Dictionary of Feminist Theory*, London: Harvester Wheatsheaf.

Hutcheson, N. (producer) (2000) *Indian by Birth: The Lumbee Dialect*, Raleigh, NC: North Carolina Language and Life Project.

Hymes, D.H. (1971) *On Communicative Competence*, Philadelphia, PA: University of Pennsylvania Press.

Hymes, D. (1972) 'Models of the interaction of language and social life', in J. Gumperz and D. Hymes (eds) *Directions in Sociolinguistics*, New York: Holt, Rinehart and Winston, pp. 35–71.

Hymes, D. (1974) *Foundations in Sociolinguistics: An Ethnographic Approach*, Philadelphia, PA: University of Pennsylvania Press.

Irvine, J.T. and Gal, S. (2000) 'Language ideology and linguistic differentiation', in P. Kroskrity (ed.) *Regimes of Language*, Santa Fe, NM: School of American Research Press, pp. 35–83.

Ito, R. and Tagliamonte, S. (2003) 'Well weird, right dodgy, very strange, really cool: layering and recycling in English intensifiers', *Language in Society* 32 (2): 257–79.

Jackson, J. (1974) 'Language identity of the Colombian Vaupés Indians', in R. Bauman and J. Sherzer (eds) *Explorations in the Ethnography of Speaking*, New York: Cambridge University Press, pp. 50–64.

Jenkins, J. (2003) *World Englishes: A Resource Book for Students*, London: Routledge.

Jewitt, C. and Kress, G. (eds) (2003) *Multimodal Literacy*, New York: Peter Lang.

JNLH (Journal of Narrative and Life History) (1997) 7, special edition *Oral Versions of Personal Experience*.

Johnson, K. (1997) *Acoustic and Auditory Phonetics*, Oxford: Blackwell.

Johnston, P. (1997) 'Regional variation', in C. Jones (ed.) *The Edinburgh History of the Scots Language*, Edinburgh: Edinburgh University Press, pp. 433–513.

Johnstone, B. (2000) *Qualitative Methods in Sociolinguistics*, New York: Oxford University Press.

Johnstone, B. and Bean, J.M. (1997) 'Self-expression and linguistic variation', *Language in Society* 26: 221–46.

Jones, C. (1997) 'Phonology', in C. Jones (ed.) *The Edinburgh History of the Scots Language*, Edinburgh: Edinburgh University Press, pp. 267–334.

Jones, M.J. and Llamas, C. (2003) 'Fricated pre-aspirated /t/ in Middlesbrough English: an acoustic study', *Proceedings of the XV International Congress of Phonetic Sciences*, Barcelona, August, pp. 655–8.

Joseph, J. (2004) *Language and Identity*, Basingstoke: Palgrave.

Kachru, B.B. (1985) 'Standards, codification and sociolinguistic realism: the English language in the outer circle', in R. Quirk and H.G. Widdowson (eds) *English in the World*, Cambridge: Cambridge University Press, pp. 11–30.

Kachru, B. (1986a) *The Alchemy of English: The Spread, Functions and Models for non-Native Varieties of English*, Oxford: Pergamon Press.

Kachru, B.B. (1986b) 'The Indianization of English', *English Today* 6: 31–3.

Kalin, R., Rayko, D. and Love, N. (1980) 'The perception and evaluation of job candidates with four different ethnic accents', in H. Giles, P. Robinson and P. Smith (eds) *Language: Social and Psychological Perspectives*, Oxford: Pergamon Press, pp. 197–202.

Keesing, R.M. (1988) *Melanesian Pidgin and the Oceanic Substrate*, Stanford, CA: Stanford University Press.

Keller, R.E. (1978) *The German Language*. London: Faber.

Kent, R.D. and Read, C. (1992) *The Acoustic Analysis of Speech*, San Diego, CA: Singular.

Kerswill, P. (1994) *Dialects Converging: Rural Speech in Urban Norway*, Oxford: Clarendon Press.

Kerswill, P. (1996) 'Children, adolescents and language change', *Language Variation and Change* 8: 177–202.

Kerswill, P. (2002) 'Koineization and accommodation', in J.K. Chambers, P. Trudgill and N. Schilling-Estes (eds) *The Handbook of Language Variation and Change*, Oxford: Blackwell, pp. 668–702.

Kerswill, P. (2003) 'Models of linguistic change and diffusion: new evidence from dialect levelling in British English', in D. Britain and J. Cheshire (eds) *Social Dialectology: In Honour of Peter Trudgill*, Amsterdam: Benjamins, pp. 223–43.

Kerswill, P. (2004) 'Social dialectology/Sozialdialektologie', in K. Mattheier, U. Ammon and P. Trudgill (eds) *Sociolinguistics/Soziolinguistik: An International Handbook of the Science of Language and Society* I (2nd edn), Berlin: de Gruyter, pp. 22–33.

Kerswill, P. (2006) 'RP, Standard English and the standard/non-standard relationship', in D. Britain (ed.) *Language in the British Isles* (2nd edn), Cambridge: Cambridge University Press.

Kerswill, P. and Trudgill, P. (2005) 'The birth of new dialects', in P. Auer, F. Hinskens and P. Kerswill (eds) *Dialect Change: Convergence and Divergence in European Languages*, Cambridge: Cambridge University Press, pp. 196–220.

Kerswill, P. and Williams, A. (1997) 'Investigating social and linguistic identity in three British schools', in U.-B. Kotsinas, A.-B. Stenström and A.-M. Malin (eds) *Ungdomsspråk i Norden. Föredrag från ett forskarsymposium (Youth language in the Nordic countries. Papers from a research symposium)*. Series: MINS, No. 43. Stockholm: University of Stockholm, Department of Nordic Languages and Literature, pp. 159–76.

Kerswill, P. and Williams, A. (2000a) 'Creating a new town koine: children and language change in Milton Keynes', *Language in Society* 29: 65–115.

Kerswill, P. and Williams, A. (2000b) 'Mobility and social class in dialect levelling: evidence from new and old towns in England', in K. Mattheier (ed.) *Dialect and Migration in a Changing Europe*, Frankfurt: Peter Lang, pp. 1–13.

Kerswill, P. and Williams, A. (2002) '"Salience" as a factor in language change: evidence from dialect levelling in urban England', in M.C. Jones and E. Esch (eds) *Language Change: The Interplay of Internal, External and Extra-linguistic Factors*, Berlin and New York: Mouton de Gruyter, pp. 81–110.

Kerswill, P. and Williams, A. (2005) 'New towns and koineisation: linguistic and social correlates', *Linguistics* 43 (5): 1023–48.

Kiely, R., McCrone, D., Stewart, R. and Bechhofer, F. (2000) 'Debatable land: national and local identity in a border town', *Sociological Research Online* 5 (2), <http://www.socresonline.org.uk/5/2/kiely.html>, accessed December 2005.

Kiparsky, P. (1979) *Pāṇini as a Variationist*, Cambridge, MA/Poona: MIT Press/Poona University Press.

Klapper, T. (1960) *The Effects of Mass Communication*, Glencoe, IL: Free Press.

Kloss H. (1969) *Research Possibilities on Group Bilingualism*, Quebec: International Centre for Research on Bilingualism.

Kouwenberg, S. and Singler, J.V. (eds) (2005) *The Handbook of Pidgin and Creole Studies*, Malden, MA: Blackwell.

Krapp, G.P. 1925 [1960] *The English Language in America* (2 vols), New York: Ungar.

Krauss, M. (1992) 'The world's languages in crisis', *Language* 68: 4–10.

Kress, G. and van Leeuwen, T. (2001) *Multimodal Discourse: The Modes and Media of Contemporary Communication*, London: Arnold.

Kristiansen, T., Garrett, P. and Coupland, N. (eds) (2005) *Subjective Processes in Language Variation and Change*, special issue of *Acta Linguistica Hafniensia* 37.

Kurath, H (1949) *A Word Geography of the Eastern United States*, Ann Arbor, MI: University of Michigan Press.

Labov, W. (1963) 'The social motivation of a sound change', *Word* 19: 273–309.

Labov, W. (1966) *The Social Stratification of English in New York City*, Washington, DC: Center for Applied Linguistics.

Labov, W. (1969) 'Contraction, deletion, and inherent variability of the English copula', *Language* 45: 715–62.

Labov, W. (1969) 'The logic of non-standard English', in J. Alatis (ed.) *Linguistics and the Teaching of Standard English to Speakers of other Languages and Dialects*, Washington, DC: Georgetown University Press, pp. 1–44.

Labov W. (1972a) 'Negative attraction and negative concord in English grammar', *Language* 48: 773–818.

Labov, W. (1972b) *Sociolinguistic Patterns*, Philadelphia, PA: University of Pennsylvania Press.

Labov, W. (1978) 'Where does the linguistic variable stop? A response to Beatriz Lavandera', *University of Pennsylvania Working Papers in Linguistics* 44.

Labov, W. (1980) *Locating Language in Time and Space: Quantitative Analyses of Linguistic Structure*, New York, Academic Press.

Labov, W. (1984) 'Field methods of the project on linguistic change and variation', in J. Baugh and J. Sherzer (eds) *Language in Use*, Englewood Cliffs, NJ: Prentice-Hall, pp. 28–53.

Labov, W. (1991) 'The boundaries of a grammar: inter-dialectal reactions to positive *anymore*', in P. Trudgill and J.K. Chambers (eds) *Dialects of English: Studies in Grammatical Variation*, London: Longman, pp. 273–88.

Labov, W. (1991) 'The three dialects of English', in P. Eckert (ed.) *New Ways of Analyzing Sound Change: Quantitative Analyses of Linguistic Structure* 5, New York: Academic Press, pp. 1–44.

Labov, W. (1994) *Principles of Linguistic Change* I, *Internal Factors*, Oxford: Blackwell.

Labov, W. (1997) 'Some further steps in narrative analysis', *Journal of Narrative and Life History* 7 (4): 1–12, special edition *Oral Versions of Personal Experience.*

Labov, W. (1998) 'Coexistent systems in African American English', in S.S. Mufwene, J.R. Rickford, G. Bailey and J. Baugh (eds) *African American English: Structure, History, and Use*, New York: Routledge, pp. 110–53.

Labov, W. (2001) *Principles of Linguistic Change* II, *Social Factors*, Oxford: Blackwell.

Labov, W. and Waletzky, J. (1967) 'Narrative analysis: oral versions of personal experience', in J. Helm (ed.) *Essays on the Verbal and Visual Arts*, Seattle, WA: University of Washington Press, pp. 12–44.

Labov, W., Yaeger, M. and Steiner, R. (1972) *A Quantitative Study of Sound Change in Progress*, Philadelphia, PA: US Regional Survey.

Ladefoged, P. (1992) 'Another view of endangered languages', *Language* 68: 809–11.

Ladegaard, H.J. and Bleses, D. (2003) 'Gender differences in young children's speech: the acquisition of sociolinguistic competence', *International Journal of Applied Linguistics* 13 (2): 222–33.

Laferriere, M. (1979) 'Ethnicity in phonological variation and change', *Language* 55: 603–17.

Lakoff, R. (1973) 'The logic of politeness: or, minding your p's and q's', *Papers from the Ninth Regional Meeting of the Chicago Linguistic Society* 9: 292–305.

Lakoff, R. (1975) *Language and Woman's Place*, New York: Harper and Row.

Lakoff, R. (1989) 'The limits of politeness: therapeutic and courtroom discourse', *Multilingua* 8 (2/3): 101–29.

Lalla, B. and D'Costa, J. (1990) *Language in Exile: Three Hundred Years of Jamaican Creole*, Tuscaloosa, AL: University of Alabama Press.

Lambert, W., Hodgson, R., Gardner, R. and Fillenbaum, S. (1960) 'Evaluational reactions to spoken languages', *Journal of Abnormal and Social Psychology* 60: 44–52.

Lameli, A. (2003) 'Dynamik im oberen Substandard', in S. Gaisbauer and H. Scheuringer (eds), *Tagungsberichte der 8*, Linz: Bayerisch-österreichischen Dialektologentagung, pp. 19–23.

Lavandera, B. (1978) 'Where does the sociolinguistic variable stop?' *Language in Society* 7: 171–83.

Lave, J. and Wenger, E. (1991) *Situated Learning: Legitimate Peripheral Participation*, Cambridge: Cambridge University Press.

Le Page, R.B. and Tabouret-Keller, A. (1985) *Acts of Identity: Creole-based Approaches to Language and Ethnicity*, Cambridge: Cambridge University Press.

Lefebvre, C. (1998) *Creole Genesis and the Acquisition of Grammar: The Case of Haitian Creole*, Cambridge: Cambridge University Press.

Leont'ev, A.N. (1981) *Problems of the Development of Mind*, Moscow: Progress.

Levin, H., Giles, H. and Garrett, P. (1994) 'The effects of lexical formality and accent on trait attributions', *Language and Communication* 14: 265–74.

Lieblich, A., Tuval-Mashiach, R. and Zilber, T. (1998) *Narrative Research: Reading, Analysis and Interpretation*, Thousand Oaks, CA: Sage.

Linde, C. (1988) 'The quantitative study of communicative success: politeness and accidents in aviation discourse', *Language in Society* 17: 375–99.

Lippi-Green, R. (1997) *English with an Accent: Language, Ideology, and Discrimination in the United States*, New York: Routledge.

Llamas, C. (1999) 'A new methodology: data elicitation for social and regional language variation studies', *Leeds Working Papers in Linguistics and Phonetics* 7: 95–118.

Llamas, C. (2001) *Language Variation and Innovation in Teesside English*. PhD thesis, University of Leeds.

Locher, M. (2004) *Power and Politeness in Action: Disagreements in Oral Communication*, Berlin: Mouton de Gruyter.

Low, E.L., Grabe, E. and Nolan, F.J. (2000) 'Quantitative characterizations of speech rhythm: syllable-timing in Singapore English', *Language and Speech* 43: 377–402.

Lucas, I. (1997) 'The colour of his eyes: Polari and the sisters of perpetual indulgence', in A. Livia and K. Hall (eds) *Queerly Phrased: Language, Gender and Sexuality*, New York: Oxford University Press, pp. 85–94.

Lyons, J. (ed.) (1970) *New Horizons in Linguistics*, Harmondsworth: Penguin.

Macaulay, R.K.S. (1977) *Language, Social Class and Education: A Glasgow Study*, Edinburgh: Edinburgh University Press.

Macaulay, R.K.S. (1978) 'Variation and consistency in Glaswegian English', in P. Trudgill (ed.) *Sociolinguistic Patterns of British English*, London: Arnold, pp. 132–43.

Macaulay, R.K.S. (1991) *Locating Dialect in Discourse: The Language of Honest Men and Bonnie Lasses in Ayr*, New York and Oxford: Oxford University Press.

Macaulay, R.K.S. (2002a) 'Discourse variation', in J.K. Chambers, P. Trudgill and N. Schilling-Estes (eds) *The Handbook of Language Variation and Change*, Oxford: Blackwell, pp. 283–305.

Macaulay, R.K.S. (2002b) 'Extremely interesting, very interesting, or only quite interesting? Adverbs and social class', *Journal of Sociolinguistics* 6 (3): 398–417.

Macaulay, R.K.S. (2005) *Talk that Counts: Age, Gender and Social Class Differences in Discourse*, Oxford: Oxford University Press.

McKenna, B. (2004) 'Critical discourse studies: where to from here?' *Critical Discourse Studies* 1 (1): 9–39.

McMahon, A.M.S. (1994) *Understanding Language Change*, Cambridge: Cambridge University Press.

McQuail, D. (2005) *McQuail's Mass Communication Theory* (5th edn), London: Sage.

McRae, S. (2004) 'Demonstrative use and variation in the Lower Garioch', in J.D. McClure (ed.) *Doonsin' Emerauds: New Scrieves anent Scots an Gaelic/New Studies in Scots and Gaelic*, Belfast Studies in Language, Culture and Politics *11*, Belfast: Queen's University, pp. 60–67.

McWhorter, J.H. (1998) 'Identifying the creole prototype: vindicating a typological class', *Language* 74: 788–818.

Mallison, C. and Wolfram, W. (2002) 'Dialect accommodation in a bi-ethnic mountain enclave community: more evidence on the development of African American English', *Language in Society* 31: 743–75.

Marshall, G., Newby, H., Rose, D. and Vogler, C. (1988) *Social Class in Modern Britain*, London: Hutchinson.

Matter, M. and Ziberi, J. (2000) 'Two patterns of dialect accommodation of Valais German speakers in Berne', in M. Matthey (ed.) *Le Changement linguistique*, Neuchâtel: Institut de linguistique, pp. 185–201.

May, S. (2005) 'Language policy and minority rights', in T. Ricento (ed.) *An Introduction to Language Policy*, Oxford: Blackwell, pp. 255–72.

Mees, I.M. and Collins, B. (1999) 'Cardiff: a real-time study of glottalization', in P. Foulkes and G.J. Docherty (eds) *Urban Voices: Accent Studies in the British Isles*, London: Arnold, pp. 85–202.

Mendoza Denton, N. (1997) *Chicana/Mexicana Identity and Linguistic Variation: An Ethnographic and Sociolinguistic Study of Gang Affiliation in an Urban High School.* PhD thesis, Stanford University.

Mendoza Denton, N. (2002) 'Language and identity', in J.K. Chambers, P. Trudgill and N. Schilling-Estes (eds) *The Handbook of Language Variation and Change*, Oxford: Blackwell, pp. 475–99.

Mercer, N. (2000) *Words and Minds: How we Use Language to Think Together*, London: Routledge.

Mesthrie, R. (1999) 'Sociolinguistic variation', in R. Mesthrie (ed.) *The Concise Encylopaedia of Sociolinguistics*, Amsterdam: Pergamon, pp. 377–88.

Mesthrie, R. (ed.) (2001) *Concise Encyclopedia of Sociolinguistics*, Oxford: Elsevier.

Mills, S. (2003) *Gender and Politeness*, Cambridge: Cambridge University Press.

Mills, S. (2004) *Discourse* (2nd edn), New York: Routledge.

Milroy, J. (1991) *Linguistic Variation and Change: On the Historical Sociolinguistics of English*, Oxford: Blackwell.

Milroy, J. and Milroy, L. (1978) 'Belfast: change and variation in an urban vernacular', in P. Trudgill (ed.) *Sociolinguistic Patterns in British English*, London: Arnold, pp. 19–36.

Milroy, J. and Milroy, L. (1985) *Authority in Language: Investigating Language Prescription and Standardisation*, London: Routledge.

Milroy, J. and Milroy, L. (1997a) 'Varieties and variation', in F. Coulmas (ed.) *The Handbook of Sociolinguistics*, Oxford: Blackwell, pp. 47–64.

Milroy, J. and Milroy, L. (1997b) *Authority in Language: Investigating Standard English* (3rd edn), London: Routledge.

Milroy, L. (1980) *Language and Social Networks*. Oxford: Blackwell.

Milroy, L. (1987a) *Language and Social Networks* (2nd edn), Oxford: Blackwell.

Milroy, L. (1987b) *Observing and Analysing Natural Language: A Critical Account of Sociolinguistic Method*, Oxford: Blackwell.

Milroy, L. (1997) 'The social categories of race and class: language ideology and sociolinguistics', in N. Coupland, S. Sarangi and C. Candlin (eds) *Sociolinguistics and Social Theory*, London: Longman, pp. 235–60.

Milroy, L. (2000) 'Britain and the United States: two nations divided by the same language (and different language ideologies)', *Journal of Linguistic Anthropology* 10: 56–89.

Milroy, L. (2001) 'Social networks', in J.K. Chambers, P. Trudgill and N. Schilling-Estes (eds) *The Handbook of Language Variation and Change*, Oxford: Blackwell, pp. 549–72.

Milroy, L. and Gordon, M. (2003) *Sociolinguistics: Method and Interpretation*, Oxford: Blackwell.

Montgomery, M. (1995) *An Introduction to Language and Society* (2nd edn), London: Routledge.

Montgomery, M. (2004) 'Solving Kurath's puzzle: establishing the antecedents of the American Midland dialect region', in R. Hickey (ed.) *Legacies of Colonial English: Studies in Transported Dialects*, Cambridge: Cambridge University Press, pp. 310–23.

Moore, E. (2003) *Learning Style and Identity: A Sociolinguistic Analysis of a Bolton High School*. PhD thesis, University of Manchester.

Morrison, K. (1995) *Marx, Durkheim, Weber: Formations of Modern Social Thought*, London: Sage.

Mufwene, S.S. (1986) 'The universalist and substrate hypotheses complement one another', in P. Muysken and N. Smith (eds) *Substrata versus Universals in Creole Genesis*, Amsterdam: Benjamins, pp. 129–62.

Mufwene, S.S. (1991) 'Pidgins, creoles, typology, and markedness', in F. Byrne and T. Huebner (eds) *Development and Structures of Creole Languages: Essays in Honour of Derek Bickerton*, Amsterdam: Benjamins, pp. 123–43.

Mufwene, S.S. (2001) *The Ecology of Language Evolution*, Cambridge: Cambridge University Press.

Mugglestone, L. (2003) *'Talking Proper': The Rise of Accent as Social Symbol* (2nd edn), Oxford: Clarendon Press.

Muhr, R. (2003) 'Language change via satellite: the influence of German television broadcasting on Austrian German', *Journal of Historical Pragmatics* 4: 103–27.

Mullany, L. (2006) '"Girls on tour": politeness, small talk and gender in managerial business meetings', *Journal of Politeness Research: Language, Behaviour, Culture* 2 (1): 55–77.

Nagy, N. and Reynolds, B. (1997) 'Optimality theory and variable word-final deletion in Faetar', *Language Variation and Change* 9: 37–55.

Nahir, M. (1984) 'Language planning goals: a classification', *Language Problems and Language Planning* 8 (3): 294–327.

Naro, A. (1981) 'The social and structural dimensions of syntactic changes', *Lingua* 57: 63–98.

Naro, A. and Scherre, M.M.P. (1996) 'Contact with media and linguistic variation', in J. Arnold, R. Blake, B. Davidson, S. Schwenter and J. Solomon (eds) *Sociolinguistic Variation: Data, Theory and Analysis. Selected Papers from NWAV 23 at Stanford*, Stanford, CA: CSLI Publications, pp. 223–8.

National Council of Social Studies, Task Force on Ethnic Studies (1976) *Curriculum Guidelines for Multiethnic Education*, Arlington, VA: National Council on Social Studies.

Nettle, D. and Romaine, S. (2000) *Vanishing Voices: The Extinction of the World's Languages*, Oxford: Oxford University Press.

Neustupny, J. (1983) 'Towards a paradigm for language planning', *Language Planning Newsletter* 9 (4): 1–4.

Newman, D., Griffin, P. and Cole, M. (1989) *The Construction Zone: Working for Cognitive Change in School*, Cambridge: Cambridge University Press.

Ng, S. and Bradac, J. (1993) *Power in Language: Verbal Communication and Social Influence*, London: Sage.

Niedzielski, N. and Preston, D. (1999) *Folk Linguistics*, Berlin: Mouton de Gruyter.

Nolan, F. (1997) 'Speaker recognition and forensic phonetics', in W.J. Hardcastle and J. Laver (eds) *The Handbook of Phonetic Sciences*, Oxford: Blackwell, pp. 744–67.

Norton, B. (1997) 'Language, identity and the ownership of English', *TESOL Quarterly* 31 (3): 409–29.

Norton, B. (2000) *Identity and Language Learning: Gender, Ethnicity and Educational Change*, London: Longman.

Nuolijärvi, P. (1994) 'On the interlinkage of sociolinguistic background variables', in B. Nordberg (ed.) *The Sociolinguistics of Urbanization: The Case of the Nordic Countries*, Berlin: de Gruyter, pp. 149–70.

Oakes, L. (2001) *Language and National Identity: Comparing France and Sweden*, Amsterdam: Benjamins.

Oakes, M.P. (1998) *Statistics for Corpus Linguistics*, Edinburgh: Edinburgh University Press.

Ochs, E. (1979) 'Transcription as theory', in E. Ochs and D. Schieffelin (eds) *Developmental Pragmatics*, New York: Academic Press, pp. 43–72.

Ochs, E. (1992) 'Indexing gender', in A. Duranti and C. Goodwin (eds) *Rethinking Context: Language as an Interactive Phenomenon*, Cambridge: Cambridge University Press, pp. 335–58.

Ochs, E., Schegloff, E.A. and Thompson, S.A. (eds) (1996) *Interaction and Grammar*, Cambridge: Cambridge University Press.

O'Connell, D. and Kowal, S. (1994) 'Some current transcription systems for spoken discourse', *Pragmatics* 4: 81–107.

Oetting, J.B. (2005) 'Assessing language in children who speak a nonmainstream dialect of English', in M. Ball (ed.) *Clinical Sociolinguistics*, Oxford: Blackwell, pp. 180–92.

O'Raigain, P. (1993) 'Stability and change in public attitudes towards Irish since the 1960s', *Teangeolas* 32: 45–9.

Office for National Statistics (2001) *The National Statistics Socio-economic Classification*, <http://www.statistics.gov.uk/methods_quality/ns_sec/>, accessed 18 December 2005.

Olson, D.R., Franklin, J.R. and Torrance, N. (eds) (1996) *The Handbook of Education and Human Development*, Oxford: Blackwell.

Olson, D.R. and Torrance, N. (2001) *The Making of Literate Societies*, Oxford: Blackwell.

Omdal, H. (1977) 'Høyangermålet – en ny dialect', *Språklig Samling* 18: 7–9.

Paardekooper, P. (2001) 'Hoe zacht is saft?' *Onze Taal* 6: 153.

Påhlsson, C. (1972) *The Northumbrian Burr: a Sociolinguistic Study*, Lund: Gleerup.

Parton, S., Siltanen, S., Hosman, L. and Langenderfer, J. (2002) 'Employment interview outcomes and speech style effects', *Journal of Language and Social Psychology* 21: 144–61.

Patrick, P. (2001) 'The speech community', in J.K. Chambers, P. Trudgill and N. Schilling-Estes (eds) *The Handbook of Language Variation and Change*, Oxford: Blackwell, pp. 573–97.

Payne, A.C. (1980) 'Factors controlling the acquisition of the Philadelphia dialect by out-of-state children', in W. Labov (ed.) *Locating Language in Time and Space*, New York: Academic Press, pp. 143–78.

Penman, R. (1990) 'Facework and politeness: multiple goals in courtroom discourse', *Journal of Language and Social Psychology* 9 (12): 15–39.

Penny, R. (2000) *Variation and Change in Spanish*, Cambridge: Cambridge University Press.

Pennycook, A. (1998) *English and the Discourses of Colonialism*, London: Routledge.

Pennycook, A. (2005) 'Postmodernism in language policy', in T. Ricento (ed.) *An Introduction to Language Policy*, Oxford: Blackwell, pp. 60–76.

Perez de Ayala, S. (2001) 'FTAs and Erskine May: conflicting needs? Politeness in Question Time', *Journal of Pragmatics* 33 (2): 143–70.

Phillipson, R. (1992) *Linguistic Imperialism*, Oxford: Oxford University Press.

Philo, G. (1999) 'Children and film/video/TV violence', in *Message Received: Glasgow Media Group Research 1993–1998*, London: Longman, pp. 56–72.

Pichler, H. (2005) 'Discourse markers in Berwick English: *I don't know, I dunno, I divvent know'*, paper presented at the Fifth UK Language Variation and Change Conference (UKLVC5), Aberdeen, September.

Pichler, H., Llamas, C. and Watt, D. (forthcoming) 'Phonological variation and claimed identities in Berwick upon Tweed'. For submission to *Journal of Sociolinguistics*.

Pollock, S. (1993) 'Ramayana and political imagination in India', *Journal of Asian Studies* 52 (2): 261–97.

Pollock, S. (ed.) (2003) *Literary Cultures in History: Reconstructions from South Asia*, Berkeley, CA: University of California Press.

Potter, J. and Wetherell, M. (1987) *Discourse and Social Psychology*, London: Sage.

Prakash, G. (ed.) (1985) *After Colonialism: Imperial Histories and Postcolonial Displacements*, Princeton, NJ: Princeton University Press.

Preston, D. (1992) '"Talking black and talking white": a study in variety imitation', in J. Hall, N. Doane and D. Ringler (eds) *Old English and New*, New York: Garland, pp. 327–55.

Preston, D. (1996) 'Whaddayaknow? The modes of folk linguistic awareness', *Language Awareness* 5: 40–74.

Preston, D. (ed.) (1999) *Handbook of Perceptual Dialectology* I, Amsterdam: Benjamins.

Pridham, F (2001) *The Language of Conversation*, London: Routledge.

Psathas, G. (1995) *Conversation Analysis: The Study of Talk-in-Interaction*, Thousand Oaks, CA: Sage.

Rampton, B. (1995) *Crossing*, London: Longman.

Rand, D. and Sankoff, D. (1990) *Goldvarb 2.0*, Montreal: University of Montreal.

Reid, I. (1989) *Social Class Differences in Britain* (3rd edn), London: Fontana.

Renkema, J. (2004) *Introduction to Discourse Studies*, Philadelphia: Benjamins.

Ricento. T. (2005) 'Theoretical perspectives in language policy', in *An Introduction to Language Policy*, Oxford: Blackwell, pp. 3–9.

Rickford, J.R. (1986) 'The need for new approaches to social class analysis in socio-linguistics', *Language and Communication* 6 (3): 215–21.

Rickford, J.R. and McNair-Knox, F. (1994) 'Addressee- and topic-influenced style shift: a quantitative sociolinguistic study', in D. Biber and E. Finegan (eds) *Socio-linguistic Perspectives on Register*, New York/Oxford: Oxford University Press, pp. 235–76.

Riesman, C.K. (1993) *Narrative Analysis*, Thousand Oaks, CA: Sage.

Roberts, J. (1997) 'Acquisition of variable rules: a study of (-t, d) deletion in preschool children', *Journal of Child Language* 24: 351–72.

Roberts, J. (2002) 'Child language variation', in J.K. Chambers, P. Trudgill and N. Schilling-Estes (eds) *The Handbook of Language Variation and Change*, Oxford: Blackwell, pp. 333–48.

Roberts, J. and Labov, W. (1995) 'Learning to talk Philadelphian: acquisition of short a by preschool children', *Language Variation and Change* 7: 101–12.

Rogers, E. (1995) *Diffusion of innovations* (4th edn), New York: Free Press.

Romaine, S. (1980) 'A critical overview of the methodology of urban British sociolinguistics', *English World Wide* 1 (1): 163–98.

Romaine, S. (1982) *Socio-historical Linguistics: Its Status and Methodology*, Cambridge: Cambridge University Press.

Romaine, S. (1984) *The Language of Children and Adolescents: The Acquisition of Communicative Competence*, Oxford: Blackwell.

Romaine, S. (2002) 'The impact of language policy on endangered languages', *International Journal on Multicultural Societies* 4 (2): 1–28.

Rumsey, A. (1993) 'Language and territoriality in Aboriginal Australia', in M. Walsh and C. Yallop (eds) *Language and Culture in Aboriginal Australia*, Canberra: Aboriginal Studies Press, pp. 191–208.

Sachs, J. and Devin, J. (1976) 'Young children's use of age-appropriate speech styles in social interaction and role-playing', *Journal of Child Language* 3: 81–98.

Sacks, H. (1972) 'An initial investigation of the usability of conversational materials for doing sociology', in D.N. Sudnow (ed.) *Studies in Social Interaction*, New York: Free Press, pp. 31–74.

Sacks, H. (1995) *Lectures on Conversation I and II*, Oxford: Blackwell.

Saladino, R. (1990) 'Language shift in standard Italian and dialect: a case study', *Language Variation and Change* 2: 57–70.

Sampson, G.R. and McCarthy, D. (2005) *Corpus Linguistics: Readings in a Widening Discipline*, London: Continuum.

Sankoff, D. (1978) *Linguistic Variation: Models and Methods*, New York: Academic Press.

Sankoff, D. (1988) 'Variable rules', in U. Ammon, N. Dittmar and K.J. Mattheier (eds) *Sociolinguistics: An International Handbook of the Science of Language and Society* II, Berlin: de Gruyter, pp. 984–97.

Sankoff, D. and Labov, W. (1979) 'On the uses of variable rules', *Language in Society* 8 (2): 189–222.

Sankoff, G. (1979) 'The genesis of a language', in K.C. Hill (ed.) *The Genesis of Language*, Ann Arbor, MI: Karoma, pp. 23–47.

Sankoff, G. (1980) *The Social Life of Language*, Philadelphia, PA: University of Pennsylvania Press.

Santa Ana, O. and Parodi, C. (1998) 'Modelling the speech community: configuration and variable types in the Mexican Spanish setting', *Language in Society* 27: 23–51.

Sapir, E. (1921) *Language: An Introduction to the Study of Speech*, New York: Harcourt, Brace.

Saville-Troike, M. (1982) *The Ethnography of Communication*, Oxford: Blackwell.

Saville-Troike, M. (2003) *The Ethnography of Communication* (3rd edn), Oxford: Blackwell.

Schegloff, E.A. (1968) 'Sequencing in conversational openings', *American Anthropologist* 70: 1075–95.

Schegloff, E.A. (2001) 'Discourse as an interactional achievement' III, 'The omnirelevance of action', in D, Schiffrin, D. Tannen and H. Hamilton (eds) *The Handbook of Discourse Analysis*, Oxford: Blackwell, pp. 247–65.

Schegloff, E.A., Koshik, I., Jacoby, S. and Olsher, D. (2002) 'Conversation analysis and applied linguistics', *Annual Review of Applied Linguistics* 22: 3–31.

Schiffrin, D. (1987) *Discourse Markers*, Cambridge: Cambridge University Press.

Schiffrin, D. (1994) *Approaches to Discourse*, Oxford: Blackwell.

Schilling-Estes, N. (2004) 'Constructing ethnicity in interaction', *Journal of Socio-linguistics* 8: 163–95.

Schirmunski, V. (1928/29) 'Die schwäbischen Mundarten in Transkaukasien und Südukraine', *Teuthonista* 5: 38–60 and 157–71.

Schuchardt, H. (1914) *Die Sprache der Saramakkaneger in Surinam*, Amsterdam: Muller.

Scollon, R. and Scollon, S.W. (1997) *Intercultural Communication: A Discourse Approach*, Oxford: Blackwell.

Scott, J. (1996) 'Class, status, and command: towards a theoretical framework', paper delivered at Hitotsubashi University, November, <http://privatewww.essex.ac.uk/~scottj/socscot4.htm>, accessed December 2005.

Sears, D. (1983) 'The persistence of early political predispositions: the role of attitude object and life-stage', in L. Wheeler and P. Shaver (eds) *Review of Personality and Social Psychology* IV, Beverly Hills, CA: Sage, pp. 79–116.

Segal, L. (1990) *Slow Motion: Changing Masculinities, Changing Men*, London: Virago.

Seggie, I. (1983) 'Attributions of guilt as a function of accent and crime', *Journal of Multilingual and Multicultural Development* 4: 197–206.

Seligman, C., Tucker, G. and Lambert, W. (1972) 'The effects of speech style and other attributes on teachers' attitudes toward pupils', *Language in Society* 1: 131–42.

Shatz, M. and Gelman, R. (1973) 'The development of communication skills: modifications in the speech of young children as a function of listener', *Monographs of the Society for Research in Child Development* 38: 1–37.

Shockey, L. (1984) 'All in a flap: long-term accommodation in phonology', *International Journal of the Sociology of Language* 46: 87–95.

Siegel, J. (1997) 'Mixing, levelling and pidgin/creole development', in A.K. Spears and D. Winford (eds) *The Structure and Status of Pidgins and Creoles*, Amsterdam/Philadelphia: Benjamins, pp. 111–50.

Silverstein, M. (1992) 'The uses and utility of ideology: some reflections', *Pragmatics* 2 (3): 311–23.

Silverstein, M. (1996) 'Encountering language and languages of encounter in North American ethnohistory', *Journal of Linguistic Anthropology* 6 (2): 126–44.

Sinclair, J. and Coulthard, M. (1975) *Towards an Analysis of Discourse: The English used by Teachers and Pupils*, Oxford: Oxford University Press.

Skutnabb-Kangas, T. (2000) *Linguistic Genocide in Education or Worldwide Diversity and Human Rights*, Mawah NJ: Erlbaum.

Smith, A.D. (1991) *The Ethnic Origin of Nations*, Oxford: Blackwell.

Smith, G. and Matthews, S. (1996) 'Pidgins and creoles', in B. Comrie, S. Matthews and M. Polinsky (eds) *The Atlas of Languages: The Origin and Development of Languages throughout the World*, New York: Facts on File, pp. 144–61.

Smith, J. (2000) 'Negative concord in the Old and New World: evidence from Scotland', *Language Variation and Change* 13 (2): 109–34.

Smith, J. (2001) '"Ye ø na hear that kind o' things": negative *do* in Buckie', *English World Wide* 21 (2): 231–59.

Smith, J. (2003–05) *Caregiver, Community and Child in the Acquisition of Variation*, Economic and Social Research Council-funded project.

Smith, J. (2005) 'The sociolinguistics of contemporary Scots: insights from one community', in J.M. Kirk and D.P. Ó Baoill (eds) *Legislation, Literature and Sociolinguistics: Northern Ireland, the Republic of Ireland, and Scotland*, Belfast Studies in Language, Culture and Politics 13, Belfast: Queen's University, pp. 112–25.

Spiers, J. (1998) 'The use of face work and politeness theory', *Qualitative Health Research* 8 (1): 25–47.

Steiner, G. (1998) *After Babel: Aspects of Language and Translation*, Oxford: Oxford University Press.

Stockwell, P. (2002) *Sociolinguistics: A Resource Book for Students*, London: Routledge.

Storto, L.R. (2003) 'Interactions between verb movement and agreement in Kuritiana (Tupi stock)', *Revista Letras* 60: 411–33.

Street, B. (1984) *Literacy in Theory and Practice*, Cambridge: Cambridge University Press.

Street, B. (1995) *Social Literacies: Critical Approaches to Literacy in Development, Ethnography and Education*, London: Longman.

Street, R., Brady, R. and Lee, R. (1984) 'Evaluative responses to communicators: the effects of speech rate, sex, and interaction context', *Western Journal of Speech Communication* 48: 14–27.

Stuart-Smith, J. (1999). 'Glasgow: accent and voice quality', in P. Foulkes and G.J. Docherty (eds) *Urban Voices: Accent Studies in the British Isles*, London: Arnold, pp. 203–22.

Stubbs, M. (1983) *Discourse Analysis: The Sociolinguistic Analysis of Natural Language*, Oxford: Blackwell.

Stubbs, M. (1986) *Educational Linguistics*, Oxford: Blackwell.

Swaan, A. de (2001) *Words of the World*, Cambridge: Polity Press.

Sylvain, S. (1936) *Le Créole haitien: morphologie et syntaxe*, Wettern: De Meester.

Tagliamonte, S. (1998) '*Was/were* variation across the generations: view from the city of York', *Language Variation and Change* 10 (2): 153–91.

Tagliamonte, S. (2006) *Analysing Sociolinguistic Variation*, Cambridge: Cambridge University Press.

Tagliamonte, S. and D'Arcy, A. (2004) '"He's like, she's like": the quotative system in Canadian youth', *Journal of Sociolinguistics* 8 (4): 493–514.

Tagliamonte, S. and Hudson, R. (1999) 'Be like *et al.* beyond America: the quotative system in British and Canadian youth', *Journal of Sociolinguistics* 3 (2): 147–72.

Tagliamonte S. and Smith, J. (2002) '*Either it isn't or it's not:* neg/aux contraction in British dialects', *English World Wide* 23 (2): 251–82.

Tagliamonte, S. and Smith, J. (to appear) 'No momentary fancy: the zero complementizer in English dialects', *English Language and Linguistics*.

Tagliamonte, S., Smith, J. and Lawrence, H. (in press) 'No taming the vernacular: insights from the relatives in northern Britain', *Language Variation and Change*.

Tajfel, H. (1974) 'Social identity and intergroup behavior', *Social Science Information* 13: 65–93.

Tajfel, H. (1981) 'Social stereotypes and social groups', in J. Turner and H. Giles (eds) *Intergroup Behaviour*, Oxford: Blackwell, pp. 144–65.

Talbot, M. (1998) *Language and Gender: An Introduction*, Cambridge: Polity Press.

Tannen, D. (1991) *You Just Don't Understand: Women and Men in Conversation*, London: Virago.

Taylor, D. (1960) 'Language shift or changing relationship?' *International Journal of American Linguistics* 26: 155–61.

Thomas, E.R. (2001) *An Acoustic Analysis of Vowel Variation in New World English*, Durham, NC: Duke University Press.

Thomas, E.R. (2002a) 'Instrumental phonetics', in J.K. Chambers, P. Trudgill and N. Schilling-Estes (eds) *The Handbook of Language Variation and Change*, Oxford: Blackwell, pp. 168–200.

Thomas, E.R. (2002b) 'Sociophonetic applications of speech perception experiments', *American Speech* 77 (2): 115–47.

Thomas, E.R. and Reaser, J.L. (2004) 'Delimiting perceptual cues for the ethnic labelling of African American and European American voices', *Journal of Sociolinguistics* 8: 54–87.

Thomason, S.G. (2001) *Language Contact: An Introduction*, Washington, DC: Georgetown University Press.

Thomason, S.G. and Kaufman, T. (1988) *Language Contact, Creolization, and Genetic Linguistics*, Berkeley, CA: University of California Press.

Thompson, R.W. (1961) 'A note on some possible affinities between the creole dialects of the Old World and those of the New', in R.B. Le Page (ed.) *Creole Language Studies* II, London: Macmillan, pp. 107–13.

Thornborrow, J. (2002) *Power Talk: Language and Interaction in Institutional Discourse*, London: Longman.

Thornborrow, J. and Coates, J. (eds) (2005) *The Sociolinguistics of Narrative*, Amsterdam: Benjamins.

Thorne, B. and Henley, N. (eds) (1975) *Language and Sex: Difference and Dominance*, Rowley, MA: Newbury House.

Tollefson, J. (2005) 'Critical theory in language policy', in T. Ricento (ed.) *An Introduction to Language Policy*, Oxford: Blackwell, pp. 42–59.

Troemel-Ploetz, S. (1998) 'Selling the apolitical', in J. Coates (ed.) *Language and Gender: A Reader*, Oxford: Blackwell, pp. 446–58.

Trudgill, P. (1972) 'Sex, covert prestige, and linguistic change in the urban British English of Norwich', *Language in Society* 1: 179–95.

Trudgill, P. (1974a) *The Social Differentiation of English in Norwich*, Cambridge: Cambridge University Press.

Trudgill, P. (1974b) *Sociolinguistics: An Introduction to Language and Society*, Harmondsworth: Penguin.

Trudgill, P. (1983) *On Dialect*, Oxford: Blackwell.

Trudgill, P. (1986) *Dialects in Contact*, Oxford: Blackwell.

Trudgill, P. (1988) 'Norwich revisited: recent linguistic changes in an English urban dialect', *English World Wide* 9: 33–49.

Trudgill, P. (2004) *New Dialect Formation: The Inevitability of Colonial Englishes*, Edinburgh: Edinburgh University Press.

Tuten, D.N. (2003) *Koineization in Medieval Spanish*, Berlin and New York: Mouton de Gruyter.

van Parijs, P. (ed.) (2004), *Cultural Diversity versus Economic Solidarity*, Brussels: De Boeck Université.

Vinson, J. (1882) 'Créole', in L.A. Bertillon, A. Coudereau, A. Hovelaque and C.

Issaurat (eds) *Dictionnaire des sciences anthropologiques et ethnologiques*, Paris: Bertillon.

Vygotsky, L. (1962) *Thought and Language*, Cambridge, MA: MIT Press.

Wardhaugh, R. (2005) *An Introduction to Sociolinguistics* (5th edn), Oxford: Blackwell.

Wartenberg, T. (1991) *The Forms of Power: From Domination to Transformation*, Philadelphia, PA: Temple University Press.

Wassink, A.B. and Dyer, J. (2004) 'Language ideology and the transmission of phonological change: changing indexicality in two situations of language contact', *Journal of English Linguistics* 32 (1): 3–30.

Watt, D. and Ingham, C. (2000) 'Durational evidence of the Scottish Vowel Length Rule in Berwick English', *Leeds Working Papers in Linguistics and Phonetics* 8: 205–28.

Watt, D. and Milroy, L. (1999) 'Patterns of variation in three Newcastle vowels: is this dialect levelling?' in P. Foulkes and G. Docherty (eds) *Urban Voices: Accent Studies in the British Isles*, London: Arnold, pp. 25–46.

Watt, D. and Pichler, H. (2004) '"We're all English really": investigating the tension between claimed identity and linguistic variation in Berwick upon Tweed', Paper presented at the Symposium on the Influence of the Languages of Ireland and Scotland on Linguistic Varieties in Northern England, Aberdeen, June.

Watt, D. and Smith, J. (2005) 'Language change', in M.J. Ball (ed.) *Clinical Sociolinguistics*, Oxford: Blackwell, pp. 101–19.

Watts, R. (2003) *Politeness*, Cambridge: Cambridge University Press.

Weldon, T. (2003) 'Copula variability in Gullah', *Language Variation and Change* 15 (1): 37–72.

Wells, J.C. (1982) *Accents of English* (3 vols), Cambridge: Cambridge University Press.

Wenger, E. (1998) *Communities of Practice*, Cambridge: Cambridge University Press.

Wengraf, T. (2001) *Qualitative Social Interviewing: Biographic Narrative and Semistructured Methods*, London: Sage.

Werlen, I., Buri, B., Matter, M. and Ziberi, J. (2002) *Projekt Üsserschwyz. Dialektanpassung und Dialektloyalität von overwalliser Migranten*, Institut für Sprachwissenschaft, Universität Bern.

West, C. and Zimmerman, D. (1983) 'Small insults: a study of interruptions in cross-sex conversations between unacquainted persons', in B. Thorne, C. Kramarae and N. Henley (eds) *Language, Gender and Society*, Rowley, MA: Newbury House, pp. 102–17.

West, C. and Zimmerman, D. (1987) 'Doing gender', *Gender and Society* 1: 125–51.

Whinnom, K. (1965) 'The origin of the European-based pidgins and creoles', *Orbis* 14: 509–27.

Widdowson, H. (2004) *Text, Context, Pretext*, Oxford: Blackwell.

Williams, A. and Kerswill, P. (1999) 'Dialect levelling: change and continuity in Milton Keynes, Reading and Hull', in P. Foulkes and G.J. Docherty (eds), *Urban Voices: Accent Studies in the British Isles*, London: Arnold, pp. 141–62.

Wodak, R. (1996) *Disorders of Discourse*, London: Longman.

Wodak, R. and Chilton, P. (2005a) *Methods of Critical Discourse Analysis*, London: Sage.

Wodak, R. and Chilton, P. (2005b) *New Agenda in (Critical) Discourse Analysis*, Amsterdam: Benjamins.

Wolfram, W. (1979) 'Towards a description of a-prefixing in Appalachian English', *American Speech* 51: 45–56.

Wolfram, W. (1989) 'Structural variability in phonological development: final nasals in vernacular black English', in R.W. Fasold and D. Schiffrin (eds) *Language Change and Variation*, Amsterdam: Benjamins, pp. 301–32.

Wolfram, W. (1991) 'The linguistic variable: fact and fantasy', *American Speech* 66 (1): 22–32.

Wolfram, W. (2003) 'Reexamining the development of African American English: evidence from isolated communities', *Language* 79 (2): 282–316.

Wolfram W., Childs, B. and Torbert, B. (2000) 'Tracing language history through consonant cluster reduction: evidence from isolated dialects', *Southern Journal of Linguistics* 24: 17–40.

Wolfram, W. and Fasold, R.W. (1974) *The Study of Social Dialects in American English*, Englewood Cliffs, NJ: Prentice-Hall, pp. 36–72.

Wolfram, W. and Schilling-Estes, N. (1999) *American English*, Oxford: Blackwell.

Wolfram, W. and Schilling-Estes, N. (2006) *American English: Dialects and Variation* (2nd edn), Oxford: Blackwell.

Wooffitt, R. (2005) *Conversation Analysis and Discourse Analysis: A Comparative and Critical Introduction*, London: Sage.

Wood, K. (1999) 'Coherent identities amid heterosexist ideologies: deaf and lesbian coming-out stories', in M. Bucholtz, A.C. Liang and L. Sutton (eds) *Reinventing Identities: the Gendered Self in Discourse*, New York: Oxford University Press, pp. 46–63.

Woolard, K. (1999) 'Simultaneity and bivalency as strategies in bilingualism', *Journal of Linguistic Anthropology* 8 (1): 3–29.

Wright, S. (2004) *Language Policy and Language Planning: From Nationalism to Globalisation*. Basingstoke: Palgrave.

Zahn, C. and Hopper, R. (1985) 'Measuring language attitudes: the speech evaluation instrument', *Journal of Language and Social Psychology* 4: 113–23.

Zentella, A.C. (1997) *Growing up Bilingual*, Oxford: Blackwell.

INDEX

Items which also appear in the Glossary are in **bold**.

The Routledge Dictionary of English Language Studies

Peter Childs and Roger Fowler

From abbreviation to zero-article, via fricative and slang, this dictionary contains over 600 wide ranging and informative entries covering:

- the core areas of language description and analysis: phonetics and phonology, grammar, lexis, semantics, pragmatics and discourse
- sociolinguistics, including entries on social and regional variation, stylistic variation, and language and gender
- the history of the English language from Old English to the present day
- the main varieties of English spoken around the world, covering the British isles, the Caribbean, North America, Africa, Asia, and Australasia
- stylistics, literary language and English usage.

Packed with real examples of the way people use English in different contexts, *The Routledge Dictionary of English Language Studies* is an indispensable guide to the richness and variety of the English language for both students and the general reader.

ISBN10: 0–415–35187–1 (hbk)
ISBN10: 0–415–35172–3 (pbk)

ISBN13: 978–0–415–35187–4 (hbk)
ISBN13: 978–0–415–35172–0 (pbk)

Available at all good bookshops
For ordering and further information please visit
www.routledge.com

Psycholinguistics: the Key Concepts

John Field

Psycholinguistics is an authoritative, wide-ranging and up-to-date A to Z guide to this important field. Cross-referenced, with suggestions for further reading and a full index, the book is a highly accessible introduction to the main terms and concepts in psycholinguistics. *Psycholinguistics* offers over 170 entries covering the key areas:

- psychological processes
- first language acquisition
- the nature of language
- brain and language
- language disorders.

This comprehensive guide is an essential resource for all students of English language, linguistics and psychology.

ISBN10: 0–415–25891–X (pbk)
ISBN10: 0–415–25890–1 (hbk)

ISBN13: 978–0–415–25891–3 (pbk)
ISBN13: 978–0–415–25890–6 (hbk)

Available at all good bookshops
For ordering and further information please visit
www.routledge.com

Key Concepts in Language and Linguistics

R.L. Trask

A comprehensive critical work, *Key Concepts in Language and Linguistics* is a highly readable A–Z guide to the main terms and concepts used in the study of language and linguistics.

Accessible and clearly presented, definitions featured include:

- terms used in grammatical analysis
- branches of linguistics from semantics to neurolinguistics
- approaches used in studying language from critical discourse analysis to systemic linguistics
- linguistic phenomena from code-switching to conversational implicature
- language varieties from pidgin to standard language.

Tracing the origin of the concept featured and outlining the key associated individuals, each entry also provides a guide to further reading and is extensively cross-referenced. Engaging and easy to use, this is an essential reference guide for undergraduate and postgraduate students, as well as anyone with an interest in this fascinating field.

ISBN10: 0–415–15742–0 (pbk)
ISBN10: 0–415–15741–2 (hbk)

ISBN13: 978–0–415–15742–1 (pbk)
ISBN13: 978–0–415–15741–4 (hbk)

Available at all good bookshops
For ordering and further information please visit
www.routledge.com